URBAN STUDIES
INSIDE/OUT

We dedicate this book to our students, past and present, who have inspired us and pushed us to keep open minds!

URBAN STUDIES INSIDE/OUT

THEORY, METHOD, PRACTICE

Edited by

Helga Leitner, Jamie Peck & Eric Sheppard

Los Angeles | London | New Delhi
Singapore | Washington DC | Melbourne

Los Angeles | London | New Delhi
Singapore | Washington DC

SAGE Publications Ltd
1 Oliver's Yard
55 City Road
London EC1Y 1SP

SAGE Publications Inc.
2455 Teller Road
Thousand Oaks, California 91320

SAGE Publications India Pvt Ltd
B 1/I 1 Mohan Cooperative Industrial Area
Mathura Road
New Delhi 110 044

SAGE Publications Asia-Pacific Pte Ltd
3 Church Street
#10-04 Samsung Hub
Singapore 049483

Chapter 1 © Helga Leitner, Eric Sheppard and Jamie Peck 202
Chapter 2 © Eric Sheppard, Helga Leitner and Jamie Peck 202
Chapter 3 © Jamie Peck, Eric Sheppard and Helga Leitner 202
Chapter 4 © Kyle Loewen, Devra Waldman and Mikael Omstedt
Chapter 5 © Dimitar Anguelov, Emma Colven and Prajna Rao 2
Chapter 6 © Tanya Matthan, Emma Colven and Hudson Spivey
Chapter 7 © Nina Ebner, Joe Penny and Andre Comandon 202
Chapter 8 © Nafis Hasan, Hudson Spivey and Kenton Card 202
Chapter 9 © Joseph A. Daniels, Mikael Omstedt and Dimitar Anguelo
Chapter 10 © Samuel Nowak and Tom Howard 2020
Chapter 11 © Tom Howard, Samuel Nowak and Fernanda Jahn-Ver
Chapter 12 © Kenton Card, Andre Comandon and Joseph A. Daniel
Chapter 13 © Tyler Harlan and Jaehyeon Park 2020
Chapter 14 © Carolyn Prouse and Fernanda Jahn-Verrii 2020
Chapter 15 © CS Ponder and Sophie Webber 2020
Chapter 16 © Prajna Rao and Andre Comandon 2020
Chapter 17 © Rachel Bok 2020
Chapter 18 © Andre Comandon, Kenton Card and Joseph A. Daniel
Chapter 19 © Helga Leitner, Jamie Peck and Eric Sheppard 20

First published 2020

Editor: Robert Rojek
Assistant editor: Eve Williams
Production editor: Katherine Haw
Copyeditor: Neville Hankins
Marketing manager: Susheel Gokarakonda
Cover design: Francis Kenney
Typeset by: C&M Digitals (P) Ltd, Chennai, India
Printed in the UK

Library of Congress Control Number: 2019938508

British Library Cataloguing in Publication data

A catalogue record for this book is available from the British Lib

ISBN 978-1-5264-3808-9
ISBN 978-1-5264-3809-6 (pbk)

At SAGE we take sustainability seriously. Most of our products are printed in the UK using responsibly sourced papers a
boards. When we print overseas we ensure sustainable papers are used as measured by the PREPS grading syste
We undertake an annual audit to monitor our sustainability.

CONTENTS

List of figures and tables   vii
List of contributors   ix
Acknowledgements   xiv
Preface   xv

PART I   REORIENTATIONS   1

1   Urban studies unbound: postmillennial spaces of theory   3
Helga Leitner, Eric Sheppard and Jamie Peck

2   Doing urban studies: navigating the methodological terrain   21
Eric Sheppard, Helga Leitner and Jamie Peck

3   Urban studies inside/out: a guide for readers and researchers   45
Jamie Peck, Eric Sheppard and Helga Leitner

PART II   METHODOLOGICAL ESSAYS   69

4   Constructing a feminist urban political economy: on Leslie
Kern's *Sex and the Revitalized City*   71
Kyle Loewen, Devra Waldman and Mikael Omstedt

5   Dreaming and scheming the 'world-class' city: on Asher
Ghertner's *Rule by Aesthetics*   82
Dimitar Anguelov, Emma Colven and Prajna Rao

6   Fluid assemblages: on Lisa Björkman's *Pipe Politics,
Contested Waters*   91
Tanya Matthan, Emma Colven and Hudson Spivey

7   Constructing and contesting the banlieue: on Mustafa
Dikeç's *Badlands of the Republic*   101
Nina Ebner, Joe Penny and Andre Comandon

8   Frustrated encounters: on Ahmed Kanna's
Dubai: The City as Corporation   112
Nafis Hasan, Hudson Spivey and Kenton Card

9   Rescaling the urban: on Neil Brenner's *New State Spaces*   122
Joseph A. Daniels, Mikael Omstedt and Dimitar Anguelov

10 Ethnography in the boundary zones: on Robert Fairbanks'
How It Works 133
Samuel Nowak and Tom Howard

11 Ethnographic exchanges: on Philippe Bourgois's
In Search of Respect 143
Tom Howard, Samuel Nowak and Fernanda Jahn-Verri

12 Grounding the housing question in land: on Anne Haila's
Urban Land Rent 154
Kenton Card, Andre Comandon and Joseph A. Daniels

13 Mapping urban governance: on You-tien Hsing's
The Great Urban Transformation 165
Tyler Harlan and Jaehyeon Park

14 Claiming rights to the city: on James Holston's
Insurgent Citizenship 175
Carolyn Prouse and Fernanda Jahn-Verri

15 Visualizing liquid cities: on Matthew Gandy's
The Fabric of Space 186
CS Ponder and Sophie Webber

16 Writing the heterogeneous city: on AbdouMaliq Simone's
City Life from Jakarta to Dakar 196
Prajna Rao and Andre Comandon

17 In search of ordinary 'elsewheres' in global urbanism: on
Ola Söderström's *Cities in Relations* 206
Rachel Bok

18 Urban comparison, quantified: on Michael Storper,
Thomas Kemeny, Naji Makarem and Taner Osman's
The Rise and Fall of Urban Economies 216
Andre Comandon, Kenton Card and Joseph A. Daniels

PART III   REFLECTIONS 227

19 Turning urban studies inside/out 229
Helga Leitner, Jamie Peck and Eric Sheppard

PART IV   RESOURCES 245

Keywords 247
Bibliography 326
Index 351

LIST OF FIGURES AND TABLES

Figure 19.1   Polyvalent knowledge cultures   235

Table 3.1   Conventions of co-authorship   53
Table 3.2   The selection of urban studies monographs   56
Table 3.3   Constructive deconstruction: prompts and
              principles   59

Table 19.1   Three classical European modes of knowledge
              production   237

LIST OF CONTRIBUTORS

Dimitar Anguelov is a graduate student in the Department of Geography at the University of California, Los Angeles. His research lies at the intersection of geographical political economy, urban development, and governance, focusing on how financialization and marketization processes articulate with development policies and practices in the European Union and Indonesia. His current research investigates the institutionalization of a market-based public–private partnership regime for infrastructure financing in Indonesia, and the hybrid outcomes of this process as it encounters the political economy and developmental legacies of the Indonesian state. His work has been published in *Urban Studies* and the *International Journal of Urban and Regional Research*.

Rachel Bok is a graduate student in the Department of Geography at the University of British Columbia. Her research interests center on global urbanism, critical urban theory, and geographical political economy. Her current research examines the globalization of the urban 'solutions' industry through methodological approaches of global ethnography.

Kenton Card is a filmmaker and PhD student in the Department of Urban Planning at the University of California, Los Angeles. His research interests include urban political economy, social movements, and housing policy. His past research has been published in *Jacobin*, *Progressive City*, *Architectural Theory Review*, and *Design Philosophy Papers*, and he has served as the Managing Editor of *Critical Planning Journal* and an advisor to the Institute on Inequality and Democracy at UCLA Luskin.

Emma Colven is Assistant Professor of Global Environment in the Department of International and Area Studies at the University of Oklahoma. As an urban geographer and political ecologist, her research explores themes of socio-ecological change, environmental expertise, and urban water politics in cities of the global South. Drawing on postcolonial urban theory, her research is motivated by the goal of producing a deeper understanding of urban political ecologies from a Southern perspective.

Andre Comandon is a doctoral candidate in the Department of Urban Planning at the University of California, Los Angeles Luskin School of Public Affairs. His research is concerned with the equity and governance implications of segregation. This research follows two paths that contribute to theories of spatial inequality. He studies, through a combination of quantitative and institutionalist methods, the changing landscape of diversity in US cities with an emphasis on Los Angeles. At the same time, he pursues the broadening of theoretical and methodological tools to understand segregation through international comparative analyses.

Joseph A. Daniels is a doctoral candidate in the Department of Geography at the University of British Columbia and the School of Geography at the University of Nottingham. His current research follows the emergence of crowdfunding as an experimental form of urban governance and its marketization as a critical part of an emerging platform capitalism. His ongoing research interests include crowd theories, collectivity, money and finance, and urban and digital geographies.

Nina Ebner is a graduate student in the Department of Geography at the University of British Columbia. Her research interests lie at the intersection of feminist political economy, critical development, and border studies. She is currently doing research on economic development and labor market participation on the US–Mexico border. She believes strongly in the importance of collaborative research, and is involved with grassroots efforts to end migrant detention, and to create more sustainable economic futures for border residents.

Tyler Harlan is Assistant Professor of Environmental Studies in the Department of Urban and Environmental Studies at Loyola Marymount University. He is an economic geographer and political ecologist with research interests in low-carbon restructuring, environmental governance, and rural and regional development, with a focus on China. His current work examines the geography and socio-environmental implications of China's energy transition.

Nafis Hasan is a PhD candidate in socio-cultural anthropology at the University of California, Los Angeles. His research interests lie in the emerging techno-politics of public bureaucracies, digital technologies, and governance. Given huge investment in ICT for governance across the global South, his research asks, if ICTs are not meeting their putative goals of ushering in transparency and accountability, what have they been doing? His current work is based in India, and examines the effects of digital technologies on the material and ideological elements of a district bureaucracy.

Tom Howard is a graduate student in the Department of Geography at the University of British Columbia. He is an urban geographer and institutional political economist with interests in economic restructuring, social regulation, and urban governance. His research has primarily focused on the dynamics of local policymaking, political–economic transformation, and the politics of urban and regional development.

Fernanda Jahn-Verri is a doctoral candidate in the Department of Urban Planning at the University of California, Los Angeles. Her research interests are focused on access to adequate housing, poor people's movements, informality, and postcolonial theory, her current work being concerned with the right to the city, displacement processes, and the role of the judiciary in practices of dispossession in Brazil.

Helga Leitner is Professor of Geography at the University of California, Los Angeles. Her research focuses on migration, cities, citizenship and communities, urban governance, and urban development and sustainability. She has published four books, including *Contesting Neoliberalism: Urban frontiers* (Guilford Press, 2007, edited with Jamie Peck and Eric Sheppard) and *Everyday Equalities: Making multicultures in settler colonial cities* (University of Minnesota Press, 2019, with Ruth Fincher, Kurt Iveson, and Valerie Preston), plus numerous urban-related articles in refereed journals. She is a former Rockefeller Fellow, and Member of the Austrian Academy of Sciences.

Kyle Loewen is a doctoral candidate in the Department of Geography at the University of British Columbia. His research interests are in economic and political geography and he is currently working on a dissertation that investigates the restructuring of logistics and work in the last mile of the supply chain.

Tanya Matthan is a graduate student in the Department of Anthropology at the University of California, Los Angeles. Her research interests lie at the intersections of economic anthropology, political ecology, and agrarian studies. Her dissertation project examines the prediction and management of agrarian 'risk' in central India against the backdrop of climate change, financialization, and market volatility.

Samuel Nowak is a graduate student in the Department of Geography at the University of California, Los Angeles. As an urban geographer, his research is broadly concerned with the political economy of urban transportation systems, and he is currently examining the politics of ride-hailing in Jakarta, Indonesia.

Mikael Omstedt is a doctoral student in the Department of Geography at the University of British Columbia. His research interests are in political economy, uneven development, and state power. In his current research he uses archival and comparative-historical methods to explore the Federal Reserve System's regulation of the uneven geographies of American capitalism throughout the 'long' twentieth century.

Jaehyeon Park is a doctoral student in the Department of Urban Planning at the University of California, Los Angeles. His research interests lie in international development studies, with a particular focus on informal settlements, urban resilience, and land governance. He is currently focusing on the rising intersection between disaster mitigation and informal settlement upgrading in Indonesia.

Jamie Peck is Canada Research Chair in Urban and Regional Political Economy, Distinguished University Scholar, and Professor of Geography at the University of British Columbia and Global Professorial Fellow, Institute for Culture and Society, Western Sydney University. His research is focused on urban restructuring, economic governance, and economic geography. As Managing Editor of *EPA: Economy and Space*, his publications include *Doreen Massey: Critical Dialogues* (Agenda, 2018, edited with Marion Werner, Rebecca Lave and Brett Christophers), *Offshore* (Oxford University Press, 2017), *Fast Policy* (with Nik Theodore, University of Minnesota Press, 2015), and *Constructions of Neoliberal Reason* (Oxford University Press, 2010).

Joe Penny is a Lecturer in Economic Geography at Queen Mary University of London. His research focuses on the governance and politics of austerity in London. He previously worked for the New Economics Foundation researching local government, social policy, and poverty/inequality.

CS Ponder is an Assistant Professor of Critical Geography at Florida State University. Her current research project uses a comparative lens to understand the urban political ecologies of the Detroit and Puerto Rico bankruptcies.

Carolyn Prouse is an Assistant Professor in the Department of Geography and Planning at Queen's University in Canada and was formerly a graduate student at the University of British Columbia. She is an urban economic geographer who works at the intersection of postcolonial, decolonial, critical race, and feminist theory. Her work focuses on the politics and economics of urban infrastructural development in North America, Brazil, and South Africa, with a particular interest in infrastructures of slum-upgrading, experimentation, and social reproduction.

Prajna Rao is a doctoral candidate in the School of Community and Regional Planning at the University of British Columbia. She is broadly interested in everyday urban life and infrastructures in postcolonial contexts. Her current research explores auto-rickshaw systems and their relationship with urban mobilities in Mumbai, India.

Eric Sheppard is the Alexander von Humboldt Chair of Geography at the University of California, Los Angeles. His research focuses on the uneven geographies of capitalist globalization, southern urban theory, and land transformations and displacement in Jakarta and Bangalore. His publications include *Limits to Globalization* (Oxford University Press, 2016), *The Wiley-Blackwell Companion to Economic Geography* (2012, edited with Jamie Peck and Trevor Barnes), *A World of Difference* (Guilford Press, 2008, with Philip W. Porter, David Faust and Richa Nagar), and *Contesting Neoliberalism* (Guilford Press, 2007, edited with Helga Leitner and Jamie Peck).

Hudson Spivey is a doctoral candidate in the Department of Geography at the University of California, Los Angeles, with research interests in environmental politics, socio-spatial theory, and technological change. His current research examines the political economy of energy transitions and the electric power industry in contemporary Japan.

Devra Waldman is a doctoral candidate in the School of Kinesiology at the University of British Columbia. Her research interests center on the intersections of sport/leisure, urban development, and (post)colonialism. Her current work focuses on the building of branded, sport-focused, gated communities in the suburbs of major metropolitan areas of India.

Sophie Webber is a Lecturer in Geography in the School of Geosciences at the University of Sydney. She is an economic and environmental geographer whose research investigates the global political economies of climate change adaptation and resilience projects. Her research is focused on the discursive and material power of circulations of finance, policy, and scientific expertise between large development institutions and their sites of intervention in South-east Asia and the Pacific region.

ACKNOWLEDGEMENTS

We are grateful to all those who worked with us, and helped us, along the path from the UBC/UCLA graduate seminar, including staff and colleagues of our respective departments and universities and at UC White Mountain Research Center, especially Dimitar Anguelov, Marwan Hassan, Kevin Kitagawa, Caroline Kong, Suzanne Lawrence, Glen MacDonald, Kasi McMurray, Bret Peterson, Elizabeth Sally, Denise Waterbury, Danny Wong, and Matt Zebrowski. The students who participated in the joint seminar, most but not all of whom are represented in the following pages, all left their mark on this project. We thank them for their contributions. We are especially grateful to multimedia artist and UC Berkeley professor Allan deSouza for permission to use his artwork on the cover and as book inserts. At SAGE, we very much appreciate the support of Robert Rojek from the earliest stages of this project, and Eve Williams for guiding it through the final stages.

Cover art and insert © Allan deSouza. Allan deSouza's speculative exhibition Through the Black Country, or, The Sources of the Thames Around the Great Shires of Lower England and Down the Severn River to the Atlantic Ocean, reenacts and upends iconic colonial narratives of discovery in Africa. The exhibition follows the expedition diaries of the Zanzibari crypto-ethnologist Hafeed Sidi Mubarak Mumbai, the fictional great-grandson of the historic figure, Sidi Mubarak Bombay – a formerly enslaved African who, upon gaining his freedom in India, returned to Africa to lead numerous British expeditions across the continent. Producing artifacts of expedition maps, photographs, diary extracts, and a sculptural base camp, Hafeed sets off in Summer 2016 during the Brexit vote to fulfill his great grandfather's unfulfilled wish to discover the fabled and elusive source of the River Thames.

PREFACE

This book began in the classroom: in and between two classrooms to be more precise. It originated in a graduate seminar jointly organized in 2016 by the geography departments of the University of California at Los Angeles and the University of British Columbia in Vancouver. Meeting simultaneously in the two departments, and combining 'local' discussions with a video-conference link each week, the joint seminar had been organized around the theme of methodological developments, challenges, and opportunities in critical urban studies, on the heels of two decades of intensifying debates around the geography and sociology of theory building and around epistemological framing, voice, and situated knowledge claims, in this diverse and dynamic field. A motivating concern for the joint seminar had been that matters of methodology and research practice had not received the attention that they deserved in a field that was opening up and diversifying as never before on the one hand, with the benefit of new voices, new perspectives, and a more cosmopolitan embrace of the majority urban world, but on the other hand was showing signs of fracture and division, as some debates polarized and some positions became apparently entrenched.

Rather than revisit these issues, the collaborative seminar set out to strike a more constructive tone, hence its title 'Researching Cities: Beyond Universalism and Particularism', with a focus on what remain substantially *shared* challenges of methodological practice across the field of critical urban studies. These range from the recurring problem of defining the urban, not just as an ontological matter but in terms of the selection, framing, and justification of case studies; a series of always-open questions around positionality, research ethics, and responsibility; the evaluation of different styles and strategies of exposition, representation, and theory making; and a host of issues relating to situated and embodied research practices in a context in which methodological talk, transparency, and reflexivity have been addressed rather intermittently, or relegated to footnotes and appendices. Correspondingly, the present volume features a collection of constructive assessments of revealed and recovered methodological practices, focused on a selection of significant monographs from across the field of critical urban studies, with a view to initiating new conversations – about methodological learning and the sharing of research practice not only about but *across* different approaches.

These are matters of concern for all those engaged in the field (and project) of critical urban studies, especially for early-career researchers, for whom the methodological choices are often as pressing as they are consequential. Hardly unusually for the field, the graduate students who joined the collaborative

UBC/UCLA seminar, the majority of whom are contributors to this volume, constituted a diverse group in terms of disciplinary backgrounds and substantive interests – not only geographers, but also those with affiliations to anthropology, architecture, economics, urban planning, and other fields. Developing effective protocols and practices for communication and collaboration were priorities from the beginning, since many in the two seminars were working together for the first time, even 'locally'. There would be only one opportunity for the Vancouver- and Los Angeles-based groups to meet face to face and in the same place, at a three-day workshop convened to conclude the seminar at the University of California's White Mountain Research Center, in the ironically bucolic surroundings of the Sierra Nevada Mountains. From the first meeting of the joint seminar through to the completion of this edited collection, it has been a priority to work collectively and collaboratively where possible, in variously configured partnerships, rather than individually. The initial separation by a distance of over 1,000 miles (1,600 km) posed a series of practical, organizational, and technical challenges that needed to be actively worked on while bringing this writing project through to completion, particularly as our collaborators scattered even farther afield.

At the end of what has been a three-year project – involving a great deal of writing and rewriting, internal conversation, and peer review, during which time some writing partnerships were reorganized while others recruited new members as lives and other commitments intervened – it is our hope that *Urban Studies Inside/Out* will live up to three aspirations. First, along with the contributors to the book, we seek to articulate a distinctive approach, that of reading for research practice and for methodology, broadly construed. This is not quite the same as merely writing a book review, or reading for theoretical or substantive takeaways. It cannot overlook the latter, of course, but it must be concerned just as much with *how* the authors achieve their explanatory and expositional goals as it is with an assessment of the value-added contribution of the final 'product'. Reading for research practice and methodology raises different (or at least additional) questions for the constructively critical reader and fellow researcher. It is to probe the question of how the monograph was made, indeed constructed. In turn, this meant asking a lot of questions of the texts and their authors, not just putting together a series of 'reviews'. A selection of well-regarded monographs in critical urban studies was chosen by graduate students in the joint seminar not in order to take the books apart, or for that matter to weigh their contribution with the cool eye of a distant critic, but instead with a view to reassembling *and learning from* their constitutive research practices. The monographs that are examined in Part II of this collection were consequently chosen not on the grounds that they might serve as convenient targets or foils for critique, but because they are valued, respected, and admired – and by extension provide constructive methodological lessons. What we characterize here as a 'reverse engineering' approach involved recovering the concrete methodological steps, data-gathering procedures, and interpretive maneuvers that the various authors used, for example by way of ethnographic studies, interview-based projects, or archival inquiries, but it also meant digging deeper. This digging deeper entailed positioning these facets of the methodological craft within the wider ambit of research practice, for instance to ask, in a positive and constructive spirit: how authors frame and bound their case studies, data-collection efforts, and fields of analytical vision; how (effectively) they marshal their empirical evidence in the context of an unfolding argument; what strategies of documentation and disclosure they use; how they engage with extant theory claims and/or how they make and sustain new ones; if and how they position themselves, as reflexive researchers and active subjects, in the text and in the research project that preceded it; how ethico-political commitments shape their research practices; and how distinctive contributions, especially compelling insights and take-home conclusions, are articulated, validated, and authenticated.

Second, with its emphasis on methodology, research practice, and the craft of critical urban studies, the present collection will hopefully speak positively to some of the things that are shared across this field, rather than those that divide it, being aimed especially at those learning the craft. The collaborative project behind the present volume was founded on the goal of learning from methodological exemplars selected from across the field, demonstrating respect for the chosen positions, research designs, and methodological strategies in the form of sustained but constructive critique, tilted in favor of what we call 'internal' critique. This entails asking what it was that the authors of the monographs discussed in Part II set out to achieve, and how (effectively) they eventually realized these objectives. In addition to bringing questions of method and practice to the surface – issues that are often submerged or marginalized in all but a small number of reflexive texts – we hope not only to contribute to what appears to be a resurgence in methodological talk in the field, but also to acknowledge the principle of mutual respect across methodo-logical (and other) differences.

Our third goal relates to the practice of this collaborative project itself, which we offer as an experiment from which others can learn, share, and build. Having attempted a similar, but rather differently focused, experiment in collaborative graduate education before, at the time when the distance between our respective departmental homes was just a four-hour drive between Madison, Wisconsin and Minneapolis, Minnesota, and when the technologies for online collaboration were not nearly so well developed, we are well aware of the nettlesome challenges as well as the intriguing potential of such efforts. This earlier collaborative seminar, convened in the Midwest of the United States, culminated in a workshop involving invited faculty along with graduate student presenters, out of which came a collection that we edited together, namely, *Contesting Neoliberalism: Urban frontiers* (H. Leitner et al., Guilford Press, 2007). Back then, the relative proximity of the two cam-puses allowed the participants to meet, work, and socialize together both at the beginning and at the end of the joint seminar – in the woods of northern Wisconsin. Since cost, distance, and logistical concerns meant that the UBC/ UCLA group was only able to get together once – at the end of the seminar but near to the beginning of the writing project that it spawned – our collaborative practices and protocols have had to be developed, sometimes laboriously, at a distance, albeit with the benefit of more robust platforms for online collaboration. We share some of these experiences, especially in Chapter 3 of the present volume, in the hope that others may be able to draw lessons and cues from them, building on them as they take forward their own experiments. For our part, we have certainly both learned and benefited greatly from this project and the opportunities that it has provided to work with graduate students across our two programs. And who knows? Maybe we too will do something similar again. But first we rest.

The editors

Los Angeles and Vancouver

March 2019

PART I
REORIENTATIONS

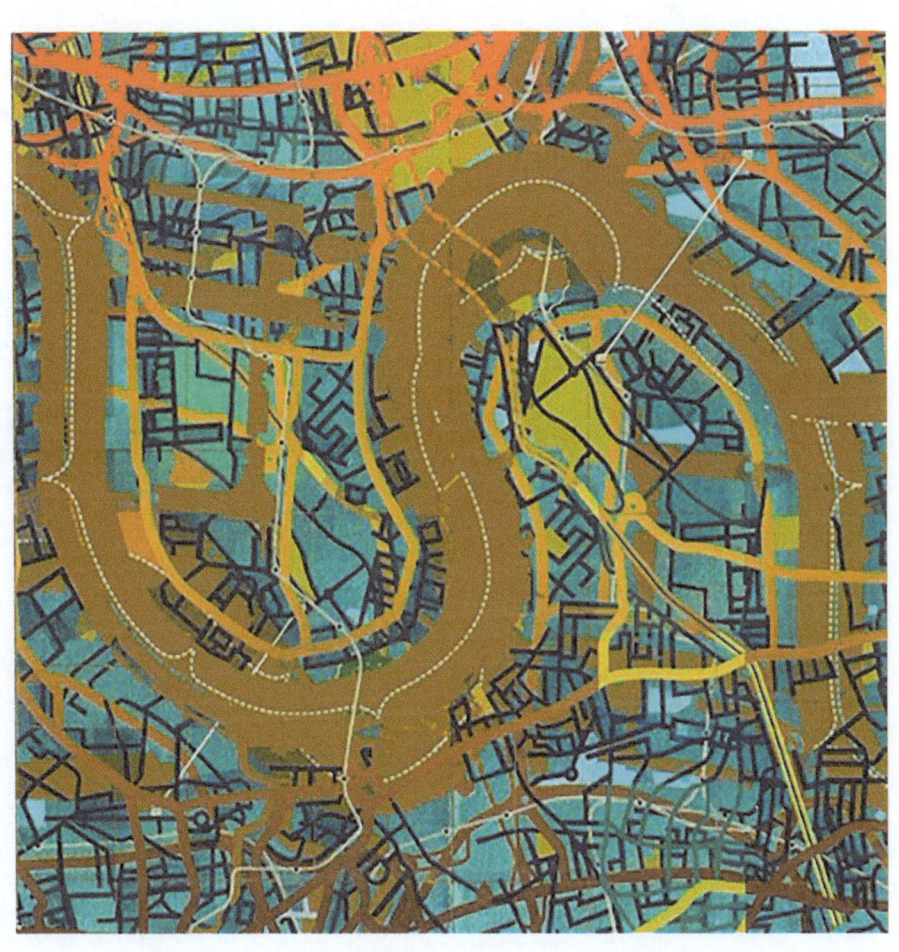

1

URBAN STUDIES UNBOUND: POSTMILLENNIAL SPACES OF THEORY

Helga Leitner, Eric Sheppard and Jamie Peck

Introduction: urban political economy, and beyond

Each of the urban monographs discussed in this book draws on one or more theorizations of the urban that have been in play since the turn of the Millennium. To contextualize the monographs, in this chapter we provide a brief overview of this theoretical landscape – an intellectual cartography of the current state of critical urban theory. In one way or another, the theoretical contributions to be discussed below each depart from a predominantly anglophone orthodoxy that dominated critical urban theory at the turn of the century: urban political economy. Before turning our attention to transformations in the field of critical urban studies over the past two decades, we provide a brief sketch of the state of the field at the turn of the Millennium, which is taken here as an inflection point of sorts despite some important strands of continuity. This represents a point of departure for the critiques and new lines of scholarship that have reshaped the field in the past two decades – the terrain explored in *Urban Studies Inside/Out*.

While the field of critical urban studies has always been characterized by a diverse and quite eclectic theory culture, by the notable absence of anything approaching singular methodological canon, and by a relatively open mandate for empirical inquiries, since the early 1980s its momentum and center of gravity were disproportionately shaped by urban political economy, notably (but not only) of a Marxian stripe. Never did this strand of work monopolize the terrain of critical urban studies, of course. A postmodern current, for example, had developed by the late 1980s (see Soja, 1989), although this too both engaged and took issue with the concerns of urban political economy. During the 1980s and 1990s, urban political economy became a dominant current or central tendency in the field, subsequently to become a locus for critique.

It is hardly an exaggeration to say that, as a critical project, critical urban studies were really made during the 1970s and 1980s, not least in the sway of a series of signal interventions from Manuel Castells and David Harvey (see Zukin, 1980; Brenner, 2009a). Influential lines of work that followed, many of them informed by various strands of (neo-)Marxist scholarship, would take up (and take on) the problematic of the capitalist city, attending in particular to the distinctive dynamics of capitalist urbanization, as well as to crises, conflicts, and contradictions rooted in specifically capitalist social relations. The 'urban process', as it would become known, was seen as an immanent and indeed active moment in the ongoing (re)production and transformation of capitalism, while cities were recognized to be on the front lines of struggles over social rights, collective services, industrial restructuring, exclusion, displacement, marginalization, and more, in ways that were variously indexed to, if never reducible to, the economic.

In retrospect, the ascendancy of urban political economy was not only framed by but also constituted through two especially important conjunctural moments, each with their own geographies. On the one hand, the 'urban crisis' of the 1960s, particularly in the United States, prompted a concern with racialized poverty, 'redlining', deindustrialization, and the flight of capital and middle-class residents to the suburbs. On the other hand, the macroeconomic turbulence of the 1970s was being linked to the emergence of new international divisions of labor, to the relocation of jobs and factories to the so-called 'peripheries' and 'semi-peripheries' of the world system, and to crises of North Atlantic Fordism.

Among the various trajectories of urban political economy that developed in the wake of these moments, two would prove to be especially influential. One was concerned with the politics of growth, the other with the implications of globalization. The catalytic notion of the 'city as growth machine' inspired a genre of critical urban studies focused on the actions and motives of growth elites, the turn toward entrepreneurial modes of urban governance, and the increasingly competitive political economy of place, as cities were reconstituted as competitive agents, hustling to attract investment and jobs, to defend and grow local tax bases in the face of economic uncertainty and the rollback of fiscal transfers, and to propagate new images and imaginaries evocative of more prosperous futures (Harvey, 1989; Leitner, 1990; Molotch, 1976). Subsequent work in this vein would run the spectrum between quite orthodox, institutionalist studies of 'urban regimes', where the focus would be placed on the network of relationships between elected officials and business elites, pretty much taking for granted the conditions of market-oriented economic development and liberal politics (Stoker and Mossberger, 1994; Stone, 1993), and a neo-Marxist strand of 'regulationist' urbanism animated by questions of 'post-Fordist' restructuring, the 'rescaling' of state capacities, and the emergence of new paradigms of socio-spatial regulation (Brenner, 1999a, 2009b; Jessop, 1997; Peck, 1995).

By the early 1990s, much of the work in urban political economy was being conducted under the sign of globalization – even though drawing on a more radical and politicized reading of globalization than that associated with mainstream notions of borderless worlds, (free) market integration, and the supposed erosion of nation-state power. The most conspicuous manifestation of this generative moment in critical urban studies came in the form of the 'global' or 'world' city, perched atop an increasingly hierarchical system of advanced global capitalism, the commanding heights of which were characterized by profound concentrations of corporate and financial power but also stark inequalities (Friedmann, 1986; Knox and Taylor, 1995; Sassen, 1991). The global cities rubric would provide the premise for new rounds of comparative urban studies, albeit typically focused on the highest peaks of the system such as New York, London, and Tokyo, along with inventive forms of network analysis, concerned not just with the attributes of top-level or 'alpha' cities but with the (re)configuration of intercity relations across the world system. In the process, not only did global connectivity, influence, and visibility become a 'treasured theoretical quality' (Beauregard, 2003: 192) in this, the 'globalization decade' of the 1990s; but so too would the seductive monikers of 'global' and 'world-class' urbanism become prized, aspirational categories, especially for a rising class of urban policymakers, gurus, and consultants. Manifestly at odds with the radical origins of this work, this instrumentalist and normative turn toward global boosterism was a byproduct of the increasingly hegemonic climate of entrepreneurial urbanism itself, with its fraught mix of competitive anxieties and promotional inclinations (Peck, 2014), but some parts of the (critical) literature were also amenable (or vulnerable) to mainstream appropriation, given their preoccupation with glitzy corporate capitals and the leading-edge operations of advanced capitalism, with the latest trends in cosmopolitan cultures and lifestyles, and with ranked league tables of urban 'success'.

Rather more heterodox and varied than their predominantly Marxist predecessors from the 1970s and early 1980s, theories of urban political economy had come to occupy incumbent status by the end of the 1990s. They represented, in effect, a critical orthodoxy of a certain kind. This was an orthodoxy attuned, inter alia: to driving processes of urban restructuring and transformation; to the pervasive consequences of power asymmetries and socio-spatial inequalities; to various forms of class analysis, crisis theory, and capital-logic explanation; to the structural positioning of cities in relation to the capitalist world system; to the circuitry of corporate power; and to macroregulatory forces; to the prioritization of predominantly economic sources of causality, along with realist and materialist forms of abstraction; and to a reliance on research sites disproportionately located in the late twentieth-century 'heartlands' of globalizing capitalism. These predispositions and priorities, in turn, would expose the field-cum-project of urban political economy to critiques of economism and explanatory overreach, often the outcome of a propensity to extrapolate from drivers of transformative change, from moments of political economic crisis, and from 'big stories' about capitalist logics, orders, or epochs. Thus the stage was set for a series of turns in critical urban studies, marked by varying degrees of sympathy or antagonism to the 'heterodoxy' of urban political economy.

In the remainder of this chapter, we organize our overview as follows. The following section begins with the fundamentals, reviewing what remain essentially unresolved debates about what the object of study should be for urban studies scholarship: what is this thing we call 'urban' that we claim to study? Next we examine the main directions of diversification, beyond urban political economy and beyond western urban theories, that have characterized the past two decades: the turn to questions of culture, identity, and subjectification; of the geography of urban knowledge production; and of the more-than-human aspects of urbanization. In recent years, debates about urban theory have become unduly heated, as new generations of scholars seeking to shift the theoretical conversation have confronted older (established white, often masculine) generations. This runs the danger of creating an intellectual environment that many of today's graduate students find uncomfortable – one where they feel forced to take sides in debates that they themselves have come to find limiting. In response to this, in the closing section of this chapter we seek to move beyond such impasses, toward a *both/and* rather than *either/or* approach to critical urban theory – the approach to which this book is dedicated.

What constitutes the urban?

What do we study when we claim to study the 'urban'? Any scientific endeavor begins with the question of what our object of study should be. In the social sciences, such objects are typically social (e.g., crime), possibly temporal, or perhaps spatial – as in the case of urban studies. Spatial objects of study have evidently posed more problems for (non-geographical) social scientists than either social objects of study or the conventions of historical analysis. Even geographers have spilt much ink determining the spatial boundaries of their object of study – an obsession of regional geographers in the mid-twentieth century. While the question of what it is that constitutes a city might seem to be intuitively obvious, this is a question that has been debated as long as there has been critical urban studies, with no settled resolution in sight. In a definitive early contribution, David Harvey's (1973) *Social Justice and the City*, the urban was simply any city, to be studied as a stand-alone object. Manuel Castells devoted a whole book to the question, writing that:

The delimitation of the urban remains ambiguous ... one might judge such a problem to be purely academic and keep to an analysis ... of space ... [given] the historical relativity of the criteria concerning the urban. [But] what is space? ... all space is constructed ... consequently, the theoretical non-delimitation of the space being dealt with ... amounts to accepting a culturally prescribed (and therefore ideological) segmentation. (1977 [1974]: 234)

Peter Saunders (1981) contended that the question of whether to approach cities through a spatial or a social lens poses a deep conundrum. Feeling that the former is limiting, he concluded that urban scholars should focus on social processes, which cannot be confined to spatial locations.

Now one might legitimately note that the same uncertainty applies also to social objects of study: certainly the question of what counts as crime, for example, depends on social conventions and definitions. Yet defining the urban has remained a puzzle for critical urban scholars, and if anything has gained increased attention, with a renewed round of debates prompted by 'urban age' rhetoric and smart-cities futurism, and by competing conceptions of planetary urbanization, 'cityness', provincialized urban epistemologies, and so forth. There is a long lineage here. In the 1960s, it was recognized that cities should be studied with respect to their hinterland – the region surrounding a city that is functionally connected to it (Berry and Pred, 1965). By the 1990s, increasing attention was being given to the study of national and international inter-urban systems (King, 1990; Knox and Taylor, 1995; Timberlake, 1985). Single-city studies remained staples in the field, to be sure, but these too were increasingly framed in 'global' terms (see Beauregard, 2003). In the context of deepening global integration and pan-urban interdependence – which is more than a matter of material linkages, being reflected also in forms of urban consciousness, ascendant ideologies, flows of ideas, practices, and much more – many have found it to be intuitively, practically, or analytically implausible to work exclusively within the city limits. Thus it has become less and less defensible to claim that it makes sense just to study what is going on within the boundaries of an individual city, as it were, in isolation (not least because borders themselves are social constructs).

Scholars from across the epistemological spectrum have sought to explode the border between the urban and the non-urban, even as they have variously retained a focus on urban issues. Writing from the post-structural perspective of performativity and non-representational theory, Ash Amin and Nigel Thrift argue: 'Time and again, the city is stressed as a site of localized flows and contact networks. Our argument ... is that the city needs theorization as a site of local-global connectivity, not a place of meaningful proximate links' (2002: 26–27).

Writing from a different post-structural perspective, that of actor–network theory, Ignacio Farías and Thomas Bender (2012) stake out a similar position. Drawing on Bruno Latour's skepticism about the utility of any scalar units of analysis, they challenge the presumption that 'cities should involve some stability of shape … entities … that can be positively identified and strictly delimited' (Farías, 2012: 9).

These ways of reconceptualizing the urban reiterate Doreen Massey's (1991) influential argument that events inside places can only be understood by studying how they are shaped by their interdependencies with events elsewhere – connectivity-based thinking (Sheppard, 2016). Considering London, Massey argues that the city's openness to the world also implies a certain ethico-political commitment. Since London's residents are dependent on, and prosper from, the actions of people in far distant places, they should be conscious of their responsibilities to the people and places affected by and affecting London:

> the question 'where does London (or any city) end?' must at least address the issue of those recruited into the dynamics of the urban economy and society by the long lines of connections of all sorts that stretch out to the rest of the country and on around the planet. (Massey, 2007: 216)

Perhaps the most geographically ambitious challenge to the urban as a delimited spatial unit of analysis has come from within geographical political economy. Neil Brenner and Christian Schmid (2015) advocate for a new epistemology of the urban, under the rubric of planetary urbanization. Taking up Henri Lefebvre's (2003 [1970]) prediction that capitalist society will become an urban society – the urban revolution – they argue that those interested in the urban, and urban transformations, cannot but study the world:

> rather than witnessing the worldwide proliferation of a singular urban form, 'the' city, we are instead confronted with new processes of urbanization that are bringing forth diverse socioeconomic conditions, territorial formations and socio-metabolic transformations across the planet. (Brenner and Schmid, 2015: 152)

While attending to the material and representational condition of our contemporary globalized world, such attempts to dismantle or transcend the city as a coherent unit of analysis have generated debate and discomfort. After all, if the world is now urban why not study the world rather than the urban? The most recent trenchant critique of such attempts to eviscerate the urban–rural frontier has come from Allen Scott and Michael Storper (Scott and Storper, 2015; Storper and Scott, 2016). Writing from a tradition melding geographical economics with political economy, they insist that a specifically urban theory is necessary. Recognizing that cities are far from isolated from their surroundings, they nonetheless argue that what happens within cities is distinctive. Any theory of cities, they insist, must therefore be grounded in agglomeration economies and the urban land nexus – the land-use patterns around a central city generated by these economies. The geographical proximity enabled by cities 'is crucial, for otherwise the time and distance costs of interaction would impede their operational effectiveness' (Storper and Scott, 2016: 1116).

Proximity itself is generative, from this perspective, enabling particularly urban relations and capacities. There is consequently a necessary role for the city, and for urban studies:

> With a conscientiously delimited and focused concept of the city it is possible to identify how the urban generates specific kinds of social phenomena and sets them apart from non-urban phenomena. This is what provides a distinctive place for urban analysis in the academic division of labour. (2016: 1118)

Proponents of planetary urbanization are skeptical of such 'methodological cityism', on the grounds that it naturalizes 'the city as the sole analytical terrain of urban analysis' (Angelo and Wachsmuth, 2015: 21), but can urban studies afford to ignore cities altogether? Brenner and Schmid (2015) retain a place for the urban within their concept of planetary urbanization, presenting the dialectical triad of concentrated urbanization (analogous to the domain recognized by Scott and Storper), extended urbanization (spanning both the everyday activities and the socio-economic dynamics of urban life, at a planetary scale), and differentiated urbanization (basically the dynamics of uneven geographical development). Yet other urban scholars working in the tradition of political economy, and with this kind of dialectical epistemology, have nevertheless sought to question this approach. Mark Davidson and Kurt Iveson contend that 'we might only be able to understand the planetary urban process through a re-engagement with the idea of "the city". Purging our vocabulary of "the city" would seem to be counterproductive' (Davidson and Iveson, 2015: 656). Similarly, Richard Walker insists that cities remain worthy of study as material objects 'of stone, concrete, breadth and depth and height', notwithstanding the fact that they co-evolve with processes extending well beyond their boundaries (2015: 185).

The question of how to hold the city in view as an object of analysis while at the same time moving to deconstruct its boundaries has also been taken up in post-structural accounts. For example, as we have seen, Amin and Thrift – contra Scott and Storper – have pressed the argument that cities should be theorized not as condensates of proximate links or agglomeration economies, but as sites of complex connectivities between the global and the local, and the urban and the more-than-urban. Nevertheless, Amin and Thrift seek to retain a sense of the 'cityness' of cities, the meaning of which they distill down to 'the combined vitality and political economy of urban socio-technical systems', the complex combination of which they believe 'define[s] the modern city' (Amin and Thrift, 2017: 3). AbdouMaliq Simone comes to a similar conclusion, his empirical work on African and Indonesian urbanism demonstrating the diverse ways in which the urban majority in these so-called 'southern' cities (and not just global capital) articulates local activities with global networks. For him, cityness 'refers to the city as a thing in the making', the making of which reflects the diverse, ever-changing, and path-breaking practices of its inhabitants – activities that 'cannot easily be channeled into clearly defined uses of space' (Simone, 2010: 3).

The various authors discussed here represent profoundly different epistemological approaches to urban theorizing, from urban economics, to political economy, to post-structural philosophy. Yet, notwithstanding these profound (and, as we will argue below, passionately defended) differences, they all face, and continue to struggle with, the same conundrum in defining the urban as an object of study. Should cities be treated as isolated spatial objects, each subject to the same processes – with the outcomes of those processes depending on spatio-temporal context? Should cities be studied as spatial objects whose internal dynamics and characteristics are shaped by processes that stretch well beyond the city? Or should we abandon the city as a spatial object of study altogether on the grounds that urbanization is everywhere? Drawing on Massey and Harvey's relational thinking about space, and what we would dub connectivity-based thinking, we incline to the second of these options: cities are understood as identifiable and distinctive spatial phenomena which nevertheless are constituted by an array of extra-local and extra-urban processes, relations, forces, and influences. They can be seen, in other words, as spatialized intensifications of these processes, relations, forces, and influences, all of which are reciprocally (re)shaped through urbanization itself.

How can and should we come to know the urban?

In this section, we consider some of the new approaches to knowing the urban that have emerged in the past two decades. Rather than return, once again, to the matter of rifts and differences in the field – which at times have appeared to be close to irreconcilable – we opt here to focus instead on three broad areas in which there has been purposive and positive development, each of which has contributed new and original insights into how we can and should come to know the urban. First, we examine the issues of difference, identity, and culture in everyday urban life; second, we turn to the question of the locations and vantage points from which to know, read, and theorize the urban; and third, we conclude this section with a discussion of the more-than-human city.

Difference, identity, and culture in the urban everyday

A complex and diverse set of interventions, from a wide range of perspectives, including feminist, post-structuralist, queer, critical-race, and settler–colonial approaches, have decentered and refocused critical urban studies in the past two decades, many of which have posed challenges to the political economic orthodoxy. We welcome these challenges because they shake up old explanatory hierarchies; we view this increasing heterodoxy not as a sign of crisis and chaos, but as an indication of conceptual dynamism and vitality in urban theorizing. By deploying different conceptual lenses and by invoking different ontological and epistemological imaginings, this increasingly pluralist heterodoxy has brought many different facets of the urban condition into focus.

What these challenges have in common is more than a decentering of the hegemonic orthodoxy, but a call for urban theorizing that: first, uncovers and theorizes difference and diversity along with multiple forms of oppression in cities; second, focuses on the mundane urban everyday; and third, has an explicit ethico-political commitment to furthering more just urban futures and the continued diversification of knowledge production. As is the case also for many political economic approaches, the aim is to explain not simply how things are but also how they should be, diversifying the geographic and social location of knowledge production.

Beyond these commonalities, the challenges these approaches pose to the orthodoxy are diverse and the boundaries between them are fuzzy. In terms of ontological and epistemological commitments we can identify two major currents. First, there are what might be considered extensions and elaborations of the orthodoxy: theoretical reconstructions that have led to new synergies and the formation of hybrid approaches that, albeit typically starting with mundane everyday practices and embodied experience, also attend to the embeddedness of these into larger, political, economic, and cultural structures (Fincher et al., 2019; Peake and Rieker, 2013). The second current, by contrast, is an ontological reorientation that makes mundane everyday practices and individual experiences the primary focus. It deploys different ontological and epistemological imaginings for the study of cities, more radically reorienting how we can and should come to know the urban.

Reconstructions of political economy have come from cultural political economists as well as feminist geographers. Cultural political economic approaches have stressed the need to pay attention not simply to the structure and workings of the capitalist political economy, but also to the ways culture shapes and indeed constitutes the economy, along with patterns of behavior, worldviews, and social relations 'in place'. They encourage us to think about an urban cultural political economy rather than simply an urban political economy, paying attention to the social and cultural embedding of economic activities. In part responding to the 'cultural turn' in the social sciences and to criticisms of economic reductionism, cultural political economists have interrogated the role of identities, discourses, representations, and institutional cultures in shaping urban economies and development trajectories (Jessop and Sum, 2010; Sayer, 2001). One of the major interventions has been to highlight the articulation between discursive representations and material processes (Oosterlynck and González, 2013). Beauregard's *Voices of Decline* (1993) was an early theoretical intervention along these lines, highlighting the power of representations (in this case negative representations of US cities) as fundamental shapers of urban development trajectories and experiential understandings of the city. Some of the subsequent work in this vein has followed the lead of Sayer, who proposed an expansive conception of a cultural political economy taking full account of the 'lifeworlds of political and economic processes – identities, discourses, work cultures and the social and cultural embedding of economic activity', together with the articulation between lifeworlds and economic and political systems (2001: 688). Building on the Habermasian distinction between system and lifeworld, which highlights communicative action and cognition, Sayer's lifeworld also includes non-cognitive and embodied elements, and goes beyond the private and public sphere to include economic and political institutions. What all these interventions suggest is that attention to the lifeworld or the everyday necessitates the need for a culture-specific analysis of urban economies and the city more generally.

Feminist geographers have been critical of the disregard by the orthodoxy of gender and other lines of social difference, and of the complexity of social relations in the operation, reproduction, and differentiation of urban capitalist economies across space and time. They have drawn attention to the importance of the embodied (gendered, raced, sexualized) nature of lived experience of the urban, but also to the intersectionality of multiple lines of difference (e.g., race, class, and gender) in shaping urban experiences and inequalities, including the encoding of these lines of difference in urban landscapes (Kern and McLean, 2017; Parker, 2011). In the spirit of reconstruction rather than abandonment, they highlight how the capitalist 'economy articulates with and reinforces gendered, racialized, and classed oppression' (Werner et al., 2017: 4). For example, they have shown how the global economy impacts and relies on the social reproduction that happens within the household, including the care and emotional labor of women. Besides pushing for explanatory extensions of political economic frameworks, feminist scholars have also advocated for scholarly commitments to social justice and feminist praxis, with the goal of overcoming injustices across the urban world (Parker 2016; Peake and Rieker, 2013), producing knowledge collaboratively, and resisting totalizing narratives (Kern and McLean, 2017: 421).

The mundane everyday has also been at the center of urban theorizing that entails an ontological and epistemological reorientation. This reorientation has involved the decentering of dominant urban theories, informed by different degrees of skepticism concerning more structural explanations of urban life, form, and dynamics. As expected, post-structural urban scholars have been front and center in this current. While still engrossed in investigating the power of discourses and representations of cities and city spaces at the turn of the century, new lines of scholarship have focused insistently on mundane and everyday practices in urban micro-spaces, including life on the street and in public spaces more generally, and in the acts of dwelling, working, recreating, and daily mobility (Blok and Farías, 2016; Farías and Bender, 2012). In line with their rejection of structural explanations, there has been a tendency in some of this literature to ignore the embeddedness of these practices in larger, political, economic, and cultural structures and their complex interconnections with systems of domination and oppression. This has also been manifest in a certain quietude concerning urban inequalities in many of these studies. Indeed, decisive contributions on urban inequality have been largely absent from this literature (cf. Goodwin-White, 2018).

Yet recent work on difference in the urban everyday shows that lived experiences are always structurally mediated (Ahmed, 2004; Fincher et al., 2019; Leitner, 2012; Theodore, 2015). For example, examining encounters between local residents and immigrants in four white settler–colonial metropolises (Sydney, Melbourne, Los Angeles, and Toronto) in different spheres of life, Fincher et al. (2019) show that while these encounters are quite particular to the different time–space contexts (e.g., at the city and neighborhood scale), they have a broader resonance because their particularity articulates with and is mediated by broader political economic structures and forms of oppression. Yet the authors do not claim that their findings constitute a universal experience.

Similarly, feminist, queer, and critical-race scholars variously have revealed and problematized the operation of power enacted through multiple forms of oppression – racism, classism, patriarchy, homophobia – in shaping the urban experience, demonstrating in the process how difference is produced, performed, experienced, negotiated, as well as contested (Woods, 1998; Pulido, 2000). This not only provides new insights into the gendered, racialized, and sexualized spaces frequently overlooked or marginalized in mainstream and critical urban studies, but also pays attention to diverse modalities of resistance and to the production of alternative imaginaries (Brown, 2008; Brown and Knopp, 2014; Doderer, 2011; McKittrick, 2006; Pulido, 2006; Roy, 2017; Valentine and Skelton, 2003; Wekerle, 2005; Woods, 2017). Notably, in this type of urban theorizing, appeals to the everyday and embodied experiences do not come at the expense of the engagement with larger power structures and forms of oppression.

Despite the differences, most of the scholarship discussed in this section cautions against universalizing research findings emerging from a narrow range of cities, especially when these are mostly located in the global North (Jacobs, 2012b; Robinson, 2006; 2011a 2013a; Roy, 2009; Sheppard et al., 2013). Those articulating this position align themselves with those postcolonial urban scholars who have questioned the assumption that urban theories and concepts developed in Europe and North America apply to cities of the post-colony. This expansive body of work, with roots in critiques of Eurocentric, 'globo-centric', modernist, and developmentalist models of the urban, has acquired a programmatic scope in the course of the past two decades, effectively reconstituting much of the field of critical urban studies, if not shifting its very axis. It is to this body of work that we now turn.

From where can and should we theorize the urban?

Knowledge production is always geographical in origin, yet the process of theorization often seeks to shake off those particular origins in the name of abstraction. The urban theories that were popularized in the 1960s bore the imprint of the Chicago school of urban sociology, developed in the 1920s under the leadership of Robert Park. Deeply engaged with the city that they called home, Park and his colleagues had theorized cities according to a locally sourced template: accordingly, a central business district was surrounded by low-income neighborhoods occupied by recent immigrants, with better-off neighborhoods further out occupied by earlier waves of immigrants who had by now assimilated to urban life and prospered. This concentric zone model was re-theorized by urban economists (Alonso, 1960), modified to account for directional effects and multiple nodes, and reanalyzed by Brian Berry and others who sought to rewrite urban social ecology as quantitative social science (Berry and Kasarda, 1977). Park himself traveled the world, envisioning 'human ecology as a universal framework to study urban processes' (Ren, 2018: 498). While he was unable to realize this research agenda, by the late 1960s this Chicago-influenced approach had become the default urban theory taught throughout the anglophone academy, and beyond. It had shed its Chicago origins to travel the world as the urban theory.

In the 1990s, the Los Angeles school of urban theory emerged, challenging this hegemony by emphasizing the limits of theorizing from Chicago. Writing from Los Angeles, its protagonists presented LA as a distinctive and globally proliferating urban form, the reading of which would require a quite different theoretical approach, later portrayed as the Los Angeles school of postmodern urban theory (Dear, 2000; Dear and Dishman, 2001; Scott and Soja, 1998; Soja, 1989; 1996; 2000). Thomas Gieryn calls Chicago and Los Angeles truth-spots, writing: 'The passage from place-saturated contingent claims to place-less transcendent truths is achieved through the geographic, architectural and rhetorical construction of a "truth-spot" ... a delimited geographical location that lends credibility to claims' (2002: 113; 2006: 29). The Los Angeles school – much like the city itself – has since dissipated.

In retrospect, the LA school can also be seen as a conjunctural product of a certain time and place. It had anticipated what would later be characterized as the globalization decade of the 1990s, albeit initially in the shape of new dynamics of Pacific Rim integration, with Japan playing a leading role. While this represented a break of sorts from the transatlantic gaze that had dominated urban studies theorizing for much of the twentieth century, the worlds of urban theorizing were about to be opened up in more far-reaching ways. Belated recognition of the explosive rates of urbanization that for some time had been registered across large parts of the global South seemed to be inaugurating new modalities of majority-world urbanism. This coincided, far from coincidentally, with the ascendancy of new lines of urban theorizing, often drawing explicitly on postcolonial thought and 'southern theory', but resonating in various ways with parallel projects in feminist and post-structuralist studies. This raised the question whether urban theories developed in the context of the global North are relevant for understanding cities and urban transformations in the global South (Edensor and Jayne, 2012). Not only did this destabilize the often taken-for-granted status that had been accorded to a small cluster of Euro-American truth-spots in urban studies;

it also prompted far-reaching debates around the decentralization and democratization of urban theory.

In her influential book *Ordinary Cities*, Robinson (2006) argued that urban
theory had become too indebted to thinking through (and indeed from) what
had become dubbed global cities – Los Angeles, London, Tokyo, and the like.
Challenging the presumption that these should be the norm against which
other cities are to be compared, she argued that all cities are global in their own
way and should be taken seriously as sites from which to theorize. She advocated for 'an urban theory that draws inspiration from the complexity and
diversity of urban life, and from urban experiences and urban scholarship
across a wide range of different kinds of cities' (Robinson, 2006: 1). Postcolonial
theory has become an expansive, interdisciplinary project, the origins of which
can be traced to subaltern studies in India. From these origins, this increasingly
diverse intellectual project has diffused across the postcolony and back to the
former seats of colonial power. Postcolonial theorists argue that the Euro-
American experience of development since 1500 cannot be taken as a universal
norm against which other societies are measured (and found wanting, subsequently to be portrayed in terms of deficits and absences), because colonialism
and its contemporary legacies have foreclosed this path of development for
formerly colonized territories (Dirlik, 1997). As a result, formerly colonized
territories have evolved distinctive characteristics that northern theorists too
often neglect, or construct as otherwise marginal – subaltern subjectivities,
surplus populations, informality, and the like – undermining the capacity of
their theories to travel to and explain cities of the postcolony (Robinson, 2006;
Roy, 2005; 2011).

In the spirit of feminist and postcolonial scholarship, especially informed by
Dipesh Chakrabarty's (2000) book *Provincializing Europe*, theorizing from
the South seeks to provincialize knowledge claims emanating from distant
centers of knowledge production. In so doing, it proposes a new comparative
analytic that decenters the universalism of dominant theories as an implied
norm or template. Provincializing urban theory thus means questioning
whether theories of urban development and form, developed in such urban
contexts as Chicago, Los Angeles, and New York, can be abstracted from those
contexts to travel elsewhere and become universally applicable. Similarly,
western cities should no longer constitute the norm against which cities in the
global South are to be judged (Watson, 2009).

Building on Robinson's intervention, urban theorists have subsequently
sought to delineate the components of 'southern' urban theory, advancing a
variety of mid-level concepts based on close studies of the urban everyday in
cities of the global South, often positioned as challenges to accounts of cities
of the global South indexed to Euro-American urban theory. Examples
include Bayat's (2000) idea of the quiet encroachment of the ordinary,
Benjamin (2008) on occupancy urbanism, Simone (2004a; 2004b) on people as
infrastructure, Yiftachel's (2009) notion of gray spaces, and Roy's (2011)
subaltern urbanism and varieties of informality. While contested from more

orthodox perspectives, including on the grounds that supposedly contextual conditions are being elevated to the status of theory claims (see Scott and Storper, 2015), these and related interventions have been triggering a rethinking of urban theories.

It is important to note that such mid-level theoretical concepts are not offered as different theories for different places (southern theories for southern cities), but as contributions to relational theorizing. Reconceptualizing features of urbanization from the south, overlooked in northern theory, may well be relevant for understanding northern cities. For example, southern urban theory that focuses on understanding informality – a pervasive feature of postcolonial cities – has the potential to bring new insights to Los Angeles, whose extensive homeless population pursues informal livelihoods similar to those in cities of the global South.

The debate on theorizing from the south has further opened up the field of urban studies resulting in, as Roy (2009) has put it, the proliferation of new geographies of theory. As we have argued in different ways elsewhere (Leitner and Sheppard, 2016; Peck, 2015), having opened things up, the question that the field faces is what the next moves should be. Postcolonial theorists have made a strong case for a more global, more cosmopolitan, and more decentered approach to understanding cities. We concur that when theories emerge from multiple sites this can productively expand our understanding of cities. Yet while acknowledging the possibilities associated with theorizing from everywhere, it is vital to do so in a manner that accounts for how cities are relationally constituted. In terms of theory development this means not only stress-testing the theories developed with Chicago or Los Angeles in mind in 'southern' cities, but also stress-testing theories emerging from the south in cities like Chicago or LA. Irrespective of whether a productive engagement and mutual learning across these differently positioned theorizations results in a better global urban theory, taking them seriously is surely the path not only to improving but also to enriching our understanding of cities.

Conceptualizing the more-than-human city

The third of our themes in this survey of postmillennial urban theorizing concerns the more-than-human. Cities are not just made up of people: other species (cats, dogs, coyotes, mosquitoes, tomatoes, oak trees) are both crucial to and deeply embedded in urban life, as are the various material and immaterial objects and technologies that humans utilize to construct and inhabit urban environments (from buildings to roads, bikes, cement, water, architectural drawings, plans, 'big data', etc.) (Braun, 2005; Cronon, 1991; Graham and Marvin, 2001; Kaika, 2005; Kitchin, 2014). The term more-than-human was coined in order to capture how humans cohabit and co-evolve with these others, a formulation that is favored over non-human, which carries the implication of inhabiting different and separate worlds. Since at least the 1970s, urban scholars have been recognizing the presence of nature in the city, initially under the rubric of urban ecology, but the last two decades have witnessed the proliferation and deepening of these lines of inquiry. In good part, this reflects our increased awareness of environmental problems and climate change, but also a re-emergent intellectual interest in making sense of the materialities of human life.

An important body of work has developed around efforts to extend urban political economy in order to incorporate the more-than-human world – not least by revisiting and reconstituting the materialism in Marx's original writings. This work has been gathered under the label of urban political ecology. Political ecology had emerged as its own sub-field in the 1980s, initially with a focus on rural environments in the third world. Critical of then-dominant approaches to cultural ecology, this ascendant project of political ecology examined how economic livelihood strategies both shape and are shaped by biophysical processes, moving on to explore how these more-than-human relationships were embedded in, while reciprocally shaping, politics and power relations (Robbins, 2004; Rocheleau et al., 2013). A distinctively urban political ecology has extended such thinking to urban environments and landscapes (Heynen et al., 2006b). This approach has called attention, first, to understanding a series of pertinent biophysical processes (how water flows, how plants grow, etc.), studying how these processes shape, but also are shaped by, human activity. Marx referred to this as metabolism – the ever-shifting exchange between humans and their more-than-human counterparts. Second, this entails the positioning of these relations within the context of the political economic system through which humans acquire what they need from their environments, under the capitalist mode of production. Third, the approach involves an interrogation of how these processes systemically favor certain social groups, and environments, relative to others – in other words, the implications for social and environmental justice (Swyngedouw and Heynen, 2003). And finally, it also means tracing the political implications, especially for those seeking to contest social and environmental injustices (Swyngedouw, 2018).

Urban political ecology currently focuses on the operation of these metabolic regimes, along with their socio-natural implications, notably in relation to neoliberalized capitalism, under which 'nature' is increasingly commodified as market logics are established as the default means to manage human–environment relations. Much of this work has focused on northern cities, but there has been significant attention to issues such as water provision in southern cities (Kooy and Bakker, 2008). Issues of identity and subjectification have only received limited attention so far, although recent work is beginning to connect questions of race and situated knowledge under the rubric of urban political ecology. The North American literature on environmental justice has exhibited a distinctly urban focus; urban political ecologists have criticized this work for prioritizing 'a liberal ... distributional perspective on justice' while downplaying the structuring role of capitalist social relations (Heynen et al., 2006a: 9). Pulido has attended to those contexts while bringing questions of race and white privilege to the fore (Pulido, 2000; Pulido and De Lara, 2018). With reference to African cities, Mary Lawhon and colleagues have sought to provincialize urban political ecology (Lawhon et al., 2014).

A second strand of critical urban scholarship has been concerned to interrogate utopian currents in mainstream thinking on how cities can be made more sustainable and/or resilient, in the process delivering the win–win of ecological and social well-being alongside economic growth – a paradigm of ecological modernist policymaking that promotes neoliberal answers to the question of whether cities can be good for the environment (for a progressive alternative, see Davis, 2010). If sustainability approaches emphasize urban mitigation, seeking a balance between environment, economy, and society, the notion of resilience calls attention to the need for cities to adapt to the 'radical uncertainties' stemming from environmental disruptions (sea-level rise and the like). Critics have argued that the political economy of neoliberalized capitalism makes it all but impossible to realize social and environmental justice under such conditions (Bulkeley and Betsill, 2005; MacKinnon and Derickson, 2012; Swyngedouw, 2007; While et al., 2004).

Post-structural urban theorists approach these issues from a rather different perspective, drawing in particular on Bruno Latour's actor–network theory and Deleuze and Guattari's notion of the assemblage. These bodies of thought begin with the more-than-human conceptualization that humans, and human action, are intimately related to everything else in the world, while stressing two other issues: first, that humans are not the only ones exerting agency on the world; and second, that power is an emergent and always-fragile feature of these more-than-human relations. Thus Latour (2005) portrays non-human agents as actants, arguing that human agents and actants are relationally connected through continuously shifting actor–networks, and that there are no pre-existing power hierarchies. Rather, concentrations of power (he calls them centers of calculation) are a contingent and emergent feature of network interdependencies, and as such are always in danger of falling apart. These are centers that do not hold. Only a limited amount of urban theory self-identifies as based in actor–network theory (ANT; Farías and Bender, 2012), but there is a deeper body of scholarship deploying assemblage theory. Colin McFarlane (2011a; 2011b) has developed this approach most fully. Gilles Deleuze and Félix Guattari's (1987) assemblage theory, influenced by dynamical systems theory (DeLanda, 2006), conceptualizes any socio-ecological entity as a machine-like combination of heterogeneous entities, whose components are not fixed but can be substituted in or out. Assemblages are constructed from the bottom up, are continually being revised, and are always emergent (never stabilizing). Applying this to urban theory, assemblage theory (like ANT) emphasizes thick description over abstract theorization, conceptualizes agency (like ANT) as distributed across 'the social and the material' (McFarlane, 2011a: 221), and stresses potentiality, emergence, change, and hope. The contrast between these approaches (emphasizing localized empirical observation rather than big-picture theorizing; change and potential rather than constraints and limits; and local agency rather than broader-scale structuring contexts) and urban political economy has generated some energetic debate (Brenner et al., 2011; McFarlane, 2011c). Nevertheless, the case has been made on both side of these debates that these can and should be seen as complementary approaches to critical urbanism rather than opposing viewpoints: *both/and* rather than *either/or*.

As noted at the outset, 'more-than-human' is not just about the biophysical world we inhabit: it also refers to the various artifacts produced by humans, artifacts that themselves also shape urban life. Often these are glossed under the term technology, with the relevant urban theoretical literature drawing from science and technology studies (STS) – an approach to the history of science that examines how the technologies that scientists produce to undertake their work feed back to shape trajectories of scientific progress – more-than-human agency again. Indeed, the biophysical and the technological intersect: the kinds of infrastructures produced in cities and what they make possible depend not only on techno-scientific knowledge but also on the biophysical properties of the materials used. McFarlane (2011b), for example, examines how houses as a technology shape urban habitation, while Farías and Bender's (2012) collection on ANT urbanism devotes a section to infrastructure.

A classic study widely credited with opening up these questions for investigation in urban studies was the book *Splintering Urbanism* (Graham and Marvin, 2001). Examining infrastructure networks that hold cities together (transport, telecommunications, water, and energy), conceptualizing the city as a sociotechnical process, and examining the influence of neoliberalism, Graham and Marvin (2001) argue that goals of equalizing access to urban infrastructure for everyone have not only proved to be elusive, but also are increasingly ignored in an era in which market forces have come to determine the production of infrastructure – thereby splintering the experience of urban residents. Indeed, just as anthropologists interested in the more-than-human world have become fascinated with technology (Anand et al., 2018), a significant stream in the literature has begun to integrate STS thinking into urban theory (Anand, 2017; Björkman, 2015; Gandy, 2014; Graham and McFarlane, 2014).

Yet many technologies are far less material than the tarmac, concrete, and metals found in roads and pipes: land use plans, architectural drawings, financial and accounting models, and, of course, digital technologies accompanied by their muscular cousin 'big data'. The increasing attention given to understanding the digitization of urban life parallels its increasingly pervasive influence. Some scholars have examined how these technologies splinter urban experiences, favoring better connected cities, and neighborhoods and social classes within cities, at the expense of the less well connected (Graham and Marvin, 2001; Wheeler et al., 2000). More recently, critical urban theorists have tackled 'smart' urbanism, embraced and propounded by mainstream policymakers as a more-than-human urban utopia (Kitchin, 2016; Marvin et al., 2015; Shelton et al., 2015).

A conclusion of sorts: from theory to practice

In this opening chapter, we have sought to do two things. First, we have pointed to several lines of development in the field of critical urban studies over the past two decades. No single chapter can do this full justice, of course; interested readers may want to explore the more extended treatments in recent book-length discussions (Brenner et al., 2012; Edensor and Jayne, 2012; Harding and Blokland, 2014; Jayne and Ward, 2016; Short, 2014; Parker, 2015). Second, we stress the importance of approaching the field of critical urban studies in the spirit of a *both/and* approach, rather than an oppositional, *either/or* mentality: one that instinctively is on the lookout for ways of putting theories and approaches in conversation with one another, even where these may be seemingly incompatible.

Some may feel that this is utopian and quixotic, far easier said than done, and certainly this is not the only possible way forward. We are open to any proposals about how to create venues for mutual learning, constructive dialogue, and autocorrection, even as we remain quite convinced that a *both/and* approach represents the most fruitful direction of travel. Far from being a flabby compromise where 'anything goes', moving toward a *both/and* approach, and away from the kind of combative, *either/or* theory culture that has marred some recent exchanges in the field, will take work. This collection is the result of one attempt to move in this direction. It does so by embracing a collaborative approach to research practice in critical urban studies, based on constructive engagements with significant texts in the field, read more for what they achieve than in terms of what they supposedly lack. To this end, there is much to be learned from positive contributions to methodological practice, as opposed to the airing of theoretical differences. It is to these issues that we now turn.

2

DOING URBAN STUDIES: NAVIGATING THE METHODOLOGICAL TERRAIN

Eric Sheppard, Helga Leitner and Jamie Peck

Introduction: questions of methodology

In this chapter, we turn from questions of theory, ontology, and epistemology to the question of methodology – of how urban scholars since the turn of the Millennium have gone about their research in order to produce empirically informed knowledge. The methodologies deployed by critical urban scholars are as diverse as their theoretical influences. Yet, while urban theory receives enormous attention, discussions of urban studies methodologies have largely remained under the radar – our motivation for this book. Indeed, for many of the monographs that are examined in Part II of this collection, the authors of the books in question generally spend little time explicating their method, necessitating the attempts herein to try to reverse-engineer what those methods were. Nevertheless, and to some extent paralleling theoretical shifts, there have been distinctive changes in the methodological culture of critical urban studies. Thus, quantitative methods have been somewhat out of fashion in critical urban research, albeit with the occasional exception (Wallace and McCarthy, 2007; Wallace and Wallace, 1998; Wyly et al., 2010). On the other hand, qualitative methods have become practically hegemonic, ranging from ethnography, intensive interviews, and discourse analysis to participatory action research. These are often approached as stand-alone alternatives, and equated with particular theoretical traditions, with mixed- and multi-method research designs becoming more popular in the recent past.

In this chapter's overview of urban methodologies, like our approach to urban theory, we cannot be exhaustive but seek instead to emphasize the role of methodology as an integrating moment in the research process. We do not wish to reduce this to a matter of the selection of tools, important though this certainly is; neither do we wish to imply that different methodological strategies imply completely separate tracks of inquiry. Just as in the preceding discussion of urban theory, we emphasize that there is much to learn from methodological strategies *not* chosen, while there are also opportunities to blend and combine different methods, sometimes to great effect. Methodology should be thought of expansively: it refers to the relationship (or hinge) between theoretical frames, methods of investigation, and evidentiary strategies.

The choice of methodology is often seen as deriving directly from a researcher's theoretical and epistemological commitments. From our perspective, however, there is no determinative relationship between theory and methodology, whereby certain methodological norms and associated research practices necessarily derive from, and are limited to, particular ontological and epistemological commitments. After all, some positivists utilize qualitative methodologies, Marxists utilize mathematical modeling (including Marx himself; Barnes, 2007) and statistical analysis, and some post-structural methodologies prioritize empirical observation. Nevertheless, certain persistent conventions have emerged within sub-fields of urban scholarship.

Consider so-called positivist approaches to urban research, dominant by the end of the 1960s and receiving some renewed attention today (Wyly, 2009; Wilson, 2014). These require a methodology for testing hypotheses against observations – generally implying the use of representative sampling and statistical inference. As urban geographers trained under the quantitative revolution abandoned positivism for Marx (himself skeptical of empiricist knowledge production), they also questioned and highlighted the limits of the quantitative methods associated with that revolution (Sheppard, 1995; 2001). David Harvey – the author of what remains the definitive text on logical empiricist geography (Harvey, 1969) – was particularly influential here, as was Andrew Sayer, whose reading of critical realism advanced qualitative methodologies as better suited to answering how and why questions concerning causality, with quantitative approaches limited to examining the extent of a phenomenon (Harvey, 1972; Sayer, 1985). This has had the lingering effect of marginalizing quantitative approaches within the methodological repertoire of critical urban studies, misleadingly associating them with an empiricist and status-quo-oriented positivism (despite the political radicalism of such early logical empiricist/positivist geographers as Fred Schaefer and William Bunge; Sheppard, 2014b).

By the same token, urban political economy is associated with methods that contextualize local urban practices, policies, and transformations by interrogating the broader-scale forces (also known as 'the context of context'; Brenner et al., 2010) and unobservable structural preconditions shaping observable local events. Sayer's critical realism has been important here, as has

Michael Burawoy's (1998; Burawoy et al., 2000) extended case method. With the turn to post-structural approaches to urban theory, discourse analysis became more popular, as did actor–network, assemblage, and performativity approaches. Feminist methodology sensitized urban studies to the need for reflexivity concerning the unequal power dynamic between researcher and research subjects, breaking down the binary divide that has long separated them (Peake, 2016).

In the remainder of this chapter, we review the current broad spectrum of methodological practices and conventions in critical urban scholarship, many of which make an appearance in the urban monographs analyzed in Part II. Seeking to trouble conventions that seemingly align methodology with ontology and epistemology, and to make space for creative methodological recombination and mixing, we organize these around four related clusters of methodological praxis: close encounters, connectivities, comparison, and conjunctural analysis. For each we note the assemblages of methods deployed by scholars working within that cluster. By *close encounters*, we reference methodological practices that stress a close engagement between the researcher and texts, and between researcher and the researched in the urban everyday: discourse analysis, urban ethnography, (extended) case study approaches, and combinations of these, as well as reflexivity and participatory action research. Methods stressing the analysis of *connectivities* reflect both the emergent interest in interrogating more-than-human networking and its effects, and connectivities operating within and beyond individual cities. Methodologies of *comparison* have a long-standing presence in urban studies, as scholars seek to understand and account for inter-urban differences and similarities – but they have taken on a new lease of life as critical urban scholars have begun to question both taken-for-granted comparative norms and different ways of conducting comparative analyses. Finally, *conjunctural analysis* has begun to receive attention as a way of unpacking how local events are shaped by their spatio-temporal positionality, notably with respect to the geopolitics of globalizing capitalism and shifting paradigms of statecraft. Again, we emphasize that these are not mutually exclusive categories, or separate methodological lifestyles. They connect with and bleed into one another in many ways, and it is often at these interfaces that innovation occurs.

Close encounters

The field of urban studies largely defines itself through its commitments to 'close' engagements with cities, to grounded and contextualized forms of analysis, to first-hand inquiries conducted in (rather than merely on) cities, and often to intimate encounters between researchers and the subjects and subject matter of their research. There are, however, many ways of getting close. This section focuses on three aspects of these close urban encounters: close readings of texts, by way of discourse and visual analysis; close encounters with the field, by way of ethnographic approaches to subjects and situations; and close engagements with the urban, including research ethics, the politics of representation, and the coproduction of knowledge.

Close readings

We begin with *close readings*. These have been particularly associated with post-structural theories that have drawn attention to the role of language in constructing/structuring a certain reality – how we see, think, and talk about the world in particular geographical and historical conjunctures. In terms of method, examining the role of language involves discourse analyses of how texts represent the world (see Lees, 2004). This may include analyzing the use of words, grammar, metaphors, analogies, and uncovering the meaning of texts (Hastings, 2014). For geographers and urban studies scholars, however, it is not only written texts that matter, but also visual representations, ranging from images and videos to the urban built environment (Rose, 2007). In each case, the meaning inscribed in a text is up for deconstruction. For example, in *The City as Text*, James Duncan (1990) shows not only how the urban landscape of Kandy, Sri Lanka, is culturally produced, but also how its built environment serves to reinforce existing power relations and hierarchies.

Significant currents in critical urban research have been inspired by Foucauldian discourse analysis (Fairclough, 2013), which emphasizes that discourses are always infused/permeated with power relations in terms of both their construction and the work they do. Foucauldian-inspired discourse analyses, with their focus on the deconstruction and the performativity of discourses, have uncovered how dominant discourses of the powerful produce a particular, selective rendering of 'reality' that comes to dominate and distort all others. Examples of such practices are selective representations of cities, such as city branding and discourses of decline. City branding, a burgeoning growth industry, is a strategy deployed by local governments and businesses that highlights certain aspects of a city's cultural, economic, or environmental characteristics for the purpose of making the city more attractive in the minds of businesses, (local as well as non-local), potential tourists, and its own citizens (Vanolo, 2017). On the other hand, pathologizing discourses have played a major role in shaping urban regeneration policy in US cities (Matthews, 2010). Robert Beauregard's (1993) *Voices of Decline* was an early study that deconstructed dominant discourses of US central cities as places ridden with various pathologies and social and environmental problems, and where residents fear to tread – not only creating a stereotypical representation of central cities but also silencing alternative representations of central cities. In step with Beauregard, Mustafa Dikeç's book *Badlands of the Republic* (2007) uncovers how the French state constructs the banlieue as a problem space, as an incubator of multiple pathologies like crime, violence, and environmental degradation – conditions held to require (and justify) repressive state intervention, which in this case has been met by counter-discourses emerging from inside the banlieues (Ebner et al., Chapter 7).

Foucauldian discourse analysis has come under criticism, however, for its concentration on dominant discourses by the state and capital at the expense of alternative discourses emerging from the grassroots. Urban scholars have shown that dominant discourses are not always successful in silencing alternative grassroots representations, for example, of inner-city neighborhoods (Martin, 2003; McCann, 2002). Such alternatives not only destabilize dominant discursive formations but also produce new ones. Further, while discourse analysis of textual representations persists as an important methodology in postmillennial urban studies, the human geographer Nigel Thrift (2008) has influentially argued for a turn away from representation toward performativity. Tracking a more general shift in post-structural theory (Butler, 2002), he proposed a turn to non-representational theory, entailing the use of qualitative and ethnographic methods to observe (and even perform) mundane everyday practices and the material relatedness of the human body to the more-than-human world.

Close encounters in the field

We turn now to a second important dimension of these up-close methodologies: *close encounters in the field*. In recent years, qualitative inquiry, ethnography, and the case study method have seen a new and expanded vitality in both urban studies and the social sciences more generally. This constitutes a revaluation of the past, when these research methodologies were often considered inferior to quantitative hypothesis testing in mainstream social science and urban studies. From this perspective, intensive case studies were constructed as being useful for the exploration of an issue or problem, and perhaps for hypothesis generation, but too limited to enable generalization since they do not involve representative sampling from a population. These assertions of methodological inferiority have been challenged, however, with the rise of other conceptions and means of generalization (Wilson and Chaddha, 2009). Theoretical generalization (based on theoretical rather than representative sampling), designed for the purpose of developing and/or improving existing theory, is now recognized as an important form of generalization. This involves generalizing from a case to a theory rather than to a population. Comparative analysis across cases and the combination and triangulation of different methodologies also have been deployed for purposes of theoretical generalization.

What do ethnography and the case study methodology bring to urban studies? With their focus on uncovering process and meaning, what actors do, and what they say in particular geographic and historical contexts, they offer insights that are not so easily obtained from quantitative surveys or structural analysis (Herbert, 2000; Sayer, 1992). Ethnographic case studies are uniquely positioned to reveal how human agency shapes, as well as being shaped by, larger structures and systems of domination, providing insights into their meaning patterns, forms, and processes. Steven Herbert (2000: 555) puts it this way: 'ethnography enables analyses of the important moments when macro and micro interpenetrate.' Robert Fairbanks' *How It Works* (2009) exemplifies this. Here, the recovery house for drug addicts becomes the site where everyday life (examined through ethnographic research) intersects with macrostructural forces (drawing on theories of neoliberalism and institutional analysis of penal poverty management), to facilitate the enrollment of drug addicts into the regulatory project of social welfare retrenchment and self-governance (Nowak and Howard, Chapter 10).

Fairbanks' book is also an excellent demonstration of the integration of ethnography with theoretical concerns. The relationship between theory and ethnography is an issue that has been forcefully pushed into the limelight in postmillennial urban studies by Loïc Wacquant's (2002) trenchant review essay on contemporary approaches to urban ethnography in North America, focusing on the contributions of Elijah Anderson (1999), Mitchell Duneier (1999), and Katherine Newman (1999). Wacquant is highly critical of these ethnographies, arguing that the disjuncture that they display between theory and ethnographic observation reduces their explanatory power. Instead, Wacquant advocates that ethnography and theory should be complementary and that 'the best strategy to strengthen the former is to bolster the latter' (2002: 1524). While Wacquant's essay raised a number of important issues regarding the role of theory in ethnographic research, the aggressive and dismissive tone of his writing contributed to a missed opportunity to address these issues more productively. Instead, what ensued was for the most part the entrenchment of pre-existing positions. Wacquant criticizes the authors for their exclusive focus on the field and the circumscribed development of mid-range concepts, at the expense of taking into account macrostructural factors that determine, for example, the social positionality of the different actors. In response, Anderson (2002) characterizes his own approach as more inductive, being designed to develop mid-level concepts such as 'code of the street' to explain the social order of an inner-city community in Philadelphia. In turn, he indicts Wacquant's approach as ideologically driven, overly deductive, and top-down, one that (over)emphasizes macrostructural factors and 'subordinates the cultural complexity he or she finds in the field to that theory' (2002: 1534).

This reiteration of age-old binaries between deduction and induction fails to acknowledge that research practice generally is an iterative process, one that combines elements of deduction and induction. This is what Burawoy (1998) advocated in his essay on the extended case method. He reiterates the need to integrate theory and ethnography, with the ultimate goal of utilizing ethnography as a means to improve theory. The epistemological mainstay of an 'extended' case method is its emphasis on the importance of attending also to the larger political and economic contexts and histories in which people, objects, and ideas are embedded. A similar argument was advanced by Akhil Gupta and James Ferguson (1997) in *Anthropological Locations*. They argue that ethnography as a methodology has to come to terms with the changed context of ethnographic work in an increasingly interconnected and rapidly changing world, in which extra-local connectivities are multiplying and deepening. Questioning the traditional ethnographic ideal of long-term field-based immersion in a particular community in a particular place, they make an argument for decentering the field as the principal site of knowledge production. 'Participant observation is ceasing to be fetishized; talking to and living with members of a community are increasingly taking their place alongside reading newspapers, analyzing government documents, observing the activities of governing elites, and tracking the internal logic of transnational development agencies and corporations' (Gupta and Ferguson, 1997: 37). They further advocate unbounding ethnographic field sites, both horizontally and vertically. A horizontal unbounding might be accomplished through a multi-sited ethnography, which would examine the connectivities among multiple sites that are crucial in the production of, for example, a particular urban form, event, or pattern. A vertical unbounding (Burawoy's emphasis) involves interrogating the embeddedness of a field site in larger scale political and economic contexts, conjunctures, and histories. Both unboundings require the development of new ethnographic and fieldwork practices.

Changing conceptions of the urban (for instance, in light of the unbounding of cities discussed in Chapter 1) and ethnography have also been associated with changing methods of data gathering and analysis. For example, urban ethnography is no longer just about documenting everyday experiences and community life (for an overview, see Duneier et al., 2014). Postmillennial urban ethnographies have been broadened to examine nature–society relations: urban environmental justice, urban environmental degradation, environmental risk and security, the production of urban environmental knowledge, urban sustainability, urban greening, and urban environmental governance. Last but not least, we have seen the development of urban multi-species ethnography (Kirksey and Helmreich, 2010), designed to uncover the role of non-human nature in structuring human agency (Rademacher, 2015). Scholars from various disciplines have also investigated the legal and property regimes regulating land transformations and natural resource claims (Leitner and Sheppard, 2018; Rademacher and Sivaramakrishnan, 2013), urban water infrastructure provision and its politics (Gandy, 2008; Anand, 2017), urban public spaces (Low, 2000), fortified urban built environments (Caldeira, 2000), urban waste work in Delhi (Gidwani, 2013), and urban infrastructure in Jakarta (Colven, 2018).

Traditional ethnographic approaches of participant observation and immersion have been complemented by discourse analysis of documents, deployed for example by Ahmed Kanna in *Dubai: The City as Corporation* to access the practices of those residents who 'inhabit the city but are reticent to speak about their experiences' (Hasan et al., Chapter 8). Multi-method research designs also have become increasingly popular in urban studies. Thus James Holston in *Insurgent Citizenship* (2008) and Asher Ghertner in *Rule by Aesthetics* (2015a) each combine historical and ethnographic methodologies to overcome the limitations of participant field observation (see Prouse and Jahn-Verri, and Anguelov et al., Chapter 14 and 15, respectively). In order to take advantage of new information sources (such as Geographic Information Systems; GIS) we have seen the development of geo-ethnography, which combines GIS analysis with ethnographic research methods (Matthews et al., 2005).

Qualitative urban researchers are increasingly deploying a wide variety of sophisticated software packages for the analysis of qualitative information such as texts and visual images contained in ethnographic fieldnotes, documents, tape recordings, interview transcripts, maps, sketches, and videos. Instead of engaging in iterative coding manually in the margins of texts (the traditional paper-and-pencil approach), software packages facilitate this process of identifying themes and/or interrogating existing themes and theories. The availability of such software packages has mushroomed, but tried and widely used packages include ATLAS.ti and NVivo (for an overview, see Silver and Fielding, 2008). In our own experience, software packages can be effective for organizing and exploring large amounts of information, but they are no substitute for careful reading of transcripts in order to avoid the decontextualization that results from when software breaks texts into segments or lines. Furthermore, there is a danger that the software packages encourage the researcher to reduce qualitative coding, with all its ambiguity, into hard and fast quantitative variables (known as quantizing; Hesse-Biber and Leavy, 2010).

Many of the urban monographs in this book demonstrate the merits of an extended ethnographic and case study approach which affords great attention to the details and nuances of everyday practices and speech, and their relation to larger economic, political, economic, and cultural contexts.

Close engagements

Turning to our third and final theme in this discussion of up-close methodologies, *close engagements*, we consider the issues of research ethics, the politics of representation, and the coproduction of knowledge. Paralleling broader shifts in the postmillennial Anglo American interpretive social sciences, qualitative urban researchers have become increasingly concerned with attending to questions of positionality with respect to their research subjects, seeking to deconstruct what historically has been assumed to be a hierarchical relationship separating the two. One aspect of this is the ethics and politics of representation. This has been followed by increasing interest in the coproduction of knowledge with actors from beyond the academy, now a widely discussed and debated topic in urban studies and beyond (Leitner and Sheppard, 2003; Nagar, 2014; Oldfield and Patel, 2016; Patel et al., 2015; Pratt, 2002).

The ethics and politics of representation associated with ethnographic and case study research are all about explicit self-reflexivity – acknowledging and reflecting on the effects of power and the researcher's own socio-spatial positionality on the practice and writing of ethnographies. Feminist scholarship, in particular, has prompted scholars to recognize and problematize the unequal power dynamics intrinsic in field research (Burawoy, 1998; England, 1994; Katz, 1994). Indeed, it has become common practice to interrogate whether urban scholars discuss how their positionality influences their research findings. Ethnographies of the urban poor, in particular, have been prone to sensationalism and exoticization. In his study of Latino men who sold crack in Harlem, *In Search of Respect*, Philippe Bourgois worries that 'the life stories and events presented in this book will be misread as negative stereotypes of Puerto Ricans' (1995: 11). In contrast, Fairbanks' study of the Philadelphia recovery house 'movement' has relatively little to say about the author's positionality (Nowak and Howard, Chapter 10).

Reflecting on one's own positionality is just a first step toward addressing the unequal power relations embedded in social science research. Feminist scholars propose taking further steps, collaborating with and learning from research participants, for example, through participatory action research. Feminists have also taken a lead in interrogating how we produce and analyze knowledge about the urban, challenging the presumption that researchers are privileged sources of understanding (Peake and Rieker, 2013). They have advocated for a research practice that incorporates knowledges and actors from beyond the university (community organizations, non-profits, activists, etc.) entailing the coproduction of knowledge. As Oldfield and Patel note: 'In this mode, the relationship between subject and object is blurred in the dynamic co-construction of knowledge, where all partners share responsibility for the research process' (2016: 508). The Sangtin Writers Collective and Richa Nagar (2006) also emphasize the deep challenges of presenting such research to others, given the very different positionalities of the co-authors. Decentering and decolonizing knowledge that is produced from the academy requires speaking across differences and working to deconstruct hierarchical engagements between the researcher and the researched. This is not an easy methodological move, as some of us have ourselves experienced (Kurtz et al., 2001), and as other testimonies from participatory action research have shown, but it is vital.

Connecting cities

In the past two decades, interest in relational thinking has increased rapidly across the critical social sciences – a development that has been characterized as the relational turn (Dépelteau, 2013). This entails an ontological shift from taking entities and categories as the default unit of analysis to a focus on the interrelations that bind and shape them. A relational approach asks how such connectivities affect the evolution of entities/categories (and reciprocally how changes in the entities affect their interrelations). In the spirit of dialectical (Sheppard, 2008) and network analysis, but also deeply influenced by feminist theorizations of positionality and intersectionality, a relational approach emphasizes how these interconnections position various socio-ecological agents with respect to one another, thereby shaping their identity, worldview, and behavior. In terms of spatialities, this entails a shift from thinking about places to thinking about their interconnections. Massey's (1991) global sense of place compellingly articulates the implications of this shift in thinking. Using a walk through London's Kilburn High Road shopping district as her case study, she argues that what happens in a place is profoundly shaped by connectivities linking this place and its inhabitants with other places. In this view, places are unbounded and internally heterogenous and, importantly, some locals are empowered by their connectivities, relative to others whose connectivities are constraining.

Taken together such connectivities form networks, so the relational turn has brought methodologies of network analysis into focus. Network analysis has moved in two directions: The first, social network analysis, is broadly quantitative, seeking to describe and explain the structure of networks, and how positionality within the network structure differentially empowers the entities (people, cities, etc.) occupying the nodes of a network (Nagurney, 2013; Scott, 2017). The second, actor–network approaches, are broadly qualitative, emphasizing the dynamic and emergent quality of networks and how internal power differentiation is contingent rather than structural (Latour, 2005). The latter is also distinctive because it emphasizes the agency of more-than-human entities in shaping network dynamics. Such entities, referred to as actants, include plants and animals and material artifacts (Callon, 1984; Law, 1996).

Networks span space without covering it, but also vary in terms of their geographical scale (Leitner, 2004; Leitner et al., 2002). In urban studies, the relational turn has somewhat bifurcated into two such scales – intra-urban and inter-urban networks – each with somewhat different methodological emphases. At the intra-urban scale, the postmillennial emphasis has been on actor–network and assemblage approaches (see Chapter 1). The latter emphasize contingency and unpredictability and are associated with post-structural social theory with its skepticism about grand narratives, predictions, and universal theories (Deleuze and Guattari, 1987; Latour, 1993). Instead, actor–network methodologies operate close to the ground – following the connectivities wherever they lead, instead of slotting them into pre-existing theoretical frameworks or claims. This epistemological approach resonates with highly inductive variants of grounded theory. At the inter-urban scale, more structural and quantitative approaches also have found favor.

The overarching metaphor describing actor–network methodologies is that they 'follow the network'. If networking and its consequences are emergent features, the researcher should approach the study as much as possible with an open-minded mentality, observing and learning from the practices of actors and actants and tracing their consequences. This implies identifying which actors seem empirically significant and deploying a range of deliberately messy methodologies (Nimmo, 2011: 113) to understand their actions (interviews, document analysis, field and participant observation, ethnographic analysis, etc.). This entails 'tracing these relationships and interactions in order to explain the observed reality, while simultaneously recognising that an alternative reality is a possibility constituted by the same actors' (Ruming, 2009: 457). Actors should include more-than-human actants (studying residential planning in Sydney, Ruming identifies squirrel gliders and landscape topography as vital actants). Yet, resonating with feminist methodologies, the researcher herself must take a reflexive approach, seeking to problematize how her situated knowledge affects not only her interpretation but the actor–network itself. This is because, by dint of her research, the researcher becomes part of the actor–network, with the power to shape how it is represented and thereby its dynamics: 'all research is the translation of a situated and selective network created by the researcher' (Ruming, 2009: 454).

A grounded and open-minded epistemological strategy also underwrites assemblage-theoretic methodologies. Tom Baker and Pauline McGuirk stress that assemblage methodologies should be open to multiple determinations of phenomena, to unpacking processes, to revealing the labors that reproduce assemblages, and to reflexivity, all of which again require an ethnographic sensibility: '[I]f an ethnographic sensibility is concerned with "how to look", and tracing sites and situations is concerned with "where to look", a methodological practice directed to the task of revealing labours of assembling is concerned with "what to look for"' (2017: 437). In terms of the spatiality of knowledge production, they stress the need to attend to multiple sites and situations (McCann and Ward, 2012). In terms of methods, the list overlaps largely with those for actor–networks, to which Ben Anderson and Colin McFarlane (2011) add montage, performativity, thick description, and stories – stressing the need for experimental methodological approaches. Lisa Björkman's monograph, *Pipe Politics, Contested Waters* (Matthan et al., Chapter 6) exemplifies assemblage methodologies. Perhaps the major difference from actor–network methodologies is a focus on sites rather than network links. A third relational approach currently popular at the intra-urban scale, paralleling a 'mobilities turn' across the qualitative social sciences, is urban mobilities research. Here, the same epistemological and methodological sensibilities are advocated, but the stress is on the researcher being also herself on the move – following the routes (Middleton, 2011). Taken together, these methodological strategies have been criticized for being too empiricist, and for neglecting processes operating at scales above that of the network or assemblage under investigation, although Colin McFarlane has responded that such extensions are both possible and desirable (Brenner et al., 2011; McFarlane, 2011a; 2011b; Tonkiss, 2011).

Those interrogating inter-urban connectivities deploy both qualitative and quantitative methodologies (a comprehensive survey is provided by Harrison and Hoyler, 2018). One kind of inter-urban networking that has received extensive recent attention is policy mobilities – the ways in which policies and governance norms move between cities, mutating as they do so (McCann and Ward, 2011; Peck and Theodore, 2015). This entails undertaking research in multiple cities – in this case, primarily through key informant interviews and document analysis. McCann and Ward (2012), using assemblage in a 'descriptive sense', argue that the appropriate methodological strategy is following the mobile policies and their human 'transfer agents', but also the policy mobility of cities themselves (in the sense that certain cities become global policy exemplars, such as the Bogota model for mass transit). They also stress the need to study sites and situations, attending to the relational situatedness (socio-spatial positionality) of sites, 'as places constituted by assemblages of the near and far, the fixed and the mobile' (McCann and Ward, 2012: 47). Peck and Theodore (2012) have dubbed the overall methodological strategy the 'distended case approach'. Whereas Burawoy's extended case study methodology moves vertically, embedding a local case in the broader conjunctural structuring context, a distended case methodology stretches horizontally, beyond and between places. In the context of studying policy mobilities, they present this as a threefold methodology: extending beyond observation to constructive engagement with and disruptive intervention into mobile policymaking; extending analysis across space and time by means of multi-site analysis; and extending out from sites to take account of 'translocal linkages, interrelations and domains' (Peck and Theodore, 2012: 27). Proponents of inter-urban policy mobility research theoretically align this more with urban political economy than actor–network or assemblage theory (for possible common ground, see McFarlane, 2011b). Yet such a distended case methodology is not just of relevance for understanding policy mobilities; it also can be deployed to study any of the ways that cities are interlinked through connectivities that shape, but also are shaped by, events in those cities. For example, examining such processes from the grassroots and positioning himself as challenging political economic tendencies to stress structuring processes from above, Michael Peter Smith has examined how Mexican and Californian cities are shaped by the Mexicans migrating between them (Smith and Guarnizo, 1998). This approach also has been extended to engage with more top-down perspectives (Krätke et al., 2014; M. P. Smith, 2005). A wide range of qualitative methods can be deployed for distended case study analysis, including multi-sited ethnography, interviews, participant observation, document and media analysis, carefully designed collaborative research involving teams of scholars embedded in the various cities, etc.

In a few cases, well-defined and available quantitative data can be collected about inter-urban connectivities – migration, financial, airline passenger or telecommunications flows and the like – making quantitative network analysis feasible. Critical urbanists have used such data to construct and analyze the global urban system, with particular attention to how these networks function to create a global urban hierarchy of more and less powerful cities. David A. Smith and Michael Timberlake (1995) have analyzed this in terms of airline passenger flows, but the most prominent body of such scholarship comes out of Loughborough University's Globalization and World Cities collaborative, analyzing inter-urban networks of corporate service firms to relationally position cities with respect to their global 'command and control' influence (Taylor and Csomós, 2012; Taylor and Derudder, 2015). Another quantitative approach, seeking to infer network connections rather than study them directly, has been cartographic and remote sensing analysis undertaken within the planetary urbanization project (Katsikis, 2018), seeking to impute global urban connectivities from maps of land use patterns (e.g., of global food production, seen as serving predominantly urban consumers).

Qualitative inter-urban research can go into considerable depth, but it is extremely time consuming and cannot realistically be extended to the globe. Quantitative network analysis can readily be global in scope but does not (and cannot) dig very deeply into what is happening in the cities thereby connected. Both methodological approaches can be criticized by those working beyond the urban political economy tradition for undertaking empirical research in ways that align with and reproduce pre-existing theory, itself disproportionately indexed to experiences in the global North. Yet there also have been recent efforts to seek common ground by engaging across such theoretical and methodological differences (van Meeteren et al., 2016).

Comparative urbanism

In urban studies, comparative methodologies typically are applied at the inter-urban scale, comparing and contrasting different cities. This need not be the case, of course; an analyst could compare central and peri-urban districts within a single city. Yet the inter-urban has been the default scale for comparative urbanism, seeking to gain additional understanding about processes of urbanization through the study of two or more sites. Before delving into the various approaches to this, it is important to note that even studying a single city has an implicitly comparative aspect. Indeed, as Guy Swanson has put it: 'Thinking without comparison is unthinkable. And ... so is all scientific thought and scientific research' (1971: 145). Since no one undertakes research without some preconceptions, all empirical work implicitly is compared against not only a researcher's theoretical expectations, explicit or otherwise, but also norms about how a city should operate. Comparative urban research has itself developed in the context of more general discussions about comparative social science methodologies. Charles Ragin (1987) defines comparative social science research as a methodological approach that operates at two spatial scales: comparing across macro-societal units and analyzing their internal properties. While the default macro-societal unit in comparative political science, history, and sociology (the main disciplines prosecuting these methodologies) has been (national) societies, comparative urbanists have down-scaled these to the metropolitan or urban scale. In this section, we address the two principal debates driving the practice of comparative urbanism in recent years: how to compare, and which cities to take as the norm for comparative purposes.

In terms of how to compare, the convention in comparative social science research, and the norm until recently in urban studies, is a place-based approach that treats cities as if they are hermetic and isolated spatial units. This approach aspires to the norm of experimental design, whereby under artificial laboratory conditions the researcher experiments with every possible combination of causal variables in order to determine their effect on a dependent variable (the outcome). Ragin divides comparative social science into a more quantitative variable-oriented approach – where statistical methods are used to test a hypothesized relationship between causal and dependent variables across macro-societal units of analysis (practically non-existent in critical urban studies) – and a more qualitative and holistic case-oriented approach (the convention in urban studies). The latter, like case study methodologies more generally, seeks to unpack the complexities and co-evolution of societal processes in place (intensive analysis, in the terminology of Sayer, 1992; 2000), deploying contextual, causal, and interpretive analysis to generate but also assess theoretical propositions. In both cases, the starting point is selection of cities to compare that are similar in many ways while differing in terms of key issues for the topic under investigation (Ward, 2010). Channeling the empiricist logic of John Stuart Mill (1843), Ragin highlights two strategies for case-oriented comparative hypothesis testing. The first compares similar places, in the sense that they experienced a common event, and seeks to identify a preceding condition, present in all of them, that can be presumed to have caused the event everywhere (the method of similarity). The second divides places into two subsets – those where the event happened and those where it did not – and seeks to identify preceding conditions that are present in the first subset and absent in the second (the method of differences). In *The Rise and Fall of Urban Economies*, Storper et al. (2015) essentially deploy the latter approach of variation finding to explain why San Francisco's urban economy has been successful, unlike that of Los Angeles (Comandan et al., Chapter 18).

Mill's approach, like experimental design, is overly mechanistic; as Ragin acknowledges, it fails in complex real-world situations where conjuncture and overdetermination matter, with multiple potential causal factors combining in different ways in different contexts to drive the same outcome (or not). Critical social scientists have come up with other comparative methodologies, with Charles Tilly's individualizing, variation-finding, universalizing, and encompassing approaches to comparison being particularly influential (the first two having been extensively deployed in urban studies; Ward, 2010). Individualizing comparison entails comparing a small number of cases in order to grasp the peculiarities of each; variation-finding comparison seeks to 'establish a principle of variation in the character or intensity of a phenomenon by examining systematic differences between instances'; universalizing comparison 'aims to establish that every instance of a phenomenon follows essentially the same rule'; and encompassing comparison seeks to explain differences across cases in terms of the effect of broader scale processes (Tilly, 1984: 82–83). Yet a shortcoming of this entire approach is its place-based starting point: the presumption that comparing cities is like observing separate experiments on a lab bench, for which the outcome is determined within the experiment itself. It always has been problematic to theorize nation states as if they are autonomous units of analysis, a problem in international relations theory that John Agnew (1994) has influentially critiqued as the territorial trap. With nation states becoming hollowed out under neoliberal capitalist globalization, this makes less and less sense, and for subnational scalar spatial units, an approach based on methodological nationalism/urbanism seems patently implausible (Brenner, 1999a; 1999b; Brenner et al., 2011). Instead, inter-urban comparative analysis needs to take into account the multiple ways in which events in cities are shaped by connectivities stretching beyond urban boundaries – a global sense of place (Massey, 1991). In a certain sense Burawoy's extended case study method takes up this challenge, but not in a way that explores the relations between cases/places. Thus, critical urban scholars have become intrigued by the possibilities of a *relational* comparative methodology.

Initial formulations of a relational comparative methodology also focused on supra-urban territorial scales. Philip McMichael (1990), taking a world-historical perspective, advocated for what he dubs incorporated comparison. Carefully distinguishing this from encompassing comparison, McMichael presents this methodological strategy as enabling the researcher to avoid preset units of analysis (defining what 'city' means as a spatial unit of analysis remains a problem in comparative urbanism; Nijman, 2007a; 2015), in order to take into account how cities are interrelated, and to make space for how cities can shape broader processes, rather than just being shaped by them (as is the case for encompassing comparison). Gillian Hart (2002) took a relational comparative approach to her 1990s empirical work in South Africa and Taiwan. For Hart, relational comparison is essentially an open-ended dialectical methodology (Harvey, 1996: Chapter 2); units of analysis (whether spatial or social) are emergent phenomena that also are shaped by (and shape) their connectivities. In spatial terms, connectivities operate across places at a certain scale (e.g., inter-urban relations) but also relationally across constructed scales – with the local both shaping and being shaped by the global (Hart, 2018; Leitner and Miller, 2007). Along with McMichael, Hart stresses the importance of a spatio-*temporal* methodological approach, one that not only teases out how places are mutually constituted at certain points in time, but also works backward in time to offer new understandings of the present and, importantly, of future possibilities.

This all sounds very abstract. How can such epistemological considerations shape how we practice comparative urban research? In recent years, a number of critical urban scholars have begun to advocate for relational (inter-)urban comparison. Kevin Ward has delineated how a relational comparative approach treats cities as open and relationally constituted phenomena, in that they are embedded in differently scaled processes where scale (including that of cities) is an emergent feature (rather than exogenous), as in more traditional approaches to comparative social science. He also stresses that 'there is an overtly political aspect to arguing for a relational comparative approach to the comparison of cities, particularly in the increasingly neoliberalizing interconnected and interdependent world in which we live' (Ward, 2010: 482). Relational comparisons cannot just shed light on recurring patterns and family resemblances across manifestations of, say, neoliberalization or urban revanchism; they can also probe the limits and contradictions of these processes, extending to the consideration of localized alternatives, networked counter-projects, and so on (Leitner et al., 2007). The living-wage movement, for example, can be seen as an inter-urban project dedicated to the goal of learning from and building on local campaigns, and 'scaling up' demands along the way.

To date, such programmatic statements about what can be gained from relational inter-urban comparison have not been matched with clear prescriptions about how to do this. Some of this is deliberate: dialectical thinking is not about recipes and best practices, unlike the experimental method. Yet this remains a challenge for practicing urban scholars. Taking the example of inter-urban comparative research, a relational methodology would involve at least three modes of analysis. First, it entails working horizontally: seeking out the various ways in which cities are interconnected, and unpacking how these connectivities shape and are shaped by events and actants to be found in cities. Second, it involves inter-scalar strategies: tracing how cities are indirectly connected through larger-scale processes that collectively affect them, as well as examining how those larger-scale processes are shaped by intra- and inter-urban processes. In *Cities in Relations* (2014), Söderström pursues this latter approach, examining how Hanoi and Ouagadougou have been differentially shaped through their shared trajectory as medium-sized capital cities of national economies transitioning from socialism to capitalism (Bok, Chapter 17). Third, it entails taking temporality seriously: examining how these interrelations connect the past with the present – attending not only to the path dependencies from which our current present emerged, but also to possible paths not taken and unrealized futures.

Thus far, we have examined two distinct ways of going about comparative urbanism, but there is a third and vital issue: which kinds of cities should become the norms against which other cities are compared, thereby creating an imaginary of what is normal and 'good' and what is deviant (and in need of improvement)? In *Ordinary Cities* (2006), Jennifer Robinson made the influential argument that the implicit norm in studying global and comparative urbanism, against which others are compared (and found wanting), has been global cities as defined by urban scholars in the global North (Robinson, 2011a). Arguing that all cities are global in their own way, and should not aspire to become a London, Tokyo, or New York, she triggered debates about southern urban theory (see Chapter 1) that decenter this norm by taking any city also as a point of departure for theorization and empirical study (Bunnell and Maringanti, 2010). In *The Fabric of Space*, Matthew Gandy experiments with this kind of flattened comparison of the evolving relationship between water, technology, and conceptions of modernity in Berlin, Paris, Lagos, London, Los Angeles, and Mumbai at distinct historical moments; this is neither explicitly relational nor variation-finding, but rather an experimental spatio-temporal comparison that puts these cities in conversation with one another (Ponder and Webber, Chapter 15).

Yet Robinson goes beyond a flattened comparison to make an explicit case for alternative normative starting points. She terms this 'thinking cities through elsewhere': 'A comparative imagination can suggest new objects of analysis by displacing ethnocentric assumptions which arise from the inevitable locatedness of all theory' (Robinson, 2016: 5). For example, whereas global urban policymakers approach cities of the postcolony in terms of how and when they can become more like US or European cities, critical urban scholars have begun to take seriously the elsewhere of 'southern' cities as alternative starting points. This might mean examining south/south inter-referencing – how some 'southern' cities look to others as their norm (Bunnell, 2015). But it also has involved attending to the worlding of 'southern' cities: how they themselves circulate as norms back to the global North (e.g., participatory budgeting, a practice invented in Porto Alegre, Brazil, but now imitated world-wide), and how what happens in southern cities also shapes urban processes elsewhere (Bunnell, 2016; Ong and Roy, 2011; Simone, 2001). When shifting the comparative norm becomes the basis for challenging mainstream and critical urban theory, the opportunities for theoretical and political opening travel with risks of unproductive exceptionalism, if analysts use alternative starting points to insist that distinct theories are needed for different cities (Nijman, 2015; Peck, 2015; Storper and Scott, 2016), particularly if 'northern' theories are represented as inert foils against which 'difference' is demonstrated. The strategic goal of postcolonial urbanism, of course, was never to produce a southern theory for southern cities, or to gather difference in the mirror of Eurocentric formulations. Rather, it has pursued the more nuanced and rela-tional ambition of asking how conjuncture matters: how theoretical insights gleaned by theorizing from southern urban elsewheres are important also for understanding northern cities, as well as vice versa (Sheppard et al., 2015).

In short, comparative urban methodologies need not only to take the relationality of cities seriously, but also to take seriously the perspectives and experiences of scholars writing from, and those inhabiting, cities around the world. A reflexive approach to comparative urbanism – the willingness to reassess conceptual starting points as we learn from the field, to ask how what we learn here may shift understandings of cities elsewhere (McFarlane, 2010), and to think through any city – can generate profoundly original insights.

Comparison also can play an important role beyond the academic sphere of knowledge production. For example, Fincher et al. (2019) in *Everyday Equalities* report on how diverse populations have learned to coexist and collaborate in everyday spaces (e.g., neighborhoods, workplaces, public spaces) and activities in four settler colonial cities, in mutually beneficial ways that transcend their differ-ences. Their main purpose is not to systematically compare the cities with one another to build some overarching theory from the cases; it is to provide readers with insights into practices and institutions that shape these positive examples of coexistence and collaboration, which they can compare against the cities they know and perhaps learn from as they seek to transform the urban everyday.

Conjunctural problematics

The emergent methodological project (or perspective) of conjunctural urban-ism seeks to problematize the spatio-temporal positionality of cities (Sheppard,

2019), cutting a path between site-specific, more introverted understandings of 'cityness' on the one hand and more expansive or generic treatments of global or universal urbanization processes on the other. A variant of relational analysis, its ontology is grounded in three animating principles. First, cities, in the plural, are each uniquely situated – historically as well as geographically – in relation to moving terrains of uneven development and structuring political economic contexts. Second, the urban scale itself is socially produced, being relationally constituted along with other scales, again in historically and geographically specific ways. And third, cities and the wider worlds of the urban that they jointly make are coproduced, with each city representing a distinctive locus, vantage point, and site of intersecting relations, rather than a microcosm or synecdoche, while the always-emergent world of cities has capacities and dynamics that cannot be reduced to the sum of its constitutive parts. In this respect, conjunctural analyses of the urban index uneven geographical development not just as an empirical truism, explanatory caveat, or source of mysterious 'out-there' forces, but as an active domain of concrete inquiry and reflexive theorization.

Understood in these terms, conjunctural perspectives on the urban are neither 'verticalist' (a hierarchically organized urban system, typically with global cities at the top), nor 'horizontalist' (a finely granulated and ontologically flat urban mosaic, animated by emergent processes and practices at localized scales). These two methodological optics remain valid and generative, if each in their own way partial. As a complement to rather than substitute for these ways of seeing the urban, the conjunctural perspective can be thought of as an orthogonal, cross-cutting or transversal one, opening up different lines of sight across the terrains of the intra-urban and the inter-urban. Pitched at this intermediate level, conjunctural analyses are consequently polycentric. Rather than deferring to ideal types, paradigmatic cases, or template models, they invite multi-sited and pluralist investigations that take full account of the terrain of the urban in its widest sense. They imply non-reductionist modes of explanation, carefully situated and rich in context but aspiring to theoretical salience. As such, they are trained as much on the limits of extant explanations as they are on their reiteration, with methodological spaces reserved for the interrogation of potentially confounding cases, boundary objects, and sites of contradiction, crisis, and conflict. Conjunctural analyses demand an open explanatory horizon, resting on a dialogic interplay between situated case studies, reflexively defined mid-level concepts, and revisable theory claims.

Drawing on Burawoy's (1998) model of reflexive science, and its favored methodological strategy of the extended case study, conjunctural approaches to urban analysis seek to situate social action, social practices, and social processes within what are invariably complex, leaky, and 'open' social systems. Exploratory in nature, they work back and forth between the investigation of concrete situations, the identification of emergent patterns, and the continuous development and revision of more abstract formulations, problematizing what must always be provisional categories of analysis and seeking to hone mid-level concepts along the way. Conjunctural approaches are characteristically rather skeptical of exclusively inductive case studies, strictly delimited and/or circumscribed, in which events are assumed to have endogenous, internal, or otherwise proximate causes, as if operating immediately behind the backs (or in the front yards) of social actors. But they are equally wary of those highly generalized, deductive, and abstracted accounts that run the risk of losing touch with contextual specificity and grounded conditions.

Properly understood as a methodological orientation rather than a theoretical disposition, conjunctural approaches to urban studies can be seen as invitations to think *through* and *out from* particular socio-spatial formations (see Clarke, 2014; Hart, 2018; Peck, 2013; Zeiderman, 2018). The preferred explanatory path is consequently an intermediate one, traced between the high-altitude atmospherics of abstract theory (with its propensity to 'read off' from theoretical propositions at the urban scale in a one-sided fashion) and contingency-laden varieties of thick description (with their tendency to alight upon adjacent sources of causality, coupled with a limited ability to identify patterned configurations across multiple sites). Instead, conjunctural explanations are sought (and constructed) on the terrain of the contextual. They entail, as Stuart Hall said of Gramsci's method, 'analyzing situations', as specific articulations of cultural, ideological, political economic, and socio-natural relations, and fundamentally, as sites of multiple determinations (Hall, 1986). In this respect, conjunctural approaches to urban studies seek to develop answers to Roy's (2016: 206) provocative question, 'What does it mean to think about contemporary urbanism via articulation rather than agglomeration?'

The appeal to 'conjunctures' certainly involves invoking existing theories and concepts ('we begin with our favorite theory' is how Michael Burawoy puts it), but we should not expect to end in the same place, after having thoroughly stress-tested those conceptual frames and theory claims that are (quite literally) in question. Rather than deferring to some overarching or already-complete theory, such as a top-down reading of neoliberalism or a systemic interpretation of financialized capitalism, conjunctural methods attend to contextual complexity 'all the way down' and all the way out, entailing the production (and restless revision) of mid-level concepts and situated theory claims that are appropriate for interrogation across multiple cases and sites, tracing the interplay between grounded circumstances, mediating conditions, and their reciprocally enabling conditions of existence. From this perspective, theory building is a cross-contextual but never a decontextualized project. It really matters, for example, that neoliberalized urbanism is a mottled, variegated, and polycentric process, and not just variations on an already-known theme, as if originating or diffusing out from a place of immaculate invention (Peck, 2013).

Conjunctural methods approach cities as sites through which to explore the localized mediation of social processes and their often-contradictory configurations. Cities are not seen as free-standing entities upon which ideal–typical models might be fashioned, nor do they merely provide convenient settings for the illustration of generalized theory claims. Instead, they are conceptualized as sites of tangled and socially embedded relations, as 'knots' in inter-urban networks, as hinges in pan-urban systems, and as spaces of political urgency and processual intensification – for social forces, emergent projects, conflicts, and contradictions. Conjunctural analysis, in this sense, addresses the 'joints of [a] social problem' (Ollman, 2003: 19). As an approach to urban studies, it begins with and then works with contextualization, reaching out from immediate and present contexts to the contexts of those contexts, and seeking expressly to position the urban on what might be thought of as a provisional, but structured, explanatory landscape. Cities are duly located in relation to wider socio-political, socio-economic, and socio-natural fields, just as urban case studies are positioned in relation to (always partial) understandings of, perspectives on, theories pertaining to the structuring and dynamics of those fields.

Conjunctural approaches to the urban are placed in the service of the purposeful *reconstruction* of explanations, working concepts, hunches, and emergent theories, not as mere illustrations (or affirmations) of what is already supposedly known, but as reflexive interrogations and stress tests of received explanations. They provide opportunities, as Hall once wrote, for 'thinking large[r] concepts in terms of their application to concrete and specific situations' (1986: 6). As such, they are neither ambivalent about extant theory nor unbendingly loyal in its defense; the purpose of conjunctural approaches (in single cities or across groups of cities) is to engage in critical dialogue with theories and concepts – with a view, ultimately, to their re-evaluation, elaboration, reconstruction, or, if necessary, rejection. In short, conjunctural analysis seeks to make a (reflexive) virtue of the theory-laden nature of social science inquiry, including the selection of research sites and methodological tools.

Conjunctural approaches to urban studies are especially attentive to the question of epistemological framing and in more practical terms to the challenging task of research design. If the logic of case studies is to preserve the 'unitary character' of social processes, encompassing the appropriate 'causal groups' of pertinent social actors and institutions while specifying, either implicitly or explicitly, relevant domains or spaces of social practice and signification (see Mitchell, 1983; Sayer, 1992), conjunctural approaches seek to extend or stretch the horizons of analysis, requiring that appropriate attention is paid to actors, institutions, and indeed social processes operating beyond the city limits. Understood as points of analytical entry, cities are conceptualized as 'complex unities' – as particular intersections in, or articulations of, wider relations of interdependency (cf. Grossberg, 1996; Hall and Massey, 2010; Slack, 1996). This does not presuppose or prescribe the choice of particular methodological practices, but certainly favors those approaches (generally qualitative and often ethnographic) that are attuned to the study of situated and contextualized social action, relationally constituted social phenomena, and recurrent or institutionalized patterns revealed *across* cases and sites. For urban studies, this suggests an approach that moves *between* the local and the global, induction and deduction, the particular and the generalized, the contingent and the structural – a kind of spiraling method that problematizes 'complexity, contingency, and change ... everywhere, and "all the way down"', all the way out, and all the way back again (Grossberg, 2015: 8, 7; Peck, 2017a; Roman, 2015: 192). From this perspective, conjunctural specificity, complexity, and contextualization do not demarcate the limits of productive theorization; they are its means and its media. Consequently, this is not a license for complexity reduction, en route to spare forms of parsimonious analysis, but rather for constructing theoretically suggestive accounts of (and through) actually existing and situated urban formations, explicitly positioned in relation to their historical and geographical contexts. These are 'structuring contexts', not in a deterministic or top-down manner, but in something akin to a structurationist fashion, in which the parts and the whole are mutually conditioning.

Conjunctural approaches seek to open up three dimensions of a necessarily more-than-urban urban studies. First, the spatial dimension: individual cities are understood in relation to the intimate and extended families that comprise closely related and sharply contrasting cases, near and far, such as to present opportunities for recognizing and interrogating the 'patterning' of processes, practices, and events across multiple sites, situations, and cases, as well as constitutive relations and network connections between them. Second, the historical dimension: positioning cases on moving, transformative landscapes means taking account of what might be called the turnover time of transformation, and a span (or reach) of historical analysis sufficient to grasp overall arcs of change, from antecedents and emergent conditions through moments of frontal advance and crisis. Third, the scalar dimension: since neither cities nor the metropolitan scale itself are stable, autonomous, or cleanly bounded, conjunctural analyses must also extend across scales, seeking to take into account the relational constitution of the urban with a host of other-scaled networks and hierarchies, including the (inter)state system, infrastructural relations, and the web of transnational connections.

Conjunctural approaches to urban studies, appropriately in so many ways, cannot be reduced to an easily recognizable formula or fully explicated framework, but instead are being shaped through ongoing practice. As such, they remain nascent, and in a persistent state of development, rather than being comprehensively codified. In fact, the style of contextualized analysis that is not only implied but demanded is not really compatible with the specification of 'portable' methodological routines or all-purpose frames, transferable from site to site and case to case. This said, there are a number of currents in contemporary urban studies that speak to some of the emergent principles and practices of conjunctural analysis. To reference two examples examined in Part II of this collection, Fairbanks' *How It Works* spirals out from the neighborhood scale of inquiry to explore the wider, framing dynamics of poverty management in the United States, while Brenner's *New State Spaces* works across a substantial number of urban locations in Western Europe as a means to probe the pervasive rescaling of competitive strategies and imperatives (see Nowak and Howard, and Daniels et al., Chapters 10 and 9, respectively).

To take a further example, a methodologically generative line of inquiry emerged in the wake of the 2008 global financial crisis: initially encountered through the situated experience of 'austerity urbanisms' in parts of Europe and North America, this has since been interpreted as one (conjunctural) moment in what has been a tendential 'financialization' of urban governance regimes, spanning reconstituted modes of statecraft across multiple scales and transformed conditions of everyday life (see Christophers, 2019; Davies and Blanco, 2017; Gray and Barford, 2018; Hinkley, 2017; Peck, 2012; 2017b). A distinctly conjunctural quality can be detected, too, in some of the burgeoning literature on Chinese urbanism. Here, particular configurations of 'local state corporatism' and entrepreneurial developmentalism have been incubated through the complex interplay of central-state directives and incentives, a selectively sanctioned mode of decentralization and experimentation, and vibrant if also patterned and channeled forms of local initiative and grassroots action (see Cartier, 2018; Harlan and Park, Chapter 13; Hsing, 2010; Lim, 2018; Shen, 2007; Wu, 2018). There is a 'configurational' quality to these variegated, yet distinctive, patterns of urban development, a quality that is evident across sites but hardly reducible to a single model, and one which appears characteristically 'Chinese' in some respects, at the same time refracting wider tropes of entrepreneurial and entrepreneurial-cum-neoliberal urbanism. Indeed, investigations variously based in and between these two macro contexts, of Chinese and North Atlantic urbanism, have been raising new questions about some of the staples of urban theory, such as the growth-machine thesis (see Hsing, 2010; Kirkpatrick and Smith, 2011; Peck and Whiteside, 2016; Zhang and Fang, 2004).

To summarize, conjunctural approaches privilege the situated, contextualized, and relational analysis of cities. They typically involve multi-sited, pan-urban, and cross-scalar inquiries, which invariably route through particular cities, not just in passing but as explanatory basing points and sites of more-than-contingent contextualization – although they rarely stop there. Working with *and through* cities, conjunctural approaches seek explicitly to suture situated modes of urban inquiry to pan-urban and extra-urban horizons of analysis, positioning specific cases in relation to structuring contexts, and problematizing their mutual interactions. The methodological ambit of the conjunctural, in this sense, extends beyond individual vectors of connectivity, single-site situations, and particular moments of transformation, seeking instead to position these within more expansive and richly contextualized readings. Contextualizing 'all the way out and all the way up' demands closely specified, concrete analyses of structuring urban contexts, not vague allusions to extraterrestrial forces or thinly drawn abstractions. In this respect, conjunctural methods tend to favor cross-cutting modes of analysis in dialogue with content-bearing, mid-level abstractions. Whereas ethnography often has recourse to thick description, conjunctural methods call for contextualized forms of 'thick theorization'.

Conclusion: for methodological enrichment

We have argued in this chapter that different methodological approaches to critical urban studies can be thought of as distinctive ways of seeing, reading, and ultimately writing the city. Up-close analyses of the intimately urban, grounded in the granular and the everyday; the transnational tracing of urban networks, flows, and intercity relations; comparative studies of cities that tease out differences large and small; and conjunctural perspectives on pan-urban configurations and more-than-urban structuring contexts: these can each be seen as a distinctive methodological optic that necessarily brings certain facets of the urban condition into focus while positioning others in the background. If all methodological approaches to the urban are in this sense partial, they are also positional. A common thread running through each of the preceding discussions of urban methodologies – close encounters, connecting cities, comparative urbanism, conjunctural problematics – is that positionality matters. In feminist scholarship and in a great deal of ethnographic practice, positionality matters in terms of ethical and political responsibilities, power relations, and the obligations to research subjects. In comparative research and network analyses, the relative positioning of cities – in relation to one another and through constitutive connections – is clearly axiomatic. Conjunctural methods, too, are motivated by a concern to situate and position cases in their historical and geographical contexts.

Alongside these overlapping concerns with positionality, it is also notable that critical urban studies is a field of methodological diversity. There is anything but a dominant approach or singular canon, while experimentation is both welcomed and valued – appropriately in our view. It follows that methodological pluralism, extending to the active appreciation of what is a rich repertoire of alternative ways of seeing, reading, and writing the urban, is both a necessary and a desirable condition of existence for critical urban studies, notwithstanding certain tendencies for specialization and segmentation. Recent debates in critical urban studies, especially those that have advanced generative critiques of universalism and Eurocentrism, along with the distinctive contributions of postcolonial, feminist, and post-structural modes of analysis, clearly have far-reaching and important implications for methodological practice in the field. And yet, as Zeiderman (2018) has observed, too often these debates have been confined to, or deflected into, the theoretical register. There are, we suggest, still-to-be-realized opportunities for methodological dialogue and enrichment in this unprecedented 'opening' of the field. To argue that the search for new articulations between theory and method might be productive is by no means to deny the value (and the indispensable role) of urban theory. Indeed, methods-talk, in a dialogic rather than declarative voice, has a vital contribution here.

In tune with this reflexive approach, the following chapter seeks further to open up questions relating to methodology, research practice, and the research 'craft' in critical urban studies. In the absence of a 'one best way', or a privileged and singular way of seeing, we proceed on the understanding that there is a great deal to be learned from the heterogeneity of research practice in the field. More specifically, there is much to be gained from bringing discussions of these heterogeneous practices to the surface, and ultimately into productive dialogue.

3

URBAN STUDIES INSIDE/OUT: A GUIDE FOR READERS AND RESEARCHERS

Jamie Peck, Eric Sheppard and Helga Leitner

The remit of this final introductory chapter is to outline the format and purpose of *Urban Studies Inside/Out*, with appropriate reference to the collaborative practices that were constitutive to its own making. Ultimately, it is our hope that this collection might provide a platform of sorts upon which new conversations, contributions, and collaborations might be convened. This we say while recognizing that the present collection can do no more than take some initial steps, although we hope steps in the right direction – toward a modified genre of research practice founded on the principles of constructive engagement; respectful dialogue across differences of perspective, position, and approach; and reciprocal learning facilitated by methodological transparency and reflexivity. In sympathy with the objective of finding ways for 'cities everywhere to be drawn into wider theoretical conversations' (Robinson, 2014: 7), this chapter sketches a framework for exploring the kinds of research practices that might productively contribute to such a goal. We do so by seeking to render transparent our *own* practice, as the editors and contributors to this volume, in approaching and asking questions of urban studies monographs, and in organizing the group's collaborative efforts.

The first part of the chapter focuses on the issue of research *practice* – understood here in a wider and more expansive sense than method or even methodology, to encompass the 'craft' of critical urban studies: the ethical and political commitments of researchers in the field; their (inter)relations with research subjects, interlocutors, collaborators, and audiences; the choices made between different styles and codes of (re)presentation, narrative, analysis, and theory making; and the communities of scholars and social action upon and to which research programs and projects are predicated and dedicated. Next, we briefly summarize the collaborative practices and procedures developed by the group of contributors to this volume, originally in the joint UBC/UCLA graduate seminar described in the Preface, including methods of peer review, writing conventions, and codes of scholarly conduct. The chapter then turns to our approach to 'deconstructing the monograph', understood as a critical but constructive enterprise based on analyses (and appreciations) of generative research practice in critical urban studies, as exemplified by significant contributions to the field. Finally, we introduce the book ahead.

Practicing research

Research practice is not just another name for the everyday, practical, and logistical challenges of conducting research, although it certainly includes those often-overlooked matters. Instead, we prefer to use the term here more expansively, to embrace the tangle of interrelated and interacting issues that run from engagements with theory and questions of conceptualization, through the challenges of research design and the mobilization of methodological tools and techniques, to a host of considerations relating to positionality and situated knowledges, analytical rigor and reflexivity, ethical commitments and responsibilities, interpretation and explanation, recording and notetaking, strategies for reading and writing, voice and tone, dissemination and sharing, and so forth. Rather than (try to) deal with these separately or sequentially – as if they are actually separate, or as if they ever really present themselves sequentially – we tackle them in the chapters that follow in Part II of this volume through the *revealed practices* of various contributors to the project of critical urban studies, with a focus on the monograph form as both signal achievement and a relative (of sorts) to the doctoral dissertation. While research practices may be more or less transparent (and therefore readily legible) across different urban studies texts, our group was motivated by the objective of recovering, constructively assessing, and learning from these often-submerged or otherwise 'underlying' research practices – some of the secrets of the craft, if you will.

It follows that research monographs are being encountered in Part II not so much as the final word or finished article (as immutable mobiles circulating in the scholarly world), but more as a series of particular windows onto generative and productive research practices. They each provide entry points into distinctive forms and styles of research practice – even as the visibility and 'recoverability' of these practices vary quite considerably from book to book, and author to author. Sometimes, the authors and their methodological labors are visibly, actively, and reflexively present in the text; in other instances, they remain partially or completely concealed, in passive-voice narratives, or behind cloaks of expertise and authority. In some cases, methodological commitments, procedures, and positions are readily discernible to, and shared with, readers and fellow researchers; in others, quite commonly, they can only be recovered in fragments, or obliquely, by reading between the lines or by positioning the text within the author's wider research program. There will be occasions where the theoretical moorings and messages of a monograph are explicitly stated or otherwise emphasized, other times when theory claims are rendered implicit, or subtly integrated, as if 'in solution' within the narrative. Moreover, there is considerable variation in both the degree and form of theoretical reflexivity: some theoretical 'commitments' may appear to be truly open to revision, reconstruction, even rejection, others less so. Sometimes, theoretical positions are confidently announced, out loud and up front, present in plain sight; in other cases, these are much more implicit, or gently carried.

Although the distinctions between these are easily exaggerated, some texts rely on analytical strategies that are deductive, whereas others are much more inductive. To recapitulate the discussion in Chapter 2: deductive approaches typically take received theoretical understandings as their privileged point of departure, deriving a series of research questions amenable to empirical investigation and 'testing'. Inductive approaches tend to be more exploratory, with theory claims and generalizations emerging in a more contextual, circumspect, and in some ways more cautious manner, in the course of the empirical inquiry itself. Stylized differences between deductive and inductive approaches are often elided with the 'divide', as it were, between quantitative and qualitative methods, but this association is too clear cut. Certainly, the two may often be found traveling together: deductive approaches being matched with quantitative methods on the one hand; inductive approaches being linked to qualitative methods on the other. But qualitative methods can also be paired with deductive, theory-interrogating approaches, as illustrated by the aspiration to theoretical reconstruction in extended case studies (see, for example, Burawoy et al., 1991; Fairbanks, 2009; Nowak and Howard, Chapter 10). Likewise, quantitative methods can be enlisted in the cause of exploratory, inductively inclined inquiries (see, for example, Bok, Chapter 17; Comandon et al., Chapter 18; Söderström, 2014; Storper et al., 2015).

Generalizing rather broadly, the current theory culture and methodological habitus of the field of critical urban studies as a whole tend to skew in favor of more inductive approaches and qualitative methods: 'dirty hands' rather than 'clean models', and granular, closely observed, and contextualized treatments rather than spare, parsimonious modes of analysis. In critical urban studies, concepts, mid-level theories, and categories of analysis are typically developed (and refined) *in dialogue* between first-hand empirical inquiries and more abstract theoretical propositions. Here, the bulk of research and writing practice is located between the two poles of inductivism and deductivism – taking heed of theoretically derived cues and questions on the one hand, and learning from local cases, grounded fieldwork, and situated actions on the other – although the field as a whole might be said to favor various forms of inductive inquiry over hard-core deductivism. Questions are typically asked in a fashion that is theoretically informed but not theoretically (pre)determined, while answers are conventionally sought in a relatively open and exploratory manner, often by means intended to inform the development of grounded, mid-level concepts and more provisional theory claims, claims that are variously sensitive to (or creatures of) those urban contexts, settings, and situations that substantially define the urban itself.

This said, a certain sensitivity to the question of more or less inductive/ deductive modes of analysis, not as a binary divide but as a matter of judgment calls and explanatory tradeoffs, can be useful to keep in mind when reading for research practice, as the chapters in Part II of this volume seek to do. A hallmark of *relatively* deductive approaches is that they will tend to carry their theoretical frameworks, their principles of analytical relevance and pertinence, and their conceptually derived hunches, hypotheses, vocabularies, and research questions, *into* their subsequent empirical investigations explicitly and visibly. These may be structured and organized accordingly, and in turn will echo and speak back to the preceding theoretical template, analytical frame, or conceptual grid. More inductive studies, in contrast, will typically carry their (prior) theoretical commitments and convictions much more lightly, constructing their understandings of causality, agency, pertinence, and so forth not only in but *through* cases, empirical situations, and datasets, often in close dialogue with research subjects, sometimes to the point of 'coproducing' interpretations, explanations, and indeed 'data'.

It follows that there is wide variation, reflecting among other things different approaches to deduction/induction, in how authors choose to extrapolate, abstract, or generalize from their respective cases, contexts, positions, perspectives, and so forth. In critical urban studies, *especially* one might say, these latter issues concerning the reference points, reach and range, and 'hinterlands' of theory claims have long been vexing issues – and properly so. It follows that contributions to the field can also be read for their differing forms (and perhaps degrees) of 'positional' consciousness reflexivity and self-awareness, in terms of the sites and situations from which theory claims are issued, how they are grounded, and the manner in which matters of extra-local or pan-urban salience are addressed. Do they (appear) to sanction generalized, 'universal', or context-independent theory claims, or are they more conjuncturally or contingently framed, for instance, in the form of (contextually indexed) mid-level concepts or provincialized theories? In short, in addition to the question of how urban studies monographs are organized on the 'inside', there are also questions to be asked about their respective domains of relevance, resonance, provenance, and applicability.

Arguably a defining feature of what we have been styling here as a postmillennial turn in critical urban studies has been an elevated level of consciousness concerning the relative *positioning* of cities (and urban case studies) in relation to both the moving maps of urban theory and the wider 'world of cities' (see Leitner and Sheppard, 2016; Peck, 2015; Robinson, 2011a; Roy, 2009). This has included provocative and far-reaching debates around the visibility and theoretical salience of 'Southern' and Asian urbanisms, the development and critique of planetary conceptions of urbanization, arguments for and against the provincialization of urban theories, critiques of economism and Eurocentrism, the advocacy of more cosmopolitan urban imaginaries and new styles of comparative urbanism, cases made for and against methodological 'cityness', overtures to conjunctural methodologies, and much more. While much is now routinely made of the differences between these various approaches, 'camps', and positions, with debates between these sometimes becoming quite acrimonious and entrenched, what they might be said to *share* has too often been overlooked. Not wishing to impose – or imagine – some underlying unity in a context in which important differences undeniably remain, in bringing this section to a close we draw attention to three lines of constructive commonality across the diverse field of critical urban studies.

First, to varying degrees and in different ways, there is an underlying acknowledgement of the *relationality* of the urban across much (if not most) of the field; that is, cities are typically understood to be relational constructions. As such, cities are variably and indeed uniquely situated in relation both to one another and to other-positioned and other-scaled phenomena, processes, and practices, just as they are differentially situated in relation to a plethora of worlding and citymaking processes, conjunctural articulations, networked connections, policymaking circuits, cultural affinities, hierarchical systems, competitive pressures, globalizing projects, and so forth. This is not to imply that the kinds of relational approaches associated with, say, actor–network theory, postcolonial studies, or radical political economy are the same, or indeed that they are readily reconcilable. Various forms of relational thinking are quite pervasive in the field, however, while recourse to ideal–typical models, 'internalist' explanations, free-standing cases, and strictly endogenous sources of causality is less commonplace. Similarly, many of the old (bad) habits of paradigmatic, this-place-is-the-future theorizing seem now to have been shaken off, just as it seems highly unlikely that some new generation of [insert city name] 'schools' will be inaugurated any time soon, in the style of the Chicago and Los Angeles schools of the twentieth century. In the place of city-centric and diffusionist perspectives, various modes of relational consciousness now hold sway, all the way from single-site ethnographies to more structural readings of the global–urban system: cities exist in a world of (different) cities; the individual parts and the emergent whole of the urban system are reciprocally related and jointly constituted; localization and uneven development, rather than being antitheses of global integration and networked connectivity, coexist with these conditions. Relational understandings of the urban, in their various forms, can thus be considered characteristic (if not constitutive) of the field.

Second, and practically without exception, there is a broad recognition of the inescapable *partiality* of each and every way of seeing the city and the urban, that each theoretical and methodological optic, vantage point, analytical framework, or line of sight represents but one perspective, take, or angle on what is an inescapably multipolar, multiplex, and multifarious urban world, with no single urban theory being in a position (realistically) to claim an analytical or explanatory monopoly. Again, this does not necessarily mean that such 'differently partial' takes on the urban are easily reconciled or combined, or that they never contradict or confound one another. Neither does it mean that analytical modesty and explanatory circumspection are evenly distributed. For the most part, though, methodological takes on the urban are widely recognized across the field of critical urban studies to be *selective* takes, each with their own priorities and principles of pertinence, while the unthinking issuance of truly universalizing, unilateral, imperialist, or 'totalizing' theory claims is rare. Methodological pluralism, then, is a second characteristic of the field, shaped by a kaleidoscopic coexistence of (particular, partial) takes on the urban, as opposed to some incipient universalism or monism.

Third, there is a corollary affirmation of a necessarily – and also productively – polyvocal theory culture in critical urban studies, echoing some of the deeply embedded characteristics of what has always been an interdisciplinary if not extra-disciplinary field in which heterodoxy and pluralism have long been normalized (if never stable or uncontested) conditions. This is to say that when sociologists, political scientists, geographers, planners, anthropologists, architects, and others engage with interlocutors in the field of critical urban studies they do so at least in part by means of a shared and indeed coproduced lingo and lexicon, the resulting vocabulary and terminology being an always-emergent product of an interdisciplinary research field that has never really been 'owned' or even dominated by a single discipline. Varieties of this critical urban studies 'Esperanto', imagined as a living and contested theory language, are spoken in the principal journals in the field, such as the *International Journal of Urban and Regional Research*, *Urban Studies*, and *City*, as well as in the disciplinary and interdisciplinary conferences in which different parts of the research community assemble, talk, and trade. None of this implies homogeneity or unity, still less an absence of dissent and debate. But these engagements and conversations occur to a significant degree on a jointly produced and multipolar terrain, across which certain codes of communication and dialogue prevail. The presence of recognized forms of (and conventions in) urban studies 'talk', in other words, can be seen as a collective achievement of this interdisciplinary field.

Summing up these observations on some of the things that connect, rather than divide, critical urban studies, this is an interdisciplinary research community that recognizes relational positionality and specificity; that acknowledges the partiality and necessary coexistence of different readings, representations, and methodological optics; and that shares a certain vocabulary, while valuing different dialects, accents, and idioms. As such, it is a field that (re)makes itself through difference, seeking to be more than the sum of its diverse parts. We highlight these threads of underlying commonality and shared purpose here for a reason. There have been occasions in recent years when long-standing traditions of (often robust) critical exchange have shaded into ad hominem portrayals, the entrenchment of partisan positions and polemically justified causes, and less than entirely respectful assertions of difference. The particular causes of these ruptures in collegial coexistence and constructive communication need not detain us, but some of their consequences may be more pertinent, such that there is (if anything) an increased premium on practices of respectful engagement, exchange, critique, and debate. Something will have been lost if those entering the field of critical urban studies feel that they must 'take sides' or take cover, or, worse still, if the perception holds that there is something to be gained *from* taking sides, by debating aggressively from fixed positions.

Heterodox and pluralist theory cultures, of course, are constructed with and across difference; by definition, they are not monocultures, but neither should they be excessively centered or one-sided. If heterodox and pluralist theory cultures are predicated on – while being constantly remade through – real differences in approach and alternate ways of seeing the urban, then they must also adopt and adapt codes of mutually respectful dialogue, communication, and even dispute. To build, value, and nurture constructive modes of engagement – across methodological traditions, theory camps, language cultures, disciplinary conventions, and so forth – should not be mistaken for a desire to suppress, or paper over, actually existing differences of perspective, approach, and orientation, less still some wistful yearning for kumbaya convergence. Rather, it speaks to an aspiration to foster productive learning and interchange in the name of preserving and treasuring a diverse community of researchers who, if they agree on little else, will most likely share the view that unification around a singular theoretical perspective or one-best-way method is neither an imminent nor a desirable prospect. There are times, of course, when signature debates or sharp-elbowed disputes represent teachable moments, dramatizing differences in the process, but just as often the different approaches (or 'sides') are liable each to be misrepresented or misconstrued. Lowering the temperature (and volume) may therefore help us to appreciate – quite literally – differences of position and approach, and to learn from and across them. This was the tack that we took in the joint seminar, and that we aspire to reproduce in the present volume.

Collaborative work

An overarching goal of the joint UBC/UCLA seminar was to create the conditions in which graduate student participants would be able to work together rather than individually, both across the two seminar rooms and in subsequent writing projects. Cultures of individualized writing, grading, and assessment are deeply ingrained in many graduate programs, including our own. Most would agree that collaboration and co-authorship are good things, like apple pie. But in the social sciences, and ironically perhaps especially in the *critical* social sciences, they are not commonplace. In situations in which researchers mostly collect and produce their own data, using 'dirty hands' methods like in-depth interviewing or ethnography, collaboration is atypical. It is often reserved for those quite distinctive situations in which the 'chemistry' is right and the stars are aligned, and normally only in small-*n* teams. Collaborative writing and joint authorship are more common, but again considerably less so when it comes to book-length projects.

This has meant that working to develop collaborative reading and writing practices has proven to be an ongoing task, both within the seminar and for this book. Even though collaborative working may be somewhat countercultural, with even co-authorship only tending to 'work' under some conditions, there are reasons to value – and to foster – these practices. They allow us to learn from and with our collaborators. They require us to find ways to negotiate (and compromise) across all manners of difference: of style, voice, theoretical preference, and so on. They allow us to realize gains from coproduction, disrupting the normative pull towards individual authorship and its associated, often pernicious, incentive systems. Our goal has been to challenge this, embracing collaborative approaches and shared writing wherever practical. In itself, this raised many issues of 'practice' that at times had to be struggled with by all involved, not unlike most collaborative projects of course.

All of the writing projects associated with the seminar were developed by two or three students writing together, often in groups that spanned the two universities. A designated lead author was principally responsible for producing an original draft, with co-authors subsequently engaging in the development and revision of the text. Within these parameters, each writing team would evolve their own divisions of labor and responsibility. Given the challenges associated with collaborative writing and joint authorship, this represented a steep learning curve for all involved. Inevitably, some writing partnerships jelled more easily than others, while in some the allocation of tasks and responsibilities was more broadly distributed than others. For some participants, changed circumstances or other commitments meant that it was not possible for them to continue with their involvement, as the plans for the *Urban Studies Inside/Out* book project were developed following the completion of the seminar. (Three graduate students from UBC and UCLA were recruited to the project later, in order to complete some of these writing tasks.) From an early stage, protocols around the proper attribution of co-authorship credits were discussed and agreed with the group (see Table 3.1), which on one level are matters of formal obligation and 'rights', but in a much deeper sense concern questions of trust and ethics of mutual responsibility.

Table 3.1   Conventions of co-authorship

Co-authorship credits should be granted on the understanding that each individual has contributed in a meaningful and substantive way to the intellectual content of the written work. In accordance with received norms concerning the attribution of authorship, each listed author should have participated in a manner sufficient to take public responsibility for its content, such that all co-authors should have been directly involved, to some degree, in all three of the following:

- planning of and contribution to some component (conception, design, conduct, analysis, interpretation) of the written work;
- specific contributions to the drafting and revision of the written work; and
- final approval of the version to be published.

Source: editors, contributors, and Yale University Office of the Provost: http://provost.yale.edu/academic-integrity/authorship

Another aspect of collaboration developed around the seminar was that of peer review. An internal peer-review system was established as a means to provide feedback and advice on written drafts. This worked well in terms of the exchange of general advice on readability and structure, the coverage of relevant issues and literatures, and the like. Understandably, there was some evidence of hesitation when it came to making especially pointed or critical comments, in situations in which the authors were not only peers but often friends. In response to this, a single-blind anonymized system of peer review (in which the authors are identified, but the reviewers are not) was subsequently adopted as the writing projects advanced toward what would ultimately become draft chapters for this collection. This functioned to sharpen and focus these assessments, and to enrich their contribution to the development of each chapter. These evolving practices for internal peer review, along with ongoing communications around collaborative writing and editorial revisions, were signs that much was learned, by all involved, about the give-and-take required in order to make a project of knowledge coproduction like this – involving so many hands – actually work.

Turning briefly to the seminar itself, the first seven weeks of the joint meetings were dedicated to the task of developing collaborative protocols and practices, in the context of an intensive (but inevitably somewhat schematic) survey of key themes, debates, and issues in postmillennial urban studies, always with an eye to questions of methodology and research practice. This included discussions of debates around postcolonial, planetary, and provincial modes of urban theory making; ethnographic modes of inquiry, from the more conventional practices of dwelling with research subjects and situations, to the growing emphasis on following or traveling with all manner of mobile actors and actants: actants were considered in the context of a variety of applications; alternative methodologies for comparative and multi-sited research were also explored, as was a range of variably competing and complementary approaches to urban studies, from assemblage to extended case methods, from more to less inductive modes of inference, and from process-based explanations to those grounded in principles like encounter. A good portion of the time in this first phase of the seminar was given over to methodologically themed reviews of contemporary debates and issues in critical urban studies, punctuated by the presentation of a series of 'keyword' papers, drafted and presented by pairs of graduate student participants, in the form of short introductions to some of the more important concepts and formulations with currency in the field (see Part IV of this volume).

A second phase of the collaborative seminar concerned the selection and subsequent interrogation of a series of monographs in critical urban studies. Following extensive discussions within the group, three monographs were initially selected in order to further explore some of the depth and range of methodological practice, and collectively hone what would become a shared approach to constructive methodological deconstruction, described in more detail in the following section of this chapter. The three books selected for review and discussion by the entire group were Ash Amin and Nigel Thrift's *Cities*, Alice Goffman's *On the Run*, and AbdouMaliq Simone's *Jakarta, Drawing the City Near* (Amin and Thrift, 2002; Goffman, 2014; Simone, 2014), in part because their methodological implications have been widely discussed across the field. An overarching goal here was to construct a mutually informed approach to interrogating the methodological premises and practices of urban monographs, including guidelines for the reverse engineering of the texts from a methodological perspective. Together with the development and discussion of urban studies keywords, this enabled seminar participants to construct a shared rubric for the purposeful and constructive evaluation of these monographs, positioned in relation to wider theoretical and methodological debates in the field.

Following these class-wide discussions, the group then divided into smaller teams, working across the two campuses in many cases, to work with their respective monographs. Working papers were subsequently drafted, each of them jointly authored, which were then peer reviewed prior to presentation, and discussion, at the three-day retreat that marked the completion of the seminar. The group's only face-to-face meeting, the retreat was an occasion to workshop each of the methodological essays, drawing out their take-home messages, as well as to refine the collective terms and tone of what would become contributions to the present volume. This also was an opportunity for the group to refine its own line on the 'constructive deconstruction' of urban studies monographs. Rather than adopting the conventional approach to writing book reviews of the chosen monographs, or accepting extant cultures of critique (not least in graduate seminars) that can tend toward the negative and partisan, we tried as a group to be as explicit and transparent as possible about the approach to constructive deconstruction, which in practice has been an ongoing process.

Deconstructing the monograph

Deconstructing the monograph, the approach developed collectively by the contributors to this volume, has been designed to open up dialogues rather than harden positions, to take away and work with positive lessons rather than merely cataloguing methodological objections, incompatibilities, or reservations. It has involved taking a selection of monographs from the diverse field of critical urban studies and then mining these for positive insights into methodological practice, expositional efficacy, and research design integrity – framing assessments of their limitations and blind spots accordingly. These selections, made by participants in our collaborative seminar through a mixture of individual choices and group dialogue, need not be 'models' or perfect specimens (not that there could be such a thing), although they were seen as significant contributions *of different kinds* to the polysemic project that is critical urban studies. Our group discussions underlined the importance of scanning the field broadly, over the previous two decades, rather than focusing only on currently 'hot' books. This longer-term perspective was helpful in positioning more recent contributions alongside those monographs, which have stood the test of time or which otherwise remain quite distinctive accomplishments. Furthermore, the bar was set high in the sense that the monographs chosen ought certainly to repay the focused attention of a group of students using these texts as windows on (generative) research practice. This implied an engaged and positive disposition, in some ways echoing Burawoy's injunction, 'We begin with our favorite theory', prior to 'stress testing' through demanding research designs.

Beginning, in our case, with a promising monograph (maybe even a favorite book) meant selecting texts that aligned with the methodological concerns and aspirations of graduate students in the seminar, but also seeing these as engines for methodological learning. From a practical perspective, a balance had to be struck here between, on the one hand, the preferences and interests of individual students in the joint seminar, who, were choosing not just any book that might be of interest but one that spoke to them in methodological terms, and on the other hand, the extremely wide spectrum of work in critical urban studies, across which the group as a whole wanted to achieve some breadth of coverage. In our group discussions, we emphasized the need to 'stretch' the extensive list of candidate monographs, in particular in the direction of a geographically wide-ranging collection of texts that reaches into the global South and global East, as well as to consider more quantitatively oriented books (since most in the group favored qualitative work). Some time was devoted to weighing candidates for inclusion, and then 'mapping' these according to methodological approach, location (and number) of case study sites, and the career stage of authors – to encompass books developed from doctoral dissertations to those produced by mid- or later-career researchers. Given the need to be responsive to the individual interests and inclinations of participants in the joint seminar, the aggregate outcome could only ever be partially successful in representing the actually existing diversity of critical urban studies, but it is indicative at least of some of that diversity. When the group reviewed the nominated monographs, the tilt in favor of 'western' cases was noted, as was the relatively small number of texts utilizing quantitative or mixed-methods approaches. The final selection (see Table 3.2) was, however, acknowledged to represent a reasonable compromise between the more immediate research interests of members of the group and the collective aspiration to reach broadly across the field of critical urban studies.

Table 3.2   The selection of urban studies monographs

Monograph	Theories (and principal spatial referents)	Methods
Björkman, *Pipe Politics, Contested Waters*	Assemblage urbanism, actor–network theory, science and technology studies, everyday urbanism (South)	Ethnography, archival research, interviews, document analysis, assemblage analysis
Bourgois, *In Search of Respect*	Cultural production theories (North–South)	Participant observation, extended case ethnography
Brenner, *New State Spaces*	Marxian political economy (North)	Institutional political economy; meso-scale policy analysis
Dikeç, *Badlands of the Republic*	Political economy, representational theory, urban politics, post-politics (North)	Institutional/policy analysis, discourse analysis, interviews
Fairbanks, *How It Works*	Political economy, governmentality studies, neoliberalization (North)	Ethnography, institutional analysis
Gandy, *The Fabric of Space*	Urban political ecology, postcolonial theory, urban morphology (North–South)	Visual and discourse analysis, literary critique, textual and archival analysis
Ghertner, *Rule by Aesthetics*	Political economy, urban politics, theory of aesthetics, cultural theory (South)	Ethnography, semiotic analysis, discourse analysis
Haila, *Urban Land Rent*	Urban political economy, urban land rent theory, housing theory, urban governance (South)	Critical genealogy, document analysis, policy analysis, institutional analysis, demographic data analysis
Holston, *Insurgent Citizenship*	Insurgent citizenship, governance, everyday urbanism (South)	Ethnography, archival research (historical analysis) institutional/policy analysis

Monograph	Theories (and principal spatial referents)	Methods
Hsing, *The Great Urban Transformation*	Polanyian and Lefebvrian political economy (South–South)	Multi-method triangulation, interviews, textual analysis, comparison
Kanna, *Dubai: The City as Corporation*	Lefebvrian spatial theory, architectural theory, southern urban theory (South)	Historical regional analysis, interviews, discourse analysis
Kern, *Sex and the Revitalized City*	Feminist urban political economy, feminist theory, gender and gentrification (North)	Interviews, discourse analysis
Simone, *City Life from Jakarta to Dakar*	Everyday urbanism, postcolonial urbanism, development of mid-level concepts (South)	Close description, participant observation, interviews, translocal analysis
Söderström, *Cities in Relations*	Postcolonial and southern urbanism, actor–network theory (South–South)	Relational comparison, economic data and document analysis, interviews, landscape analysis, actor–network analysis
Storper, Kemeny, Makarem and Osman, *The Rise and Fall of Urban Economies*	Urban economic theories of development, geographical economics, institutional theory (North–North)	Quantitative data analysis, document and network analysis, comparative case study

The process of sifting and selection having been completed, the monographs were then each 'read for method', and for indications of research practice, by groups of two or three collaborating researchers – groups that in nearly all cases continued on to write the jointly authored chapters included in Part II of this volume. The charge to read the monographs for method and practice was in one respect a literal one, since it entailed a close examination of methodological statements, rationalizations, and traces in the text itself. With some notable exceptions, this first-cut examination often yielded only scattered insights, however, since both the conventions of academic book publishing and to some degree customary approaches in the field of critical urban studies tend to mitigate against anything beyond relatively cursory, compressed, or footnote-status discussions of methods, methodology, and research practice. This is most certainly not to imply that corners are somehow being cut. Instead, it is arguably more a reflection of tacit understandings and writing conventions in the field, coupled with the fact that publishers and editors tend to be more interested in prioritizing the (net) scholarly contribution of books over their mode of production per se.

Furthermore, it is not entirely unusual, it must be said, for 'methods-talk' to become somewhat submerged within established scholarly communities, especially where certain conventions are broadly (if perhaps implicitly) shared (see Barnes et al., 2007), exceptions being instances of concerted methodological innovation or disputation, or studies embedded in research cultures where reflexivity and the recognition of positionality are constitutive to research practice such as ethnography, participatory action approaches, and feminism.

Acknowledging this variability in the degree (and form) of methodological transparency, reading for method and research practice involved posing a host of probing questions of the text, and of the author's underlying design, approach, and strategy. What can the text and its underlying methods of construction teach us about various approaches to, and styles of, critical urban studies? To which scholarly conversations does the book seek to contribute, and how is it positioned in relation to these conversations, their interlocutors, and their respective methodological approaches? What research design sits behind the text – involving what kinds of articulations of theory and method, what kinds of relationships with (established and emergent) conceptual frames, formulations, and frameworks? What strategies for data collection, processing, analysis, and representation were involved, and implying what kinds of engagements with research sites, sources, and subjects? How does the author's own voice come through, and in what relation to others in the text? How is the argument structured and sustained, with the aid of what narrative and expositional strategies? How (effectively) are substantive conclusions and theory claims developed and delivered? And how does the book address and engage with its audience(s)? Finally, what reception did the book anticipate and ultimately meet, in scholarly and in more 'public' communities?

Given that every urban theory is based on certain principles of explanatory pertinence and analytical relevance, just as every act of empirical representation will give voice to certain subjects or priority to certain events and situations, it follows that authors cannot but confront choices of focus and prioritization on the one hand, and silencing and exclusion on the other. But what are the implications of these – inescapable – choices of explanatory and representational selectivity? What is placed in the foreground, and presented as active, driving, consequential, or causal? What is left out, left unsaid, skimmed over, or quietly pushed into the background? Which figures, actors, and settings are drawn most richly, in three dimensions, and which ones are portrayed in 'flatter', more singular, and less rounded terms? To ask such questions is not to call authors to account for bracketing or bounding their inquiries, as such bracketing and bounding is always necessary. Rather, it is a way to draw out and appreciate explanatory and presentational priorities, and to ask what ingredients went into the construction of the monograph, how they were combined, and to what effect.

Addressing questions such as these, intended to 'open up' the chosen monographs from a specifically methodological perspective, required practices of close but constructive reading and critique. This involved the articulation and discussion of practices of constructive engagement with the texts, some of the principles and prompts of which are distilled in Table 3.3. In contrast to what are often the default approaches, socialized habits, and received practices in many graduate seminars and reading groups, *internal* critiques were expressly prioritized over external critiques. Internal critiques are not just sympathetic, friendly, or otherwise 'lite' critiques. First and foremost, they attend to the goals and objectives articulated by authors themselves, in relation to theoretical positions, debates, and what have been called 'belts' of discourse in the research literature (cf. Paige, 1999), seeking to gauge the extent to which both the text and the research project behind it are effective *in their own terms*. What is it about the overall research design and strategy in (and around) the book that is most effective, and in what ways is the monograph most compelling? Where is evidence, argumentation, and conceptualization brought together most persuasively? The focus here is placed on what is 'positively present' in the text, in relation to its underlying research practices, rather than what was left out, skirted over, or marginalized. Having addressed these questions, authors would *then* turn to ask to what extent there are holes, lapses, missing links, or moments of insufficient substantiation in the book, and the extent to which this impinges upon the central argument. These questions are asked not to score points against the book, to poke holes, or to undermine its contribution, but on the contrary to highlight what it is that really *works* about the text and its attendant research practices, again allowing appropriately for the author's framing of, and goals for, the text, read as an object of constructive, internal critique.

Table 3.3 Constructive deconstruction: prompts and principles

Assess the goals, objectives, and overall purpose of the text: What is the author setting out to achieve? What questions, concerns, problems, or puzzles guided the research project behind the text? With what literatures, fields of inquiry, and debates is the author engaged? Are the author's ethical and political commitments acknowledged and discussed?

Read sympathetically: What is effective or persuasive about the argument or case presented? What organizational and narrative strategies does the author employ, and to what ends? What is the overall arc of the argument? How does it build and culminate? What are the positive contributions of the text in these terms?

Situate and position the text: In relation to what theory cultures, methodological traditions, and discursive communities is the text located? What are the spatial and scalar coordinates of the argument, the theory claims, and the empirics? Are these bounded and specific, or more expansive? How are the author and the text positioned in the worlds of urban studies?

(Continued)

Table 3.3   (Continued)

Reverse-engineer the methodology: By means of what methodological practices, analytical routines, and data-collection strategies did the author construct the foundations of the book? What research design did this imply and entail? What are the strengths, accomplishments, and positive achievements of the research practices enacted in (or 'behind') the book? What evidentiary strategies are used and how (effectively) are findings organized and presented? What are the takeaway lessons for method and research practice?

Read for reflexivity: To what extent does the author demonstrate a reflexive approach to research practice, representation, and engagement? Is there evidence of adaptation, learning, and (self-)evaluation in the text? To what extent does the text itself internalize a critique of alternative approaches or contributions to the field?

Prioritize internal critique: How does the author articulate her own argument, and how is this worked out through the text, understood in its own terms? How effective are the chosen methodological and representational strategies in realizing these goals? In which respects (and where in the text) is the book at its best?

Consider lines of external critique: Which issues, actors, processes, situations, and practices are positioned in or out of focus in the analysis? Which are most/least closely drawn? Which are explicitly problematized, and which are sidelined or afforded less attention? Are there notable silences or exclusions? Who is/is not given voice in the text? How might the text be assessed from different – complementary or more contrary – theoretical viewpoints?

Source: editors and contributors

Far from holding back, letting things pass, or shying away from tough questions, this kind of internally oriented critique can actually be deeply probing, since external critiques can too often lead to premature foreclosure. We are all no doubt familiar with the tropes (and tenor) of external critique in seminars and reading groups – that the author chose the 'wrong' theoretical framework, that the author missed this or that current in the literature, or that certain variables or dimensions were neglected or marginalized in the analysis. These tropes certainly are valid in assessing the limitations of any monograph, but they can also foreshorten discussion, and the opportunity to learn from each text. Our strategy of asking graduate students to select, and to a certain extent 'stand up for', the texts in question had the effect of limiting any quick recourse to arm's-length, oblique, or external assessments. 'Recovering' and then traveling with the author's methodological strategy produced a closer engagement, not to say a more engaged one. Prioritizing internal critique in this manner involves exploring, in a searching but also more constructive register, what the authors were able to accomplish in the context of their own chosen terms, tools, and terrains of analysis, positioning the text in relation to its own explanatory goals and parameters, as well as within its own methodological paradigm, while also holding it to account in these terms. Reading for positive methodological lessons (what worked well in the text, how this was achieved in the preceding research strategy, how it was realized, etc.) not only departs from prevailing conventions of external critique but also (with its insistent focus on research design, execution, and practice) is subtly different to reading *primarily* with an eye to substantive conclusions or theoretical insights.

The texts examined in Part II of this collection are consequently encountered from the perspective of fellow travelers in the community of researchers, rather than with the lukewarm and more distant attitude of the skeptical reader, waiting to be convinced or impressed. As such, they are engaged by rigorous but supportive reader/researchers with an active interest in learning from creative and productive responses to shared methodological challenges, problems, and opportunities. Reading with methodological curiosity and generosity, and with the empathy of a co-researcher, also has the potential to contribute to the tonal shift that we seek to emphasize. In an urban studies field in which differences sometimes threaten to become fractures, with dialogue likewise veering at times toward the fractious, assessing the value of contributions in their own terms and reading for constructive insights into research practice can be seen as modestly countervailing maneuvers.

Furthermore, if these facets of constructive deconstruction primarily concern 'internal' matters of how an individual monograph (with its underlying research designs and strategies) can be approached, evaluated, and discussed, there are also implications for how monographs, in the plural, can be placed into conversation with one another. To once again borrow Jennifer Robinson's aphorism, it is important to acknowledge not only that cities exist in a 'world of cities', but also that monographs about cities exist in a world of monographs about cities. Such is the scope of methodological diversity and pluralism in critical urban studies that a premium surely must be placed on the continuous development of dialogic practices that span, connect, and respect methodological difference, in all its registers. The training, expertise, and predilections of particular researchers will often lead them to favor one methodological approach and theoretical perspective over another, just as different sites, subjects, questions, problems, and situations may sometimes (seem to) favor one such approach over another. But exclusivity and partisanship have little to recommend them: it certainly does not follow that the strengths of one approach reflect (or resolve) the shortcomings of others, that rigor or reflexivity can only be realized in one way, that some methods or theories are intrinsically and universally superior, or that a certain methodological approach is suitable for every context and problem. If methods are understood as alternative devices for seeing, reading, and interpreting, then they (can only) exist in a world of alternative ways of seeing, reading, and interpreting. In a heterodox field like critical urban studies, methodological pluralism may be inevitable, but surely it should be leveraged as a strength. There is room for discourse analysis *and* statistical inference, for participatory action research *and* elite interviewing, as well as for all manner of ethnographical approaches and genres. A principle of parity of methodological esteem should accord value to all these individual techniques, approaches, practices, and perspectives, among others.

The wager on which this collection is premised is that there is much to be gained – and little or nothing to be lost – from an enriched dialogue *across* methodological approaches, research traditions, and monographs, and also much to be gained from the cultivation of reading practices across such differences for what they each bring, not for what they supposedly lack. Taken in aggregate, albeit still only a highly selective one, the monographs featured in Part II can be read in this way. Of course, the selection here can (also) be read for what it misses – and in the diverse field of critical urban studies that is inevitably a great deal – but if it cannot claim to be exhaustive, or a representative sample, perhaps it can be taken as a preliminary illustration of the principle that the sum of this methodological diversity exceeds that of its separate parts. And to the extent that there is value in this style of methodological probing, with an orientation toward exacting, internal critique, then the approach followed here might provide a template for further applications and extensions, in practice and in print, in student assignments, seminar rooms, and conference halls.

The book ahead

The next section of the book, Part II, features a collection of short essays, each concerned with questions of methodological practice. In the spirit of the approach sketched out here, these essays seek to reach beyond narrow understandings of method-as-technique to attend to the intricate connections between theory, research design and practice, empirics, expositional style, and normative–ethical commitments. It is hoped that there is indicative value in the reflexive and transparent modes of production and presentation evident in these essays, each of which in their own terms seeks to model constructive approaches to evaluation, critique, and assessment, in conjunction with the consideration of such more conventional matters as the veracity of substantive claims and the bases upon which attendant theory claims can be said to rest.

The sequencing of the following chapters is neither arbitrary, nor conventional. They are loosely sequenced according to the degree of 'distance' from the doctoral dissertation work of each author, beginning with monographs that to varying degrees were 'converted' from dissertation projects, to mid- and later-career contributions usually drawing on post-dissertation research projects and programs of various kinds. Here we provide brief introductions to the monographs featured in *Urban Studies Inside/Out*, calling attention to their distinctive methodological features and to some of the insights gleaned from these 'constructive deconstructions'.

In the first of the following collection of methodological essays, Chapter 4, Kyle Loewen, Devra Waldman, and Mikael Omstedt offer an evaluation of Leslie Kern's *Sex and the Revitalized City*, an original contribution to feminist urban political economy that seeks to bring gender into the study of gentrification in a way that moves beyond the rather calcified division between production-oriented and consumption-oriented approaches to the latter. Kern demonstrates the constitutive role of gender relations in shaping the condominium-based model of development and the design features and marketing strategies with which it has become associated, using interviews and textual analysis to draw out the ways in which these are refracted and reproduced through lived, everyday experiences. It is through an interrogation of the everyday that Kern brings together her concerns with development rationalities and capital logics on the one hand, with the (re)production of gendered subjectivities on the other, although an opportunity is missed to trace the consequences for those marginalized and excluded by the condo development model.

In Chapter 5, Dimitar Anguelov, Emma Colven, and Prajna Rao reflect on Asher Ghertner's *Rule by Aesthetics*, in which a multi-method approach is deployed in order to uncover how aesthetic norms based on 'world-class city' appearances are forged into a hegemonic order for governing space in Delhi, as well as the ways in which the city's slum dwellers simultaneously partake in and resist this. Theoretically, the book moves beyond the familiar terrain of political economy, delving into linguistic studies, semiotic analysis, and cultural theory to explore the sensory registers through which Delhi's residents and government officials interpret and perform aesthetic visions of the city. Methodologically, it illustrates the merits of an expanded conception of ethnography that goes beyond the excavation of fieldnotes. However, the authors argue that more might have been made of how this vivid depiction of Millennial Delhi could be mobilized in the service of a deeper challenge to the explanatory power and provenance of what are mostly western theories.

Turning to Chapter 6, Tanya Matthan, Emma Colven, and Hudson Spivey interrogate Lisa Björkman's *Pipe Politics, Contested Waters*, a study of water, technology, and everyday life in Mumbai. Through an in-depth ethnographic study – interviewing various participants maintaining and using the water infrastructure but also attending to more-than-human agency Björkman analyzes why city residents face erratic and uncertain water supply even in a context in which water itself is not actually scarce, and how they access water on an everyday basis. By 'following the infrastructure' she provides a historicized understanding of infrastructural shambles while complicating easy analytical binaries, yet her determination to avoid ascribing all agency to social factors runs the danger of overemphasizing technical and material factors to the neglect of issues of social power and justice.

Badlands of the Republic, by Mustafa Dikeç, is the focus for Nina Ebner, Joe Penny, and Andre Comandon in Chapter 7. This is an object lesson in the insights and the potential of a critical and theoretically informed approach to discourse analysis, while also highlighting some of its limitations. Dikeç begins by deconstructing how French urban policy has imagined, articulated, and constructed the banlieue (French suburban neighborhood) as a problematic space, as a badland riven with pathologies in need of repressive state intervention. He then discusses how these representations of the banlieue are contested by those demanding social justice from below. Yet an over-reliance on the discourse analysis of existing policy documents and texts risks ascribing too much power to these at the expense of the experiences and agency of actors, for example, of those contesting these negative representations – challenges of discourse analysis that can be overcome and remedied.

In Chapter 8, Nafis Hasan, Hudson Spivey, and Kenton Card assess *Dubai: The City as Corporation* by Ahmed Kanna, a study of the construction of contemporary Dubai. Combining historical analysis and ethnographic investigation, the book reconstructs how Dubai is produced spatially, and how the city is experienced by residents. Kanna's focus on architecture brings attention to how urban form is quite literally produced, presented as a challenge to western and modernist depictions of Dubai. Effective use is made of interviews with local elites and the architects they hired, as well as with middle- and working-class South Asian residents, along with an analysis of architectural practices and discourses. But analysis of local subjectivities is somewhat truncated and the author is unable to convey how these issues play out in everyday life – particularly for non-Emiratis.

Joseph A. Daniels, Mikael Omstedt, and Dimitar Anguelov tackle *New State Spaces* by Neil Brenner in Chapter 9, a book notable for its twin concerns with the urban as a (relationally defined) scale and as a significant domain of state restructuring. Recognizing the value of this pioneering approach to mid-level theorization, working as it does across a large number of metropolitan cases and indeed countries, the authors also call attention to what is sacrificed at the level of the concrete, including the specificities of (local) institutional restructuring and contestation, grassroots politics, and the identification of counter-projects. As a result, state action may come across as more coherent, coordinated, and purposeful than is truly the case, while less attention is paid to the indeterminate outcomes of regulatory struggles and implementation practices at the local scale.

In Chapter 10, Samuel Nowak and Tom Howard present an assessment of Robert Fairbanks' theoretically and methodologically novel contribution to understanding urban poverty in the United States in *How It Works*. This critical ethnography with a distinctly multiscalar reach interrogates the relations between political economic structures and institutions, and everyday life and practices, in Philadelphia's recovery houses. Fairbanks' critical ethnography is extremely successful in exposing these complex linkages, persuasively showing how processes of state restructuring reach into the lives of the poor. The analysis is limited, however, by Fairbanks' lack of reflection on his own positionality and on the effects of unequal power relations in ethnographic practice.

In Search of Respect, by Philippe Bourgois, is the focus for Tom Howard, Samuel Nowak, and Fernanda Jahn-Verri in Chapter 11. This is the result of a participant observation ethnography of the crack-dealing business in the largely Puerto Rican community of East Harlem, New York City. Against both pathologizing and sanitizing narratives of the urban poor, Bourgois develops an original and compelling analysis of the everyday reproduction of masculinized identities and behaviors, understood as a kind of oppositional culture. The author struggles quite explicitly with dilemmas of representation, to which there is no easy resolution in what are deeply marginalized communities, scarred by social violence. In the context of recent debates in critical urban studies, the book is credited with pioneering a distinctive approach to relational analysis that in a sense transcends conventional North–South binaries, offering as it does a revealing examination of Puerto Rican cultures relativized and recontextualized in New York City. It also provides insights into the politics and ethics of positionality in what is a challenging setting for both researchers and research subjects.

Anne Haila's *Urban Land Rent* is examined by Kenton Card, Andre Comandon and Joseph A. Daniels, in Chapter 12. This is an analysis of how Singapore became a property state. Combining a genealogical analysis of the western literature on land rent with an institutional history focused on state-led institutional reforms, Haila analyzes historical and media documents, and demographic data and policies, complemented by direct observations. She makes the case that Singapore's success in good part is due to the state's active deployment of land and property, reminding urban scholars of the importance of attending to the interrelated urban land and urban housing questions. Yet a theoretical framework that privileges top-down analysis tends to neglect the perspective of urban majorities and peripheries.

You-tien Hsing's *The Great Urban Transformation* is the subject of the methodological essay by Tyler Harlan and Jaehyeon Park in Chapter 13. The book presents the results of a long-term study of land and property politics in China, covering a significant span of the country's extended period of marketization. This is a mixed-methods, multi-site study providing multiple vantage points on the interactions between the political economy of (central) state-led implementation and complicity, co-optation, and contestation at the local scale. Placing theoretical propositions in ongoing dialogue with her empirical findings, Hsing is able to offer a persuasive analysis of land and property markets as an 'instituted process', even in a context in which secondary data are notoriously unreliable and where methodological 'saturation' is effectively unattainable.

In Chapter 14, Carolyn Prouse and Fernanda Jahn-Verri investigate James Holston's *Insurgent Citizenship*, a multiscalar/multi-method study of Sao Paulo's urban peripheries at the turn of the last century. Holston's historical analysis of land policy and constitutional citizenship in Brazil provides insights into how and why urban peripheries have developed as spaces marked by the auto-construction of dwellings and a particular repertoire of insurgent practices. This ethnographic investigation shows how urban peripherality, especially auto-construction, has also provided both the means and substance for struggles around rights to the city, and more generally around emergent forms of democratic citizenship at the national scale. While Holston's project can be credited with opening up these issues in new ways, it could have benefited from greater methodological attention to issues of intersectionality and the differential experiences of being poor, specifically along racial and gender lines, and to how the interrelated processes of racialization, colonization, and patriarchy shape insurgent citizenship.

Matthew Gandy's creative contribution to urban political ecology, *The Fabric of Space*, is the focus for CS Ponder and Sophie Webber in Chapter 15. The book tackles the interrelated issues of social and environmental transformation by way of a multi-city study of the entangled politics of water and modernity, stretching from the nineteenth century through the present and into the future. Highly evocative accounts of six different cities, including Weimar Berlin, Lagos in the 1940s, and a future version of London, are read here as examples of provocative juxtaposition rather than formal methodological comparison. Gandy's analysis makes use of literary sources and visual culture in a way that is both novel and effective, although there is relatively little in the way of methodological codification or explicit reflexivity in the book.

In Chapter 16, Prajna Rao and Andre Comandon assess AbdouMaliq Simone's transnational unraveling of the livelihood practices of 'urban majorities' in *City Life from Jakarta to Dakar*. Through up-close observations coupled with deep personal engagement with those occupying the urban majority, Simone displays a facility for shaping extremely fluid mid-level concepts most notably relating to mundane – if also consequential – urban practices. He conceptualizes cities and cityness as bound together by the inventiveness and everyday industry of urban inhabitants, framed always by a web of uncertainties that they can only but navigate. This places oft-neglected urban populations and peripheries at the center of participatory-style urban studies, one that does not conform to the conventions of ethnography but which is especially effective in bringing to light often unseen practices and connections. However, Simone provides little in the way of a legible template, or map, for how his distinctive research design might be replicated.

Ola Söderström's relational comparison of the cities of Hanoi and Ouagadougou in *Cities in Relations* is Rachel Bok's concern in Chapter 17. The book positions these two cities in relation to the broader fields of extra-urban relations through which they are jointly constituted, making use of economic statistics, document analysis, interviews, and an actor–network sensibility to unpack how objects within the city are made and circulated. Notably, Söderström seeks to place these cities in conversation with one another rather than with northern cities, and their developmental and cultural norms. However, his disproportionate reliance on northern theorists and on a selection of relatively powerful local informants, together with insufficient attention to issues of reflexivity, raises questions about how disruptive the analysis might be in relation to the norms of northern urbanism.

In the last of this selection of methodological essays, Chapter 18, Andre Comandan, Kenton Card, and Joe Daniels discuss Michael Storper, Thomas Kemeny, Naji Makarem, and Taner Osman's co-authored study of economic divergence between San Francisco and Los Angeles, *The Rise and Fall of Urban Economies*. Based on an exacting research design, this comparative case study utilizes quantitative data to critique theories of urban economic development, combining this inventively with qualitative data on institutional networks in the two metropolitan areas to argue that the differential effectiveness of these networks is the underlying cause of the divergent economic fortunes of the two cities. The institutionalist approach can be considered to be somewhat narrow, the role of the state is neglected, and the possibilities of a relational comparison are not explored, but the authors' transparency about assumptions and method is laudable.

Following this collection of methodological essays, Part III of the book presents some concluding thoughts on the practice and purpose of *Urban Studies Inside/Out*, which we hope will be read as a constructive contribution to the ongoing conversation about methods and research practices in the field. Finally, Part IV closes the book with a selection of co-authored keyword 'primers'. Initially developed as orientating devices and as foci for discussion in the joint graduate seminar, these are intended to provide a balanced and informative explication of a sampling of key concepts and formulations in the field of critical urban studies. Each keyword provides a critical genealogy of the term along with a brief commentary on its applications and currency in critical urban studies, including a sense of the situated context from which the concept emerges, its explanatory scope, patterns of usage, and so forth. The keywords are invigorated (where appropriate) with concrete examples, illustrations, and vignettes, also referencing foundational works in the area that provide a springboard for deeper inquiry. More substantial than typical dictionary entries and more focused than conventional encyclopedia entries, these keywords are particularly concerned with methodological issues, albeit in a wide range of applications and contexts. Our goal is that this section of the book can function as a 'deep index' for the collection, in that the keywords are referenced where appropriate in the methodological essays that comprise Part II, as well as being a resource in its own right. The number of keywords was limited by the size of the collaborative seminar, and once again skews to some degree to the pattern of interests of those participating in the UBC/UCLA seminar, but our hope is that these might serve as a 'template' of sorts for student assignments that can be developed in conjunction with the book.

PART II

METHODOLOGICAL ESSAYS

4

CONSTRUCTING A FEMINIST URBAN POLITICAL ECONOMY: ON LESLIE KERN'S *SEX AND THE REVITALIZED CITY*

Kyle Loewen, Devra Waldman and Mikael Omstedt

KEYWORDS: gentrification, neoliberal urbanism, urban citizenship, urban governance

Introduction: the everyday as hinge

Leslie Kern's *Sex and the Revitalized City* (2010) excavates Toronto's condominium boom in the early 2000s, drawing particular attention to the gendered aspects of **neoliberal urbanism**, shifts in **urban governance** structures, and **urban citizenship**. Building on her dissertation at York University's School of Gender, Sexuality and Women's Studies, Kern begins by demonstrating how the city's economic and regulatory environments encouraged the development of owner-occupied housing over rental properties. She then interrogates the role of gender in **gentrification** through four cases: the values and experiences of homeownership; constructions of community in condominium developments; relations between security, fear, and the city; and the myths of urbanity surrounding condominium development. Setting two main goals for her project, Kern wants, first, to integrate gender analysis more deeply into gentrification scholarship by examining changing everyday relations in the city, and, second, to utilize this feminist analysis of gentrification to understand how opportunities for social transformation and democratic citizenship are being reshaped.

One way to assess the theoretical and methodological significance of the book is to situate its arguments in relation to strands of feminist urbanism and urban political economy, the latter tending to focus on class, capital, and the state, while the former typically centers gender relations. In gentrification scholarship, a similar divide between class processes and gender relations can be traced to the long-standing distinction between production and consumption-oriented approaches. Production-oriented approaches prioritize the role of real-estate capital and the state in gentrification, often resulting in a class-based analysis of urban development (Smith, 2002; Lees et al., 2007). As Neil Smith argues, 'class for Marx is the first and foremost social category. It is the social relations of class that mobilize specific economic relations and not the other way around' (2000: 1027). He goes on to argue that gentrification is driven by logics of capital investment, realizing profit by targeting working-class neighborhoods and displacing local residents. The neoliberal state's role in this process often involves removing protections of public space, paving the way for privatization and the exclusion of working-class residents (Smith, 1996; Hackworth and Smith, 2001). Through these dynamics of redevelopment, capital steers the discourses of public space away from understandings of a 'public good' and toward the 'highest and best use' for middle-class consumers (Blomley, 2004).

On the other hand, consumption-based theories of gentrification tend to more fully problematize the identities and motivations of the gentrifiers themselves. From this perspective, change in the postindustrial city is driven by the aggregated individual decisions of a professionalized middle class. These scholars highlight the diversity of gentrifiers' gender, race, sexuality, and the extra-economic agency exerted by the middle classes in gentrification. Inspired by humanistic geography, this consumption approach is one of the few perspectives that have taken gender identities seriously as an active force in urban redevelopment. Liz Bondi (1999) for example argues that gender (as a social relation) has frequently been neglected within gentrification research and that women (as a category) have often been subsumed within class frameworks. Likewise, scholars such as Damaris Rose (1984), Robert Beauregard (1986), and Alan Warde (1991) have all emphasized the role of single professional women and dual-earner relationships in driving gentrification processes, while arguing that a greater understanding of who gentrifiers are requires a focus on gender divisions of labor instead of an exclusive focus on sociologically 'empty' accounts of capital and class.

Cutting through this long-standing divide between production and consumption explanations of gentrification, Kern insists that gender is a constitutive aspect of the cycles of capital investment and circulation that drive gentrification. That is, Kern reworks the analytical divisions that she inherited, not by approaching urban redevelopment as a relatively autonomous process that adversely affects and/or creates new opportunities for women simply after the fact. Instead, she argues that 'from the start' gender is a crucial factor in how developers and planners decide on where and how to invest in the built environment of the city. In this sense, gender is a necessary part of production-oriented analyses of gentrification, rather than sidenote, after-effect, or secondary phenomena. This means that gender analysis need not be positioned simply in opposition to class analysis. At the same time, neither does Kern straightforwardly follow those consumption-oriented approaches that understand gender through the frame of identity. Rather than focusing on how pre-given identities motivate or dissuade individuals to migrate to the city, she focuses on the ongoing processes of subject production that occur through the experiences, opportunities, and constraints encountered in everyday life. It is this broad-based production of gendered subjects, not already established and essentialized identities, that plays a constitutive role in capital-led processes of gentrification.

Kern makes this analytical contribution to gentrification scholarship by methodologically prioritizing the everyday in her research, utilizing it as a hinge between the macro-analysis of Toronto's regional political economy and the micro-analysis of gendered subject production. She used three main methods to better understand the everyday lives of single professional women who own condominiums in Toronto. First, she utilizes visual and discourse analysis of condominium advertisements, city documents, and provincial documents in order to situate the day-to-day lives of women condo owners within a regional political economic context. Second, she draws on key informant interviews with developers and city planners in order to understand how these actors who shape capital's investment patterns think about, plan for, and accommodate women condo owners in their own activities. Finally, she conducts personal interviews with female condominium dwellers in order to understand the everyday experiences, encounters, and thought processes of women who live in Toronto's new-build condominiums.

In this chapter, we interrogate the potential and limits of *Sex and the Revitalized City*'s feminist political economy through its methodological use of the everyday. To do this, we consider the extent to which Kern's approach was able to realize her own goals of bringing gender into gentrification scholarship and finding opportunities for social justice in the neoliberal city. First, we evaluate Kern's success at demonstrating the constitutive role of gender in a production-oriented analysis of gentrification. We find that the everyday has significant potential for enhancing our understanding of the logics of capital accumulation and demonstrating the inextricable relationship between economic processes and social difference. We then move to consider how effectively Kern was able to elucidate opportunities for social justice in neoliberal cities, including the emancipation of women from the patriarchal family form. Here we argue that her methodological focus lent itself more to understanding how gentrification foreclosed opportunities for social justice, rather than finding new openings. In considering whether this is a function of Kern's methodology or the constraints of neoliberal governance, we look at some methodological adjustments that she could have made to push at, or overcome, the limitations that she encountered. Following feminist and postcolonial scholars, we suggest that the scope of *Sex and the Revitalized City* might have been extended to incorporate the everyday lives of those *excluded* by processes of gentrification, in order to open up a wider set of questions around social justice.

Gender as constitutive of the city

In *Sex and the Revitalized City*, Kern conceptualizes everyday life by combining a Lefebvrian understanding of the phrase as 'inhabiting the city, working in the city, creating the city' with a feminist perspective on how the seemingly mundane spaces of women's lives are central to social struggle (Kern, 2010: 8). Through this approach, she is interested in how 'the everyday' expresses, challenges, or reproduces neoliberal ideas about privatization of the social, as well as how 'daily meanings and practices revolving around home, family, work, leisure, and other activities' are structured and mediated through condominium dwelling (2010: 8). In order to tether this analysis of the everyday with a political economic take on neoliberal **urban governance,** she turns to Foucault's concept of governmentality. In the process, she is able connect the ways that women condo owners came to understand their own subjectivities in part through the economic rationalities of profit maximization, with the ways that planners and developers conceptualize 'single professional women' as target consumers of condominiums.

To get at the everyday experiences, encounters, and thought processes producing the social subject of the female condo owner, Kern primarily relies on semi-structured interviews with these women. By interrogating the 'everyday meanings' women attribute to condo ownership, Kern's interviews with female condo owners reveal that their preference for ownership is almost exclusively framed in terms of economic benefit, reflecting a broader culture of property ownership as a moral imperative. As one interviewee states, 'I don't think I'd ever go back to renting. It just feels so much better to invest in something that you're going to get your money out of later, and then some ... I think it's kind of ridiculous to be renting' (2010: 76). Similarly, another interviewee explains: 'I should buy a place here, just as an investment ... I can always sell it, and make money off it, and do it that way ... I think that would be a wiser decision, for me to actually move in ... and do that' (2010: 73). These kinds of interviews enabled Kern to examine the everyday meanings of homeownership and demonstrate how women are enrolled as entrepreneurial subjects who view their home primarily as an investment.

This entrepreneurial subjectivity was extended to the relationships that the women have with those in their communities. For example, one of Kern's interviewees decided to join her condominium board because of a desire to protect the value of her own condo, arguing that:

> [t]he first year of a condo the developer gets to appoint an arm's-length property manager ... It was absolutely corrupt from the get go ... She [the manager] was not doing a service to us, she was doing a service for him

[the developer]. Making sure that work wasn't getting done ... just doing all sorts of stuff. It took me months and months of battling ... and that's how we ended up getting the new security and the new property manager ... I think my job's done ... I've protected my asset. (2010: 120–121)

Significantly, Kern compiles many interviews like this one in order to demonstrate the similar ways that condo owners think about their homes in terms of an investment and a return on that investment. By layering these similar rationalities together, Kern is able to push her analysis beyond anecdotal conjecture in order to consider the kinds of subjectivities that women are forming through condo ownership. For example, by understanding that condo owners conceptualize their own home as an asset, Kern can logically step beyond what her interviewees explicitly say in order to think about how owners' conceptualizations of their homes redefine their broader social relationships. By viewing herself as a protector of her condominium's market value, the interviewee above was not interested in participating in the governance of the building as an expression of democratic participation, seeing it instead as an instrument of financial self-interest and market position.

To connect this everyday production of women condo-owner subjectivities with a broader political economic context, Kern relies primarily on interviews with city planners and condominium developers, along with analyses of commercial advertising and city documents. These interviews are particularly important because they provide her with material to demonstrate not only that gentrification has gendered effects *after the fact*, but that gender itself is a constitutive aspect of capital's decisions on where and how to invest in the city. To do this, she maintains her focus on the everyday lives of potential women condo owners in interviews with planners and developers. These interviews make it clear that they conceive of 'single professional women' as a target market of potential buyers, to whom they need to cater in their developments. As one of the developers who Kern interviews states:

It's much more difficult being a woman today ... Do you become a family individual? Do you become a professional? There's just so many different rifts. The reality is women are getting married ... at an older age. By the time someone is out of school ... they're ready to buy a place. (2010: 67)

Through multiple conversations with developers that had similar responses, Kern was able to demonstrate that they view 'single professional women' as ideal real-estate consumers. Developers consistently articulated a view of women as 'long-term' thinkers, who are getting married later in life and therefore want to buy a house before they get married. This figure of the 'single professional woman' as a long-term planner was contrasted with single men, who are believed to be short-sighted and more likely to rent rather than buy. These readings of single professional women were not after-thoughts of the investment and development process, but played an active role in influencing the design and location of buildings. As one developer stated, 'The building ... provides the opportunities for communities to form. We try to facilitate that ... [one project] for example has a large courtyard space. We have a yoga studio ... It's about a ... lifestyle, people sell lifestyle' (2010: 103).

By consistently maintaining a focus on the everyday lives of women in interviews, not only with the female condo owners themselves but also with developers, Kern effectively draws out the constitutive role of gender within a production-sensitive analysis of gentrification. On the one hand women condo owners are being invited to view themselves as economically rational individuals looking for lucrative investments, while, on the other, condominium production is being tailored to the perceived lifestyle preferences of 'single professional women'. The everyday provides Kern with a hinge to connect the construction of gendered subjects with the production of the city's built environment. Through this mutual construction of the city and 'single professional women', Kern makes clear that the patriarchal relationships between women, the city, public space, and marriage are no doubt being remade; however, it is uncertain what potential this remaking holds for social justice. This leads us to the second goal of Kern's project.

Seeking social justice

Building on her analysis in gentrification, Kern also wants to understand opportunities for social justice in neoliberal cities. Most of her analysis of political opportunities revolves around the ways that condo ownership alters women's relations to the city on a day-to-day basis. Her interviews show that the experience often brings a sense of freedom from marriage, economic dependence on a man or parents, and segmentation into unwaged domestic labor. In this sense, condo ownership has the potential to disrupt some norms of patriarchal social relationships. Interestingly, though, this disruption did not occur by challenging gendered divisions of labor in the home itself; instead, it worked by outsourcing masculinized labor previously undertaken within the family unit to the governance and maintenance structures of the condominium building. For example, the interviews showed that owning a condominium was attractive to single professional women because they would not be individually responsible for broader maintenance repairs. One condominium dweller states:

> I'm not interested in landscaping or gardening or any of those things, so the fact that I don't have to worry about that at all, and the fact that I don't have a roof that could start leaking or a basement that could flood ... I'm not at the point where I would really see the benefits of having any of those things. (2010: 81)

Here we can see the effectiveness of interviews at creating space for research participants explicitly to compare and contrast their current situation with alternative living arrangements, real or imagined. This is particularly helpful in Kern's research where gender and homeownership norms are often taken for granted, being considered normal and unexceptional for most participants. The interview format creates a good opportunity for interviewees to identify for themselves what the key distinctions are between alternative relations and arrangements. By comparing the responsibilities involved in owning a single family home versus a condo, this interviewee makes clear that condo ownership is less important to them as an opportunity to disrupt gendered divisions of labor in the home and more as an opportunity to achieve homeownership and economic advancement without depending on a husband or parent. This dynamic is corroborated in Kern's interviews with developers, who are keen to sell to single professional women not just a home, but the opportunity to 'grow up outside of a heterosexual partnership' (2010: 79). Kern concludes from these interviews that while liberation is sold to women condo owners, and often experienced by women as part of homeownership, patriarchal divisions of labor are nonetheless reproduced in different forms at the level of everyday life. This means that gentrification functions not in a subversive way but in reality to 'facilitate the economic goals of creating an enterprise culture', along with neoliberal conceptions of freedom (2010: 70). In practice, there are few openings for progressive politics here.

Of greater concern in this context is the way that neoliberal subjectivities enroll condo owners, and their visions of freedom, into the securitization of their buildings and the criminalization of surrounding neighborhoods. Kern describes how developers seek to create *and* sell 'secure' urban spaces through the discursive representation (and subsequent provision) of physical gates, security features and personnel, and surveillance technology. In her interviews, she drew on the discourses of the condominium development industry, including through marketing materials, as a way to explore women's perspectives on the importance and value of these security features in their daily lives:

> The concierge is actually a really big thing. I don't feel like I'd feel as comfortable living right [in] downtown Toronto. I mean, I love the location, but there's just a fair number of homeless people and not that far away there's drug dealers and prostitutes … the pass-codes, things like that, there's card entry … surveillance cameras … all that stuff contributes to making it feel comfortable living here. (2010: 133–134)

Through this approach of bringing circulating discourses and development-industry narratives into her interview questions, Kern is able to connect issues like securitization and building design with women's everyday lives and world-views. She concludes that the opportunities that condominium living provides, for some women, to escape patriarchal family norms are dependent on the securitization of these privatized living spaces, the effects of which extend out to surrounding neighborhoods through the othering and criminalization of unhoused communities, drug dealers, and sex workers.

Kern's approach is therefore very effective at articulating the constitutive role of gender in gentrification. However, it is not as successful at achieving its second goal of finding opportunities for social justice. Condominium developments can provide the material conditions for disrupting patriarchal norms concerning the home and women's life trajectories, but they do this by enrolling women as neoliberal subjects and redefining certain city neighborhoods as 'unsafe'. Yet it would be naive for us to claim that this frustrated search for social justice openings and opportunities is simply a function of Kern's methodology. Decades of neoliberal policies have placed significant constraints on radical and progressive urban politics, and it is difficult to know if her findings concerning these apparent foreclosures or limits are the result of extant conditions of city life or her methodological approach. With this caveat, it is worth considering if other approaches to researching the city could help move beyond these limits.

Gentrification's others

So far, our evaluation of Kern's methodology has stayed within the terms and goals she defined for her project. However, *Sex and the Revitalized City* relies on a foundational methodological choice to study the lives of women condo owners, which we believe warrants further consideration in light of the limitations in her approach. As we have argued, the decision to focus on these subjects was effective in bringing gender relations into the foreground, and doing so through an innovative focus on the everyday. But what are the political implications of this exclusive focus on gentrifying subjects, as opposed to those that are being displaced?

Kern's decision to research gentrification from the perspective of women gentrifiers was a decision to study gentrification from the position of its 'internal' processes, logics, and functioning rather than engaging more expansively with the question of gentrification's 'outside' – and those displaced by or otherwise excluded from condominium developments. Of course, it is impossible and in many ways undesirable to include everything within a research project. However, decisions regarding the parameters of research projects always raise political as well as analytical issues, if sometimes only indirectly. As Tom Slater (2006) argues, much academic attention on gentrification has been on the 'why' of this process, largely at the expense of a focus on the experience of non-gentrifying groups in gentrifying areas. Methodologically, feminist and postcolonial scholars have long argued that an exclusive focus on the internal functioning of processes like capitalism and gentrification can be problematic. This is because an exclusive focus on the 'inside' sets up an analysis where there is a dominant process or subject that on the one hand is all-encompassing and constitutive of itself (Maldonado-Torres, 2007), and on the other hand erases or reduces alternative subjects and rationalities to an opposition of the dominant term (Plumwood, 1994).

In many ways Kern's focus on gentrification's inside is reflective of Slater's (2006) observation that recent scholarship in the field has drifted away from highly critical accounts of the damaging effects of gentrification, in favor of analyses of gentrification processes as dominant and all-encompassing. Correspondingly, in *Sex and the Revitalized City* just about every potential opportunity for social justice turned out to actually enroll women condo owners as neoliberal subjects. To her credit, though, Kern did not let this potentially encompassing construction of neoliberalism and gentrification erase gentrification's other. For example, her analysis of security in the city focused on how public discourses mobilized binary logics of safe condominium buildings and unsafe surrounding neighborhoods. In this sense, Kern recognizes not only that gentrification has others, but also that it reduces these others to something akin to the opposite of condo owners. To this extent, Kern's approach is relatively consistent with the postcolonial and feminist critique of binary thought.

However, while her discussion of the issues surrounding securitization of the city pointed to concerns around the wider implications of gentrification, these were not fully pursued. Furthermore, Kern makes her arguments firmly from gentrification's 'inside' by focusing on the everyday lives of condo owners, rather than attempting to understand the everyday experiences of those that gentrification others, marginalizes, excludes, and displaces. This is evident in that all of her interviews are with condo owners and developers, and her textual and documentary analysis focuses heavily on material targeted at potential condominium buyers. While this enabled her to articulate how public discourse creates an other to 'revitalization', she was not able fully to unpack the negative framing of drug dealers, the unhoused, and sex workers as oppositions to condo owners. This framing of those who are *not* condo owners as, in effect, their binary opposites served to reinforce, or at least to leave untroubled, the all-encompassing conception of neoliberalism and gentrification.

As an alternative approach, Kern could have designed her project in such a way as to hold together, or in tension, the everyday lives of those excluded by gentrification with the subjects appropriated through this process. This fuller picture of the everyday coproduction of gentrification's subjects would likely have helped undo the othering of those excluded by gentrification, and possibly enabled a fuller understanding of Toronto's opportunities for social justice by looking at the everyday knowledge, livelihood strategies, social formations, and the solidarities among those displaced (Cahill, 2006). To be clear, we are not arguing that it is politically untenable for gentrification scholarship to study gentrifiers. Instead we are suggesting that in order to address some of the political limits that Kern encountered, scholars should consider focusing their attention on the everyday co-constitution of both the dominant and othered subjects of gentrification.

There are many examples of research in geography and urban studies that situate their projects right at these articulations of the inside and the outside.

Jennifer Bair and Marion Werner's (2011) methodology of 'disarticulation' provides one example in economic geography. They start from a parallel critique of global production network approaches: that these privilege those places and workers incorporated into global production. Their alternative disarticulations perspective calls attention to the fact that the flipside of this inclusion–integration process is that some workers and places find themselves on the outside, being excluded and disinvested from the circuits of global production (Bair and Werner, 2011). Along similar lines, Aihwa Ong (2006) argues that analyses of the impacts of neoliberalism are best understood when one considers the 'hinge' between the neoliberal practices/policies by the state and corporate actors, and those who are excepted, displaced, and excluded from the benefits of neoliberal decision-making. Paying close attention to the simultaneous interplay of giving/denying value and inclusion/exclusion opens up ways to destabilize and challenge the spatial fragmentation of the city and perhaps different avenues for social justice (Ong, 2006). These examples are suggestive of methodological frames that might expand Kern's analysis of the everyday in gentrification, by way of a fuller account of its excluded subjects, along with processes and practices that exceed the economizing logics of neoliberalism.

Conclusion

In light of Leslie Kern's success at demonstrating the constitutive role of gender within gentrification, albeit alongside a frustrated attempt to identify real opportunities for social justice in this case, what are some of the methodo-logical lessons that we can learn from this valuable and important contribution? Our first conclusion from *Sex and the Revitalized City* is that methodological innovation can provide an important tool for analytical innovation. Kern's work makes clear that methodology is not simply about the accuracy of researchers' accounts of the city, but also that it deeply affects the kinds of analytical claims they can make and knowledge that they are able to produce. Kern utilized a methodological focus on the everyday in order to argue that gender is a constitutive aspect of capital's reinvestment in the city. Mediated through interviews with developers, planners, and owners, it is Kern's insistent focus on women's everyday lives that allowed her to hold together, analytically speaking, these processes of subject production on the one hand and the logic of capital circulation on the other. This provided a means to overcome the stub-born divide between production- and consumption-oriented approaches to gentrification, not by ignoring them, or favoring one over the other, but by positioning them in productive tension.

Our second conclusion from *Sex and the Revitalized City* is that methodo-logical choices are always political choices, and that the political stakes of a research project must be given as much weight as academic concerns – from the formulation of research designs through research practice to analysis and dissemination. Kern's project reinforces this point in multiple ways. First it is explicitly political in its attempts to bring some of the subjects traditionally excluded or marginalized in urban research into the analytical foreground. Furthermore, she did this with the goal of not only pushing urban studies in new directions, but also developing a fresh approach to the strategic challenge of social justice in neoliberalized cities. The book models a reflexive approach to the politics of knowledge production, in and beyond the academy. At the same time, by focusing on those women with privileged access to the condominium market, much less is said about the everyday lives of those displaced and othered by gentrification. As Kern keenly understands, the consequences of this are significant not only in terms of the text itself, but also in terms of the political possibilities that are opened and foreclosed.

5

DREAMING AND SCHEMING THE 'WORLD-CLASS' CITY: ON ASHER GHERTNER'S *RULE BY AESTHETICS*

Dimitar Anguelov, Emma Colven and Prajna Rao

KEYWORDS: postcolonial cities, urban citizenship, urban informality

Slums in/out of place in the world-class city

Historically pathologized as problems justifying external, remedial interventions, slums have long been a target of state efforts to rationalize urban space in order to render it legible and governable. In the late twentieth century, slums became synonymous with **postcolonial cities** of the global South, interpreted as the lack of state control and spatial discipline (Rao, 2006; Roy, 2011). In *Rule by Aesthetics* (2015a), Ghertner instead explores slum management practices as constitutive of Delhi's political economy, engaging with the institutional, legal, and especially the discursive and sensory registers through which the state pursued a vision of a world-class Delhi – a clean, beautiful, and slum-free city.

Developed from his doctoral dissertation at the University of California, Berkeley, Ghertner's book primarily tracks the shift in Delhi's spatial governance from 'rule by records' – based on statistics, surveys, censuses, maps – to what he calls 'rule by aesthetics' – or the production of an aesthetic normativity based on vague but dominant understandings of beauty and cleanliness, ugliness and unbelonging. His overarching approach is to combine a political economic account that examines changing governance structures in Delhi with a govern-mentality approach that examines how residents' subjectivities and conduct are aligned with and deployed to enact such aesthetic orders. Further, he draws on Rancière's theory of aesthetics to explore how a certain sense of aesthetics is normalized across diverse groups and practices. To do so, he examines various institutions and technologies, ranging from poverty statistics and land markets to resident welfare associations and civil courts, while excavating the nuances in the everyday language and speech of his interlocutors. In particular, he shows how slums and slum dwellers were rendered out of place by Delhi's middle class and political elites in the conjuring of a world-class aesthetic: a modern, sanitized, and slum-free Delhi. However, Ghertner demonstrates not just how the world-class aesthetic is forged into political economic orders to benefit the propertied classes; he also highlights the complex and contradictory ways in which those displaced by such an order – the unpropertied poor – aim to partake in it.

Ghertner carried out his fieldwork in Delhi over 24 months, beginning in 2007. His ethnographic account focuses on the institutional spaces of Delhi's courts and a government–citizen initiative called *Bhagidari*, as well as the slum settlement of Shiv Camp. He deploys different methods towards different ends: (a) a quantitative analysis of poverty data in Delhi to uncover the statistical myths and speculative discourses framing Delhi's vision of a world-class city; (b) 'institutional ethnography' combining participant obser-vation at *Bhagidari* workshops with interviews to examine how these new institutional spaces empower Delhi's propertied middle class and their aesthetic sensibilities; (c) direct observation of court proceedings and hearings combined with discourse analysis of planning and court documents to show how these sensibilities gained performative force; and (d) participant observa-tions of everyday life and speech in Shiv Camp, and interviews with slum dwellers to examine how they partook in the world-class aesthetic.

The book is partitioned into two broad sections: the first focuses on how the vision of a slum-free Delhi is forged into an aesthetic order, and the second examines the implications for those displaced by this order. Moving beyond the common focus within (urban) political economy on the institutional and material, Ghertner examines how these forces intertwine with the sensory and aesthetic registers of a multiplicity of actors. By uncovering the powerful role of aesthetics in world-class city building and its encoding in law, land, and everyday life, Ghertner makes an important contribution to studies of contem-porary urbanization. At the same time, this focus on aesthetics comes at the analytical expense of the material interests shaping city building as well as the organizational politics and potential of the urban poor to resist these interests. This is a tension we examine in the rest of this chapter, which is organized as follows. First, we highlight and evaluate the effectiveness of the methodological approaches deployed in uncovering the transformation of Delhi's spatial order. Second, we discuss the limits of this approach, before lastly turning to a discussion of the book's methodological lessons.

The making of a new order

In the first chapter, Ghertner examines the making of the 'world-class city' as an inherently speculative project premised on future imaginaries of economic growth, but deeply entangled with the political economy of land in Millennial Delhi. He shows how statistical projections of economic growth overstated a boom of the Indian middle class, thereby presenting a future of high growth and endless opportunity. These projections were aggressively disseminated by global consultancies (such as McKinsey & Company), think tanks and government agencies in order to influence investor confidence and justify enormous amounts of foreign investments into real estate. Yet Ghertner demonstrates how they understated the persistence of poverty. Performing his own calculations from National Sample Survey data, he documents an actual increase in poverty levels between 1983 and 2005. By overlaying statistics for the number of absolute poor in Indian cities onto McKinsey's graph of India's supposedly growing middle class, he shows that the urban poor have been subsumed into middle-class categories. Combining this meticulous quantitative analysis with Roland Barthes' (1972) interpretation of myths, he makes the case that poverty graphs were operationalized not just as calculative tools, but also as aesthetic images, which constructed a myth of a prosperous economic future by visually bloating the rise of Delhi's middle class and their demand for property. This myth served to reinvent the poor as future consumers, to critique socialist land policies as a distortion of market dynamics, and to rationalize land market liberalization in the interest of a projected prosperous population. Moreover, it served to recast slums and slum dwellers as obstructions to be cleared for the future, not as citizens warranting equal protections.

While this future-orientated myth provided a rationale for slum clearance, Ghertner shows how the world-class aesthetic was institutionalized. Convinced that the middle-class vision of a slum-free Delhi could only have gained traction through a reconfiguration of urban governance structures, he examines how the propertied class gained exclusive access to the state machinery and utilized their power to transform their class aversion to slums and slum dwellers into a broader rationality for governing (and ultimately controlling) space. Specifically, he observes *Bhagidari*, a government–citizen partnership designed to foster closer ties between civil society and government, while also incorporating citizen participation in governance in order to increase transparency and reduce corruption and inefficiency. Critically, this initiative excluded unpropertied residents of slum settlements and unauthorized colonies from participating – instituting 'propertied citizenship' as a central principle of **urban citizenship** in Millennial Delhi.

Through participant observations of *Bhagidari* workshops and monthly meetings, he examines how this initiative provided the institutional space for bureaucrats and property-owning members of resident welfare associations (RWAs) – mobilized around issues of neighborhood security and quality of life – to cultivate relationships and establish consensus over visions and interventions in Delhi's development. It also allowed RWA members to raise neighborhood grievances to district officials. Surveys and interviews with RWA members revealed how they felt empowered, partly due to their direct access to higher-level bureaucrats, which in turn provided them with significant influence over government planning practices and agendas. As a result, the political space which had previously provided Delhi's poor residents with informal access to lower-level bureaucrats was effectively gentrified by the middle class, a process Ghertner (2015a: 46) calls the 'gentrification of state space', drawing on Neil Brenner's concept of 'new state spaces' (Daniels et al., Chapter 9). This gentrification made RWAs de facto citizen representatives with quasi-official authority in planning decisions, including that of slum removal. While Ghertner has elsewhere offered forceful critiques of the application of western-derived concepts such as gentrification to contexts such as India (cf. Ghertner, 2015b), here he uses 'gentrification' in a broad and largely metaphorical sense to describe the strengthening of ties between the propertied classes and the state. This metaphorical use does not diminish his argument, yet by restricting his optics to the *Bhagidari* spaces in which the RWA members circulate, it fails to account for the ways in which the urban poor's interactions with elected officials and bureaucrats were actually affected.

Expanding upon how the propertied class consolidated its vision into a systematic process of spatial exclusion and expulsion, in chapter 3 of his book Ghertner examines the sensory and meaning-making processes through which the aesthetic consensus gained legitimacy. Here he focuses on 'nuisance talk', or the everyday speech through which residents depicted slums as dirty, uncivil, and out of place. Nuisance functions as an aesthetic register based on visual and olfactory dimensions associated with sensory disgust. Building on Julia Kristeva's (1982) psychoanalytic framing of 'the abject' as an object of repugnance, Ghertner claims that the construction of the slum as an 'abject object' became necessary for maintaining and enacting the world-class aesthetic. Through interviews with RWA members and analysis of local media content he shows how the 'nuisance talk' in which the propertied middle class engaged (such as 'that slum stinks') extended beyond class aversion and became a 'sensory framework' for governing space. By tracing the circulation of nuisance talk in the speech of RWA members, in public statements by the police and in media coverage, he shows its transformation into a general discourse which assigned visual and sensory notions of proper and improper, and equated slums with public nuisance.

In his chapter 4 Ghertner shows how this discourse gained performative force, illustrating its deployment by the judiciary and state departments, and its codification into 'nuisance law'. Through discourse and visual analysis of court and legal documents, RWA petitions, petitioners' photographs of slums, and observations of court proceedings, including over 50 slum and encroachment-related hearings, he examines both the discursive devices deployed in such documents and the practices of lawyers and judges in courts. For example, he traces particular phrases, such as 'slums are illegal' or 'illegal encroachment' (2015a: 105), and references to the need to 'clean up' Delhi, observing their repeated use in judicial discourse. This had a performative effect, presenting slums and slum residents as out of place, and demolitions as a logical solution to the 'nuisance' slums embodied. Crucially, this discourse enabled judges faced with a vast number of pending cases visually to distinguish informality and formality, in the context of an otherwise largely unintelligible urban landscape. This analysis – illustrating how the aesthetic appearance of slums was equated with illegality and informality – could have been productively put into conversation with critical accounts examining **urban informality** as a differential practice of state planning, where both property developments (elite informality) and slums are equally shaped by informal practices (Roy, 2009).

In sum, rather than assuming aesthetic visions as top-down impositions by political elites or as purely grassroots initiatives of the propertied class, Ghertner's analysis shows the complex and iterative dynamics between government officials, bureaucrats, property-owning middle-class residents, judges and news media through which a consensus about a slum-free Delhi emerged. While *Bhagidari* was a government-sponsored initiative aimed at enrolling citizens into government, empowering propertied residents and cultivating their aesthetic sensibilities, realizing the vision of slum-free Delhi also depended on residents' everyday encounters with slums, and the articulation of their sensory experience into a powerful discourse. While the power of RWAs to influence bureaucrats and judges (at the expense of the unpropertied class) is convincingly shown, what falls out of view are the political processes through which slum residents may engage in efforts to construct their own coalitions or pragmatic alliances with the state (cf. Appadurai (2001), writing on Mumbai; Miraftab (2009), writing on Cape Town). Instead, Ghertner's focus shifts to the way slum residents sought to partake in and appropriate the emerging vision of a world-class Delhi, to which we now turn.

Participating in the world-class aesthetic

In the last two chapters of the book, Ghertner draws on his ethnographic engagements with Shiv Camp dwellers to explicate a central argument: that slum dwellers 'took the world-class city up in their own imagination' (2015a: 20). Noting instances of resistance to demolition to be the exception rather than the rule, he focuses on how the residents of Delhi's slums related to the world-class imagination through their everyday actions and speech. Drawing on an ethnographic study in the courtroom and in Shiv Camp, where residents were able to secure tenure and obtain voter ID and ration cards through political connections, he makes a twofold argument.

First, he argues that slum dwellers partook in the same world-class aesthetic that displaced them. He observes a recurring theme in residents' statements: the acceptance of a vision of a slum-free Delhi, which would appear to be against their interests. Ghertner draws on Rancière's notion of the 'distribution of the sensible', which explores how aesthetic consensus is established among a community, and who gets to participate in it, arguing that residents took up the language of the world-class aesthetic in order to have their speech recognized and heard – a form of 'aesthetic politics'. Recalling a court hearing related to Shiv Camp's defense, Ghertner recounts one resident's (Motilal) response when asked by lawyers what he thought of resettlement: 'Everyone sees what is appropriate. Where is there room for [squatter settlements] in Delhi today?' (2015a: 148). For Ghertner this statement about slum unbelonging does not indicate consent; rather it signals how Motilal adopted the language of the world-class aesthetic in order to secure his involvement and consultation in the legal proceedings. In aligning their aspirations with the world-class aesthetic, he argues that slum dwellers are not simply consenting to it, but seeking to be included.

Second, and following from this, Ghertner argues that slum dwellers sought to participate in the world-class aesthetic by appropriating its registers of cleanliness, privacy, and propriety. For example, by reimagining resettlement as lush, privately owned bungalows, displayed in posters of beautiful homes adorning their walls, residents reinterpret the world-class aesthetic and their futures in it. By imbuing the world-class aesthetic with these meanings, slum dwellers engage in an act that Ghertner labels appropriation. Further, he observes how residents envision that resettlement plots will transform their lives in quite specific ways, for example by telling him:

> If we receive a plot, all our problems will go away. Our men will stop gambling and will find good work; our children will get good educations; our daughters will marry good boys. There, life will be good. We will have big houses and maybe even a car. (2015a: 159)

Ghertner thus concludes that residents are free to reinterpret the world-class imaginary as a future city in which they are included, thereby distinguishing residents' attempted participation in the world-class aesthetic from consent to its hegemonic order.

Through this attention to linguistic nuance Ghertner recovers the agency of slum dwellers to the extent that they are not passive bystanders in Delhi's transformation. Slum dwellers appear to have internalized the vision of the world-class aesthetic, and Ghertner is convinced that their statements do not signal resignation; rather they represent slum dwellers' experimentation with the visual and discursive registers of the emergent aesthetic order, so as to be recognized as legitimate subjects able to take part in its future. In the following section we examine the limits to this interpretation, particularly taking into account the broader historical context of Delhi's political economy.

The explanatory limits of aesthetic politics

While Ghertner provides convincing evidence that slum dwellers participate in the world-class aesthetic by 'speaking sensibly', his claim that Shiv Camp residents successfully 'appropriated' the world-class aesthetic appears over-extended. His suggestion that the residents may be able to alter the direction of the world-class city to produce a more inclusive vision of Delhi appears overly optimistic, as he offers no evidence for how they influence the material outcomes of court proceedings or resettlement interventions, or even in their everyday lives.

This optimistic reading may in part reflect Ghertner's research subjectivity. As a white American male, Ghertner does not sufficiently examine his own (perceived) positionality in his interactions with middle-class residents and slum dwellers, and how this might have shaped their responses to his questions about slum demolitions and slum unbelonging. For example, noting the privileged access his position as a westerner grants him, Ghertner describes how middle-class residents were enthusiastic to meet him and demonstrate their knowledge of, and admiration for, the west, often assuming that he shared their view of slums as out of place. Yet, he does not consider the possibility that slum dwellers, internalizing the aesthetic norms that circulate so powerfully in Delhi, may have similarly been eager to demonstrate their recognition that slums were out of place. Instead, he reads their responses as evidence of strategic attempts to ensure their inclusion in the world-class city.

Indeed, residents of Shiv Camp continued to face precarious conditions, with the threat of displacement looming. On his return to Shiv Camp in 2012, Ghertner found that RWA action led to the closure of a toilet block, resulting in lines so long that people were forced to defecate in public. Further, many Shiv Camp residents continued to face marginalization and endure extremely difficult living conditions. In retrospect, an engagement with collective action may have offered insights into how slum dwellers seek not only to appropriate the world-class aesthetic, but also to directly challenge it. As Ghertner updates his analysis through an engagement with Delhi's urban politics at the time of writing, he himself notes the success of collective mobilization by slum dwellers demanding their inclusion in the world-class city, especially after the Delhi Chief Minister's promise in 2008 to build 60,000 flats for the urban poor was exposed as falsely made.

Ghertner could also have expanded the scope of his study beyond Millennial Delhi, to consider Delhi's historical role as the capital city and the object of grand aesthetic visions of modernity and mega-interventions. Such an account could produce a richer analysis, offering a deeper understanding of the institutionalization of rule by aesthetics and potentially reveal continuities and divergences between historical and contemporary modes of governance in Delhi. For example, tracking the shift from rule by records to rule by aesthetics, Ghertner suggests that enforcement of rule by records would have effectively rendered most of Delhi illegal, given that 70% of the city's built form (including elite shopping malls and townships) violates building codes and development norms. Realizing a world-class vision as impossible in this way, Delhi's government changed course toward a vaguely defined rule by aesthetics. Thus by his own account, rule by records ended up being an impediment to, rather than a tool for, world-class city building.

Yet, his own cases suggest that rule by aesthetics did not fully replace rule by records; rather they appear to be deeply intertwined. Ghertner admits that rule by records enabled slum dwellers to contest their displacement. He observes that demolitions slowed down in recent years, partly due to new legislation requiring the relocation of slum dwellers prior to evictions, prompting a revival of surveys and land-based record procedures. A deeper engagement with how aesthetic and calculative modes of governmentality interrelate – sometimes in cohesion, just as often in dissonance – would have offered richer insights into the workings of postcolonial cities, which are often overwhelmed by the demands of technocratic procedures and legal regulations. Furthermore, a methodological focus on the middle class and slum dwellers may have narrowed his explanatory capacity by overlooking a range of other significant actors. The emphasis on the aesthetic sensibilities of Delhi's propertied class and the institutionalization of their interests may give them too much explanatory power, while ignoring the role of the 'movers and shakers' of Delhi's property market, including developers, global financial firms, and the infamous 'land mafia' (cf. Goldman, 2011; Shatkin, 2014).

Methodological reflections and lessons

Rule by Aesthetics is an innovative and multidisciplinary account that seamlessly combines theories of governance and governmentality with linguistic and semiotic theories to uncover the aesthetic order shaping Millennial Delhi and the lives and dreams of its inhabitants. Ghertner's ethnographic approach engages in a novel fashion with the sensory registers and affective experiences underpinning the world-class aesthetic, as well as the institutional spaces, practices, and actors through which it is realized. Paying careful attention to language, rhetoric, everyday speech, and the sensory perceptions of Delhi's propertied middle class, Ghertner effectively shows how aversion to slums (sensory disgust) becomes codified into a general framework for identifying and enacting spatial dis/order: a 'rule by aesthetics'.

Drawing on Rancière's conceptualization of aesthetic politics, Ghertner further examines how slum dwellers take part in the very hegemonic order that displaces and marginalizes them, with the apparent goal of influencing that order. Yet, the evidence he marshals does not necessarily support such a conclusion. His methodological and ethico-political commitments to recovering the agency of marginalized slum dwellers against the overwhelming force of world-class city making risks misreading their participation in it as strategic appropriation, rather than internalization of the allure of a slum-free Delhi. A more nuanced understanding of slum dwellers' claims and how they interrogate, appropriate, or are subjectivized by the world-class aesthetic could offer greater scope for examining and explaining its performative force, or slum dwellers' resistance to it.

This focus on aesthetics also appears to come at the expense of historical contextualization. Ghertner distinguishes between aesthetic and calculative modes of governmentality when he argues that a calculative mode ('rule by records') prevailed before and after the advent of aesthetic governmentality in Millennial Delhi. His account presents these modes as temporally separate, understating the importance of persisting calculative rationalities in shaping Delhi's spatial order, and the potential imbrication of the two. This is especially the case for Delhi, which has been a site for aesthetic and calculative–administrative preoccupation as a seat of colonial powers and national governments. As a result, the recent return to calculative governmentality in Delhi that Ghertner notes in the book's conclusion appears to diminish the explanatory power of aesthetic governmentality in world-class city making.

These limits notwithstanding, it is precisely this account of aesthetic governmentality that offers most insights for urban studies, against dominant political economic explanations of urban governance and governmentality. Yet Ghertner does not elaborate how his findings from Millennial Delhi might generate broader theoretical insights, or challenge the explanatory power of the mostly western theories on which he draws (cf. Ghertner, 2015b). This despite a growing literature in urban studies inspired by postcolonial theory that has sought to engage cities in the postcolony as sites of theory construction, rather than simply theory testing (Robinson, 2006; Roy, 2009; Sheppard et al., 2013). For a former student of Ananya Roy, one of the key proponents of this literature, this is surprising. Ghertner's concluding hypothesis that the world-class aesthetic will become an important lens for understanding world-class city making in the twenty-first-century metropolis would have benefited from such a discussion on the potentials and limits of theorizing from Delhi.

Overall, the book illustrates the merits of an ethnographic approach that affords great attention to the details and nuances of everyday speech and texts, and their relation to sensory experiences. While inviting overly optimistic readings of slum dweller participation in the hegemonic project of world-class city making, this is an innovative methodological enterprise that enables Ghertner effectively to make a case for the significance of the aesthetic dimensions of urban governance, and it demonstrates the ways in which the world-class aesthetic penetrates the dreams and schemes of slum dwellers and the propertied middle class alike.

6

FLUID ASSEMBLAGES: ON LISA BJÖRKMAN'S *PIPE POLITICS, CONTESTED WATERS*

Tanya Matthan, Emma Colven and Hudson Spivey

KEYWORDS: assemblage urbanism, infrastructure, more-than-human, post-colonial cities, uneven urban development, everyday urbanism

In contemporary Mumbai, water engineers hunt helplessly for a trunk main laid in 1976 whose location no longer corresponds with landmarks on official maps. Finally, a drunk homeless man sleeping by the side of the road – who turns out to be a former valve operator – leads them to its precise site. Elsewhere, policemen follow lines of sleepy men riding their bicycles, armed with jerry cans, to the homes of illegal water vendors in ritualized pre-dawn raids that end in the confiscation of suction pumps and the cutting of pipes. Such stories populate Lisa Björkman's ethnography of Mumbai's crippled water **infrastructure**, a study of the everyday work of water distribution in the Indian city. In her book, Björkman sets out to answer two key questions: First, why do city residents face erratic and uncertain water supply even though there is no overall water scarcity in Mumbai? Second, given these unpredictable flows, how do people access water in their everyday lives?

Building on a growing literature on infrastructure (cf. Star, 1999; Larkin, 2013; Harvey and Knox, 2015), and elaborating on her doctoral dissertation in politics at the New School for Social Research, Björkman attends to everyday encounters with infrastructure to understand why and how city residents face and negotiate erratic and tenuous water supply. She follows a diverse group of actors, ranging from engineers and plumbers to social workers, brokers, slum dwellers, and luxury apartment dwellers, as they engage in the everyday work of facilitating flow. Björkman's methodological approach emerges in part from her observation that city residents across social hierarchies – slum dwellers and elites alike – are compelled to cope with the risks of water shortage. Thus, she argues that existing analytical frameworks cannot explain Mumbai's dry taps; these theories are rooted in a critique of Eurocentric urban planning in **postcolonial cities**, accounts that emphasize the universalization of capital, or analyses that laud urban informality as sites of resistance.

Whereas popular accounts of Mumbai's water woes tend to blame corruption, informality, or illegality, Björkman suggests a more complicated story. On the one hand, water engineers lay the blame on technical factors or natural causes (airlocks or supply shortage), which are hard both to prove and disprove. On the other hand, city residents point to state corruption and water mafias, positing the idea of an all-powerful state apparatus or a murky underground economy. Björkman maintains that more robust explanations can be found through 'attention to water infrastructures themselves: to the sociopolitical and material landscapes through which water flows are produced and within which infrastructures are embedded' (2015: 8). By infrastructure, Björkman is referring to the relationship between people and water in Mumbai as mediated by material things (pipes, valves), forms of knowledge (maps, news reports), and broader structural forces (financial instruments, interest rates) (2015: 12). In the daily work of infrastructural maintenance and use, she observes a gamut of practices that leak across categories of analysis such as formal/informal, slum/world-class, legal/illegal, and private/public forms of water distribution. Her methodological approach for illustrating the historical, material, and discursive *production* of erratic and uneven water supply is thus centered upon making water infrastructures 'simultaneously an object of inquiry, as well as the medium and methodological entryway' (Björkman, 2017: 1).

In this chapter, we engage with Björkman's use of what she calls 'infrastructure as method' (2017), and examine the theoretical contributions that emanate from this approach. Drawing together **assemblage urbanism** and ethnography, we tease out the possibilities and limitations of her methodology for de-centering conventional analytical categories in urban studies (such as class and community, or rights and rules) for a greater focus on infrastructure. We begin by examining the centrality of site selection to her approach, which crucially shapes her explanations of the city's 'hydraulic shambles' (Björkman, 2015: 82). Then, we interrogate the methodological value of bringing ethnography's emphasis on detailed empirical observation into conversation with assemblage theory's focus on materiality and contingency. Finally, we raise questions about the attribution of agency and the placing of responsibility, and about the analytical and political limits of 'following the water' (2015: 15).

Produced dysfunction, unpredictable flows

The first half of the book situates Mumbai's pipe politics within a broader context of **uneven urban development**, explaining the destruction of the city's water distribution system through liberalization-era policies, fantasies of world-class city building, unplanned construction, and rapid urban growth. Marshalling oral historical research with urban planners and water department engineers, Björkman demonstrates how Mumbai's 'hydraulic shambles' were produced through (ultimately failed) late twentieth-century projects of privatization and marketization. Until the early 1990s, detailed surveys and recording of water network expansion were integral to the working of the municipal corporation. However, the circulation of global policy discourses lauding the virtues of market logics underwrote the slow destruction of the water department's '*informational* infrastructures', its human systems of mapping, surveying, and recording water flows (2015: 25, authors' emphasis). Further, Björkman shows that new development rules incentivizing private sector participation in slum redevelopment programs triggered a rush of large-scale construction projects, creating a disastrous material disjuncture between the city's above-ground built space and its below-ground water networks.

In the second half of the book, Björkman illustrates how residents, faced with erratic or absent supply, resort to diverse strategies to acquire water: pre-paying to be a member of a certain tap system, purchasing water time from a tap owner, buying water by the can from a vendor. These informal arrangements give rise to a host of new actors – water sellers, brokers, plumbers – who leverage their experience and expertise in 'getting water' to shore up small profits and considerable political authority. For instance, in an account reminiscent of AbdouMaliq Simone's (2004b) description of 'people as infrastructure', Björkman describes how *chaviwallas* (literally, key-holders; valve operators), plumbers, and brokers emerge as key actors whose informal, place-based knowledge of the water distribution system has become crucial to its everyday functioning (particularly with official records in a state of disarray). People come to rely on 'elaborate knowledge-exchange networks' (Björkman, 2015: 131), rather than placing faith in engineering or legal entitlements to deliver water. In Björkman's formulation, this fragmentation of knowledge has ushered in a transformation of neighborhood and city politics. Water is enrolled into a distributive and performative politics, in that several local political leaders begin their careers as social workers who organize for connections, mediate with police regarding illegal pipes, and build a sought-after base of knowledge about the ebbs and flows of Mumbai's hydro-political network.

Infrastructure as method

Björkman adopts what she terms a 'pipe-political approach to urban water' (2015: 15). In methodological terms, this entails tracing flows of water across space and time as well as the inquiries of actors encountered through this process. Her approach exemplifies the descriptive emphasis of assemblage urbanism, within which explanation emerges through thick description (McFarlane, 2011a; 2011c). Assemblage urbanism lends itself well to ethnography; indeed, Björkman (2015: 15) suggests that it might 'even require' such a methodology. The richness of her ethnographic data point to the value of 'being there', of observing, day after day, the tankers going by, the valves being opened, the water being sold, the leak being fixed, and the political protest being staged. This ethnographic detail shapes her emphasis on the range of semi-official, quasi-(il)legal practices that comprise infrastructural activity. This approach also allows her to analyze the practices of both those who create and maintain infrastructures and those who use them daily, placing both sets of practices within a coherent whole.

The monograph itself is largely based on research conducted in Mumbai over 18 months between 2008 and 2010 within a single geographical region, the M-East Ward: a contiguous administrative, electoral, and hydraulic unit, which receives water from a single reservoir. This selection is critical to Björkman's intervention, as it allows for a focus on the workings of the water network as a whole, rather than the ways in which it works in a single neighborhood (such as a 'slum' or 'gated enclave'), or among a single social group ('middle-class' residents or 'Muslims') (2017: 5). This, Björkman argues, enables an examination of hydro-social relations, beyond specific social categories that carry a-priori assumptions about why and where water flows (or not). A substantial portion of her fieldwork thus involved trailing water engineers engaged in the work of fixing and maintaining the water system, a privileged and insightful entry point into questions of access and distribution, albeit with perspectival limitations (as we discuss below).

M-East Ward is distinctive in that it is a relatively new suburban development. For most of the nineteenth century, the area comprised agricultural settlements and fishing villages. Following India's economic liberalization, the ward underwent remarkable growth due to its status as a favored site for resettling 'project-affected people' displaced by the construction of mega-infrastructure projects, shopping malls, and office towers in the city center. The pace of development in the ward is so alarming and the distribution system has become so unmanageable that engineers try to avoid being posted there. One engineer tells Björkman that she had picked 'the wrong ward to study' (2015: 98) since this area, filled with unplanned, 'illegal' neighborhoods, was not representative of the department's work in Mumbai. To Björkman, it is precisely these dynamics that make this ward a valuable case study. Indeed, moments and sites of interruption and dysfunction form a valuable entry point into the often invisible and taken-for-granted processes that undergird the **everyday urbanism** of Mumbai. Studying an infrastructurally 'dysfunctional' ward is a methodological strategy intended to illuminate both the causes of erratic water supply and the forms of expertise, technical improvisations, and political mobilizations through which residents and government staff keep the water flowing.

Within this unit of analysis, Björkman deploys a range of methodological devices primarily rooted in ethnographic research, including participant observation, oral histories, and interviews, further supplemented by analysis of policy documents, development plans, consultant reports, and maps. This diversity of sources allows attention to both everyday relations surrounding water availability and access, and the political economic structures producing hydrological chaos in this particular ward.

Following the matter

Throughout, Björkman vividly describes the material qualities of water and the pipes that distribute it through the city, since these materialities play a role in how water flows, where, and with what effects. As Mumbai's water engineers repeatedly note, they require water of a certain pressure in order to do their work of facilitating flow. Several other qualities of water are pertinent to her analysis: its flows create specific relations between uphill and downhill sites and users; they can be siphoned off with little difficulty; are embedded within a high-cost and labor-intensive distribution and transport infrastructure; and, most importantly, they comprise an underground, and thus opaque and largely illegible, network of flows (2015: 15). In attending closely to the dense materialities of the water system, she maintains that her approach is informed by neo-Deleuzian assemblage urbanism and Latourian actor–network theory. These conceptual frameworks, which emphasize the coproduction of the social and material worlds, imagine urban forms as contingent assemblages of human and non-human actors.

Through detailed empirical observation, Björkman aims to illustrate the ways in which materiality matters: that it holds meaning and produces particular effects. To give one example, whether a pipe is made of galvanized steel or plastic is a matter of tremendous political import. Björkman points out that illegal connection-cutting drives are directed almost exclusively at plastic pipes, even though they are permitted. This is because older pipes – installed prior to administrative 'cut-off dates' defining il/legality – are made of steel, while newer ones tend to be plastic; more simply, steel pipes look older than plastic ones, and plastic pipes are much easier to cut with a saw (2015: 262).

For the most part, however, Björkman refrains from any detailed discussion of the agency of **more-than-human** components of the hydraulic network that has animated debates around assemblage theory in urban studies (see Farías, 2011; McFarlane, 2011c). Rather than attribute any intrinsic agency to the fluidity of water or the plasticity of the pipe, she emphasizes that specific material qualities of substances have multiple, unpredictable effects. While at times her writing alludes to the agency of the water or the pipes, on the whole her description centers human actors as the authors and objects of 'pipe politics' (2015: 148).

Björkman's engagements with the materiality of Mumbai's water distribution system enable her to extend the extensive scholarship on Mumbai's water system that has emerged in the last decade (Anand, 2011; Gandy, 2008; Graham et al., 2015), which has largely examined inequality in access to water along axes of socio-spatial difference. Björkman adds a more explicit focus on Mumbai's water infrastructure as an emergent assemblage of people and things, emphasizing the uncertain and precarious nature of world-class city building. As she notes, making water flow in Mumbai is a significant achievement, 'one that requires continuous production and maintenance', and is dependent on 'dispersed and intimate assemblages of knowledge, power and material authority' (2015: 3, 97).

The reader bears witness to several such instances of contingent achievements and unanticipated outcomes. The building of a pumping station and a change in water supply timings, expected to solve water problems in one neighborhood, unexpectedly increased water pressure in a neighboring locality and subsequently led to the drying of those same taps. Builders understand that engineers can only guarantee water supply to new buildings for a short time, after which 'anything can happen' (2015: 96). Such moments of uncertainty demonstrate the ways in which securing uninterrupted flow is a precarious political achievement, made possible by the 'complex rhythm of assembling and reassembling' (McFarlane, 2011a: 216) on the part of myriad hydraulic actors.

Knowledge is power

Throughout the book, Björkman displays dazzling knowledge of the socio-technical operations of the water system. Illustrating, often in excruciating detail, the mundane workings of pipes, pumps, and valves, as well as bureaucratic and legal procedures, she demonstrates that the devil is indeed in the detail – of planning, policy, and practice. This reflects one of the key strengths of her ethnography: Björkman's unbridled access to the water bureaucracy, which enabled her to undertake fine-grained observation of the everyday work of department staff. In a methodological supplement published online, detailing her research design including her methods of access, Björkman (2017) reflects that while she initially believed that the bureaucracy would be impenetrable, this site came to be the most accessible due to a connection with a senior engineer. Interestingly, Björkman herself becomes imbricated within these networks of knowledge within the water department and beyond; for instance, she comes to be regarded by other engineers as someone 'in the know' because, unlike them, she is able to gain access to private water maps.

Perhaps it is not surprising that Björkman is especially sympathetic to the water department, given that the substance of her fieldwork was conducted with the department's staff. This raises interesting questions regarding the implicit alliances of the ethnographer who, after spending a substantial amount of time with a particular group of interlocutors, comes most readily to identify and empathize with this 'insider's' point of view. This concern, which has long animated debates on ethnography within anthropology, appears evident in Björkman's claim that 'it's the engineers and the staff that keep the system functional at all' (in Björkman and Campion, 2016).

At the same time, the book devotes significant attention to the residents of M-East Ward. It describes how their erratic hydraulic system is being used to justify slating their neighborhood for slum rehabilitation, and also traces the strategies through which ward residents attempt to navigate this system. While the farcical dysfunctionality described in the book appears to preclude the possibility of socially just infrastructural change, Björkman's concluding remarks highlight the (limited) democratic potentialities brought into being by this hydraulic chaos. With control over everyday water supply no longer in the hands of international experts or senior bureaucrats, the downscaling of expertise to neighborhoods is producing new political actors and novel constellations of power, often articulated through the messy and compromised – yet promising – politics of electoral democracy.

The limits of infrastructure as method

While close observation of water department engineers and residents within a single ward yields considerable insight into the everyday (mal)functioning of the water system, this methodological choice comes at the expense of others who might have revealed different dynamics. For instance, given that a central premise of Björkman's research question and argument is that water scarcity affects all neighborhoods and social groups in this ward, regardless of 'caste or class', her examination of elite water access practices is surprisingly thin. Apart from a short passage on a luxury apartment building in M-East Ward – where residents recreate in swimming pools and arrange installation of prohibited 200 liter bathtubs – her primary data are drawn from the middle-class housing society where she stayed during her fieldwork. Even here, detailed information about water flows was closed to her, and she was 'never able to insinuate [herself] into that network of power relationships beyond [her] positionality as a "paying guest" and a "foreign researcher"' (2017: 30).

In the housing society, an elaborate system of upward pumping and downward flow means that residents' taps had constant pressure at all times, even though the housing society's pipes were pressurized for only two hours a day (2015: 154). Nevertheless, the contentious politics of water supply affected middle-class homes. Certain houses received less water than others, spurring rumors about the installation of 'online' pumps by some households, and inspiring informal water-policing missions conducted by housewives to listen for such pumps. While such vignettes make it clear that elite access to water is not without its own tensions and negotiations, assertions of 'class-blind hydrologies' (2015: 54) would certainly benefit from a more sustained exposition.

Björkman emphasizes that water shortages affect all residents, while under-playing the unequal ways in which residents are affected by it.

Even though the taps in elite homes also dry up on occasion, the question remains of who can get (plentiful) water despite the vagaries of the hydraulic infrastructure. This leads to the crucial question of culpability: who (or perhaps what) is responsible for the fitful taps? In the first half of her book, Björkman squarely lays responsibility for the city's hydraulic shambles at the door of privatization debates, and the messy politics of land and housing. These material disjunctures are not framed as the inevitable product of informality in southern cities, nor of the elusive agency of material things. Rather, they are produced by privatization agendas, liberalization policies, and a booming real-estate market that crippled the water bureaucracy and weakened the existing material infra-structure. By highlighting this, Björkman is able to historicize the city's hydro-politics and, thereby, politicize the pipes.

The fixing of accountability becomes more difficult in the second half of the book, however, as she turns to investigate everyday practices of access. As scholars have argued, in its distribution of agency across human and non-human actors, 'assemblage troubles ... where we assign responsibility and causality when we conduct critique' (McFarlane, 2011a: 218). As mentioned earlier, Björkman rarely uses analytical categories such as actant, agency, or non-human, even when focusing on specific material forms. Yet, we are repeatedly informed of the mysterious volatilities of the pipes, the illegibility of the grid, and the intractability of flow. To be sure, these are critical qualities of water and its distribution networks that make it a particularly 'uncooperative commodity' (Bakker, 2003). Nonetheless, the question of how to integrate volatile materi-alities into urban analyses, without attributing authorship and blame to non-human 'things', remains a critical one with high political stakes. What, for example, are the policy and legal implications of an account that minimizes the ways in which social hierarchies shape access to water?

At times, Björkman almost appears to concur with technical (and rather a-political) explanations of the uneven geographies of water supply, noting that it is hydraulically impossible to manipulate the valves with such precision as to purposefully discriminate against a single locality. Elsewhere, however, she cautions against narratives of 'technical challenges' that serve to discursively naturalize hydraulic dynamics as properties inhering in the pipes (2015: 260). This necessitates a return to her theoretical and methodological approach. Rather than social structures dictating material outcomes, she argues: 'Effective claims to water ... cannot be predicted or accounted for by prior categories of identity: class, community, rights, or rules. Instead these categories them-selves are contingent, discursive *effects* of infrastructural practice' (2015: 231; emphasis in original).

While Björkman certainly does not assign responsibility to the pipes, her circumvention of class, caste, language, and religion as explanatory categories in a city such as Mumbai is puzzling. Although she concurs with the observation of one interlocutor that 'when water comes, it's because of politics, and when water doesn't come, it's because of politics' (2015: 12), the substance of that politics, and its entanglement with social differentiation and inequality, are inadequately examined. Björkman listens to conversations among water department staff that this or that 'slum' area has only illegal connections, and rumors that a North Indian Muslim-dominated neighborhood was intentionally not being supplied water. In these moments, she hypothesizes that it is possible that shortages were being deliberately engineered, observing that 'personal or political connections, cash payments, ethno-linguistic chauvinism, and socio-spatial elitism (among other things) are brought to bear on water and its infrastructures'. Yet ultimately she maintains that 'these categories in themselves are distinctly unreliable as predictors of water flow' (2015: 197). Her emphasis on the water infrastructures themselves may therefore come at the expense of a deeper engagement with how inequalities continue to shape access to water, albeit in unpredictable ways.

Conclusion

Björkman's research offers new insights into an extensive literature on water in Mumbai. This analytical move is made possible by her refusal to presume beforehand that water practices neatly map onto social categories, exploring instead the complex fields of power through which water access is materially produced (2017: 5). 'Following the infrastructure' leads her to elusive maps and hidden pipes, which then enable her to undertake a historicized under-standing of infrastructural shambles while complicating easy analytical binaries. However, this also engenders important limitations: a near over-determination of technical and material aspects substitutes for the over-determination of the social that Björkman finds so problematic as an explanation for Mumbai's dry taps.

The vast and illegible materiality of the system has epistemological impli-cations, too. In the wake of her own indefatigable efforts to know the system, she becomes convinced of the impossibility of grasping it as a whole, ultimately coming to terms with the 'deeply fragmented nature not only of my own knowledge of the underground network but of the grid's very knowability' (2015: 176). Like the water engineer, and despite adopting what she initially describes as a 'holistic' research approach, the ethnographer also finds it impossible to fully grasp the water system (2015: 15). Indeed, it appears that its complexities make it quite impossible to convincingly know why water does or does not flow:

> The opacity of the water distribution system – in which water flows are hidden inside pipes that are buried underground, where the laws governing legal supply of water are in turns contradictory and vague and where the legal status of residents themselves is deeply political and constantly in flux … renders water access … fraught with unknowns (and unknowables). (2015: 163)

Like the social worker, broker, and plumber, the ethnographer's knowledge is distinctly place-based and experiential, generating critical insights yet partially obscuring the ways in which social positionality and enduring inequalities shape meaning and practice. This facet of her work demonstrates both the promise and perils of employing 'infrastructure as method'.

7

CONSTRUCTING AND CONTESTING THE BANLIEUE: ON MUSTAFA DIKEÇ'S *BADLANDS OF THE REPUBLIC*

Nina Ebner, Joe Penny and Andre Comandon

KEYWORDS: post-political city, right to the city, urban citizenship, urban social movements

On October 27, 2005, three young men from a Parisian suburb, Clichy-sous-Bois, took refuge in a power station to evade police capture. Two of them were electrocuted and died. Soon after, uprisings erupted in *banlieues*[1] across several French cities, resulting in a national state of emergency and almost 3,000 arrests. The conditions that made possible these tragically unnecessary deaths, as well as the uprisings that followed, are at the heart of Mustafa Dikeç's intellectual project, providing urgency to his drive to understand the spatial dynamics of policing and politics in France's urban peripheries. As his first stand-alone monograph, *Badlands of the Republic* (2007) (henceforth *Badlands*) represents a significant milestone in this project, an attempt to differently make sense of urban space and its geographies of violence and contestation.

In *Badlands*, Dikeç is animated by two concerns. First, he sets out to show how French urban policy has imagined, articulated, and constructed the banlieue as a problematic space – a badland – requiring increasingly repressive state intervention. Second, he explores how the discursive rendering of these spaces is contested by 'alternative voices from below' demanding spatial justice. Methodologically and politically, *Badlands* therefore speaks to an enduring challenge for those invested in the project of critical urban studies. That is, the book works to expose the variegated dynamics of capitalist and authoritarian social relations as they operate in and through the urban, while simultaneously shedding light on the 'possibilities for alternative, radically emancipatory forms of urbanism that are latent, yet systematically suppressed' (Brenner, 2009a: 204). His method for achieving this is discourse analysis – the analysis of language, its form of presentation, the ways in which it frames issues and spaces, and the cultural, institutional, and ideological contexts within which it does so.

In this chapter, we use *Badlands* as an entry point to reflect on the possibilities and limitations of using discourse analysis as a method of social inquiry and as a tool of critical urban theory. By scrutinizing Dikeç's methodological choices and method, we show how a reliance on discourse both illuminates and obscures certain ways of seeing, reading, and articulating political possibilities in the so-called **post-political city**. Within this volume, *Badlands* offers an interesting counterpoint to ethnographies of subaltern urban spaces and peoples by detailing how discourse analysis is mobilized to critically interrogate the discursive strategies, and therefore power relations, that produce the banlieue 'from above'. However, we also suggest that the use of discourse analysis, both within this book and more generally, is not without its challenges. While Dikeç uses discourse analysis to effectively deconstruct French urban policy, he also reproduces three common methodological shortcomings associated with this method, which ultimately constrain his specific engagement with the politics of the banlieue, and suggest limitations of the method as a tool of critical urban theory more generally. These shortcomings are: (1) a lack of openness and reflexivity concerning how discourse analysis is done, and what is at stake when choosing to use this method; (2) the tendency to ascribe too much agency to policy texts and their discourses at the expense of the agency of actors who, at multiple levels and in different institutions and places, (re)articulate, (re)circulate, and (re)work them; and (3) a limited engagement with 'alternative discourses' and the different ways in which they are articulated and inscribed in, and across, space.

Throughout this critique we stress that while these shortcomings are common in many discursively oriented urban policy studies, they do not represent reasons enough for jettisoning discourse analysis altogether. Indeed, we are convinced it has the potential to expose the variegated dynamics of capitalist social relations and amplify alternative politics. Finally, we include Dikeç's (2012) own reflections on *Badlands* and the constraints he faced writing the book during his transition from graduate student to early-career researcher. We are conscious that many people reading this book will be graduate students, perhaps beginning the process of research for the first time. Therefore, throughout this chapter, as we describe the challenges of using discourse analysis, we propose constructive ways of addressing these within the confines of graduate student research.

From 'autogestion' to 'repression': constructing the banlieue

Dikeç organizes *Badlands* in three parts. In Part I, to conceptualize how the banlieue has been constructed through urban policy and in relation to processes of state restructuring, Dikeç draws on the political thought of Jacques Rancière and contemporary debates concerning the nature of neoliberalization. This section is lucid and engaging, providing one of the enduring contributions of *Badlands* – his novel use of Rancière's concept of the 'police order'.

Rancière's understanding of the 'police order' exceeds the familiar institutional understanding of the police as a repressive organ of the state, maintaining 'law and order' through hard power and its disciplinary logic. More expansively, it encompasses the soft aesthetic power of 'common sense' logics; the various technologies and choreographies of policy development, decision-making, and problem solving; and the institutional arrangements of governance through which logics and routines are rehearsed and managed. Dikeç mobilizes the concept of police order to describe how political and policy elites in France have made use of urban policy to actively construct a common sense of how urban space is both imagined and governed. French urban policies, according to Dikeç, function as a spatial police order 'designating areas to be treated, associating problems with them, and generating a certain discourse (though not the only one) about them' (2007: 21). Concretely, the spaces 'to be treated' for their ills are the banlieues, neighborhoods on France's urban peripheries. Constructed from a system of 'sensible evidences' – a term Dikeç uses to describe policy documents, spatial designations, mappings, categorizations, namings, and statistics – this spatial police order reflects and reproduces the perceptive givens of urban policy 'within which strategies and techniques of power can be defined' (2007: 20), and from which normative interventions are progressed and justified, and out of which is constructed the banlieue as a badland.

In Part II, Dikeç uses this theoretical orientation to parse almost three decades' worth of urban policy, analyzing close to 90 national urban policy documents and mainstream newspaper commentaries and conducting half-a-dozen interviews with key central government actors involved in the policy process. In doing so, Dikeç charts the evolution of the discursive construction of the banlieue as badland through urban policy, identifying a shift from socialist approaches, such as the 1977 program *Habitat et Vie Sociale* (created to alleviate inequalities linked to economic crises), to increasingly securitizing repertoires, designed to deal with the 'problem' of the banlieue as a threat to the integrity of the French Republican state.

For Dikeç, the emergence and evolution of urban policy's treatment of the banlieue is also tied to specific moments of revolt and the spaces in which they are enacted. He begins with the 'hot summer of 1981' when social unrest in the banlieues of Lyon first made headlines, prompting a national debate on immigration and years of subsequent territorial stigmatization of the banlieue. The space of the banlieue became central to understanding these riots and the policies and programs that followed. After the 1981 uprisings, in a state-led process of urban policy experimentation, the French state attempted to increase the involvement of local civil society organizations and municipal actors in designing and implementing policy. Espousing Lefebvrian idea(l)s of the **right to the city** and autogestion, whereby people strive to manage their own affairs collectively without hierarchical state rule, urban policy signaled the decentralized, democratic currents of the time.

Through the 1990s and 2000s, however, further unrest seemingly revealed the shortcomings of these previous rounds of urban policy experimentation and prompted a shift in the tenor and type of intervention. As national discourses on the question of immigration turned more overtly xenophobic, the 'banlieue question', echoing and in part responding to a rightward tilt across governing parties, was framed in terms of a heavily racialized spatial security threat to the integrity of the Republic and French Republicanism. Urban policy became increasingly technocratic and repressive: the emphasis on local knowledge and experimentation in the 1970s and 1980s was replaced by a focus on generalizable statistics and the establishment of pernicious policing practices, including aggressive stop-and-search and racial profiling.

In Part III, Dikeç explores forms of politics as 'alternative voices' generated from the banlieue. He begins by describing Agora, a politically engaged association created by immigrant youth, and Le Choix Vaudais, a political party, in Vaulx-en-Velin, a suburb of Lyon. Drawing on Rancière's conceptualization of politics as that which ruptures or exceeds the logic of the police order, inaugurating new ways of being, Dikeç suggests that their discourses and actions represent 'an attempt to open up political spaces in a context where the space of the political seems well delimited' (2007: 147). Against the spatial police order of the Republican state and its construction of the banlieue as inherently insecure, Dikeç presents Agora, Le Choix Vaudais, and the 2005 revolts as political formations which create new relations, orders, and meanings out of established commonsense regimes. For instance, as part of a push to improve living conditions for banlieue residents, Le Choix Vaudais and Agora worked to redefine **urban citizenship**, in particular contesting limited modes of participatory governance and official urban policies of 'social mixing' that sought to address state-perceived issues of immigrant ghettoization and 'attract another, "better" type of population' (2007: 138).

Next, Dikeç turns to the uprisings of 2005. After 2005, the state worked purposefully to render banlieues as sites of delinquency and violence, turning 'voices into noises' by naming the revolting youth 'scum' and 'rabble' and fixating on the production of 'urban violence' statistics. Dikeç argues, contra popular, sensationalist, and pathologizing accounts, that these revolts should be understood as unarticulated spatial justice movements 'addressing at once material, categorical and political conditions that are spatially produced' (2007: 155).

Dikeç critically deconstructs the police order as it was discursively constructed by the state, tracing its mutation through several decades of national urban policy. His use of discourse analysis is essential to what he is able to accomplish here, enabling him to demonstrate how certain urban spaces are produced and 'othered' from above. Discourse analysis as a method illuminates and contextualizes both the words and actions which represent and produce space. In *Badlands*, Dikeç analyzes both national-level urban policies and alternative voices coming from the banlieue as contested, spatial, place-making practices – 'what the official policy discourse constitutes as "badlands" also become sites and organizing principles of political mobilization with democratic ideals' (2007: 7). In what remains of this chapter, we turn to consider three limitations of Dikeç's approach to discourse analysis, which also speak to the wider challenges of deploying discourse analysis in the service of critical urban theory.

Opening up the black box of discourse analysis in urban studies

The use of discourse analysis in urban studies dates back at least to the 1990s, when a discursive turn saw researchers more readily embrace representational and interpretive analyses (Lees, 2003). Yet, despite becoming a methodological mainstay since then, deployed by countless scholars, discourse analysis often appears as a 'black box'. That is to say, there is a dearth of open and reflexive discussion about it as a method – the nuts and bolts of how discourse analysis is conducted – and methodology, including underlying 'bedrock views on the nature of "reality" (ontology) and knowledge (epistemology)' (Lees, 2004: 107) for understanding the urban. In step with other urban researchers who use discourse analysis, Dikeç spends almost no time in *Badlands* interrogating his use of the method, reflecting why he chose it, and what it offers as a tool for pursuing the theoretical and political aims of his project, as well as its limitations. This presents a set of challenges which ultimately limit the extent to which Dikeç is able to achieve his aims.

Notwithstanding detailed formative accounts of critical discourse analysis as a method in other disciplines (see Fairclough, 1995), in urban studies there is a general lack of transparency with regards to *how* scholars do discourse analysis. Jason Dittmer (2010) suggests that to some extent this is because it is a craft – a kind of 'artisanal' pursuit that cannot be easily distilled into a step-by-step guide. However, as challenging and perhaps unhelpful as it may well be to codify discourse analysis into a dry and replicable formula, appeals to the creative nature of discourse analysis cannot come at the expense of reflections on how it has been done and could be done better. The current 'black box' tendency matters, not so much because it makes it harder for other researchers to check and/or replicate what the author has done, but because it prevents us from learning from one another and sharing good practice. This is especially problematic for graduate students using discourse analysis for the first time, but it also holds back methodological reflection and development in the wider field of urban studies.

Methodologically speaking, there are two approaches to discourse analysis – political economic (structural, Marxist) and constructivist/subjective (Foucauldian) (Lees, 2004). But urban researchers seldom locate their own methodological choices explicitly within one (or both) of these strands, and so rarely discuss the epistemological and ontological assumptions which underpin them. As Lees writes, 'there are important theoretical tensions between the idea of discourse as constitutive and a commitment to agency that geographers have sometimes not even acknowledged ... While these are theoretical tensions, they find their clearest expression in questions of method' (2004: 103). Similarly Dittmer (2010) argues that, ontologically and epistemologically, clarifying which tradition informs your analysis matters because these different approaches lead us to think quite differently about agency: the agency of discourse itself, and the agency of those whom discourse is supposed to act on, or through. The main distinction between the two strands is that structuralists take the subject of ideology as ontologically prior to the effect of discourse – powerful actors and institutions produce discourse intended to be consumed as common sense by pre-existing social classes[2] – whereas constructivists understand discursive subjectivities as emergent and active. Researchers can mix both approaches, as long as they are clear how (Dittmer, 2010; Lees, 2003; 2004).

Dikeç's analysis sits somewhere between both traditions. Within the more structural and empirically oriented tradition, Dikeç applies discourse analysis to privileged policy actors, texts, and media commentaries as a 'tool for uncovering certain hegemonic ways of thinking and talking about how things should be done that serve vested interests' (Lees, 2004: 102). In a constructivist vein, he presents the banlieue as actively constructed through discourse. In *Badlands* the 'state's statements' and 'sensible evidences' function as a powerful, almost all-encompassing regime of truth, or a 'partition of the sensible' in Rancière's words, shaping 'the acceptable formulation of problems and solutions to those problems' (Lees, 2004: 103). Yet, in presenting an analysis of the 'state's statements' overwhelmingly from the perspective of central government texts and actors, Dikeç never fully commits to the Foucauldian insight that the power to (re)construct such spaces is decentered. His lack of clarity and reflection on issues of agency here helps to explain imbalances and shortcomings in the application of discourse analysis as a method, and in the analytical and political power of the arguments that flow from it, as we further explore below.

Mediating discourses: from state statements to state practices

A common pitfall of discourse analysis is the tendency to over-ascribe a determinant agency to key texts and their discourses, especially those emanating from elite circles. In *Badlands*, policy texts as finished products are well critiqued, but their mediation by other actors involved in, or working against, the policy process is rarely addressed. Here, an over-reliance on an analysis of privileged policy documents makes it seem as though the 'state's statements' flow unproblematically from text to implementation. Elucidating the municipal context of the urban policy process and seeking out interpretations, readings, and implementations from local state and subaltern actors would have afforded a more variegated understanding of the multiscalar (re)production of France's spatial police order.

Discourse analysis has the power to reveal oppressive state logics constructing banlieues as problematic spaces of intervention. In Part II of his monograph, Dikeç demonstrates how the banlieue has been discursively constructed from above through a shift in language and rhetoric. Focusing on central government discourse, he demonstrates how we can discern a shift in 'perceptions of interests and issues' and how this shift came to 'define the object of policy attention' to 'promote particular policy agendas' (Rydin, 1998: 178). Dikeç thus presents French urban policy as both reflecting and reproducing centralized state power, while also implying that this power is all-encompassing. That is to say, he does not problematize the diffuse workings of power through the state at multiple levels of governance. This focus on national policy documents, the selection of two prominent national newspapers, and his incorporation of just three interviews with local policymakers in one case study location elides diverse institutional and social contexts, including the spaces and practices of negotiation, translation, and contestation through which these policies emerge and are implemented. As a result, his analysis gives the impression that the state is a univocal, monolithic actor, whose power flows unproblematically from the center to the peripheries, and from 'state statements' to state practices.

Dikeç, therefore, misses an opportunity to nuance our understanding of how the 'police' is co-constituted between scales of governance and by its discontents. Existing literature on French urban policy from the 1980s suggests that local actors within the state worked to 'enable multiple local solidarity regimes' (Dahmann et al., 2012: 326). Despite recognizing that national urban policy was created with input from municipal actors, Dikeç does not explore how local governments reinterpreted or reappropriated these national-level directives at a time of decentralization. He hints at the ways in which the desires of the local government in Vaulx-en-Velin were reflected in policy creation, stating that 'local reverberations of urban policy vary, to be sure' (2007: 148), also adding that 'there may be unchecked discrepancies between the stated aims of urban policy and their local interpretations' (2007: 139), but in not extending his analysis to the local level, he is never fully able to explore this process of translation. By locating his analysis predominantly at the national scale he reproduces a 'methodological nationalism' (Brenner, 2004).

For researchers interested in exploring the power of policy discourses and their effects, we emphasize the importance of paying attention to the active ways in which actors (re)articulate elite discourses across space. Urban policy is constructed and implemented in different, albeit patterned, ways across varying local institutional contexts. Policy implementation in practice never involves simply following the policy script 'from above'. At least to some extent, it involves place-based creativity, improvisation, and negotiation. While recognizing the constraints of graduate study, we believe that those employing urban discourse analysis should pay attention to the multiscalar and variegated production, circulation, and translation of powerful discourses. To do this in a project such as *Badlands* would require a multi-sited case study, deploying interviews and observations.

Amplifying alternative voices through discourse analysis

If scholars are committed to using discourse analysis as a tool of critical urban studies, creative approaches are required that can reach beyond the 'state's statements' or discourses of powerful elite actors to recognize and amplify subaltern discourses. In this section, we point to ways that Dikeç could have better extended discourse analysis to uncover 'alternative voices' that contest and politicize the state's construction of the banlieue from below.

In Part III, Dikeç goes beyond official discourses 'to give voice to alternative discourses formulated' (2007: 5) in the banlieue. He does this by engaging with Agora, Le Choix Vaudais, and the 2005 revolts. In his investigation of the politics of the banlieue, Dikeç analyzes recorded and unrecorded conversations with a select few members of Agora and young banlieue residents. He positions these conversations as ways in which people from the banlieue speak out against the violent injustices of French urban policy and demonstrate an alternative, insurgent urban citizenship against a racist, postcolonial Republicanism.

Additionally, Dikeç presents his interpretation of the 2005 uprisings as 'unarticulated justice movements', signaling that the uprisings are of a different nature and quality than **urban social movements** conventionally conceived; those taking part did not take to the streets with a defined set of claims or demands on the social order. Nevertheless, he insists that their actions are politically meaningful, even if the French state's response sought to aggressively disavow them of any such meaning.

Yet, empirically, this is the thinnest section of the book. It relies on the voices of a small number of actors and the author's interpretive agency, only partially making visible how the banlieue is politicized through the diversity of ways in which different actors articulate, perform, and inscribe their resistance to the spatial police order.

To explore the banlieue as a rich space of political discourse and mobilization, *Badlands* would have benefited from either an ethnographic engagement with the space and the inhabitants of the banlieue, or a more diverse reading of discourses produced 'from below'. Reflecting on methodological constraints, Dikeç recognizes that an ethnographic approach would have illuminated the everyday lives of banlieue inhabitants, but reveals that the book started as a policy analysis, and that a concern with feasibility rather than 'a theoretical or political preference for one form of inquiry over another' ruled out a 'richer ethnographic account' (2012: 332). We are sensitive to the constraints and tradeoffs faced when conducting research in the early-career stage, and it is facile to suggest that he should have conducted an ethnography or interviewed hundreds of people who were involved in the uprisings.

However, there were other ways he could have extended his use of discourse analysis to engage with 'alternative voices from below' without over-committing time or resources. He might, for example, have looked to the 'alternative voices' that are enunciated and inscribed in the graffiti, music, poetry, literature, and cinema of banlieue residents, and/or in online spaces. Whether they be tagged on walls, printed on CD jackets, or uploaded onto the Internet, counter-narratives are inscribed publicly across diverse fields as the 'staging of artistic ruptures' (Garbin and Millington, 2012: 2079) that do not necessitate a deep ethnographic engagement to be appreciated.

In their work on Parisian banlieues, Garbin and Millington (2012: 2076) emphasize the importance of counter-narratives that challenge territorial stigmatization, and show how residents engage in a continuous struggle to challenge how their neighborhoods are represented. Banlieue youth and other residents make their mark on the public arena 'to stress the extent of their marginalisation, and to express a collective claim for social existence'. One way is through music. Gündoğdu, for example, points to how young people living in banlieue seek

> to build connections between their actions and the French republican tradition of protest ... Music, especially rap, was crucial in providing alternative narratives that represented the 2005 revolt as an extension of the French revolutionary tradition. (2018: 216)

Gündoğdu (2018) also draws our attention to the case artwork on an EP entitled 'Insurrection' released by a collective of artists during those uprisings. The artwork depicts

> a black man with a turban holding a tricolour flag alongside an image from the French Revolution of a woman wearing the red Phrygian cap worn by the famed *sans-culottes* ... Above them is written '*La France*

aux humains' (France for all humans) and, underneath, '*Sans-Culottes* 2006'. (2018: 216)

Dikeç might also have found alternative discourses in a survey conducted by a political organization, the Association Collectif Liberté, Egalité, Fraternité, Ensemble, Unis, created in the wake of the uprisings. It surveyed young people to create a *Cahiers de doléances*[3] (again riffing on French revolutionary symbolism) and presented the list to the French National Assembly in October 2006.

As noted above, Dikeç is concerned with reclaiming the 2005 uprisings from their popular political and media narrations as inchoate and mindless acts of vandalism. He rightly refuses to reduce the voices of banlieue residents to noise and their actions to senseless violence. Yet, while Dikeç's interpretive reading of the 2005 uprisings is at pains to counter lazy stereotypes of young people, it nonetheless tells the reader what the author *thinks* they signify more than it demonstrates what they mean from the participants' perspectives, *in their own words*. In characterizing the uprising as 'unarticulated', he elides the ways in which youth *do* articulate grievances. Rather than muting the voices of these young people, Dikeç could have used discourse analysis to amplify them. This is not to say that academic interpretation is in itself problematic. Rather, the point here is that in critical urban theory, it should not be used to elide the voices of those being studied. In *Badlands*, the risk of unreflexive discourse analysis is an 'exaggeration of the power of academic interpretation ... diminishing the agency of "ordinary people"' (Jackson, 1999, in Lees, 2003: 108). Given the importance of reclaiming the banlieue as a political space and of uncovering alternative voices to the ethico-political project of the book, this methodological limitation proves consequential.

Conclusion

In this chapter we have explored the possibilities and pitfalls of discourse analysis for critical urban theory by deconstructing Mustafa Dikeç's *Badlands of the Republic*. While we have celebrated the ways in which Dikeç deploys discourse analysis to powerfully chart and critique the regressive mutation of French urban policy, we have also used the book to highlight some common limitations in how the method is used in practice by urban scholars. These limitations are: (1) the lack of reflexive openness about operational, epistemological, and ontological questions; (2) the risk of eliding subaltern voices by privileging elite texts and/or the academic's interpretive agency; and (3) the tendency to ascribe too much power/agency to texts and their discourses (at the expense of the voices, experiences, and agency of those who, at multiple levels and in different institutions and places, (re)articulate, (re)circulate, and (re)work with and against them). None of these limitations, however, are inherent to discourse analysis as a method; they are challenges that can be overcome or worked around. Echoing Lees (2003; 2004), some 15 years later, we advocate for more methodological candor and discussion about how and why discourse analysis is done. We also suggest, in the spirit of critical urban studies, that scholars need to find ways of going beyond elite discourses, be that by complementing discourse analysis with multi-sited case studies, or by extending discourse analysis to more prosaic and non-elite forms of discourse.

Notes

1. Generally, banlieue is a term that refers to a neighborhood located in the urban periphery of French cities. More than simply another word for 'suburb', since the 1980s, the idea of banlieue has become synonymous with issues of spatial exclusion, immigration, insecurity, and threats to the social (and spatial) order of the French Republic. The 'danger' of the banlieue is also tied to the racialized populations inhabiting these neighborhoods. Dikeç intentionally uses the term banlieue rather than suburb in his monograph, to emphasize the term's origin and its geographical connotations. French urban policy has become increasingly concerned with governing the banlieue, as part of a larger project to reduce the socio-spatial fragmentation of French Republicanism, and to reproduce the social and political integrity of the state.

2. It is important to note that Gramscian approaches to discourse analysis tend to be more mindful of the active role that subaltern classes play in the production of common sense, although their existence as a class is often taken for granted.

3. The *Cahiers de doléances*, or list of grievances, were drawn up by the three Estates in France between March and April 1789 in the build-up to the start of the French Revolution, which began that year.

8

FRUSTRATED ENCOUNTERS: ON AHMED KANNA'S *DUBAI*: *THE CITY AS CORPORATION*

Nafis Hasan, Hudson Spivey and Kenton Card

KEYWORDS: everyday urbanism, neoliberal urbanism, urban governance, urban sustainability

In the early 2000s, the internationally recognized Dutch architect Rem Koolhaas proposed a 6.5 square mile (17 km²) artificial island off Dubai's coast that would contain beachfront resorts and an 82-storey coiling tower evoking classical Arabic architecture, called the Spiral. Around the same time, stories about the inhumane living and working conditions of migrant laborers in Dubai began to circulate globally in popular media. Rooms designed for one person were packed with 14 to 15 workers. Without electricity for months, workers were forced to sleep on the roofs of their dwellings to avoid the suffocating heat inside. Ahmed Kanna's *Dubai: The City as Corporation* (2011) epitomizes the spatial inequalities produced by these contradictory examples of urbanism and **urban governance**.

The book is an anthropological critique of alliances forged between elite state actors and western architects leading to the spatial transformation of Dubai, until the 2008 financial meltdown. Kanna employs Henri Lefebvre's concept of 'the production of space' to chart out a theoretical and methodological framework to decode the political agendas and material implications of this transformation. Turning his gaze toward Dubai also as a site of **everyday urbanism**,

Kanna provides valuable insights into the linkages between macro processes of spatial transformation and the texture and fabric of human experience resisting it. In doing so, he shows how paying attention to the intensification of these spatial processes – as well as their human outcomes – can provide an opportunity to study the relatively recent phenomenon of urbanization in the Arab world.

Methodologically, Kanna's text is illustrative of the challenges and workarounds in researching a city that on the one hand is governed like a corporation – power in the hands of a few, an apotheosis of neoliberal values of contemporary capitalism – while continuing to hold onto kinship-based solidarity and conservative views on race and gender. Making use of the tools of ethnography, Kanna also shows us the limits of and alternatives to the traditional ethnographic approach of participant observation in a situation where a fear of losing their place in this corporate machine makes some people suspicious of researchers. He thus employs interpretive techniques, and analyses of representational discourse, to characterize the lifeworlds of those who inhabit the city but are reticent to speak about their experiences.

In this chapter we make the claim that Kanna's strategy of looking at Dubai from both above and below – as the 'spatial representation' of capital through which hegemonic space is produced and the 'spatialization' effects this has on residents – provides insights into the methodological choices that such a framing entails and the significance of these choices and their limits. After situating the book within urban studies and anthropology, we describe Kanna's theoretical approaches and methods, following this with a critical analysis of the book and its usefulness for future urban scholars.

Influence and contribution

While Kanna's work can be situated within a well-trodden Lefebvrian tradition of thinking about how space is produced under political economic regimes, it analyzes Dubai from a less common frame. Rather than studying urban morphology, which is how spatial representation is often approached (e.g., Ren, 2011), Kanna chooses to focus on the politics of Dubai's spatial design: the western architectural practices that guide the city's development, not only as aesthetic choices, but as professional practices that manifest both western architects and Dubai's ruling dynasty's (hereafter Maktoum) political ideologies. Whereas Ren focuses on how transnational architectural practices shape the globalized form taken by cities in China (in terms of spatial structures, ownership, and control), Kanna is more interested in identifying the ideologies that undergird western architectural practices.

Trained as an anthropologist, but also steeped in critical theory (Walter Benjamin, Fredric Jameson, and Sigmund Kracauer are his favorites), Kanna is able to provide an interpretive analysis of public representations, putting him in the company of a growing body of urban geographers who seek to integrate the study of language and culture into urban geographical analysis (cf. Lees, 2004).

As an Arabic-speaking American citizen of Iraqi origin, Kanna is privy to public representations of culture in Arabic newspapers and other local media, just as he has access to the representation of western architecture in the global media. This allows him to distinctly apply western critical theory to local contexts.

Kanna's use of ethnographic methods (e.g., sampling, participant observations, interviews) to provide insights into the lived world of Dubai's sub-populations can be seen as a critique of political economic analyses of place-making that ignore specificity and the intersections of gender, race, and class in relation to space. As such, he can be located among a group of cultural anthropologists mobilizing ethnographies of space and place (paralleling notably Low and Lawrence-Zuñiga, 2003), who offer a cultural analysis of spatial processes as opposed to a largely quantitative political economic focus on variables and inanimate categories. He thus joins a small but important group of anthropologists who provide a unique account of the processes of subjectivation under neoliberalism; as Tejaswini Ganti (2014) points out, this is a much needed contribution to the anthropology of neoliberalism. Further, his knowledge of Arabic and access to local scholars and scholarship allows him to productively historicize the social production of contemporary Dubai, joining a host of scholars thinking about relational approaches to space and time (Harvey, 1996).

Importantly, while urban anthropology itself is an emergent sub-field within anthropology, studying the Middle East as an urban phenomenon is even rarer. As Lara Deeb and Jessica Winegar (2012) point out, there remains an abiding representation of Arab majority societies in anthropological scholarship as being 'tribal, exotic, and isolated'. Kanna's urban focus helps displace some of this bias by bringing to light a little-known account of Arab urbanism, contributing to accounts of place making outside of the west. With Dubai now central in the shifting of regional influence in matters related to urban design and architecture within the Middle East (Davis, 2006; Kanna, 2011), Kanna's work also can be seen as a theoretical and methodological guide for researching other cities in the region.

Key arguments and methods

Kanna's investigation of Dubai revolves around two theoretical terms that frame the book: 'spatial representations' and 'spatialization'. These allow him to understand the city both from above, that is, from the perspective of 'urbanists' – western architects and the elite Maktoum – and from below, through the eyes of a heterogeneously defined set of residents in Dubai. These theoretical choices lead to a set of methodological strategies, which we unpack here and subsequently assess in terms of their efficacy in illuminating Kanna's claims about the city. Pairing theoretical choices with methodological ones reveals both possibilities and limits of his research design.

Spatial representations

Kanna employs Henri Lefebvre's notion of 'spatial representations', understood as the representation of capital through space, as a guiding frame to
describe the work of urbanists. For Kanna, like Lefebvre, urbanists are all
manner of 'experts' who come together to act on space, including not only the
Maktoum and the western architects, but also 'urban planners and real estate
developers, along with various kinds of intellectuals, from academics to jour-
nalists' (2011: 4). Borrowing from Lefebvre, Kanna suggests that these actors
represent a kind of 'class urbanism' (2011: 90), by which he means that their
political projects coincide and that they have the power and ability to impose
their ideas onto space. Importantly, Kanna locates this 'coming together' of
western and Arab urbanists in the Maktoum's desire to reinvest finance capital
from the 1970s oil boom; in the particular strand of US geopolitics post-9/11
that identified Dubai as the site of 'good Muslims'; and in the historical
ethnocentric 'bargain' that the Maktoum struck with Dubai's Emiratis leading
to its hegemonic control of land.

In addition to highlighting this political and economic context, Kanna also
focuses on the star architects entering Dubai during this time – a relatively
small group of globally dominant, aesthetically bold, and politically complicit
architects. As a cultural anthropologist, Kanna approaches their rhetoric of
urban entrepreneurialism, the development of Dubai as *tabula rasa,* and the
discourse of sustainability with suspicion. Thus he asks: What kind of space
is produced in the interaction of local elites and western architects? How does
this further an elitist agenda? What representations of ethnic identity are
produced in these interactions? What notions of culture are portrayed in this
production of space? What is concealed in this process? (2011: 83–85).

In order to investigate these questions, Kanna engages in two kinds of
empirical work. First, by drawing upon the work of historians and political
scientists of the region (the Emirati political scientist Abdulkhaleq Abdulla, the
Emirati historian Fatma Al-Sayegh, both based in the UAE, and Christopher
Davidson, a scholar of Middle East politics) he charts out the particular
historical trajectory through which the Maktoum gained hegemonic control
over space in Dubai. Kanna, citing Abdulla, calls this a 'political deactivation
of the populace' (2011: 54), which the Maktoum were able to carry out in the
period after the oil boom by making Emiratis 'materially prosperous in
unprecedented ways' (2011: 55), through rent sharing, social security benefits,
and concessions on financial, industrial, and commercial activities. As a result
of this co-optation the Maktoum could offer the space of Dubai as a clean
slate to western architects, while also actualizing a spatial segregation between
'pure' Emirati and 'outsiders'. Reading some of these scholars in the original
Arabic, Kanna's methodological strategy is to counteract urbanist ideology
with 'local voices [that] have long been critiquing Dubai's turn towards
Western style free market' (2011: 21).

Kanna's second approach is to directly engage the material carrying the rhetoric and discourse of star architecture. He undertakes a discourse analysis of this material from diverse sources: the website of Koolhaas's architecture firm; a documentary film commissioned by the Maktoum, *The Sand Castle*, that recounts the competition among four Norwegian architects to build a new city in the Emirates; BBC talks by faculty at the American University of Sharjah, UAE; a workshop at Harvard's Center for Middle Eastern Studies devoted to the theme of **urban sustainability and resilience** in the Gulf, which was attended by American and British specialists in sustainable architecture and two real-estate developers from the UAE; a fawning review of Koolhaas's work in the *New York Times*; and a description of the Arab landscape in the architecture webzine, *Arcspace*.

Using this material, Kanna shows that the transformation of space through architectural designs is legitimized through repeated reference to a stereo-typed authentic Arab culture. For instance, he writes that 'a sympathetic reviewer of Koolhaas' Waterfront City proposal notes "that the plan's geo-metric grid gives way to an intimate warren of alleyways, like a traditional souk" (Ouroussof)' (2011: 84). Further, Kanna writes, 'urbanists almost automatically reach out for such cultural stereotypes when writing about or theorizing spaces in non-Western societies' (2011: 84). Similarly, he shows how, in *The Sand Castle*, urbanists work to produce an image of the space of Dubai as a clean slate or *tabula rasa* on which they can act. This is done by invoking the Arab desert as landscape, 'empty', 'romantic', with an 'authentic Arab tradition':

> The local culture is steeped in 'tradition', ironically represented by exotic, aesthetic expressions of identity; the architect and his local elite clients are visionaries who will excavate the landscape's hidden potential, trans-forming it from its intuitive, primal immanence into its concrete final shape. (2011: 100)

The discourse of ecological sustainability at the Harvard workshop also relies on the presentation of a stereotyped Arab culture. According to Kanna, this leads to 'the abstract, technical framing of problems of urban sustain-ability, and the conflation of orientalist or other ethnocentric stereotypes with locally situated problems of environmental impact that the UAE seemed to present' (2011: 93). One way in which this was done was to invoke 'traditional house gardens', displaying values of 'self-fertilization', 'personal freedom', and 'longevity' – 'values that the architect sees rooted in Gulf culture' (2011: 93).

In Kanna's interpretation, star architects are depoliticized from the context in which they work, and rely on orientalist clichés and a rhetoric of radicalism to reduce architecture to pure aesthetic experimentation, unwittingly playing handmaiden to local hierarchies of power.

Spatialization

Drawing on the work of anthropologists Akhil Gupta and James Ferguson, Kanna employs the term 'spatialization' to show how this urbanist ideology is experienced by Dubai's residents. For Kanna, spaces are always politically contested; in the case of Dubai, this phenomenon is represented by the ways in which ordinary residents (referred to as Dubayyans) contest the spatial representations of the city's urbanists. In order to illuminate the heterogeneous experience of spatial representations, Kanna chooses to divide Dubai's population into subgroups based on ethnic and occupational characteristics, allowing him to depict the multiple interests at play in the city and the different ways in which they resist these spatial representations.

These subgroups consist of older Emirati men, younger Emirati men and women mostly working in corporations, middle-class South Asian men and women in business and corporate jobs, and working-class female South Asian immigrants. In forming these subgroups, he is constrained by limited access to Emirati family life and an inability to speak with Emirati women, even when their increasing presence in public life is a cause of concern. He thus devises methodological strategies to work around these constraints to ask: In what way do Dubai's residents experience spatial representations? Is the project of spatializing capital resisted? Is this experience differentiated by ethnicity and socio-economic class?

To investigate these questions, Kanna conducts 'between forty and fifty interviews' with the subgroups of Dubayyans, in addition to 'dozens of other more informal conversations over coffee, drinks or meals, at formal receptions and in offices' (2011: 11). While this may sound like he had equal access to each of these groups, Emiratis appear reticent to speak to him about their family life, due to what he sees as his 'US affiliations'. Given this difficulty of access, he turns to critically analyzing 'cultural materials' to comment on their experience of a transforming Dubai:

> Along with what Westerners would recognize as the normal contents of such pages (academic and intellectual opinions, editorial reflections on major current events, and so on) they are forums for what would seem to Western readers as materials with a tenuous claim on serious editorial attention. Examples include poems submitted by readers, essays reflecting on the nature of parenthood, odes to the supposedly wise and visionary rulers, short stories written by readers, and jokes and comics, usually mocking the petty foibles of society at large or of stock characters, such as the neglectful father or the wayward wife, which are understood by Emiratis as objects of mirth and metaphors for social ills. (2011: 112)

Based on these materials, he shows that privileged Emiratis, having internalized the ethnocratic thrust of the Maktoum, are anxious and nostalgic for a 'lost village' of traditional life and an idealized, racially pure Arab past, which in their eyes an urbanizing Dubai is moving away from. Ironically, this desire for hyper-ethnicity, or what Kanna terms 'neo-orthodoxy', is used to tacitly critique the family state, which itself bases its spatial imagination of Dubai on a stereotyped vision of Emirati identity. For these privileged Emiratis, the Maktoum's modernizing policies do not adequately respect traditional practices. One of the key sites where this is revealed is a prevailing attitude toward women and their increasing public presence in shopping malls, represented in these cultural texts as a 'narrative arc and characters which we now can see as conventional – the ungoverned wife abandoning the husband, in turn inviting corruption, familial and cultural, by way of the foreign domestic' (2011: 127). These representations of women help Emirati men critique the hyper-modernizing tendency of the family state, thereby resisting the domination of spatialized capital.

If privileged Emiratis challenge the spatial transformation of Dubai by pointing to its ill effects on women and domestic life, middle-class South Asians challenge its neoliberal character by pointing to its ethnic bias. Through semi-structured one-to-one and group interviews, Kanna asks open-ended questions pertaining to identity and racism that allow him to elicit deep-seated anxieties. He concludes:

> the issue is mainly one of economic belonging. Especially, among middle-class South Asians, there is no desire for inclusion into the community of citizens … the desire is for a fair shake in the economic sphere, a feeling that economic inclusion should be based on merit and not on other factors, such as ethnicity and nationality. (2011: 183)

In order to illustrate this point spatially, Kanna collects anecdotal evidence based on conversations with home 'rental office agents' (2011: 185) to show that the main beneficiaries of upscale residential projects in New Dubai are 'foreign nationals, mostly from Great Britain, South Africa, Australia and New Zealand' and in some cases very wealthy South Asians, who in turn 're-rent the properties to expatriates'. Excluded from this 'hierarchically-ordered, privatized space', most wealthy middle-class South Asian immigrants experience a deficit of the neoliberal values of consumer citizenship (2011: 185).

A third group of people who Kanna engages with are young Emirati men and women who resist being boxed into the ethnic categories that their older counterparts espouse. Kanna finds that this group fashion their identities in the interstices of multiple discourses, dubbing them as 'flexible citizens' – drawing on Aihwa Ong's (1999) characterization of citizens under globalization with flexible allegiance to nation states. While wavering in their allegiance to the Maktoum's ideas of ethnocracy, they consistently support its neoliberal policies and are proponents of Dubai's modern transformation. Kanna pays attention to how their symbolic construction of identity is carried out, observing the manner in which language is used, the claims made to ethnicity, how young people dress, what they have to say about religion, how they navigate across different ethnic and gender identities, and, most importantly, what meaning they give to their experiences. He shows that while these residents are the most significant proponents of the city-as-corporation, their neoliberal subjectivities and consent to the project of **neoliberal urbanism** emerge out of a contested process. Kanna begins to realize that his interlocutors are presenting to him a version of their neoliberal selves, assuming (wrongly, given his long affiliation to the United States) that he espouses neoliberal values. Part of what he observes is thus a performance, in direct response to his presence there. Kanna also notes that the relationship he forms with these interlocutors makes him unable to speak to them about those aspects of Dubai that in their minds do not correspond to neoliberal urbanism, such as issues related to the exploitation of migrant workers or Dubai's political economy, highlighting another methodological challenge.

The final group of people that Kanna engages with are poor middle-class South Asian migrants. A single case study of two South Asian women migrants who were domestic workers reveals that their experiences in Dubai are dominated by fear and anxiety. He reflects on his inability to provide a more compelling account of the lives of working-class migrants by pointing to his own positionality as a person with 'immense privilege', intimately connected to the Arab community, triggering fear of deportation among the working-class people he approached. Unlike the young Emirati, who perceived him as neoliberal, these working-class informants perceived him to be conservative and anti-immigrant. Even though he tries to put them at ease by taking his wife along for these conversations, in the hope that these women would reveal more about their lives in the presence of another woman, he is unable to allay their fears.

In sum, Kanna employs techniques of ethnography (sampling, (semi-structured and focus group) interviews, and observation) and deploys interpretive techniques to analyze publicly circulating media when met with resistance, to show the multiple ways in which the hegemony of urbanists is contested and rearticulated, while constantly also juggling his respondents' contradictory perceptions of himself.

Reflections

Kanna's interpretive and archival approaches to critiquing urbanist ideology are innovative and useful methodological strategies that complement his ethnographic work. Historicizing the spatial transformations of Dubai by analyzing the work of regionally focused scholars allows the reader to see how contemporary social processes in Dubai relate to past spatial forms, and to place contemporary land transformations in relation to these past processes. This relational view helps throw light on the ongoing annihilation of space by capital (Harvey, 1996), puncturing the 'clean slate' image purveyed by urbanists. Similarly, his methodological strategy of using cultural materials enables him to challenge not only what he calls 'western writings on the UAE' (2011:107) that tend to naturalize the development of both the federal and Dubai states as dynastic, authoritarian, and 'pro-western', but also the presumption that the Maktoum elicit uncontested support from the Emirati population.

Yet a focus on this multi-method approach is at times detrimental to the ethnography. First, Kanna's reduction of the demographic diversity of Dubai to ideal types prevents his analysis from developing a relational, inter-subjective account of city life. His presentation of subjectivities associated with 'neo-orthodoxy' and 'neo-liberalism' as occupying two opposite poles at times feels too rigid, since these poles may not account for interactions between subject positions. For instance, one does not get a sense of whether there are spaces where conservative Emiratis and younger neoliberal Emiratis interact. More importantly, although Kanna spent over a year interacting with some of his interlocutors, his ethnographic discussion does not reveal the texture of his subjects' everyday lives. The conversations he presents appear mechanistic at times, relating only to the specific argument he seeks to make. While this partly reflects the reticence of his subjects towards inquiry, it also results from an ethnographic approach that does not quite provide the kind of thick description of people's changing experience of Dubai that has become a hallmark of ethnographic work (Geertz, 1973).

Further, Kanna is not equally methodologically creative with all the subjects he engages with. While he is challenged by the reticence of both economically poor South Asian migrants and rich Emirati families (albeit for different reasons), he does not attempt to study the former through the interpretive techniques devised for studying the latter. He also does not attempt to fill this conspicuous absence of ethnographic material on the lives of working-class domestic servants and laborers by interrogating forms of media, such as newspapers, which in his own words 'are an especially rich, and generally ignored (at least by anthropologists), source of data on the ways everyday people concretely engage and imagine more abstract, diffuse realities, such as the state and the community' (2011: 14). South Asian migrant communities, such as the sizeable proportion from Kerala in India, have newspapers and radio channels dedicated to the community (Vora, 2013).

More generally, since Kanna's interpretive strategies for analyzing representational discourse are as important to him as his ethnographic framework, the book would have benefited from a greater detailing of the theoretical and methodological assumptions underlying that analysis. As Lees (2004) points out, notwithstanding the growing discursive turn in urban research, very few scholars discuss how they undertake discourse analysis. Lees notes two main strands of discourse analysis: a Marxist tradition of political economy and ideology critique, and a Foucauldian approach to discourse as part of a process through which identities get constructed. Kanna's discourse analysis of the work of elite urbanists, as a tool for uncovering certain hegemonic ways of thinking and talking about how things should be done that serve certain vested interests, points towards Lees' second approach. However, it does not elicit the more general ideological context within which these discourses have been produced. For example, the reader is not informed about the context in which the articles glorifying star architects and their work is produced, nor how film-makers and other creative artists are interpellated into this elite urbanist hegemonic project. These individual sources are simply deployed as evidence for his arguments.

In reviewing anthropological studies of neoliberalism, Ganti argues that there is a tendency among anthropologists to treat concepts like state, market, and neoliberalism itself as 'self-evident' categories rather than interrogating these terms (2014: 99). Kanna's overbearing fidelity to these concepts prevents him from allowing his ethnographic insights to speak for themselves. Focusing on how neoliberalism shapes subjectivities, he does not consider the possibility that his interlocutors may be responding to other forms of domination and authority. Even his substantial discussion of patriarchy is subsumed within his discussion of neoliberalism.

Conclusion

These critiques notwithstanding, in identifying architects as primary agents of an urbanist ideology, and conducting a discourse analysis of their representations in public life, Kanna productively brings interpretive and anthropological methods of analysis to bear upon architectural systems and design. His use of textual and visual material to interrogate both the dominant ideology and how people make sense of these ideologies is an innovative approach to studying the urban, which can be applied across multiple geographies and social contexts. Kanna's work demonstrates the possibilities and challenges that ethnographic methods hold for researching a city caught in the throes of rampant transformation. It also highlights the multiple ways in which a researcher's identity is laid bare or mistaken, or becomes a hurdle to understanding life in the city. Most of all, his work reveals the inadequacy of approaching the urban from a single methodological standpoint, pointing to the need to constantly innovate across disciplinary boundaries in order to unpack the divergent strands that make up a city.

9

RESCALING THE URBAN: ON NEIL BRENNER'S *NEW STATE SPACES*

Joseph A. Daniels, Mikael Omstedt and Dimitar Anguelov

KEYWORDS: comparative urbanism, planetary urbanization, uneven urban development, urban governance

One of the most influential contributions to urban studies in recent years has been the assertion by Neil Brenner and his colleagues that the field's traditional preoccupation with the territorially bound 'city' should be abandoned (Brenner and Schmid, 2015). In its place, they have put forward the '**planetary urbanization**' thesis, which reconceptualizes the urban as a multiscalar process encompassing both the agglomerations that are traditionally associated with urban life and the extended processes of connectivity, energy, and materials provision that sustain them. By arguing for an 'urban theory without an outside' (Brenner, 2014), this approach has provoked concerns about the potential abandonment of the concrete and particular for the abstract and universal (Derickson, 2015). However, in response to these critics Brenner (2018) claims that the planetary urbanization thesis must be understood primarily as a *meta-theoretical* intervention, which seeks to develop an epistemological framework capable of accounting for the ongoing reconstitution of the urban. In this sense, it is also a call for methodological innovation and reflexivity.

The precursor to such an approach can be found in Brenner's influential monograph on the remaking of **urban governance** in Western Europe, *New State*

Spaces (2004), hereafter *NSS*. Like the planetary urbanization thesis, this book does not seek to stand in for concrete research but is concerned with building a conceptual framework by theorizing *across* multiple cases. The result is an ambitious and innovative account of urban governance not only as a phenomenon to be explained, but also as a terrain through which to examine the restructuring of the modern state. Brenner is not simply concerned with the essential 'content' of the urban nor with a particular city, but with how the urban can be deployed as a methodological lens for understanding pan-urban and cross-scalar processes. As such, *NSS* reconceptualizes the urban by foregrounding the role of urban governance in state restructuring, and by redefining urban governance as the multiscalar regulation of urbanization *processes*.

In the discussion that follows, we explore the methodological insights offered by *NSS*, beginning with a synthesis of the book, and tracing how the empirical argument is sustained across cases through Brenner's 'meso-level' method. We then highlight the potential and limits that this multiscalar methodological orientation brings to analysis of the urban, emphasizing the important dialectic between concrete research and abstract theorizing. A conclusion draws these reflections together and assesses the relevance of the book in light of contemporary debates on planetary urbanization.

Remaking urban governance

NSS investigates the post-war remaking of urban governance in Western Europe and its subsequent transformation under conditions of inter-urban competition. As such, the book unfolds both as an intervention into state theory and as a reconceptualization of the nature of urban governance, and, by extension, the urban itself. Opening the book, Brenner argues that we need to rethink received understandings of the state as a nationally scaled territorial unit (a tendency he calls 'methodological nationalism'), in favor of an approach that conceptualizes the state as co-constituted across a range of national, subnational, and supranational scales. To understand why the state takes specific forms in certain conjunctures, Brenner draws on Martin Jones' (1997) spatialization of Bob Jessop's (1990) 'strategic–relational' state theory to argue for a processual notion of state space as an interplay between 'state spatial projects' that produce certain administrative geographies and 'state spatial strategies' that shape socio-economic processes.

Arguing that these are articulated in both scalar and territorial terms, Brenner asserts that by examining the evolution of urban policy one can understand how Western European states since the crisis of Fordism in the early 1970s have been transformed from post-war models of 'spatial Keynesianism' to variants of a 'Rescaled Competition State Regime'. While the goal of the former was to spread out economic activity in order to alleviate **uneven urban development**, the latter seeks to enhance the nation's competitiveness in global circuits of capital by strengthening the position of leading city-regions.

State policies have privileged global city-regions as scales of governance and sites of investment, resulting in a rescaling and reterritorialization of statehood. In effect, the power of the state has been recentered on the urban scale so that urban governance 'has served as a major catalyst, medium, and arena of state rescaling processes' (Brenner, 2004: 174), producing new state spaces. Reading state transformation *through* the urban, consequently, becomes Brenner's focus as *NSS* departs from theoretical elaboration to engage with empirics.

Brenner argues that spatial Keynesianism in Western Europe sought to equalize economic growth across a nation's territory, privileging the national scale as the main scale of regulation. A key strategy anchoring this state spatial project was the development of compensatory regional policies in the 1950s–1970s. These included West Germany's Spatial Planning Law of 1965 which mandated the state to promote 'equal life conditions' regardless of geography, Italy's Southern Development Agency which sought to support the country's lagging *Mezzogiorno*-region, and France's designation of cities like Marseille, Lyon, and Nantes as 'countervailing metropoles' – provincial growth-poles that could balance the economic might of Paris. The goal was to 'redistribute employment within national boundaries, and thus, to induce the spatial integration of the national economy as a whole' (2004: 133). Along with the broader centralization of intergovernmental relations, these policies of spatial Keynesianism meant that cities and regions were instrumentalized primarily to act as administrative sub-units in a standardized national project of state welfarism. They were 'enclosed within *nationalized* interscalar rule-regimes ... [subordinated] to the centralizing regulatory controls of *national* governments and ... position[ed] ... within *nationally* configured spatial divisions of labor' (2004: 160–161, emphasis added).

Similarly, Brenner examines the Rescaled Competition State Regime that succeeded spatial Keynesianism in terms of its (new) approach to urban policy and governance. Under this regime, cities and their metropolitan regions are remade as semi-autonomous engines of growth in service of the national project of territorial competitiveness. In contrast to the previous emphasis on national standardization and centralization, this involved administrative devolution, including the introduction of city-regional governance structures to coordinate investments and the establishment of agencies tailor-made for specific localities and scales. Examples of these state spatial projects include: the granting of more autonomy and responsibility to the *Länder* of West Germany throughout the 1980s; the Danish government's formation of the Metropolitan Development Board to strengthen the Copenhagen city-region as the nation's major growth engine in the early 1990s; and the urban development corporations and enterprise zones established in the 1980s by the Thatcher government in the UK. Rather than seeking to equalize and redistribute economic growth, these localized regulatory spaces allowed for the mobilization of 'entrepreneurial' development strategies in cities across Western Europe, aiming to create competitive environments for capital accumulation.

Meso-level comparison

Brenner develops these arguments by reading *across* cases, illuminating shared development trajectories of political decentralization by synthesizing a range of secondary sources, but largely foregoing more conventional primary research methods. This represents a distinctive approach to **comparative urbanism**, not as side-by-side cases but as a meso-level analysis spanning multiple cases. Brenner examines the major urban governance trends in particular periods and places, drawing on extensive secondary literatures along with further illustrations derived from policy texts, spatial planning maps, and quotations sourced from various state actors. Working to identify trends and family resemblances across cases, as well as to specify subgroupings, Brenner distills the particular national policies and plans into synthesized categories, text-boxes, diagrams, and tables, which he then juxtaposes in order to draw out the similarities and differences in development trajectories across Europe. The example of Brenner's Box 5.4 on the 'return of the regional problem' (2004: 186) illustrates this approach. Here, he draws on local scholarship to show how a growing 'North/South divide' manifested across the UK, Germany, and Italy in the 1980s, demonstrating that while the era of spatial Keynesianism was one of spatial convergence, its breakdown in the 1970s produced new rounds of 'inter-metropolitan polarization' (2004: 183). Other text-box summaries illustrate the role of intergovernmental reforms in enhancing the competitiveness of cites in the Netherlands (Box 5.9), or the shift from geographical equalization to greater promotion of regional 'self-reliance' in the spatial planning regime of the unified Germany (Box 5.11). Together, these trends point toward the (uneven) restructuring of an entire state system in the face of crisis in the Keynesian regime.

The reason that the empirical argument takes this form becomes clear in Brenner's discussion of methodology in *NSS* and elsewhere (Brenner, 2009a). Drawing on a critical-realist notion of different levels of conceptual abstraction, he distinguishes between an abstract level that posits general dynamics between capitalism and the state, a meso-level emphasizing how these dynamics articulate with historically specific and medium-term temporalities, and, lastly, a concrete level concerned with local diversity during particular conjunctures and events. As a method positioned '[b]etween generality and diversity' (Brenner, 2004: 17), this meso-level approach combines 'both abstract concepts and concrete evidence to propose a broad periodization of state spatial development patterns across western Europe during the 40-year period under investigation' (Brenner, 2009a: 128). This allows Brenner (2004: 20) to generalize from a diverse set of national political debates, policies, and urban outcomes in order to point toward a more systematic process that reveals 'the underlying regularities that tie together … variegated contexts within a shared historical-geographical configuration'.

Through text-boxes, diagrams, and graphical summaries Brenner compiles evidence for his theory claims, grounding emergent concepts with illustrations spanning numerous cases and countries, revising and replacing received concepts along the way. For example, while the concepts 'urban growth machine' and 'urban entrepreneurialism' are found to be instructive for understanding a particular set of actors, institutional forms, and practices, they are less suited for understanding (or explaining) the generalized and multiscalar process of restructuring. This is because their methodological approach tends to treat urban governance transformations as localized responses to supranational constraints. Similarly, while the term 'glocalization' better captures the dynamics between the general and the particular, Brenner (2004: 45) finds its focus on two scales (the 'global' and the 'local') limiting. In this light, the somewhat ungainly concept of the Rescaled Competition State Regime is deployed as a more accurate representation of the fluidity of scalar structuration, and as a mid-level concept that draws together the experiences of European cities despite the apparent diversity of their 'growth machines'.

While the focus is on the meso-level of patterned and systemic transformations, Brenner (2004: 22) is keen to emphasize that this should 'not be constructed as a denial of the institutional diversity that can be readily observed at the concrete level'. Rather, while notions of institutional convergence are challenged by persistent diversity at the concrete level, the meso-level illuminates the shared 'context of context' within which this diversity unfolds, highlighting the constitutive relations that tie local specificities together in the *uneven but systematic* restructuring of urban governance (cf. Peck and Theodore, 2007). This meso-level approach does not come along with prescriptive methods but rather *methodological orientations* that inform how theory and empirics can be mobilized to reveal the mediated and dialectical relationship between general processes and particular outcomes.

Multiscalar methodologies

The cross-case methodology of NSS highlights not only the systematic restructuring of urban governance, but also the 'interscalar' relations through which the urban is constituted. As such, it reflects a decade-long attempt to refine the conceptualization of scale. In order to counter the tendency in traditional accounts of the state to reify scale (i.e., methodological territorialism) and thus mask 'the profound mutual imbrication of all scales' (Brenner, 2004: 7), NSS mobilizes a 'multiscalar methodology'. Drawing on geographical scholarship on the political economy of scale (see Smith, 1992; Swyngedouw, 1997), Brenner argues that scales never exist independently; rather, they are shaped relationally 'in terms of [their] upwards, downwards and sidewards links to other geographical scales situated within tangled scalar hierarchies and dispersed interscalar networks' (2001: 605). These ongoing (socially produced) scaling processes are temporarily stabilized in 'scalar fixes' – the set of historically and geographically specific institutional forms and practices 'through which each [historical] round of capital circulation is successively territorialized, deterritorialized, and reterritorialized' (Brenner, 1998: 461).

To explain how the state is reconstituted at the subnational scale through the urban policy interventions of the Rescaled Competition State Regime (RCSR), Brenner (2004) reconceptualizes urban governance as a phenomenon exceeding 'local' governance in cities, and extending to larger (and uneven) processes of urbanization associated with all scales of state activity. In contrast to the 'methodological cityism' (cf. Angelo and Wachsmuth, 2015) of those approaches to urban governance that explain the rise of urban entrepreneurialism as 'localized, often business-led, responses to newly imposed, supranational economic constraints' (Brenner, 2004: 254), urban governance is understood as multiscalar politics. As a result, urban policy is seen to encompass any state activity aimed at regulating the uneven process of urbanization, including regional development policies, systems for fiscal redistribution, and the construction of infrastructure networks.

It is here that the continuities between NSS and the concept of planetary urbanization become most clearly evident. As a generalized methodological orientation, the shared emphasis on the multiscalar in NSS and planetary urbanization shifts attention from what Brenner (2001: 599–600) calls a 'singular' notion of the politics of scale – examining urban questions strictly localized within cities – to a 'plural' alternative, focusing on how cities are positioned in processes of 'production, reconfiguration or contestation of particular differentiations, orderings and hierarchies *among* geographical scales'. Aiming to open up geographical imaginations of the urban, planetary urbanization echoes this call to pay attention to the 'churning of urban configurations at all scales' (Brenner and Schmid, 2015: 165, italics in original).

In reconceptualizing urban governance in terms of the interscalar regulation of capitalist restructuring and as a process through which the state apparatus has been rescaled, NSS shows that the dialectical relations between scales are central for understanding the production of the contemporary urban condition. It is through multiscalar methodologies that the co-constitutive role of cities as drivers and outcomes of this broader process can be revealed. However, this approach does not come without some risks and tradeoffs, to which we now turn.

Methodological limits

Brenner's (2004) creative mobilization of the urban as a locus for (multiscalar) state restructuring and as a methodological orientation for analyzing pan-urban processes has secured the status of NSS as an original and influential text. In reviews, it has been referred to as one of the 'most stimulating' and 'seminal' works of urban research (Le Galès, 2006; Walks, 2006). Yet, while Brenner's methodological approach enables us to understand the tendential and systemic changes impacting a wide range of places, his mobilization of meso-level analysis carries with it some significant risks – namely, a relative lack of attention to concrete agents and social forces (Beauregard, 2006; Martin, 2006).

This partly relates to Brenner's use of methods. In order to overcome the expositional challenges of theorizing across (many) cases, NSS relies heavily on secondary sources. Abstract theorization tends to take precedence over the concrete investigation of specific institutional settings and policymaking domains at the 'local' level. Brenner's treatment of national rescaling processes is illustrative: he mobilizes a range of case studies of urban governance trans-formations by seemingly accepting secondary material and policy documents at face value, going on to condense these into text-boxes in order to illustrate a set of larger arguments concerning systemic shifts in state spatial selectivity. Mostly absent here is any real concern with the fraught processes of imple-menting policies, the account tending to blur the distinction between policy ambition and actually existing outcomes. This compromises the meso-level dialectic between the concrete and the abstract, with the appearance of abstract theories of the nature of statehood driving the argument, and empirical change largely there for illustration and validation.

While Brenner (2004: 22) anticipates that '[e]xperts on specific states, regions, and cities may find that [NSS] neglects important contextual details', this means that his generalizations are vulnerable to critique from those oper-ating on a more concrete level. Such critiques can, however, always be leveled against attempts to theorize from multiple cases, particularly if they vary as widely as Western Europe. In order to engage with the book's method on its own terms, a more apt critique would shift focus from a concern with local diversity to instead interrogate the issue of abstraction itself; in particular, ask-ing whether a focus on the meso level of conceptual abstraction is suitable for understanding the state as dynamic, undetermined, and socially produced.

Drawing on a strategic–relational approach to the state, Brenner cites Jessop's (1990: 270) influential formulation: 'the power of the state is the power of the forces acting in and through the state'. However, NSS gives the reader only a sparse sketch of the character of these forces. The level of abstraction that is privileged does not place much explanatory weight (or devote much expositional space) to socio-political forces and conflicts, and to the specific actors and institutions involved in these. While Brenner (2004: 16) repeatedly refers to 'political and territorial struggles' over state spatial selec-tivity, evidence of the substantive social and political content and consequences of these struggles is notably lacking. By focusing primarily on the production of patterned state forms, Brenner relegates the political – in its more visceral, social, and granular form – largely to the background, mostly subsuming con-crete contradictions and struggles under the churn of structural transformation.

This omission undermines Brenner's conceptualization of the state: focusing on meso-level trends rather than concrete institutional analysis limits his ability to go beyond state-centric explanations. Instead of giving the reader a sense of the social forces that surround and animate the restructuring of the state, it appears as if the 'state' itself becomes the agent of rescaling. This approach paradoxically reifies the state as a self-conscious and monolithic actor, despite continual references to the contrary.

This black-boxing of the state also has implications for the revelation of political alternatives. In the concluding chapter, Brenner highlights – by way of secondary accounts – some of the alternative political rescaling strategies (e.g., neighborhood-based anti-exclusion projects, metropolitan reform programs, and inter-urban networking initiatives) that have emerged in response to the uneven development of RCSRs. Rather than generating progressive alternatives, Brenner argues that such experimentation represents a form of crisis-management to the regulatory failure of urban locational policies, co-opted by powerful interests and contributing to de-politicization. Yet, while noting the need for progressive political alliances 'to locate strategic openings within the institutional landscape of RCSR' (2004: 301), his treatment of these cases as already subsumed in the institutional folds of RCSR runs the risk of obscuring the processes and politics through which they emerged, perhaps foreclosing opportunities for unearthing such alternatives.

This notable absence of concrete-level analysis has more to do with the challenge of operationalizing this framework than with its methodological injunctions. Indeed, analysis of meso-level processes must be coupled with careful investigation of the concrete ways in which they are co-constituted across scales in order to account for socio-spatial outcomes, as well as the potential for change. As Brenner recognizes in his later work, multiscalar analysis must 'spiral dialectically among the relevant levels of abstraction in order, simultaneously, to deepen theoretical understanding ... to illuminate meso-level tendencies ... and to decipher concrete-historical conjunctures and struggles' (2009a: 129). A multiscalar methodology must further take account not only of the local and national but also of supranational scales of governance as well (cf. Swyngedouw, 1997). Yet, despite Brenner's attempt to capture the most important institutional changes in urban policy, governance, and the churning 'scalar structuration' of Western Europe, the European Union (EU) is largely absent from his analysis. While he foregrounds national-state restructuring as a response to the economic pressures of the 'European Single Market', without concrete discussion of the EU as a supranational administrative apparatus, the analysis remains underdeveloped in terms of this vital dimension.

Coda: methodological lessons and the future of urbanization

NSS stands as a significant contribution to critical urban studies that has opened up new avenues for examining and understanding the co-constitutive nature of state transformation and the urban process under globalizing capitalism. It has boldly staked out the position that urban studies need not be a secondary venture to scholarship on economy and society writ large. According to Brenner, urban scholars are well placed to tackle questions of contemporary capitalism and its restructuring through time and space. The book invites urban studies scholars to embrace multiscalar methodologies that do not assume the fixity of scales, nor dismiss their real effects as the complex outcome of social practice. This is more than a question of methodology. To understand the urban as a scaling process is also to reveal how possibilities for political action are conditioned, constrained, and enabled by the ongoing production of scalar fixes. In other words, it is to understand the material constraints on political action and to foreground the need to generate progressive political projects that are socially reproducible in the face of powerful countervailing forces. The goal of such an approach is to enable a critical urban theory that can 'excavate the emancipatory possibilities that are embedded within, yet simultaneously suppressed by' modern capitalism (Brenner, 2009a: 203).

Furthermore, Brenner's approach encourages scholars to be attentive to the empirical and theoretical scope (and scale) of their analyses, suggesting a way to mobilize the *meso*-level as a critical space for analyzing the mediations and tensions between the concrete and the abstract. This is a plea for reflexive abstraction. Yet, operationalizing these methodological lessons involves some tradeoffs, including the expositional challenges of accounting for multiple cases and regimes, coupled with a certain risk of downplaying the role of concrete social practices (and all their contingencies), along with the scope for political alternatives. The gap between the empirical analysis that Brenner offers and the potential of his theoretical intervention reflects the difficulty of striking a dialectical balance between the abstract and the concrete when operating at the meso-level. Nevertheless, the methodological lessons that the book offers outweigh these risks. The extensive scholarship catalyzed by *NSS* highlights its productive influence on the critical social sciences, with numerous studies taking up the challenge of examining the actually existing dynamics that received less attention in the original formulation (see Boudreau et al., 2007; MacKinnon and Shaw, 2010; Smart and Lin, 2007). These contextual applications of Brenner's framework have filled out some of these under-specified facets in his story, highlighting the role of political struggles in particular. They demonstrate the need for engaged and critical dialogue between complementary scholarly approaches as well as across levels of conceptual abstraction.

Finally, *NSS* can be read as a precursor to the planetary urbanization thesis in that it anticipates and encapsulates many of the epistemological concerns of the latter framework. In particular, its critique of 'methodological nationalism' and treatment of the dynamic and multiscalar nature of transformations in urban governance parallels the critique of 'methodological cityism' advanced by planetary urbanization. Yet, planetary urbanization goes further, arguing for a systematic analytical delinking of urbanization from the bounded unit of the 'city' in light of what Brenner and his colleagues understand as the continued extension of urban processes on a planetary scale. As a result, it has been widely critiqued for allegedly subsuming the diversity of urban experiences under an all-encompassing umbrella, and erasing the constitutive outsides against which capitalist urbanization, and urban theory, have long been defined (Peake et al., 2018).

Polarized debates around planetary urbanization have been marked by misunderstandings concerning the level of abstraction at which the argument is mobilized as well as the particular claims to generalization that are made. Responding to criticism against the purportedly universalizing assumptions of their claims, Brenner and his colleagues insist on the inescapably (and significantly) variegated nature of planetary urbanization, as well as the meta-theoretical nature of their undertaking. Far from seeking to 'explain everything', their goal is to develop a framework for exploring the dialectical interplay between the changing nature of urban processes on the one hand and the concepts through which these transformations are understood and explained on the other. Yet it remains the case that while variegation and relationality have been invoked at the epistemological level, the methodological strategies for the operationalization of these somewhat abstract principles have been less well specified. This exposes the planetary urbanization thesis to overdrawn critiques of theoretical totalization and universalization, leaving much of the subsequent debate polarized along the lines of unhelpful dualism between generalization and difference (Goonewardena, 2018).

The methodological injunctions of NSS can be instructive for overcoming this impasse. Working at the meso-level, combining abstraction with concrete research necessarily entails mobilizing a variegated analytic that does not render the particular incompatible with the general, but seeks to articulate their mutual interconnectedness. Rather than simply a form of generalization that identifies empirical similarities in different contexts, the meso-level allows Brenner to construct a relational account of how localized regulatory experimentation and continent-wide processes are coproduced, for instance, through RCSRs. In his view, identifying such meso-level commonalities 'is entirely consistent with an insistence upon continued empirical diversity and politico-institutional variation among those contexts' (2004: 22).

Returning to NSS in this moment helps to highlight the potential of planetary urbanization as a framework for grasping socio-spatial dynamics behind 'urban' processes far beyond the city itself, and the implications of this for revealed patterns and parameters of local diversity. It does so by mobilizing the meso-level and scalar mediations as domains for relational analysis. In this sense, revisiting NSS may provide the planetary urbanization thesis with a more solid counter to claims that it is melting 'the city' into air. Urban studies – planetary or otherwise – has to traverse a difficult methodological and empirical terrain in order to reveal the relational unity that binds general processes with their co-constitutive differences. *New State Spaces* is a powerful methodological argument for why multi-scalar relations and meso-level commonalities are indispensable way-stations for such a journey.

10

ETHNOGRAPHY IN THE BOUNDARY ZONES: ON ROBERT FAIRBANKS' *HOW IT WORKS*

Samuel Nowak and Tom Howard

KEYWORDS: everyday urbanism, neoliberal urbanism, postcolonial cities, urban governance, urban informality

In his book *How It Works: Recovering Citizens in Post-Welfare Philadelphia*, Robert P. Fairbanks II presents an analysis of 'urban poverty management' (Wolch and DeVerteuil, 2001), unearthing the mechanisms and relations by which poor, addicted subjects are enrolled into the regulatory project of social welfare retrenchment and self-governance. Fairbanks (2009: 13) takes as his focus the city's recovery house 'movement' – an unregulated, for-profit archipelago of informal institutions based in Philadelphia's burgeoning supply of vacant row homes, which offer temporary housing and self-help 'recovery' programs for poor drug addicts and alcoholics. Fairbanks' focus is twofold. At the municipal level, he is concerned with how the institution of the recovery house has managed to both endure and proliferate across Philadelphia despite an absence of formal regulatory oversight and a serial failure to produce 'recovered' subjects. At the level of **everyday urbanism**, Fairbanks analyzes how neoliberalism is reproduced through the subjectivities of poor addicts themselves as they navigate recovery programs based on principles of personal responsibility and self-governance. With close analytic detail and robust theorization, *How It Works* excavates the ambiguous space of the recovery house, charting the dilemmas and contradictions expressed in its relationship to the self, the street, the city, and the state.

Fairbanks' study draws on both meso-level institutional analysis and a wealth of micro-level ethnographic research conducted between 2002 and 2004. His primary focus for the latter is Always Have a Dream (AHAD), a pseudonymized recovery house located amidst persistent clusters of racialized poverty in Philadelphia's Kensington neighborhood. In bringing together a broader tapestry of political economic restructuring with street-level insights from one of the city's estimated 400–500 recovery houses, Fairbanks also attempts to bridge long-standing but resurgent debates in urban studies on epistemological approaches, methodological priorities, and research agendas. The space of the recovery house appears for Fairbanks as a site where everyday life intersects with macrostructural forces, self-governance converges with neoliberal statecraft, biopower articulates with state regulation, and theories from the global South meet northern contexts. Put otherwise, Fairbanks conceptualizes the recovery house as a sort of 'boundary zone' of urban theory and practice: an ethnographic case located at the intersection of seemingly opposed methodological and theoretical orientations, capable of supporting mutual exchanges between them. By analyzing recovery houses through a combined frame of regulationist-inspired political economy, Foucauldian notions of governmentality, and postcolonial conceptions of informality, Fairbanks' analysis aims to create generative exchanges between diverging scales of analysis, communities of inquiry, concepts of power, and geographical divides. This chapter is concerned with the following question: to what degree does Fairbanks' ethnographic methodology enable him to facilitate links between competing, or even conflicting, research practices and priorities?

The title of the book *How It Works* operates on multiple registers. On one level, Fairbanks is concerned with how recovery houses 'work': the actors, subjectivities, activities, value systems, and policies that allow for their reproduction. Yet on another, he is also concerned with their persistent failures in terms of individual recovery. Fairbanks details how relapsing individuals are trapped between low-wage work, the predatory tendencies of the recovery house market, and spatially concentrated poverty. Failure to 'recover' then leads to regulatory encounters with the state through the criminal justice system, workfare programs, and the social welfare system, in effect producing a new mode of poverty management based on spatial containment and self-governance. In short, Fairbanks investigates how it works, even when it does not. In this chapter, we take our lead from Fairbanks in considering how his ethnographic method 'works' on two registers. On the one hand, we examine the strengths of Fairbanks' method insofar as it enables him to pull together disparate conceptual and methodological approaches in urban studies. On the other, we consider what the limitations of his approach can tell us about the enduring challenges for ethnographies of urban poverty, and current debates in urban theory.

Constructing a dense site of poverty management: recovery and regulation

How It Works follows the story of AHAD and its operator, Malik,[1] as he struggles to convert an abandoned row house in Kensington into a functioning recovery house. After following the workings and tribulations of AHAD's first 18 months of operation, Fairbanks expanded his purview beyond AHAD to engage in participant observation at 10 other houses and in-depth interviews with an additional 25 residents and operators throughout the neighborhood (2009: 11). Complementing this street-level ethnographic research, Fairbanks also conducted in-depth interviews with officials from various regulatory institutions, and analyzed popular media sources. In interpreting this data, Fairbanks brokers a conceptual rapprochement between governmentality studies and state regulation theory, arguing that recovery houses persist through the (re)production of a system of power/knowledge that aligns with the post-welfare urban restructuring in Philadelphia. The analytical and conceptual work of this core argument proceeds through describing three interrelated, multiscalar forms of urban poverty management. We take each in turn to briefly summarize the book's arguments.

First, Fairbanks details the workings of the recovery house market as an organizing force for recovering bodies. The vestigial form of welfare provision known as recovery houses was first enabled by the Pennsylvania Welfare Reform Act of 1982, which created a new category of destitution that allowed for 'chronically needy' substance abusers involved in licensed treatment to receive $205 for nine consecutive months[2] in General Assistance (GA). Dramatically insufficient for a single individual, when pooled together this sum supports a market for collective living: an individual can rent, buy, or appropriate one of Philadelphia's estimated 30,000 abandoned row homes, start a 'recovery program', and begin to collect around $205 for each client they can house. 'Bodies', as Malik puts it so simply, 'is what makes it work' (Fairbanks, 2009: 44). Market competition for addicted bodies creates downward pressure on operators and compels a search for cost-savings practices. Resultant configurations of 'overcrowding, property neglect, interhouse competition, coercion and exploitation of clients both in-house (volunteer labor) and externally (via day-labor sub-contracting)' effectively transfer risks from operators to other inhabitants (Fairbanks, 2011b: 2568). Such practices generate a core tension within recovery houses that resurfaces throughout the book, namely, between the 'programmatic idealism' of the recovery concept and the 'economic pragmatism' of cutting costs to increase revenue (Fairbanks, 2009: 41).

Second, recovery house operators (re)produce a particular form of poverty politics – 'imaginaries, representations, and judgments of who is poor and why, as well as laws, rules, policies, and everyday practices that govern class subjects' (Elwood et al., 2015) – that ascribes addiction and poverty to personal and moral failure. Transformation into responsible and productive members of society through techniques of self-governance thus comprises the milieu of recovery houses. Inhabitants are subject to a disciplined schedule, compelled to attend their outpatient treatment, expected to 'give back' through free labor, and are informally case-managed by operators to re-enter the wage labor market, open a bank account, pay child support, or apply for Section 8 housing. Drawing on theories of governmentality, Fairbanks shows how these technologies of the self constitute 'recovering' subjectivities, 'first as pathological subject, then as modern citizen' (2011b: 2562) who takes responsibility for their own poverty. In this sense, he argues that recovery house operators like Malik become 'able partners' of welfare retrenchment and neoliberal devolution, insofar as they reformulate subjectivities compatible with these projects (2009: 143).

Lastly, Fairbanks explores the strategically selective non-intervention of the local state – the ways in which the city benefits from the continued lack of regulation for recovery houses and, further, how regulatory inaction itself operates as a mechanism of statecraft. Through interviews with city officials, Fairbanks shows how recovery houses provide an inexpensive alternative to the rental market by effectively 'warehousing' homeless addicts who would otherwise be on city streets, inadvertently contributing to the city's anti-blight campaign to fill vacant row houses. Fairbanks sums it up concisely:

> [w]ho else would take homeless drug addicts and alcoholics in off the street … house them for less than $205 a month … and feed them three times a day on $139 in food stamps? In what other housing situation would these addicts also be monitored and *required* to attend formal drug and alcohol treatment? (2009: 208–209, emphasis in original)

Further, he shows how the recovery houses' ambiguous status extends regulatory mechanisms into the lives of poor addicts, if not the house itself. Thus, rather than 'unregulated spaces', Fairbanks theorizes recovery houses as the product of multiple, overlapping regulatory forces: the formal addiction treatment sector, welfare discipline, the carceral state, workfare programs, and the predatory market of the recovery houses themselves (2009: 230).

Ethnography shoulders a heavy load for Fairbanks' prosecution of these arguments. Within his methodological formulation, ethnographic practice in the boundary zones can pull together conflicting epistemological traditions and concepts, problematize them through grounded empirical research, and refine them to make general claims about urban processes, all while avoiding the representational and ethical challenges of ethnographies of urban poverty. The remainder of this chapter assesses the extent to which Fairbanks is successful in these goals and, where he is not, what this can tell us about the state of urban theory and the enduring challenges of urban ethnography. We proceed in two parts. First, we situate the book in a longer tradition of the challenges faced by ethnographies of urban poverty, before turning to the question of how

Fairbanks responds to them. Second, we interrogate Fairbanks' ethnographic reflexivity – how he critically reflects upon the relations of power between himself and his participants, and between himself and the field of urban studies. By way of conclusion, we distill these arguments into two methodological lessons we learn from Fairbanks: the importance of critical ethnography for theory refinement in an era of conceptual proliferation; and the continuing need for reflexive attention to the effects of power in ethnographic practice.

Urban ethnographies of poverty and their 'perennial pitfalls'

Ethnographies of poverty have a long tradition in urban studies, with significant impacts on urban policy and the politics of welfare provision in US cities.[3] Reflecting on these histories, critical poverty scholars have argued that much academic 'poverty knowledge' influencing popular discourse and public policy has tended to reflect anxieties about the purportedly essential social habits of often racialized, poor communities (Goode and Maskovsky, 2001; O'Connor, 2001). Such approaches have ignored the impacts of economic restructuring and institutional racism, thus obscuring the structural dynamics of urban poverty. Equally important, they have produced moralizing, pathologizing accounts that have reinforced biases and discrimination of the urban poor (cf. Howard et al., Chapter 11).

In a particularly incisive polemic, Loïc Wacquant (2002: 1520) links these 'perennial pitfalls of urban ethnography' to a disconnection between ethnographic practice and a reflexive approach to theory. Without subjecting empirical findings to theoretical scrutiny, and vice versa, Wacquant contends that researchers tend to uncritically report (rather than analyze) their subjects' perspectives and 'folk theories'; mold their data to preconceived notions or political goals; or structure their analysis around dominant public discourses of poverty instead of theoretical concepts (Wilson and Chaddha, 2009). Wacquant furthermore argues that these tendencies not only undermine the potential for critical understandings of social oppression, but also are complicit in the production of poverty knowledge that bolsters neoliberal **urban governance** and punitive forms of urban poverty management. Alongside earlier critiques, Wacquant's intervention – and the subsequent rounds of debate that it provoked – raise a series of pressing questions for urban ethnographers: What is the relationship between ethnographic observation and theory? How do asymmetrical power relations inform relationships between us and our subjects, the knowledge we produce, and our field of study? How do we construct a middle path between naive empiricism and theoretical predetermination?

Aware of such critiques, Fairbanks grapples with these long-standing methodological, representational, and political challenges. As he writes, 'to confront the problems of urban ethnography that long preceded it, this book integrates two approaches to welfare and urban analysis that have developed in relative isolation from each other: studies in governmentality and welfare state regulation theory' (2009: 20). In this formulation, regulation theory guards against romanticizing the agency of the poor while 'a governmentality approach has the potential to address the traditional pitfalls of moralizing or pathologizing the poor that have long plagued urban ethnography, precisely by opening us up to the ways in which liberal governance ... presupposes rather than annuls the agency of poor subjects' (2009: 20). It is with this conceptual framework that Fairbanks attempts to chart a path through pitfalls of ethnographic studies of urban poverty in order to investigate how the production of 'recovering' subjectivities articulates with the broader political economy of welfare retrenchment in Philadelphia.

In this sense, Fairbanks argues for a theoretically guided ethnography that remains open to conceptual revision and extension. As he writes elsewhere, 'I am suggesting that we engage in ethnographic fieldwork that is in a sense *already theorized* ... but nonetheless still capable of inductive work at the level of general claims-making in order to build theory' (2012: 562; our italics). Such theoretically primed – and theory-generating – ethnographic practice is, of course, the basis of Michael Burawoy's (1998: 16) extended case method in which '[w]e begin with our favorite theory, but seek not confirmation but refutations that inspire us to deepen that theory.' The extended case method 'deploys participant observation to locate everyday life in its extralocal and historical context' through extending observations in the field over space and time to understand social processes and, subsequently, from social processes to macro-scale social forces – all while deepening the theory with which the researcher began (Burawoy, 1998: 4). Fairbanks implicitly mobilizes the extended case method, working to construct a boundary zone case that can refine some leading analytics of urban theory – regulation theory, governmentality, and informality – through linking street-level analysis to structural forces without falling prey to the perennial pitfalls of urban ethnography. The methodological, conceptual, and empirical goals Fairbanks sets for himself are therefore considerable.

Though demanding, Fairbanks mostly rises to the task. Recovery houses provide a strong case for integrating regulation theory with insights from governmentality. His ethnographic analysis shows rather than explicates how 'self-craft' articulates with 'statecraft' in ways that make the long-standing debates between these epistemological traditions seem almost overstated (cf. Barnett, 2005). In doing so, he offers a substantial empirical and theoretical contribution to understanding poverty management under **neoliberal urbanism**, while also attending to how street-level actors (re)produce a poverty politics of self-regulation. Methodologically, Fairbanks navigates through the hazards of urban ethnography with great skill. He does not sanitize or overlook activities that do not fit neatly into a representation of urban poverty that best serves his political interests. Rather, he constantly fact-checks his subjects stories, often providing insightful analysis of discrepancies between his subjects' narratives and empirical observations (see, for example, Fairbanks, 2011a: 29). Nor does he simply perform a photo-negative analysis by swapping the trope of the irrational, immoral poor subject with a righteous paragon of morality. Instead, he wades into the ambiguous moral boundary zones of recovery house operators and inhabitants, upending preconceived binaries of moral/immoral, deserving/undeserving, and street/decent. What emerges on the other side is a complex exploration of the multiscalar dimensions of subjectivity, recovery, welfare reform, urban governance, and poverty.

Reflexivity and ethnographic practice

While Fairbanks implicitly references the extended case method as his guiding methodology, he is relatively silent on its methodological limitations. Burawoy (1998: 22–25) terms these the 'effects of power': the ways relationships of unequal power inevitably shape the process and practice of ethnography through *dominating* and *silencing* research participants, and *objectifying* and *normalizing* complex social processes into seemingly static 'categories that can be investigated, sites that can be evaluated, people that can be controlled' (1998: 24). Within the text, Fairbanks largely obscures these relationships of power in that he does not critically reflect upon on how his own positionality as a researcher might have led to the domination and silencing[4] of his participants. In short, the book lacks a certain depth of ethnographic reflexivity, referring to 'an awareness of reciprocal influence between ethnographers and their settings and informants ... [and] self-conscious introspection guided by a desire to better understand both self and others through examining one's actions and perceptions in reference to and dialogue with those of others' (Anderson, 2006: 382). This section interrogates the methodological implications of this lack of explicit self-reflexivity in the text.

Ethnographers cannot avoid *domination* in gaining access to subjects and in relating to them during fieldwork (Burawoy, 1998: 22). On both accounts, Fairbanks obfuscates these processes. Nowhere does he reveal how he gained access to the recovery house network, outside mentioning that he met Malik through Bilal (though we are not told how he met Bilal, also a recovery house operator). If, as Burawoy (1998: 22) suggests, 'entry [into a social group] is often a prolonged and surreptitious power struggle between the intrusive outsider and the resisting insider', then we do not see even glimpses of how Fairbanks 'struggled' to gain access to the recovery house network. Fairbanks is also remarkably silent on how his positionality as a white, comparatively wealthy, educated man impacted his fieldwork in predominantly poor, minority neighborhoods. Only occasionally does he acknowledge his outsider status. His whiteness, for example, is mentioned only in passing, as in a case where Malik walks him to the train station under the pretense that 'Tuesday is rob the white boy night' (Fairbanks, 2009: 107). In the text, Fairbanks moves

on immediately from this remark without using the ethnographic encounter
to reflect on how his experience of the recovery house network and/or interactions with Malik may have been shaped by asymmetrical power relations
and structures of social domination.

This leads to Burawoy's second effect of power, *silencing*. As an ethnographer 'extends' observations over space and time, they abstract many events
into social processes. In doing so, the ethnographer inevitably privileges some
voices, processes, and relationships while marginalizing or excluding others.
This process has methodological as well as ethical considerations. As Burawoy
(1998: 23) writes, '[s]ince silencing is inevitable, we must be on the lookout for
repressed or new voices to dislodge and challenge our artificially frozen configurations, and be ready to reframe our theories to include new voices.' In this
regard Fairbanks is less successful. For example, gender is rarely discussed. On
the one hand, given that recovery houses are separated by gender, and AHAD
is a 'men's house', this is understandable. On the other, the number of 'women's
houses' in the city is nearly the same as, if not larger than, men's houses, yet
readers are rarely afforded a glimpse into the experience of women in recovery
(Fairbanks, 2011a: 37). Moreover, when the experience of women is mentioned it is almost exclusively in reference to Blanche (Malik's wife), yet, even
then, her opinions and experiences are most often filtered through Malik's
words (see, for example, Fairbanks, 2009: 77). Though the process of abstraction into social processes inevitably silences, Burawoy reminds us of the
methodological significance of remaining constantly open to recalibrating our
understandings through the inclusion of other voices, a point which Fairbanks
does not take up.

Reflexivity demands critical consideration not only of the ethnographer's
positionality in relation to participants, but also of the relationships between
the ethnographer, their communities of inquiry, and the geographies of theory.
In recent years, postcolonial scholars have challenged the universal assumptions
of urban theories emerging out of the North Atlantic region, arguing that 'the
distinctive experiences of the cities of the global South can generate productive
and provocative theoretical frameworks for all cities' (Roy, 2009: 820).
Perhaps the most important conceptual innovation of this project has been
theorizing **urban informality**. Drawing on this literature, Fairbanks shows the
co-constitution of the informal and formal regulatory mechanisms that operate through recovery houses, arguing that 'urban informality becomes both an
effect of retrenchment logic and an instrument of an ever-transforming matrix
of state regulatory power' (2009: 227). In short, he demonstrates what Ananya
Roy (2003a: 138) calls territorialized flexibility – 'a context of regulatory
ambiguities that allows the state and political parties tremendous flexibility in
controlling the poor'. Counter-intuitively, the ambiguous relationship between
recovery houses and formal regulatory structures serves a regulatory function,
insofar as it contains addicts within institutional circulations between the carceral
state, low-wage labor markets, welfare administration, and the self-disciplinary
poverty politics of the recovery house.

Yet, despite his heavy reliance on concepts emerging out of postcolonial urban theory, Fairbanks is remarkably silent about this body of literature as such. He does not explicitly situate the concept of territorialized flexibility within its postcolonial origins, nor does he describe its relationship to the Euro-American urban theory – that is, as emerging out of the conceptual limitations of the Euro-American canon in explaining urban processes in **postcolonial cities** (Roy, 2003a; 2016). This is a lost opportunity to make connections between the geographical and theoretical divides of urban studies. Ethnographies in US cities so rarely draw on theories emerging from outside of the North Atlantic region, most frequently producing and refining concepts that cyclically speak back to 'mainstream global urbanism' and reinforce its often insular nature (Sheppard et al., 2013). In conceptualizing informality as a form of statecraft, Fairbanks poses 'Third World questions of the First World' (Roy, 2003b: 466) but does so without making those connections explicit. Whereas he emphasizes repeatedly that *How It Works* builds bridges between regulation theory and governmentality, the conceptual linkages he constructs across the geographical divides of urban theory are understated, but no less significant. Fairbanks shows the possibility for ethnography to do so, but obliquely in that he neglects the methodological importance of reflexive attention to the relationships between place, theory, and power.

Conclusion

We close with two interrelated methodological lessons learned from the strengths and weaknesses of *How It Works*. First, the book is a compelling example of the capacity of critical ethnography to refine leading analytics of urban theory, while successfully navigating its representational and political pitfalls. Fairbanks offers a rich case of neoliberal poverty management that documents the ways in which everyday urban informality deepens state regulation. Methodologically, the challenge here is always to connect how processes of urban restructuring reach into the lives of poor subjects, even as the state devolves responsibility for welfare provision. Ethnography is well suited to providing evidence for this claim often explicated in institutional political economy, but only occasionally shown through grounded empirical research. As Jamie Peck et al. (2013: 1094) write, 'there are few substitutes for theoretically informed ethnographic approaches that use contextualized investigations to illuminate the operations and projections of neoliberalization.' *How It Works* offers a persuasive example of how ethnographic methodologies might offer great potential for reworking our understandings of (neoliberal) urban governance and urban restructuring (Fairbanks, 2012).

Second, the mandate of theory refinement must not be taken up at the cost of ethnographic reflexivity on effects of power. The nullification of the effects of power is a receding horizon, necessary to travel toward, but never fully attainable. To reach for that horizon is to be reflexive and explicit about unequal relationships of power in our research practice, and to critically question the ways in which they render our ethnographic knowledge partial. By omitting more substantive reflections on his own positionality and the power-laden geographies of theory, Fairbanks reminds us of the importance of ethnographic reflexivity and explicit attention to the effects of power at multiple scales.

Ultimately, *How It Works* operates in the boundary zones of urban theory and practice, as an area of overlap, exchange, and co-constitution. At the beginning of this chapter, we questioned the extent to which Fairbanks' ethnography in the boundary zones enabled him to build generative connections between disparate conceptual traditions in urban studies. Throughout, we have argued that he is in large part successful. He persuasively forges ethnographic linkages between governmentality and regulation theory; street-level description with structural forces; and theory with observation. Breakdowns in exchange, however, occur at two points: between the researcher and self-reflection on the effects of power; and between the geographical divide of postcolonial concepts and North American urban ethnographies. Yet, in both the connections he makes in the boundary zones and the breakdowns, *How It Works* holds valuable lessons for ethnographers of urban poverty. As urban theory continues to develop at a high level of theoretical abstraction, critical ethnography holds great promise for grounding and refining the ever-growing field of conceptual innovations. In *How It Works*, Fairbanks demonstrates this potential, but also reminds us that it will not be realized without also reaching for the receding horizon of nullifying the effects of power in ethnographic practice.

Notes

1. As with most operators, Malik is also a recovering addict.

2. According to his informants, GA recipients are easily able to informally extend this for up to five years (Fairbanks, 2009: 90).

3. We draw on American cases here for their salience to our argument, while at the same time acknowledging that academic studies of urban poverty in other contexts – such as the monumental study coordinated by Pierre Bourdieu (1993), focused largely on French cities – have been likewise influential beyond the academy.

4. Fairbanks is more attentive to normalization and objectification, but less so to domination and silencing. For purposes of space, we expand only on the latter two as examples of how Fairbanks fails to make explicit how the effects of power shaped his ethnographic practice.

11

ETHNOGRAPHIC EXCHANGES: ON PHILIPPE BOURGOIS'S *IN SEARCH OF RESPECT*

Tom Howard, Samuel Nowak and Fernanda Jahn-Verri

KEYWORDS: comparative urbanism, everyday urbanism, postcolonial cities/ subaltern urbanism, uneven urban development, urban governance, urban informality

Introduction: cities in crisis

In 1985 Philippe Bourgois moved with his family to an East Harlem tenement, intending to research 'the experience of poverty and ethnic segregation in the heart of one of the most expensive cities in the world' (Bourgois, 1995: 1). Budgetary austerity in the aftermath of New York's 1970s fiscal crisis had by then withered what remained of a local social safety net, while long-roiling processes of deindustrialization and economic restructuring had meanwhile evaporated large swathes of low-barrier, well-paying jobs across the city. Though the majority-Puerto Rican East Harlem had long been a site of racialized exclusion and concentrated poverty, deteriorating economic conditions had been associated with deepening poverty and widening social divisions in the neighborhood in the years preceding Bourgois's arrival. Initially, Bourgois imagined his still-protean study would focus on how residents negotiated these pressures through a repertoire of informal subsistence tactics. Within a year, however, it was evident that one informal sector played a dominant role in defining the social life and supplementing the incomes of East Harlem residents: an emergent underground economy centered on crack cocaine.

Bourgois would spend the next five years conducting ethnographic research with a community of Puerto Rican crack dealers and users in the neighborhood. The culmination of this research is his landmark ethnography, *In Search of Respect* (1995). Through extensive participant observation in the tenebrous spaces of East Harlem's crack economy – much of which took place in a drug house disguised as a video arcade – Bourgois elucidates the dynamics of structural oppression and cultural meaning-making that shape his informants' struggles for dignity and subsistence. The social reproduction of marginalization, rather than illegal drugs per se, is Bourgois's central focus. Drawing from the cultural production theories pioneered by Pierre Bourdieu (1980) and Paul Willis (1977), Bourgois outlines how his informants navigate both entrenched racial hostility and the pressures of New York's post-Fordist transition through what he terms an 'oppositional street culture'. By constructing a political economy of the conditions of emergence, causal logics, and generative effects of this culture, *In Search of Respect* shows how marginalization both within and beyond East Harlem's crack economy is shaped by subjective negotiations of broader structural forces.

Attempts to locate the relative role of culture in reproducing oppression raise several pressing questions about the politics of representation and theory construction. In his prefatory remarks to *In Search of Respect*, Bourgois acknowledges that such inquiries risk confirming 'culture of poverty' stereotypes, which ascribe the condition of poverty to the supposed pathologies of the 'unworthy' poor (1995: 16). By situating the **everyday urbanism** of 'oppositional street culture' within broader historical currents and political economic structures, Bourgois seeks to destabilize pathologizing narratives and relativize the agency of his informants. Against the consolidated hegemony of moralistic victim-blaming in popular discussions of poverty and drugs, however, Bourgois constantly guards against constructing a narrative that supports the actual oppression of his research subjects.

In recent years, similar concerns have been central to a growing critique of mainstream urban theory. Drawing variously from postcolonial and feminist approaches, numerous critics have assailed the normative assumptions and epistemic foundations of prevailing urban-theoretical frameworks as extensions of neocolonial ways of knowing and acting in the world (Derickson, 2015; Leitner and Sheppard, 2016; Roy, 2016). Among other concerns, these critics have questioned the universalizing analytical frames that have been applied to urban processes in the so-called global North and South; the problematic ways in which the latter are often represented; and the relation between these phenomena and material processes of marginalization (see Parnell and Robinson, 2012; Peck, 2015; Sheppard et al., 2013). We argue in this chapter that *In Search of Respect* provides critical resources for confronting two ethico-political challenges raised by these debates.

Our discussion proceeds in two parts. The first part considers Bourgois's reconstruction of cultural production theory as a tool for addressing presumptions that cities in the global North and global South are characterized by essential(ized) differences which make them fundamentally incomparable. We argue that Bourgois's method of following changing cultural practices across disparate geographies opens up new horizons for **comparative urbanism** and relational analysis that can productively disrupt such binaristic and obstructive geographical imaginaries. We then explore the politics of representing the relationship between marginalized groups and their conditions of oppression. Here, we suggest that *In Search of Respect* illustrates how efforts to represent this relationship in non-sensationalist, three-dimensional terms are constrained by issues of positionality and research design. Inasmuch as the violence of structural oppression is an unavoidably distressing phenomenon, we position *In Search of Respect* as something of a 'limit case' for representational politics.

Transnational tensions

While recent postcolonial-inspired critiques of urban theory cultures are diverse and irreducible to a single agenda, they are animated by several common themes and concerns (Derickson, 2015). One central line of critique focuses on how most available urban theories have been based on research in a small coterie of European and North American cities. Critics argue that the *explananda* and *explanans* of conventional urban theories are structured to reflect (select) Euro-American experiences, thereby falsely universalizing certain causal forces – such as the interplay of **urban governance** structures and capitalist imperatives – as a monist basis for explaining urban dynamics globally (Parnell and Robinson, 2012; Roy, 2016; Sheppard et al., 2013). Among other consequences, these norms underwrite pervasive 'assumptions of incommensurability' between cities across global North–South lines (Robinson, 2011a: 15). Global North cities are accordingly positioned as not only the normative reference points for urban modernity, but also the 'natural' terrain for constructing generalizable urban theories. By contrast, **postcolonial cities** in the global South are conventionally rendered as developmentally deficient iterations of, or deviations from, 'normal' urbanization patterns, unsuited for the development of broader theory claims (McFarlane, 2012). To the extent that such sites are considered appropriate for theory building, they are often related through exoticized concepts (such as megacities, **urban informality**, and peri-urbanization) rarely extended back to the metropolitan heartlands of the urban-theoretical mainstream.

New forms of comparative urbanism tracking across global North–South boundaries are a productive starting point for reconfiguring these geographical imaginaries. Rather than seeking lateral contrasts and empirical variations between cases, such comparisons might focus on the common processes and mutually transformative flows – of capital, population, policy expertise, and the like – through which cities are connected (Robinson, 2011a, 2016; Sheppard et al., 2013). Attending to these connections can both stress-test established presumptions regarding causality and disrupt received notions of unbridgeable difference between outwardly dissimilar cities (Peck, 2015; Robinson, 2016). While *In Search of Respect* was not explicitly formulated as a comparative exercise, we argue that it nevertheless contains important lessons for bringing seemingly incongruous research sites into 'stronger analytical and not simply empirical relation' (Robinson, 2011a: 15; cf. Bok, Chapter 17).

The foundations of this approach are found in how Bourgois weaves the material context of Puerto Rico into his analysis of post-Fordist East Harlem. Most of his neighbors and research participants are 'Nuyoricans' descended from the 1.5 million Puerto Rican migrants – nearly a third of the island's population – arriving at New York City in the two decades following World War II. Many of these earlier migrants were smallholding peasants and semi-subsistence farmers displaced by US-sponsored land reforms, whose labor was subsequently absorbed by New York's manufacturing sector in its twilight years. A significant portion of these uprooted Puerto Ricans would have been considered *jíbaros*, a cultural identity evoking 'traditional' social values – autonomy, patriarchal authority, and community solidarity bound by webs of interpersonal *respeto* (respect) – associated with rural subsistence livelihoods.

Noticing that young men in his study sometimes refer to each other and themselves as *jíbaros*, Bourgois asks his central informant, Primo, a low-level dealer, to explain. Primo's response points to how *jíbaro* identities and diasporic experiences shape subjective self-identification of second-generation migrants: 'My father was a factory worker. It says so on my birth certificate, but he came to New York as a sugarcane cutter. Shit! I don't care; fuck it! I'm just a *jíbaro*. I speak *jíbaro* Spanish. *Hablo como jíbaro*' (Bourgois, 1995: 52). There are multiple connotations to *jíbaro* identity. On the one hand, the term carries 'an ambiguously pejorative connotation', signifying social backwardness in a similar manner to the English term 'hillbilly'. On the other hand, in the face of 'foreign influence, domination, and diaspora', Bourgois (1995: 5) argues that the figure of the 'ruggedly independent subsistence farmer' has emerged as a symbol of 'Puerto Rican cultural integrity and self-respect'.

By collecting oral histories with Primo and his colleagues, Bourgois explores how young Nuyorican men rework categories of identity received from rural Puerto Rico within the seemingly 'incommensurable' context of New York's formal institutions. His informants relate a common experience of shame and rejection in their recollections of primary school. In the eyes of a 'mainstream, middle-class, white-dominated bureaucracy', affections and dispositions learned from transplanted *jíbaro* parents – accents, language skills, and even bodily comportments – are misapprehended as signs of insolence, low intelligence, uncooperativeness, or some combination thereof (1995: 174–177). Censure from teachers and authority figures is experienced as a profound violation of cultural dignity and personal respect, to which Bourgois's informants respond through expressions of an 'oppositional culture' characterized by transgressive language, open disobedience, sexual profligacy, petty crime, and violence (cf. Willis, 1977). Several of these young men also begin selling drugs in school not only to compensate for their parents' limited means, but also to achieve a sense of masculine authority and relative autonomy.

The challenge of securing respect is likewise seen in the attempts of these men to enter a formal economy practically antithetical to the terms of *jíbaro* identity. Both subsistence farming and the macho shop-floor cultures of factory production provide arenas for realizing and expressing a relative sense of independence, mutual respect, and masculine authority (Willis, 1977). In the context of deindustrialization and economic restructuring, however, the most readily available job opportunities for Primo and his cohort are found in 'feminized' low-level office work. Drawing on Bourdieu's (1980) notion of symbolic capital, Bourgois argues that such jobs demand high levels of tacit knowledge regarding contextually 'appropriate' forms of speech, appearance, and physical comportment. The dearth of outlets for class or cultural solidarity (such as unions) within low-level service and office-support jobs compounds serial racialized humiliation in these workplaces, where an absence of 'Anglo, middle-class cultural capital' leads bosses and colleagues to perceive Bourgois's informants as incompetent, threatening, or even illiterate (Bourgois, 1995: 145). As 'males who are socialized not to accept public subordination', they struggle to manage workplace discipline, particularly from women (1995: 115). Reprimanded by a female boss for answering the phone at an office job ('because objectively a Puerto Rican street accent will discourage prospective clients and cause her to lose money'), Primo expresses how the internalized humiliation imposed by chronic disrespect is reworked into both misogynistic rage and reaffirmations of 'Puerto Rican-ness' as an oppositional strategy:

> There are so many different kinds of people out there in New York City that've got a crazy accent. ... But that bitch didn't like my Puerto Rican accent. ... I used to answer it pretty well, man. But then after that – after she dissed [*disrespected*] me – when I did pick up the phone, I used to just sound Porta'rrrrican on purpose. (Bourgois, 2003: 145–146)

Such experiences draw upon and reinforce oppositional cultural identities which had earlier emerged as both 'a triumphant rejection of social marginalization and a defensive ... denial of vulnerability' (2003: 158). While offering a bulwark against recurrent traumas of class and race-based humiliation, these cultural identities predispose the men for 'the systemic and effective use of violence' demanded and rewarded by crack economy employment (2003: 24). Through its structures of violent discipline and *compadre*-style kinship networks – which act as central organizing principles for managing risk and securing loyalty – the crack economy thus offers a forum for (self-destructively) realizing the forms of respect, autonomy, community, and power demanded by *jíbaro* culture. While binging on cocaine with Primo, fellow dealer Caesar offers the following assessment on his recent decision to cease looking for work in the service economy: 'Really, I'm happy with my life. [sniffing] Like no one is bothering me. I got my respect back' (2003: 118). This reflection underscores Bourgois's argument that East Harlem's street culture is an ironic force that both rejects and reaffirms structural oppression. While its oppositional valences provide terms for asserting masculine dignity and securing subsistence (qua crack economy employment), they ultimately foreclose (admittedly scarce and remote) opportunities for upward mobility in the formal economy.

Like the cultural production theorists upon whom he draws (Bourdieu, 1980; Willis, 1977), Bourgois renders oppressed subjects as active (if unintentional) participants in their own structural oppression, rather than passive victims. The crucial innovation of his method, however, lies in how he illuminates the diasporic connections behind the 'oppositional' culture central to this process. By showing how the subjective terms of cultural identities from rural Puerto Rico are reworked against the objective political economic pressures of post-Fordist New York, Bourgois sketches what Cindi Katz (2001) calls 'contour lines': lines of connection which maintain the distinctiveness of separate places while showing their mutual imbrication in a common process (such as globalization, **uneven urban development**, colonial rule, etc.). Bourgois's contour lines do not join two explicitly urban places. Yet much like the way global South cities appear in mainstream urban theory, rural Puerto Rico appears decidedly incommensurate with New York's paradigmatic aura of urban modernity (cf. Robinson, 2011a). Insofar as Bourgois highlights the ways in which each of these sites plays an active role in the production of both subjective experience and material economic circulations, Puerto Rico and New York are rendered as jointly constituted, relational geographies.

This method could be extended to comparative studies involving global North and global South cities. Rearticulations of cultural identities and practices among the mobile subjects traversing such contexts – such as globe-trotting policy consultants, NGOs, investment professionals, peripatetic labor forces, and displaced populations – can be used to draw relational ties across them, thereby undercutting notions of unassailable difference or hermetic disconnection. Given the length of time required for Bourgois to build access and rapport within a single research site, the question of ethnographic depth available for research across multiple contexts is indeed an open one, particularly in a field that 'remain[s] dominated by "lone scholar" models of enquiry and generally small-scale collaborations' (Peck, 2015: 170). Attempts to use such models of inquiry to draw relational contour lines, particularly across contexts of violence and deprivation, must furthermore confront numerous representational dilemmas. It is to these we now turn.

Representation at the margins

The dislocations of post-Fordist transformation and pervasive social suffering were not the only crises shaping the project behind *In Search of Respect*. In a

context of revanchist welfare reform and accelerating War on Drugs milita-
rism, popular discussions of poverty and drug use had been dominated by
victim-blaming narratives, polarizing around issues of self-worth and personal
responsibility (Katz, 1996). By Bourgois's estimation, a protracted crisis of
representation in his home discipline of anthropology (see Clifford and
Marcus, 1986) had meanwhile compelled academics to retreat from studying
the relations between social agency and racialized urban poverty. Fearful of
confirming racialized stereotypes or ascribing marginality to personalized
moral failures, Bourgois argues that researchers had by then succumbed to an
imperative to 'sanitize the vulnerable' by endorsing roseate 'representations of
the oppressed that those who have been poor, or lived among the poor, know
to be completely unrealistic' (1995: 15).

Recent rounds of feminist and postcolonial urban research have likewise
critiqued how scholarly and popular discourses of marginality tend to polarize
around the binaries of victimhood and heroism. Critics argue that although
invocations of structural oppression are often intended to counter reactionary
forms of victim-blaming, such gestures risk glossing the agency of marginalized
populations (Varley, 2013; Schütte, 2014). The sensationalist, quasi-apocalyptic
terms often deployed in mainstream discussions of global South poverty have been
subject to particularly acute critique in this regard. Among other effects, framing
poor districts in cities of the postcolony as 'rapidly emerging doomscapes' effaces
the organizational capacities, political demands, and mundane community-build-
ing practices of oppressed groups, reducing their experience to passive victimhood
(Benjamin, 2008: 722; McFarlane, 2012). By the same token, however, attempts to
subvert such narratives by lionizing the qualities of poor subjects – or (mis)reading
'resistance' into their everyday practices – also produces distorted representations
of poverty. Effusive celebrations of subaltern creativity and resilience not only risk
minimizing the effects of social marginality, but furthermore obscure how
structural oppression is reproduced at the level of lived experience (Roy, 2011).
These critiques highlight how the task of overcoming jejune binaries of victimhood and heroism amidst marginalized groups are paralleled by the challenge of
accounting for social suffering without minimizing or spectacularizing its effects.

Ananya Roy (2011: 232) has argued that these unhelpful binaries can be
overcome by attending to the 'paradoxical forms of social agency' that
characterize subaltern urbanism. In Search of Respect can be read in such a
way, illustrating how oppositional street culture and the crack economy provide figures like Primo and Caesar with 'alternative[s] to their own social
marginalization', but in so doing often transform them into 'the actual
agents administering their own destruction and their community's suffering'
(Bourgois, 1995: 143). The question of how to represent this suffering, however,
is a challenging one. If Bourgois's subjects actively participate in their own
marginalization, how can their experiences of suffering and violence be
depicted without vilifying their behavior or sensationalizing their plight?
And whose voices should be recognized and represented in these depictions?

These issues are brought into sharpest relief when Bourgois confronts the gendered dimensions of violence in East Harlem. Where Nuyorican men experience 'rapid historical structural transformations as a dramatic assault on [their] sense of masculine dignity', Bourgois observes an emergent 'crisis of patriarchy' which 'expresses itself concretely in the polarization of domestic violence and sexual abuse' (1995: 215). Denied status in their domestic lives as bread-winning father figures and humiliated in workplaces by female bosses, some of these men lash out at wives and girlfriends. But such patterns of domestic abuse build on learned structures of misogyny that are irreducible to economic pressures alone: in discussing public-schooling experiences, for example, Bourgois finds that many of his subjects have participated in gang rapes as part of their adolescent socialization. Through these brutal rituals, Primo, Caesar, and their male peers bond over violent assertions of patriarchal dominance and position sexual violence at the center of their developing senses of (threatened) masculinity.

Bourgois openly airs his uncertainty about how to proceed with these violent histories. Reticent to create a 'forum for the public humiliation of the poor and powerless', and fearful 'readers would become too disgusted and angry with the crack dealers and deny them a human face', he admits that there was a temptation to omit them. But considering that the prevalence of rape is masked by social taboos preventing its discussion, Bourgois ultimately concludes that 'a failure to address sexual violence in street culture would be colluding with the sexist status quo' (1995: 207–208). The dynamics of gender relations in East Harlem, alongside Bourgois's own subject position and research design, impose substantial limits on this commitment. His informants relate their histories as rapists only after he has earned their *confianza* (trust) through long-term participant observation in male dominated spaces such as the video arcade. Where his informants' marginalization entails a crisis of masculine authority, private conversations with women might have appeared improper, suspicious, or even lascivious. Though Bourgois eventually secures interviews with a handful of rape survivors, he cannot forge the 'kinds of long-term relationships with these individuals to allow for the detail and confidence of a meaningfully contextualized life-history interview or conversation' (1995: 207). Still committed to confronting the problem of sexual violence, Bourgois runs the risk of reinscribing the enforced silence of rape survivors by relating their stories only through the voices of male perpetrators and complicit witnesses.

The structure of Bourgois's analysis reflects his struggle with this dilemma. To avoid lapsing into sensationalist retellings or accusatory moralizing, he contextualizes rape within both broader structures of patriarchy ('there is nothing specifically Puerto Rican about rape') and the specificities of a *particular* crisis of masculinity situated in East Harlem, where it exists on a spectrum of violence ranging from gendered insults to physical abuse (1995: 208). He also follows his expositions on sexual violence with two chapters outlining how crack and masculinist street culture articulate with struggles over changing family structures and women's access to public space. Aside from highlighting the 'structurally induced wrenching of traditional gender roles' accompanying the breakdown of the male-dominated *jíbaro* household, these chapters allow women to emerge in more complex, three-dimensional, and dynamic ways than that of the textually mute(d) victim (1995: 215).

An example is found in Bourgois's extended analysis of Candy, a mother of five, on-and-off lover of Primo, intermittent crack dealer, and survivor of chronic abuse at the hands of lovers and family members alike. To supplement sporadic formal economy wages, Candy assumes a leading position in a local crack network after shooting her then-husband during one of his serial episodes of domestic violence. The respect garnered by this act allows her to participate in the otherwise masculine spaces of crack-copping corners and the video arcade, where Bourgois builds rapport under the distant supervision of male drug dealers. Through extensive interviews and observations of her domestic life with Primo, Bourgois narrates Candy's struggle for respect and economic autonomy against cycles of enforced conjugal dependency, dysfunctional bureaucracies, ongoing domestic violence, and shifting familial responsibilities. Candy employs a diverse range of survival strategies to manage violence, including romantic elopement, drug use, bargaining with public officials, and both emulations and inversions of masculine street culture. Highlighting the ambiguous and contradictory relationship between these strategies and structures of patriarchal authority conveys a complex ensemble of responses to trauma that are reducible to narratives of neither heroic resistance nor passive victimhood.

Candy's narrative is important, but also exceptional. It takes Bourgois over two years to construct a sufficient level of *confianza* to conduct his first tape-recorded interview with her, which he is still compelled to conduct within eyesight of Caesar. Candy's unique position in the crack economy creates opportunities for securing her confidence and discussing issues of intimacy and violence in a manner otherwise beyond Bourgois's reach. At one point, Bourgois elicits the collaboration of Eloise Dunlap, a black sociologist colleague, to conduct joint interviews in the hope that her gendered and racialized positionality might help him attain access to a broader community of women. While this effort provides material for a parallel project (Bourgois and Dunlap, 1993), the challenges of forging deep rapport through this strategy – to say nothing of collaborating with another researcher committed to their own full-time agenda – are evinced by Bourgois's sole reference to it (1995: 284). To the extent that Bourgois can secure access, he incorporates the voices of women from a variety of subject positions, including spouses and (grand)mothers, the homeless and precariously housed, addicts and dealers, and teenagers and the elderly. These maneuvers helpfully expand the range of subjectivities typically considered in poverty research (cf. Varley, 2013), but in comparison to the extended quotations and visceral details characterizing his narration of men's lives, Bourgois's accounts of women's lives are tellingly composed of abbreviated observations and quotes lacking the detail generated through long-term trust.

In his attempts to uncover what Roy (2016) calls 'paradoxical forms of social agency' among the oppressed, Bourgois encounters patterns of violence that plainly challenge ethical as well as expositional conventions. Beyond Candy's narrative, he struggles to represent the experiences of the women who are most vulnerable to the violence associated with the crisis of masculinity in East Harlem. If his earned trust with the neighborhood's men allows him to capture the paradoxes of their agency, his inability to secure access and rapport with a larger group of women leaves him unable to fully overturn the victim/hero binaries to which they are subject. Here, *In Search of Respect* illustrates how both the confines of single-author research designs and (unavoidable) discrepancies between the positionality of ethnographers and their subjects ineluctably constrain representations of social marginalization. Collaborative research designs incorporating researchers from diverse subject positions surely have a role to play in pushing these boundaries and recovering more comprehensive expressions of social agency. Articulating the links between structural pressures (such as situated crises of masculinity) and patterns of violence is furthermore a viable, if limited, strategy for deemphasizing the sensational qualities of social oppression.

Fully avoiding sensationalism is, however, a far more intractable problem. As evinced by *In Search of Respect*'s narrative, 'suffering is usually hideous; it is a solvent of human integrity' (Bourgois, 1995: 15). The potential for sensationalist readings of social misery can be suppressed, as through Bourgois's contextualizing moves, but never fully effaced. Yet 'to ignore or minimize' either the gravity of social suffering or conditions of its reproduction – even when it implies marginal groups themselves – is, as Bourgois argues, to be 'complicitous with oppression' (1995: 12). There are no easy or comfortable terms for representing extreme cases of deprivation and violence. Yet there is more political value to be found in compromised accounts of oppression than in the decision to avoid representing such processes altogether.

New geographies of theory

The politics of representation and academic knowledge production are complex, multifaceted issues. In this chapter we have focused on two issues that have been raised in recent critiques of urban theory: on the one hand, developmentalist presumptions of incommensurability between global North–South contexts; and on the other, a constellation of interlinked questions about representing marginality. With respect to presumed incommensurabilities across global North–South lines, Bourgois's strategy of following the changing cultural practices of displaced populations provides one potentially fruitful method for connecting and theorizing disparate geographical contexts. Ethnography is for Bourgois the basis of this project insofar as it offers a robust platform for relating abstract political economic forces to the terrain of embodied, culturally mediated experience. Here, categories of social identity are taken less as markers of irreducible or essentialized difference than as historically and geographically particular phenomena that provide opportunities for unravelling diasporic relations across time and space. These 'contour lines' (Katz, 2001) can in turn illuminate the shared geographies of metropole and (post)colony, rendering them decidedly more 'commensurable'.

In Search of Respect offers a less certain, but nonetheless crucial, response to representational dilemmas. While cultural production theory offers a means for short-circuiting distorted, binaristic framings of oppression, Bourgois's analysis demonstrates how such research can entail confrontations with patterns of violence that are at once difficult to represent in non-sensationalist terms, yet politically necessary to confront. Bourgois responds to this challenge by situating violence within broader structural conditions and life trajectories, showing how violence articulates with broader processes of identity-formation and meaning-making. But where women are the most structurally vulnerable cohort within Bourgois's research community, his access and a-fortiori ability to represent them are compromised by his own subject position. *In Search of Respect* can therefore be read as something of a 'limit case' for representational politics, insofar as it asserts that the causes and consequences of social suffering must be explored as an ethical imperative, while simultaneously showing how differences in positionality between researchers and their informants undermine such attempts. To the extent that *In Search of Respect* helps identify these limits, if not ways of managing them, it is a productive point of departure for reconstructing more robust, reflexive, and responsible approaches to urban inquiry.

12

GROUNDING THE HOUSING QUESTION IN LAND: ON ANNE HAILA'S *URBAN LAND RENT*

Kenton Card, Andre Comandon and Joseph A. Daniels

KEYWORDS: financialization, neoliberal urbanism, right to the city, the housing question, urban citizenship, urban governance, urban social movements

Urban Land Rent (2015) is Anne Haila's magnum opus on a Singapore's success in transforming the state institutions governing land, property, and markets over the past half-century. During this time, Singapore became a 'property state', wherein the government owns 90% of the land, providing 'affordable owner-occupied public housing for the majority of its population' (Haila, 2015: 4). Haila's designation of Singapore as a 'property state' signifies much more than sanctifying property rights; it also suggests the active deployment of land and property to achieve state objectives. In that process, she claims, Singapore outperformed most other cities in terms of per capita economic productivity – especially those fitting squarely into 'capitalist' or 'socialist' economic paradigms – while maintaining comparatively low unemployment rates. She explains this success through a revised and expanded land rent theory applied to a purely urban context.

Haila develops what we term a critical genealogical analysis of land, rent, and property that results in a powerful synthesis of urban land rent, illustrated through a historical account of the political economy of Singapore's city-state institutions. The broad scope and long-term engagement of her methodological analysis, neither purely qualitative nor quantitative, serves as an excellent expository through which to see a non-essentialist land rent theory in action. The craft of forming a meta-theory extrapolated through a real site – a purported actually existing alternative to **neoliberal urbanism** – makes an impressive contribution that others can learn from.

We begin by stressing why Haila's book centers land and housing within capitalism today. Next, we outline the structure of the book and its arguments. Then we summarize the methodological strategy of the book, discuss her twinned methodologies of a critical genealogy of rent theory and an institutional history of transformation in Singapore, and finally highlight ways that her methodology – while theoretically innovative and empirically illuminating – has limitations. Haila's *Urban Land Rent*, in addition to making substantial contributions to extending rent theory into current and future trajectories, provides a valuable example for developing a theoretical language that can be applied to empirical case studies.

Land and housing in capitalism today

Haila's most basic goal in *Urban Land Rent* is to impress upon the reader the importance of land in urban studies. Land, she postulates, has an inextricable connection to how modes of accumulation, techniques of capital extraction, and forms of **urban governance** regulation co-evolve under finance capitalism: a phase of capitalism where growth stems from leveraging and speculating on assets rather than commodity production. It is now commonplace to attribute the 2008 global financial crisis to the proliferation and default of risky, subprime mortgage loans, but urban scholars are only recently reemphasizing the roles of housing and land as central components of contemporary capitalism (Aalbers and Christophers, 2014; Saegert, 2016). Haila's strength is her breadth of approach, ranging from, for instance, Marxist urban theorist Henri Lefebvre to Keynesian economist Joseph Stiglitz, to understand Singapore and contemporary **financialization**-driven capitalism. While Lefebvre (2003) foresaw the shift from industrial production (the 'primary circuit' of capital) into real estate (the 'secondary circuit'), the role of land has remained a blind-spot among economists, like Stiglitz, who privilege the analysis of real-estate bubbles and strategies to mitigate their effects.

Haila's argument

Urban Land Rent proceeds in two stages. The first half unpacks the state of land rent theory, tracing various 'representations of land' (Haila, 2015: 21), or what we might think of as the 'mythology of land': the stories behind the various traditions of thinking about land. Myths ground 'theories of land' and how land becomes 'property', which ultimately 'justif[ies] landownership' (2015: 21). The second half traces Singapore's development, in which Haila embeds her analysis of land within a series of social institutions, actors, and

politics that meld into the unique 'preconditions' of Singapore's property state
and its subsequent 'housing success' narrative.

Haila examines how urban scholars have underemphasized the importance
of land and property over past decades (major exceptions include Harvey's
(1973) *Social Justice and the City* or Scott's (1980) *Urban Land Nexus and the
State*). Challenging the hegemonic position of neoliberal urbanism in academic
discourse on land restructuring, she destabilizes the 'blind faith' most urban
economists place in private property as an essential prerequisite to fluid land
market transactions. Influenced by Karl Marx, Friedrich Engels, and notably
Henry George, she centers the role of the state as essential to improving 'market'
efficiency.

Singapore functions as Haila's 'laboratory for testing land rent theory'
(2015: 19), chosen because of its unique combination of features relating to
land. The city-state has to contend with a scarce land supply within a confined
urban setting, maintains a high proportion of public ownership, and makes
substantial provisions for housing. Indeed, land functions within a political
'land logic', inscribed into the state apparatus by the People's Action Party (the
nearly unrivaled ruling party since independence in 1965). She works to
unravel *how* Singapore elides normative, false-dichotomous framings of urban
governance as 'capitalist' or 'socialist', and urban economies as 'free market'
or 'command', laissez-faire, or welfare.

Haila's examination of Singapore draws on the **housing question** as postu-
lated by Friedrich Engels (1872), which addresses the inadequacies in the
production and provision of affordable, decent housing in a capitalist economy
of low wages and unequal political power. She argues that Singapore has
'solved' the housing question because around 90% of the population (Singaporean
citizens or permanent residents) owned their flats by 2013 (2015: 101), most
of them in public housing. Whereas 'public housing' means state-owned housing,
for most urban scholars, she argues that the Singapore city-state has gradually
changed incentives through institutions that encourage the transition of tenure
from state-owned to a hybrid model that has most features of individual ownership. One example is the creation of a compulsory pension saving system, in
which residents can apply toward purchasing their flat, while preserving government control of the land (through approximately 99-year leases). This
process of rent 'manipulation' by the state is why Haila undertakes this extended
analysis of land rent theory and its contemporary relevance.

Methodology: land rent theory in action

Haila derives her theoretical inspiration from the political economy of land and
housing institutions. She uses a variety of methodological strategies to connect
her theoretical framework of land and rents to the evolution of Singapore as a
property state, with particular attention to critical genealogy and institutional

history. *Critical genealogy* unpacks concepts (in this case land, rent, and housing) from a variety of intellectual traditions, interrogates their assumptions, refines the terminology, and then illuminates material manifestations of those components. Once these intellectual fields are tilled, Haila works to sow the seeds through observing Singapore's governance practices. She unfolds her *institutional history* to tease out spatial–historical, material manifestations of land and housing practices, markets, and policies in Singapore through the lens of institutional changes. Contrasting her approach against 'single-city ethnographies and comparisons between cities', she aims 'to analyze land and land ownership, and explain urban development processes' (2015: 46).

Haila asserts that her approach is distinctive from those of other scholars researching Singapore, which she divides into four categories: from the West, from the East with an Asian cultural perspective, as a global city, and as a developmental state. For her, none of these provide satisfactory explanations for Singapore's success, in large part because they neglect the history and consequences of the city-state's governance of land.

Critical genealogy: the life of rent

Haila's methodology of *critical genealogy* is rooted in a process of categorical excavation, wherein she returns to alternative theories of property, and shows how they have not always been as marginal as they may seem today. For Singapore, she demonstrates how such a heterodox lineage can be more effective in elucidating the functioning of land institutions. Her other goal in tracing the genealogy is to develop a language that can be used in an 'intercultural, neutral, and general sense' (2015: 51).

Critical genealogy is a methodology of theoretical excavation. This is a technique that can stand alone (as demonstrated in Haila's (1990) previous writing), but is best used in tandem with an empirical application. Haila's overview of the rent literature is systematic, extracting meaning and theoretical constructs in a way that is instrumental to the empirical work to come. One of the key contributions of her critical genealogy is to destabilize contemporary paradigms, in this case: 'first to show the embeddedness of today's dominant justification story in European history and European philosophies; and second to introduce alternative stories' (Haila, 2015: 56). This involves an exhaustive engagement with a broad literature, historicizing the sources.

This is most readily illustrated in her critique of Douglas North's scholarship, which has been foundational in reemphasizing modern ideologies of property rights. Haila identifies several inconsistencies in the empirical and logical basis of his arguments, proceeding to refute them one by one with the support of relevant academic studies. As with every theoretical branch she engages with, the thoroughness and clarity of her critique forms the basis of her method. She breaks down the assumptions underlying North's theory into a set of points that she examines in turn. What sets her method apart is that she uses this process, central to any critical scholarship, to synthesize decades' worth of research and to organize relevant literatures via a uniform structure to support her argument (e.g., in the form of tables, for example). This allows her to mobilize the relevant literature to draw out the validity of a different conceptualization and even paradigm.

The crux of Haila's critique of North is the concept of 'efficiency', a concept that she returns to throughout the book to tell the story of Singapore in a more 'neutral' way. She uses the term to distinguish liberal economics from radical political economy. Liberal economics – in its classical, neoclassical, and neoliberal variants – emphasizes private property rights as foundational to individual incentives and fluid market transactions. She stresses the influence of John Locke, for whom property is foundational to individual liberty, focusing on North's claim that private property is more economically efficient than other forms of land ownership (2015: 34). Yet she also engages theories of land beyond 'neoclassical economics' (2015: 37–44), from Proudhon, Hume, Pufendorf, and Rousseau to Kant, who contest private ownership and situate land's 'propertiness' within social relations. For example, challenging the 'natural' notion that land must be privately owned, Hume recognized that 'property depends on the laws of society' (Haila, 2015: 37). Haila's methodology of reconstructing 'debates on genealogies' demonstrates that Locke's notion of private property, extended today 'to all sorts of alienable things and universalized as a hegemonic ideology' (Haila, 2015: 44), was contested and unascertainable among classical political economists.

To expand conceptions of property, Haila turns to Marx, Engels, and George. She is particularly concerned with land rent, arguing that 'rent theorists pay attention to social causes and consequences of land reforms', 'complicating' land and property by seeing 'rent as a social relation involv[ing] a power relationship and social control' (2015: 63, 59). Marx and Engels understood land rent as fundamentally a class relationship, arguing that land should be nationalized, which Haila considers a radical proposal because the government could most equitably distribute its usage. George was more politically pragmatic (Haila calls this progressive). Believing that nationalizing land would trigger catastrophic social conflict, George argued for taxing land, because 'rent is "unearned" and therefore would be legitimate to confiscate' (Haila, 2015: 55). A land value tax would be 'assessed on land values separately from the value of buildings and improvements … confiscating the land rent' (2015: 79, 67). Haila then connects land rent theory to urban development, painstakingly cataloguing and differentiating the diverse uses of rent (at least 13) of varying significance.

More than an exercise in theoretical exegesis, Haila challenges how concepts are often 'neutralized'. Her goal is to (re)define terms like rent-seeking or rent-manipulation so they can apply in places like Singapore with its fundamentally different conceptualization of property, without its system of governance being rendered deficient. Challenging its pejorative treatment in the literature, rent-seeking – the 'manipulation of the law or government in order to obtain profit' (2015: 58) – plays an important role in her institutional analysis.

Chapter four of her book serves as a pivot between the critical genealogy and the institutional history, blending key ideas from her theoretical excavation with the intellectual history of Singapore's leaders. For example, Haila connects George's political economy of land with Singapore through the history of two of the country's most influential leaders. She notes that Lee Kuan Yew, Singapore's first prime minister, who remained in office for over 30 years, and Goh Keng Swee, the second deputy prime minister, both attended lectures at the London School of Economics by Harold Laski, a Fabian socialist heavily influenced by the land economics of Henry George. This helps set the stage for understanding the fluidity of change in state institutions that she describes in the second half of her book.

Institutional history

One of Haila's central arguments is that Singapore's leaders were able to define a distinctive style of land efficiency through the rapid and versatile development of 'land institutions' to govern its economic and social uses. Unlike North's account of efficiency, which is entirely embedded within a capitalist and individualistic rights framework, she contends that Singapore demonstrates that an alternative conception is possible, based on balancing capitalist imperatives against social good. She examines the emergence of institutions designed to mediate the interactions between the state, global and national capital, and residents. Her analysis of institutions focuses on the context shaping their emergence and the issues precipitating change, including the role of actors working to shape the institutional trajectory of the country.

Haila's account of institutional change, focused on unintended consequences and endogenous change, is congruent with traditional forms of institutional analysis in political science. Yet, she attempts to shift the focus from political power to 'problem solving'. She highlights the pragmatism of Singaporean politicians and developers, sometimes at the expense of a more nuanced understanding of institutional stickiness and contestation.

This is clearly visible in her chapter 5, where Haila uncovers the institutional webbing connecting different aspects of policy, government, and economics with the housing question. Haila moves quickly from one institution to the next, stating the problem and the solution as if one followed fluidly from the other. In the process, she offers illustrations of her theoretical framework on the ground and deploys it to explain the situation in Singapore.

Haila seamlessly narrates the state-led institutional reforms, additions, and adjustments implemented to adapt to changing economic and demographic circumstances facing Singapore, drawing a direct connection between the ideological content of these institutional changes and the radical European land rent theories known to its policymakers. This is animated through secondary historical sources, newspapers (mostly English language), demographic data, policy analysis, and direct observation. By combining these sources, she creates a comprehensive picture of how the diverse organizations became involved in realizing the state's institutional vision.

Haila analyzes the role of institutions in shaping land use through a focus on statutory boards, government-linked companies, and globally operating investment corporations. Her 20-year engagement with the city, formally and informally interviewing numerous officials, developers, bankers, and civil servants, enables a rich analysis. At the same time, the narrative often includes parallels to comparative cases with which Singapore shares important institutional features, especially China and Hong Kong, but also European countries in order to illustrate where Singapore departs from such conventional housing typologies as with the inverse relationship between the size of the public housing sector and homeownership.

Haila argues that this sprawling institutional complex has enabled the state to facilitate the ease of entry of international businesses through clear expectations and low establishment costs, to ensure that land is devoted to the right mix of industrial, commercial, and housing uses to keep the costs of labor reproduction low (enhancing attractiveness for investors), and to tamp down land speculation. Noting how mainstream economists have extensively utilized rent-seeking to explain the supposed shortcomings of Asian economies, particularly their lack of entrepreneurialism (2015: 122), she argues that while Singapore's developer lobbies use political manipulation, the institutional context within which they are embedded prevents them from acquiring monopoly rents. In making land available only through auctions, the state can impose restrictions on how land can be used, and for how long. Paradoxically, this heavily regulated land market is thus critical to insuring that the state can flexibly match land use to land needs through densification and redevelopment. It also prevents speculation by putting a timeframe on development (avoiding vacant lots) and restricting resales within five years, limiting property flipping. Halia argues that these anti-speculation rules were significant in enabling Singapore to bounce back very quickly after the 1997 Asian financial crisis (2015: 205). Simultaneously, she suggests, Singapore's economic success has resulted from a coupling of land regulations with smooth business practices, allowing domestic or international companies to enter the city and invest quickly.

While urban economic theory might suggest that this approach would be inefficient, slowing economic growth due to over-burdensome management, Haila argues that Singapore has demonstrated an actually existing 'correct mixture' of highly regulated urban environment that can foster economic growth. Through this analysis, she seeks to provide a framework for understanding not only land governance in Singapore, but also one that is relevant for other cities.

Limitations of Haila's methodological strategy

An unfinished genealogy

Haila's methodological choices align with a specific set of goals. She set out to synthesize land and rent theory and apply it to an overlooked aspect of one of the most puzzling case studies of modern urban development. Her larger goal is to provide the foundation for theorizing across land and rent paradigms, proposing a framework for elucidating state-led development and individual property rights systems. The book is a step in this direction, not a complete blueprint.

With regards to transcending intellectual boundaries, Haila asserts that she is offering an alternative to the four dominant lenses through which Singapore has been analyzed. Yet there is a sense of irony when she equates the western theoretical lens with the property rights framework, only to use another set of European thinkers to develop her alternative. In essence, she is bringing a western framework marginalized in the European context to the context of Singapore, where it provides novel insights.

The land rent theory that she develops is incisive, opening new avenues of inquiry into Singaporean exceptionalism. Yet this is in tension with her stated desire for her approach to be applicable to other cities. In one sense, Haila fails to engage with a genealogy that takes the position of her case in Singapore seriously, to consider alternative approaches to 'property' that do not fit her fourfold typology. Singapore is exceptional because it offers a way to 'purify' an abused or maligned rent theory, but she does not consider that a generalizable rent theory might require detours into non-western theory, only non-western empirics.

While *Urban Land Rent* brings insights into the synergy between land regulation and an ultra-liberalized market, her methods distort some of Singapore's complexity. For example, gaps remain in how the Singaporean version of homeownership relates to the private property rights framework. At the micro-level, the incentive structure the Singaporean system provides for individual homeowners and its implications for how they navigate the economic system are vague. This raises questions regarding the lack of fit with prevalent theories: is the mismatch theoretical, or is it due to Singapore's exceptionalism? Haila argues that Singapore is better understood through the lens of land rent theories, but what this approach obscures may be as important to understanding Singapore as what it illuminates.

Haila excels in showing how classical economists take for granted both institutions like property rights and the larger capitalist structure. Yet she does not demonstrate how rent theory is empirically superior to liberal economic accounts. Her laser focus on the role of land and property governance in Singapore's development makes her causal argument persuasive to the extent she shows that any account of Singapore's success would be incomplete without the factors she emphasizes. Yet this focus makes it difficult to see how her framework would perform better in a different context.

Top-down institutional history

Haila's methodology is less persuasive when she unravels Singapore's institutional history because much remains left out. As noted above, her primary empirical strategy is intermixing interviews, newspaper clippings, and secondary historical source material to present and analyze the emergence of this property state. There is considerable detail that is very precise and includes emergent themes relevant to land in contemporary urban studies (real estate investment trusts, securities, derivatives, anti-speculation strategies, etc.). Yet, whereas Haila emphasizes complementarities between the various political and economic systems, much of the data fails to connect to critical aspects of Singapore's development. In adopting a retrospective approach to Singapore, presenting it as a model state in resolving the housing question, she tends to present the road taken as a teleological trajectory, with no other possibilities, wrong-turns, or contestations.

Furthermore, Haila's institutional narrative fits into a classical approach to institutions where change is seen as the result of exogenous factors, a framing to which Singaporean state leaders themselves often turn to when rationalizing their actions. Given the expanse of institutions she covers, she cannot provide a more nuanced account of the fluctuations in power dynamics that shape all these organizations' and actors' incentives over time. For example, her chapter 5 lists the dozens of government agencies that were created to regulate land and housing, but without establishing clear parameters for their creation. This gives the impression that the state has been able to respond to changing conditions rapidly, sometimes predict problems, and unwaveringly adapt to new challenges. Yet such a trajectory seems unlikely in light of the apparent failures that both democratic and authoritarian (Rodan, 2012) regimes inevitably run into, including Singapore (for a discussion of the limits of the racial quota system, see for example Sin, 2002). This creates a kind of selection bias; because Singapore succeeded, Haila can retrospectively retrace all the correct steps.

This bias is reproduced in her choice of interlocutors for the interviews sprinkled throughout the text: primarily major figures. Her analysis thus lacks the perspective of non-experts, or attention to how resistance or **urban social movements** might have contested dominant institutions. She acknowledges the mass evictions that characterized Singapore's transition from a city of informal *kampungs* to one whose population became concentrated in dense, newly constructed, high-rise flats. Yet, by leaving no room for considering alternative possibilities, this implies that this end justified evictions as the means. The process itself was problematic and the outcome is not without salient concerns. The city mitigated evictions by offering displaced populations public housing and subsidies (Haila, 2015: 99), but this might just shift the question of displacement from access to housing toward political and cultural access to particular housing forms. For example, migrant workers are confined to poor dormitory-style housing, with little means to claim access to the housing they are responsible for building.

By definition, critical urban scholarship seeks to integrate the perspectives of the most dispossessed in cases where they are directly implicated. Less influential informants – such as tenants, marginalized citizens, and non-citizen migrant workers – should have been interviewed and would have likely enriched the conclusions. Singapore, like many other city-states with limited populations of citizens, has notorious issues with migrant workers who provide much of the day-to-day labor for the state, particularly in the construction industry that makes housing development possible.

Haila does not completely ignore the most precarious experiences, highlighting how immigrant laborers often live in overcrowded housing with 30 people sharing a flat. Yet she claims that Singapore has solved the housing question and that tenants have a **right to the city**, while seemingly omitting the perspective of those at the margins. This is best illustrated by the section she devotes to inequality in Singapore, which pushes aside potential issues in four short pages (2015: 165–169). Her argument here is unclear about whether the housing question has been resolved, or the right to the city achieved, for precarious populations who are clearly living in poor conditions with limited access to the city and basic human rights. Indeed, Engels' (1872) original discussion of the housing question criticizes dealing with the housing shortage by simply extending ownership of housing to the working classes, describing this as a bourgeois socialist solution that does not confront the real problem – the capitalist mode of production. In overextending her claims, Haila seems to be making the case that inequality has been adequately addressed in Singapore, displacing, if not silencing, dissent in the process.

Summarizing, Haila's political economy of land remains a top-down, somewhat functionalist analysis, failing to incorporate perspectives from those who her theory aspires to emancipate: the most vulnerable. Ananya Roy (2014) has written that the paradox of inclusive growth in cities like Singapore is that the city-state is ultimately dependent on an underside of immigrant labor who are silenced, displaced, and denied **urban citizenship**. In repeatedly highlighting the near universal access to public housing and ownership, questions persist as to who is left out. It might be suggested that the 'unfinished' nature of her genealogy of urban land rent in Singapore triggered the empirical blind-spots of Haila's institutional history. In framing her land genealogy so tightly around the Fabian socialist rent theory, justified by their (limited) connection to a very select few (albeit important) Singaporean elite, the analysis is set up as a top-down approach. Haila's conclusions raise a warning for scholars not to overstretch the implications of urban scholarship at the risk of silencing vulnerable populations or neutralizing broader language of urban emancipation. It is also important to emphasize, as Haila acknowledges (perhaps without sufficient emphasis), that Singapore's single-party 'democratic' system over the past half-century poses ongoing challenges for how to 'think through' the exceptionality of Singapore as an applicable case study for other cities as well.

Conclusion: a model to selectively replicate

Notwithstanding these concerns, *Urban Land Rent* is an inspiring example of a project demonstrating actually existing alternatives to failing urban governance policies associated with neoliberal urbanism worldwide, policies that have contributed to widening inequality. It also is a crucial reminder that urban studies and urban economics must fuse housing and finance in order to understand the central role of land within global capitalism.

Reflecting on Haila's motivations, it is important to reiterate her commitment to the production of knowledge within the tradition of critical urban scholarship. She demonstrates how one might seriously synthesize and extend a theoretical tradition in urban studies, while also illuminating those ideas through a multi-decadal research commitment to a globally oriented city-state. In systematically examining a broad scope of literature through the lens of the empirical issue of interest, she shows how to construct an original argument through which to approach empirical work. *Urban Land Rent* thus stands out as an excellent example of translating a theoretically informed perspective into an in-depth case study.

Haila's approach comes with important reservations, however. By overcommitting to a theoretical framework that privileges top-down analysis, her analysis obscures elements relegated to urban peripheries. In this era when urban theory is of such central concern, it is tempting for scholars to commit to a theoretical framework and then feel the need to fit their empirical findings within its confines, rather than approaching empirical work with an open mind – asking how empirics may challenge received theory. Haila's critical genealogy exemplifies this temptation, against which its limitations offer a warning. The problem is not methodological: institutional analysis is uniquely well adapted to studying issues of disparate power and representation and also tends to inductively breed theory from observed empirical regularities. But her institutional analysis is embedded within her theoretical commitment.

Urban Land Rent is an essential read for students investigating rent theory, housing studies, or the role of land and finance in cities today (and especially for those thinking outside the orthodoxy of neoliberal urbanism), but we recommend that readers proceed with caution. Haila's critical genealogy and institutional history serve well to illuminate urban land rent theory and Singapore as a 'property state', yet her conclusions remain contingent on her top-down approach.

13

MAPPING URBAN GOVERNANCE: ON YOU-TIEN HSING'S *THE GREAT URBAN TRANSFORMATION*

Tyler Harlan and Jaehyeon Park

KEYWORDS: displacement, right to the city, urban governance, urban social movements

You-tien Hsing's *The Great Urban Transformation* (2010) offers a new framework for understanding China's unprecedented experience of rapid urban expansion and rural land conversion. Since its publication in 2010, this work has invigorated theoretical debates about the nature of Chinese urbanism and inspired a number of empirical studies (Herrle et al., 2014; Meyer-Clement, 2016; Rithmire, 2013; Tang, 2015; Tomba, 2012; 2017; Wai Wong, 2015; Yeh et al., 2013). However, while Hsing's theoretical contribution has received wide attention, few studies have considered her methodology (for exceptions see Chuang, 2014; Fu and Lin, 2014; Song et al., 2016). Moreover, those studies that do engage with Hsing's methodology see her approach as a response to data constraints, rather than a conscious epistemological choice. The aim of this chapter, then, is to examine the thread that ties Hsing's underlying epistemological stance and theoretical framework to her chosen research methodology. The thread, in this case, is Hsing's spatial and territorial understanding of Polanyian political economy that she uses to unearth and map the complex nature of the urban land politics in China (indeed, the title of Hsing's book is inspired by Polanyi's masterwork *The Great Transformation*). We believe that Hsing's theoretical and methodological contributions are highly instructive for those engaged in the field.

Theorizing Chinese urbanization

Hsing's book captures a specific temporal–spatial transitional moment in China from the late 1980s to the 2000s. This period, called the post-Mao or reform era, was characterized by land marketization that was ignited by the enactment of the Land Management Law in 1986, followed by the establishment of the land leasehold market in 1988. These legal and institutional changes allowed the state to separate land use rights from their ownership rights in urban areas, thereby collecting land rents by leases. As urban land became lucrative, more and more farmland was converted to urban land. In the process, urbanization replaced industrialization as *sine qua non* of the central government's national development agenda.

A body of research from the early to mid-2000s seeks to analyze the form and dynamics of this rapid urbanization process (for example, Lin, 2002; Pannell, 2002). This scholarship views urbanization as a causal effect of macro-level forces from above, especially state policy. Pannell (2002) highlights population growth, rural-to-urban migration, and economic restructuring as the main drivers of urban change in China. Lin (2002) focuses on the number, size, population, and distribution of cities that resulted from political decentralization and economic policy shifts. Given their focus on the macro-level, however, these studies tend to overlook local-level interactions and contestations, with but a few exceptions. For example, in Lin's (2007) more recent work, he notes that the accumulation of cheap peri-urban land became increasingly attractive to municipal governments who needed extra-budgetary revenues following fiscal decentralization. Lin illustrates this new 'land-centered urban politics' by examining massive land conversion for non-agricultural purposes at the national level, and he calls for a central government response (Lin, 2007: 1832). Other studies in this vein include Guo (2001) on protests in rural China, He and Wu (2005) on **displacement** from inner-city redevelopment, and Read (2003) on homeowners' **urban social movements** in Beijing.

For Hsing, this view from above is insufficient to understand the temporal and spatial dimensions of China's rapid urbanization. Instead, she posits that urban transformation is shaped by the politics of control over land between different interest groups, and at different scales. Within their ill-defined administrative and jurisdictional boundaries, local governments and village cooperatives seek to expand their territory through urban construction. Social groups protect themselves from land confiscation and eviction through different strategies, ranging from land bargaining to outright resistance. Black markets for rural construction land abound in southern China, muddling established notions of the separation of rural and urban. Existing theoretical frameworks of China's urbanization fall short in analyzing what Hsing calls these 'muddy realities'.

Hsing's alternative theoretical framework draws heavily on Polanyian political economy. Polanyi (2001) recognized that market exchange is not a 'natural' way of organizing the economy; rather, he argued that the market is an instituted process, embedded in social relations. Polanyi's concept of 'double movement' recognizes that the marketization of society is often met with opposition from below. Here, Hsing applies the double movement of market–society relations in the context of urbanization instituted through the socialist land market, along with civic responses to urbanization. Drawing on Lefebvre's (1991) notion of 'space as a force', she views instituted urbanization as an exercise of territorial power that occurs across spatial units and scales. The novelty of this framework is that Hsing recognizes the symbiotic, ubiquitous relationship between urban space and local state power, or in other words, local state control over its territory. Expressed through state-led urbanization, this pervasive modality of state power is subsequently contested and negotiated by local actors. Hsing's (2010: 23) research questions are thus 'How does the state and society shape and become shaped by the unprecedented urban trans-formation of post-Mao China?' and 'How does space, in the form of territoriality, play a role in these contested processes?'

To answer these questions, Hsing views the metropolitan region as a dynamic container where players with different degrees of power struggle over territory, along with the meaning and form of **urban governanace**. In this conceptual model, the ability of local governments (and other holders of land use rights) to develop urban land is enabled and constrained by jurisdictional boundaries. However, local actors also seek to expand their territorial control through preemptive – and sometimes illegal – urban construction, such as the redevelopment of inner-city neighborhoods or residential construction on peri-urban farmland. This territorial control over land translates to increased state power, which drives local governments to pursue urban development at all costs – in Hsing's words, urbanizing the local state. It is competition over land between different levels of government and different spatial jurisdictions that drives the territorial dynamics that Hsing seeks to capture.

Hsing does this by conceptualizing a tripartite geography, consisting of the urban core, the urban edge, and the rural fringe. Within each of these zones, she identifies the main power actors from the state and society in urban governance, ranging from high-ranking state agencies to municipal, district, and township governments, inner-city protesters, village collectives, and dis-placed peasants. These are, in her view, the sites where the Polanyian double movement of instituted urbanization and civic response manifests through urban land politics. The juxtaposition of the state and civic groups in her tripartite urban geography is the conceptual model that she employs to advance her theory. As such, it is also the crux of her methodology as well as the main narrative structure of the book. In the following sections, we analyze how

Hsing arrived at this model through the interplay of theory and methodology, and the benefits and tradeoffs that such an approach involves.

Methodology: the co-construction of theory and method

Hsing's theoretical framework stresses the dialectical relationship between state and society on the one hand, and the territorial politics of urbanization on the other. This framework does not arise out of a singular method, or for that matter a case study of one field site. Instead, Hsing employs a mixed-methods, multi-site methodology, conducted over many years in different cities in China. Her methods consist of policy analysis, summaries of official statistics, and, most importantly, interviews and ethnographic observation with state officials, private developers, and community members across the city. Through these methods, Hsing aims to understand the subtle tensions and often extra-legal nature of land accumulation and dispossession through the eyes (and actions) of the actors involved. This type of grounded methodology is missing from much of the scholarly work on urbanization in China.

But it would be a mistake to see Hsing's methodology as simply proving or disproving a theoretical framework that she developed prior to going into the field. Rather, Hsing's theory and method are intertwined, in dialogue with the scholarly literature while building on one another to explain empirical phenomena. Burawoy (1998: 5) calls this approach a 'reflexive model of science', in which objectivity 'is not measured by procedures that ensure an accurate mapping of the world but by the growth of knowledge; that is, the imaginative and parsimonious reconstruction of theory to accommodate anomalies'. Hsing's work draws on the extended case method, the application of reflexive science to ethnography in order 'to extract the general from the unique, to move from the "micro" to the "macro", and to connect the present to the past in anticipation of the future, all by building on preexisting theory' (Burawoy, 1998: 5). Unlike a positivist approach to data collection, which tries to assemble data from a large number of cases in order to approach a state of saturation, Hsing's method examines a handful of cases from multiple perspectives, and then aggregates them into an understanding of social processes. Instead of appealing to notions of positivistic 'detachment' from research subjects, this reflexive approach actively confronts questions of positionality in both theory and method.

How does Hsing deploy this method while building her theory, using a relatively small number of case studies? In other words, how does she aggregate case studies into an understanding of social process – specifically the instituted process of the socialist land market? Here, we break down her approach into two types of triangulation: data triangulation and methodological triangulation. Data triangulation refers to the expansion of the time, space, and sources of data (Denzin, 1978). Hsing did this, first, by extending her fieldwork for over 10 years, from 1998 to 2007. Her aim was not to reside in the field continuously: this would have been impractical given her professional and other obligations, and is in any case unnecessary. Rather, the extended timeline enabled her to develop a longitudinal reading of China's protracted transition from socialist land control to market-driven urbanization. By visiting her chosen sites iteratively over years, Hsing was able to trace the evolution of power dynamics and territorial control in different metropolitan regions. This approach also meant that she was attuned and responsive to policy changes, such as during the period 2003–2007 when several new land policy decrees were issued at the national level, disrupting local land politics.

Second, Hsing purposefully expanded the number and diversity of research sites during her 10 years of fieldwork. Having begun with a focus on China's three major coastal cities (Beijing, Shanghai, and Guangzhou), she later added several provincial capital cities on the coast and in the interior, totaling more than 10 municipalities. Her justification for these multiple sites is that they reveal different degrees, speeds, and techniques of local state land grabs and civic responses to those grabs.

A distinction is drawn between first-tier and second-tier (and, in some cases, third-tier) cities. Hsing's selection of second-tier municipalities allows her to examine how pressure on the local state and party leadership to 'catch up' shaped even more rapid land development, extra-legal confiscation, and displacement of rural residents. In these municipalities, the demand for new housing mainly came from local buyers, in contrast to the first-tier cities of Beijing, Shanghai, and Guangzhou, where foreign investors and developers have played a much larger role in the market. Because land and housing require large up-front investments, and can take years to prepare and develop, local governments in second-tier cities take more aggressive steps than their coastal counterparts to secure buyers. These steps include lowering the mortgage rate and granting *hukou* (household registration) to rural migrants to stimulate new demand. Furthermore, second-tier cities are more forceful in demolishing inner-city neighborhoods, because displaced households will likely relocate to the urban fringe where they create demand for new housing. Hsing calls this process 'the economy of demolition and relocation' (2010: 108). In these second-tier cities, unlike the largest cities, relocation is less likely to cause grassroots resistance, as those relocated can rent their new rooms to others, such as college students. Nanjing's 'New City' projects for building university towns are one example of these new dynamics around relocation.

Notably, Hsing adopts a multi-site approach both *within* and *between* cities. Within the city, her tripartite conceptual model of the urban core, the urban edge, and the rural fringe establishes the key sites for fieldwork in each metropolitan region. Each of these areas of the city experiences instituted urbanization in different ways, and to different degrees. Her approach is to analyze the sometimes symbiotic, sometimes fraught, relationships between the state, society, and territory in each of these spaces. In the urban core, where the property value is the highest, Hsing examines the municipal government's relative inferiority to central state agencies in accumulating premium land, which incentivizes the municipality to expropriate land from inner-city residents. On the urban edge, she details how urban district governments legitimate their dominance over township governments through urban development. Some villagers, she notes, are able to take advantage of rapid urbanization by solidifying their collective land rights, a distinctive **right to the city** claim, using these as a bargaining chip. At the rural fringe, where the property market is still inchoate, and where urban governments have little presence, Hsing finds that township governments suffer from a lack of legitimacy due to their lower status in relation to their urban counterparts, which leads them clandestinely to implement unauthorized development projects and issue ownership certificates on the black market, thereby increasing their territorial power over rural land. She also notes that village elites often collude with the state, such that many rural peasants have been displaced and dispossessed, while their protests have frequently been fragmented and thus frustrated.

Hsing also triangulates her methods by using more than one technique to gather data. The crux of this approach is in-depth interviews paired with ethnographic field observation. This represents a distinctive approach, in relation to prevailing patterns of scholarship on China's urbanization, which tend to rely on large-scale surveys and official statistics. But this unstructured, ethnographic approach is appropriate to Hsing's understanding of urbanization as an instituted process shaped by territorial politics over time and space. She focuses on urbanization from both above (by interviewing experts and state officials, and citing state statistics) and below (by interviewing households and conducting ethnographic observation), allowing her to better grasp the particulars of the double movements of state and society. The historical and contemporary narratives that she gleans from interviews illuminate the mechanics and experiences of urbanization that are often hidden in large-scale surveys and official statistics.

Hsing also analyzes secondary qualitative sources. A good example here is her use of interview recordings collected by other scholars to examine the motivations of property-rights protesters in the urban core of Beijing (see her chapter 3). These protesters were originally private homeowners before the Cultural Revolution in the 1960s and 1970s. During the Revolution, however, their properties were expropriated and converted to standard-rent housing by the state, and inner-city homeowners were downgraded to the status of renters. By drawing on the interview data of doctoral students and professors who were colleagues at her local affiliated institution, Hsing is able to illustrate the efforts of protesters to recover their housing and land use rights in opposition to the state's demolition threats for urban redevelopment. She does not explain in the book why she uses prerecorded existing interviews, rather than her own, but is likely because the Cultural Revolution is largely a prohibited topic for discussion. Using raw, primary data sources allows Hsing to recover the historical narratives from the time before she undertook her own fieldwork.

Hsing's multiple field sites, mixed methods, and extended period of research allow her to conceptualize urbanization as an instituted process, contested from below, which articulates with territorial power and its material manifestations in different parts of the city. Yet, her dialectic of state and society and tripartite spatial model run a risk of obfuscating relations between actors that do not conform with the framework of top-down implementation versus grassroots mobilization in specific places. Of course, generalizations are inherent to any theoretical framework, and are useful for drawing out commonalities between cases and the processes that shape them. But co-constructing theory and method also demands ongoing reflexivity in relation to the (inevitable) specificity and selectivity of each research strategy, which are shaped just as much by one's positionality as by local contexts and data constraints.

Reflexivity: contextualizing and refining theory and method

Hsing consistently acknowledges possible biases and omissions of her theoretical framework and conceptual city typology. She is not seeking to 'prove' a particular model of urbanization in China, but rather to identify and explicate the *processes* by which power is instituted and contested through urbanization, in different areas of the city. These processes, Hsing recognizes, will play out differently in different municipalities, with the result that further evidence is required to elucidate specific exercises of territorial power and resistance. Thus, it is important that Hsing contextualizes her methodology by pointing out major differences between cases, inconsistencies between techniques, how she arrived at data saturation, and her own positionality as a US-based scholar.

Hsing is forthright about situations in which findings from one case diverge with another, using these as opportunities continuously to reconstruct her theory. For example, she finds that residents of state-managed rental housing in inner-city Beijing tended to fail in their protests against the state, while the residents of standard-rental housing were more successful, despite their very similar socio-political status in the urban core (her chapter 3). She addresses this divergence by contextualizing the successful strategies of standard-rental housing protesters in the decades-long history of inner-city housing rights in Beijing, and their continued legitimacy today. The success or failure of those two rights-based protests, she concludes, resulted from the level at which political actors variously mobilized and articulated their claims to legitimacy: standard-rental housing at the municipal level, and state-managed rental housing at the central level. The property rights claims of standard rental-housing protesters, advanced through collective legal and media action, broadly coincided with the political imperatives confronted by many municipal governments, notably where there was an urgent need to find resolutions to these issues. However, those of state-managed rental-housing protesters, despite similar mobilization strategies, were obstructed at the central level and thus ignored at the lower level. By contextualizing these cases, Hsing avoids overgeneralizing the success of one group of urban core protesters to other cities or China as a whole. In other words, she recognizes that the power relations that her theoretical framework highlights do not always materialize in the same way, nor do they have the same outcome.

Yet Hsing is somewhat less vocal about the place specificity of her analysis of village corporatism on the urban fringe (her chapter 4). She mentions that successful village territorialization mainly occurs in southern China – particularly near Guangzhou and Shenzhen – and outlines different collective strategies used by the local state to capitalize on opportunities for urban development through the construction of rental housing for rural-to-urban migrants. However, it is unclear whether local governments and village corporations use similar strategies in northern or western China, and thus what a Polanyian double movement on the urban fringe may look like elsewhere. Sally Sargeson (2011), for example, is unconvinced that corporatist village strategies such as shareholding cooperatives, lineage balance, and collective identities universally serve as the variables that shape non-confrontational and successful distributive land politics. Beibei Tang (2015) complicates Hsing's selective case studies too by highlighting several historically and policy-dependent factors that contribute to different forms of village corporatism.

Hsing also encounters inconsistencies and contradictions between her secondary quantitative sources. To resolve this, she collects as much statistical data as she can across a wide spectrum of government, academic, media, and unpublished materials. Because Chinese official statistics are often inaccurate and exaggerated, she then cross-checks official figures with data derived from other sources, including her own interviews. She does this, for example, when estimating the number of displaced people in a particular locality. However, Hsing does not offer much explanation for how she combined interviews with quantitative measures, which sometimes makes it difficult to match statistics with particular local case studies. For example, while narrating her ethnographic observations and findings, she often cites statistical data relating to other places than those she is describing. Of course, it is well recognized that statistical data in China are imperfect and often inaccessible, and that claims made in interviews cannot always be backed up by hard numbers. Nonetheless, one gains the sense that Hsing drew on quantitative data merely to fill the gaps in her interviews, rather than assiduously pursuing both channels of data collection simultaneously.

With so many months spent in multiple sites, using a variety of methods, how does Hsing know when she has enough data? She does not provide a clear answer to this question, but hints at it in the closing section of the book, suggesting that she reached data saturation when additional findings were no longer improving or disproving her theoretical framework. Of course, such a claim is always open to scrutiny and critique: one can always do *more* field-work in order to refine one's theory. Indeed, Hsing might have conducted additional interviews and ethnographic observation on the urban fringe in northern China, using her findings to further contextualize those from southern China. She might also have extended her fieldwork period, as indeed she found it necessary to do, for example, in order to examine the effects of the introduction of a new program of land-focused macroeconomic adjustment policies in the mid-2000s, especially following the massive property-value correction after the 2007–2008 financial crisis. Yet, co-constructing theory and method eventually requires making a decision to aggregate case-study findings to an understanding of process – a decision that is never perfectly timed, nor perfectly applicable to all cases. We might quibble with some of her case selections and suggest conducting more interviews, but believe that her framework still holds explanatory power for understanding Chinese urbanization.

Conclusion

As Zhang (2013) claims, a Polanyian perspective is timely and necessary to understand China's gradual transformation from state socialism to a 'socialist market economy'. This perspective sees marketization not as a natural progression, but as an instituted process, one which engenders civic backlash in the form of a double movement. In *The Great Urban Transformation*, Hsing takes this Polanyian perspective one step further, by demonstrating how instituted urbanization in the form of the real-estate market shapes and is shaped by territory. On one hand, local states avariciously take over land within and even outside their jurisdictions as a means of both revenue generation and territorial control. Here, urban and rural governments compete with each other, and with central-level 'socialist land masters', to acquire development and usage rights over land, which in turn 'urbanizes the local state'. On the other hand, urban residents and peasants employ various strategies to contest state land grabs and to retain control over land and livelihoods. This chapter has argued that Hsing's Polanyian theoretical framework and methodological approach offer novel insights into those ongoing processes of land accumulation and confiscation that are drivers of urbanization in China.

Since the book's publication, urban studies researchers have interrogated Hsing's theoretical claims in different locales and among different groups – with results that do not always align with her framework or findings. Comparing the northern cities of Dalian and Harbin, Meg Rithmire (2013: 874) observes that some local governments are unable to successfully territorialize urban land due to challenges mounted by non-state actors, an outcome that she refers to as 'territorial fragmentation'. Her conclusion is that Hsing's framework of instituted urbanization and bottom-up mobilization does not entirely capture the myriad power relations that are unique to each site. In another example,

Miguel Hidalgo Martinez and Carolyn Cartier (2017) analyze urbanization through the lens of central-state changes to subnational territory, which directly impact the ability of municipal, district, and rural governments to colonize space in different cities. This central state-led process is largely absent from Hsing's work. Elsewhere, Zhu Qian (2013) adds nuance to Hsing's framework by highlighting the heterogeneity of pro-growth coalitions, involving as they do a range of state and market actors, which drive the variegated implementation of urban master plans. And finally, Sargeson (2013) complicates Hsing's spatially binary abstraction of the rural fringe as based on distance from the urban core, demonstrating instead the temporal and organizational differences between rural areas that lead to divergent political outcomes. This conclusion calls into question Hsing's sharp contrast between the relative success of urban resistance and the failure of rural protests. Such critiques suggest that her theory and conceptual model have less broad explanatory power than she claims in the book.

Yet we have argued in this chapter that Hsing's methodological approach – her co-construction of theory and method – is highly instructive for other scholars, despite the geographical limitations and oversimplification of power relations described above. It is better, we believe, to build theory and explanatory concepts rather than simply highlight difference. Hsing largely succeeds on this front, putting her theory in dialogue with her methods, using each to inform the other. Rather than seeking to prove a particular hypothesis, she utilizes a range of data sources together with methodological triangulation in order to refine her theory and to apply it reflexively in the field. In so doing, she keeps her research questions relatively open, gathering empirical evidence through an iterative journey of fact-finding and reconceptualization, thereby constantly interrogating and refining her theoretical and methodological framework based on this reflexive epistemological stance. You-tien Hsing's *The Great Urban Transformation* is an especially suggestive example of how to leverage a Polanyian framework and reflexive methodology to unpack and explain what are multifaceted, polymorphic, and complex spatial economies.

14

CLAIMING RIGHTS TO THE CITY: ON JAMES HOLSTON'S *INSURGENT CITIZENSHIP*

Carolyn Prouse and Fernanda Jahn-Verri

KEYWORDS: comparative urbanism, displacement, ordinary cities, postcolonial cities, right to the city, uneven urban development, urban citizenship, urban encounters, urban social movements

When Zé, a resident from an autoconstructed neighborhood of São Paulo's periphery, came to the city in the 1970s, he – like many other Brazilians – felt that 'law was for the enemies' (Holston, 2008: 203). Elites astutely used legal codes and ambiguity over property titling to accumulate land, while the residents of the urban periphery were threatened with forced evictions. Yet, 30 years later, these residents were using the law and the courts to fight for legal tenure and for a more general **right to the city**. As one São Paulo resident explains to James Holston, 'If you don't run after your rights, how are you going to make them happen?' (2008: 253).

What changed during the three decades? How did the experience of building homes in Brazil's autoconstructed urban peripheries constitute new subjects, citizenships, and understandings of urban rights? And how has Brazil's historically entrenched model of citizenship created the conditions for new forms of insurgence? These are the core questions that guide James Holston's *Insurgent Citizenship*. In this monograph, the anthropologist documents how residents of São Paulo's urban periphery have for decades experienced precarious land tenure.

As a result of building their own homes and communities on this land – a process he calls autoconstruction – they have become insurgent citizens, fighting for land rights and taking a central role in Brazil's **urban social movements**. In so doing, these insurgent citizens have challenged and unsettled centuries of unequal distribution of rights, particularly through participating in the crafting of Brazil's new, democratic Federal Constitution of 1988, while also being impacted by transformed modes of violence under this new and precarious democracy.

Holston arrives at this argument through his distinct historical and ethnographic methodology, which was inspired by his experiences working in São Paulo's urban peripheries in the late 1990s and early 2000s. Here, the anthropologist bore witness to and even participated in residents organizing against evictions. The more Holston followed residents through their local resident associations and the courts, the more he realized that it was the *historical* character of land rights, 'illegal' occupation, and indeed **urban citizenship** itself that was central to these present-day contestations. As he recounts, fighting for land rights could only be understood 'as a strategy … in relation to the centuries of land occupation in Brazil that made illegal settlement the norm of residence' (2008: 33). Holston thus turns to both *historical* methods – detailing the development of a particular, Brazilian form of citizenship – and present-day *ethnographic* practice. In so doing, he is able to show how sites of historical differentiation became those of insurgence: 'how the past always leaks through the present' (2008: 34) in São Paulo's peripheries.

Insurgent Citizenship is organized chronologically and largely divided according to his methods. In the first half of the book, Parts I–II, Holston uses archival data and secondary literature to track changes in citizenship models and to situate contemporary land conflicts in a larger historical context of ambiguous land rights. Here he argues that Brazil's citizenship has been inclusively inegalitarian: it includes all Brazilians born in the national body, but restricts the distribution of resources and rights – specifically voting and land rights. In the second half, Parts III–IV, Holston conducts ethnographic work in two autoconstructed neighborhoods of São Paulo's periphery – Lar Nacional and Jardim das Camélias. He shows, first, how the state and citizens alike draw on complex histories of occupation to (often violently) negotiate land rights; second, how these contestations over land ownership have created a new insurgent citizenship that shaped the Citizens' Constitution of 1988; and third, how these modes of insurgence have unsettled elite privilege, thus patterning new forms of violence, exclusion, and impunity, a 'coincidence that represents the perverse paradox of Brazil's democratization' (2008: 271).

In this chapter, we deconstruct the historical and ethnographic methodology that underpins these arguments. In the first section, we recount Holston's main theoretical interventions. Next, turning to Holston's methodology, we work chronologically through the book and discuss the methods that he deploys, the evidence he marshals, and the arguments these allow him to make. The following section offers a more general reflection on this methodology, and in it we pose some questions that remain for us of the work. The chapter closes with a discussion of the take-home lessons: what is effective about Holston's methodology and what could be improved by students looking to undertake a similar historically informed ethnography?

Brazil's entrenched and insurgent citizenship

Holston's argument hinges on a nuanced conceptualization of citizenship. Citizenship, in his framework, is a set of recognitions and rights conferred by the state, but is also, crucially, a social practice enacted by residents in their daily lives. Holston argues that, as state recognition, Brazil has developed an 'inclusively inegalitarian' citizenship, in which all Brazilian-born are recognized as citizens, but not all share the same privileges. In other words, formal citizenship (i.e., belonging to the nation state) in Brazil is fully inclusive, while substantive citizenship (i.e., the distribution of entitlements) is highly unequal. The histories of these citizenships produce a highly differentiated terrain of access to rights and resources – particularly land and homeownership – that shapes present-day conditions and forms of what the author calls entrenched citizenship. But entrenched citizenship does not create passive subjects; rather, Holston argues that the experiences of precarious ownership, housing, and rights have, since the 1970s, fomented practices of insurgent citizenship: 'a counterpolitics that destabilizes the present and renders it fragile' (2008: 34).

Urbanization, industrialization, and displacement from the core of Brazil's cities have made the urban peripheries both 'the context and substance of a new urban citizenship' (2008: 4). Holston argues that in the global South, mundane spaces, where **urban encounters** take place, are the primary arena for struggle; it is on 'illegalized' land in the peripheries, for instance, that 'São Paulo's workers became property owners, taxpayers, and modern consumers [and thus] came to see themselves as contributor-citizens entitled to stakeholder rights in the city' (2008: 23). In other words, historically entrenched processes of differentiation and unequal distribution of rights have made the peripheries precarious and, as a consequence, a privileged site of mobilization:

> In effect, the very urban conditions of segregation and inequality in the peripheries made this development possible: remoteness enabled a certain off-work and out-of-sight freedom to invent new modes of association, at the same time that illegality motivated residents to demand inclusion in the property, infrastructure, and services of the legal city. (2008: 247)

This process is consistent with what Teresa Caldeira (2017) – from whom Holston has drawn substantially – calls 'peripheral urbanization', in which autoconstructing homes in the urban peripheries of **ordinary cities** in the South has 'produced deep political transformations' (Caldeira, 2017: 9). In Holston's case, specifically, autoconstruction and its subjects (insurgent citizens) have contributed to national-level urban social movements. Thus, in contrast to Arjun Appadurai (2001: 28), who argues that the poor's 'general invisibility in urban life [makes] it impossible for them to claim any rights', Holston finds that it is precisely this relative invisibility that has incited the construction of new peripheral futures and a new insurgent citizenship.

However, as the fight for their rights to land ownership attests, insurgent citizens do not always upend hegemonic forms of propertied citizenship. Holston draws on liberal philosophy to argue that in Brazil, much like elsewhere, there exists an ideological relationship between owning land and achieving person-hood, where 'property ownership is the means to establish such fundamental qualifications for citizenship as independence, respect, and responsibility' (2008: 113). Poor peoples' movements paradoxically tend to disturb and sustain the apparatus of property (Roy, 2017). Indeed, in using the courts to fight for what they think of as their *own* property ownership rights, insurgent citizens in São Paulo's periphery are not necessarily 'revolutionary' subjects but they may (re)create, in transformed fashion, 'modern' notions of being and relations to the land, thus reproducing contemporary regimes of propertied citizenship.

Holston argues that Brazil's form of (insurgent) citizenship is *particular*. He intervenes in theories of modernity and democracy that take as their norm North Atlantic countries, and that tend to frame the Brazilian experience as being an incomplete or failed version of these 'standards'. Instead, Holston wants to take an 'assemblage' and 'comparative' approach that foregrounds the 'particularity of Brazil's engagement with modernity', from which 'North Atlantic formulations appear as particulars as well, though often presented as universals' (2008: 14). He argues, for instance, that the violence that exists alongside democratic rule is not a function of incomplete democracy; rather it is a result of the historically situated process of democratic rule in Brazil, where insurgent citizens have disrupted the entrenched, with the 'old' defend-ing the loss of their power, often to extreme degrees. To understand how these specific, historical forms of citizenship have fomented present-day insurgence, Holston very explicitly crafts a historical and ethnographic method, which we discuss at greater length in the following section.

History of the present: Holston's historical and ethnographic method

Holston's book is organized chronologically, shifting from historical to ethnographic method as he proceeds. Because his argument hinges on the assertion that Brazil's historically entrenched citizenship shapes present-day insurgence, he uses the opening half of the monograph (Part II) to establish this historical context. He engages both primary and secondary historical sources to construct a 'genealogy' (2008: 13) of formal citizenship and the differentiated distribution of rights. For instance, to demonstrate Brazil's claim to universal inclusivity of citizenship, in contrast to American and French models, Holston analyzes different iterations of the Constitution that codify formal citizenship in shifting ways, and quotes specific constitutional articles and lawmakers' speeches to demonstrate Brazil's model of inclusivity. To account for the differential distribution of rights, Holston traces access to political, land, and labor rights through three periods in Brazil's history: the colonial (1500–1822), the imperial (1822–1889), and the republican (1889–present). Drawing on primary and secondary archival material, he documents the differential and shifting access to political rights; initially restricted to land holders and 'good men', they were then extended to higher-income earners while denying voting rights to the illiterate. Holston is careful, however, to acknowledge the 'precarious quality' of demographic information (2008: 91). He also does not equate enfranchisement with political power and influence.

Arguably more important to Holston than enfranchisement is how land rights, policies, and access have been differentially distributed and have informed contemporary insurgent struggles for land ownership. Again, he draws on historical sources, such as quotes from eminent politicians and codified legislation, to investigate how the Brazilian state and elite transformed land policy to sustain shifting accumulation and labor regimes. Privileging the *longue durée*, Holston outlines the 'various installments of a relation between land and law first developed in Portuguese land policy as an instrument of colonization' (2008: 33), then turns to how these relations were remade in imperial and republican moments, and how, more recently, elites have used the law to support industrialization and manage the industrial workforce.

Holston's focus between 1930 and 1980 turns predominantly to the scale of the urban generally, and São Paulo specifically, to describe **uneven urban development** and centrifugal patterns of segregation in the city. Quoting from task force publications calling for the scientific management of São Paulo, and city/state legislation, Holston shows that workers were forced to the outskirts of the city through hygienist and Haussmann-inspired beautification movements. He reproduces maps of Brazilian scholars (cf. Caldeira, 2017) and income statistics by Brazil's IBGE (the Brazilian Institute of Geography and Statistics) to demonstrate the growth of the city's peripheries over time. Using these sources, Holston argues that, through constant **displacement** and resettling, the urban poor experienced the 'center–periphery paradigm of growth' (2008: 157) that ejected them to the outskirts of São Paulo.

It is not until the second half of the book that Holston uses ethnography to show how this historical genealogy 'erupts' in the present. This is where the book comes alive. He focuses specifically on forms of land contestation and ownership in two peripheral neighborhoods of São Paulo – Lar Nacional and Jardim das Camélias – the two neighborhoods in which he and Caldeira have conducted extensive ethnographic work.

Holston first documents how municipal and state eviction campaigns galvanized residents to form local chapters of the Societies of Friends of the Neighborhood (SAB), Christian Base Communities (CEB), and their own resident associations to fight for their legal standing to the land they inhabit: in other words, how state actions fomented an insurgent citizenship. The author then compellingly (if somewhat exhaustingly) follows court cases in these two neighborhoods – at which he has been a participant–observer – to explain how the historical land policies he documents in the first half of the book have created competing court claims between multiple stakeholders. He follows contestations over a parcel of land in Jardim das Camélias, specifically, to show how myriad stakeholders, including the federal government and local families, all have seemingly legitimate claims on this space due to historically entrenched ambiguity. In other words, colonial-era legislated expropriation and various sales of the property as both physical and deeded space have made it very difficult to ascertain a specific owner of the land. Residents of Jardim das Camélias and Lar Nacional have used this ambiguity and the lengthy court process to hold on to their land: Holston's experiences in court show how claimants rely on this drawn-out process to unsettle the state's and other elites' claims to property. Because the legal proceedings are often not resolved (or at least not in a timely fashion), residents are able to continue living on the disputed lands for the interim. Yet it is ultimately this ambiguity that makes residents of the urban periphery vulnerable to eviction threats in the first place.

Insurgent citizens of São Paulo's periphery have also developed their own strategies outside the justice system to forward their agenda. Holston draws on his experiences in the courts, alongside interviews he conducts with community leaders, to show how Lar Nacional residents adopted a 'guerilla strategy' (2008: 245) to track politicians at public events and secure the latter's attention. Additionally, he documents how the residents of Jardim das Camélias fought land fraud performed by *grileiros* (those who deceive and sell somebody else's land), by continuing to make deposits into the *grileiros'* court-sanctioned bank accounts and thus to delay (and, eventually, stop) eviction.

Holston extrapolates from his ethnographic observations in São Paulo's periphery to make a more general argument about insurgent practices of land transformation and ownership, and their effect on national citizenship and democracy. He argues that it was experiences such as those in Lar Nacional and Jardim das Camélias that motivated citizens to articulate concerns through the Urban Forum, the latter being central to the formulation and pas-sage of Brazil's 1988 Federal Constitution and the 2001 City Statute. Holston does not draw a direct link between the leaders and activists in these neighbor-hoods and broader social movements, but argues that similar contestations were taking place throughout the country – peripheral movements joined laterally to demand popular participation in nation-building. In other words, Holston uses São Paulo as a *representative case* of insurgent citizenship throughout Brazil, and generalizes urban social movements beyond these two communities.

Toward the end of the book Holston draws primarily on participant observation, interview material, and written manifestos to argue that citizenship continues to have different meanings and violent manifestations under democracy. He provides quotes from residents' interviews in Jardim das Camélias and Lar Nacional to show how they understand citizenship. His analysis reveals that they assign three different meanings to the term citizenship: as moral and social category (e.g., as 'honest worker'); as deriving from stakes in the city (e.g., through paying taxes); and as textually based rights written in the new democratic Constitution. He argues that, following these conceptions, citizenship in Brazil is ultimately a mix of old (the first conception) and new (the latter two conceptions). Yet it is not just residents in the periphery who draw on and deploy various notions of citizenship in their everyday lives. Holston discursively analyzes narco traffic and military police manifestos to show how these state and non-state actors each use new democratic citizenship- and human rights-based language to justify their extreme violence – such as when gangs invoke 'prisoners' rights' as they shut down local commerce and set buses on fire to protest prison conditions.

Methodological reflections and ongoing questions

Holston's project is methodologically ambitious, combining historical and contemporary methods in the analysis of citizenship at multiple scales. In this section we reflect on this methodology and discuss its effectiveness, paying particular attention to scale, evidence, embodied experience, and positionality. We also pose questions that the methodology inspires, and point to some unresolved tensions in the book.

Holston's analysis is at once historical, contemporary, and interscalar. He privileges a different scale at each temporal period, but seeks to make connections across all scales and moments. Central to his methodology is the mutual constitutive relationship between formal citizenship at the national (often constitutional) scale, and everyday citizenship practices at the urban scale (Staeheli et al., 2012). The monograph is largely structured around these different scales and moments – switching scales as it temporally shifts to the present. In other words, his historical work is focused predominantly at the national level (although he also documents historical patterns of segregation in São Paulo's urban periphery) while his contemporary ethnographic research privileges the urban scale, more specifically the spaces of the urban peripheries. Yet Holston also tries to connect these contemporary practices in Lar Nacional and Jardim das Camélias to national legislation – to the 1988 Federal Constitution and its popular constitutional amendments, specifically (although he does not show how Lar Nacional and Jardim das Camélias were directly connected to events at the national level). This methodological interscalar tack allows Holston to

make a broader theoretical argument about the political. Echoing much feminist scholarship, he argues that the political operates beyond electoral politics
and the public realm, and theories about democracy need to account for actions
in the domestic sphere, the peripheries, the everyday, and embodied experiences
of city building.

Holston's multi-method approach provides rich description and analysis.
For the most part, he is successful in using different lenses to articulate citizenship:
he stitches together a multifaceted picture of different modes of (non-)belonging,
from constitutional legislation and urban segregation practices, to national
policymakers' codifications; to everyday lived experiences. His work is most
compelling and rich at the ethnographic scale: from sitting in courtrooms to
experiencing domestic workers' interactions in elevators, Holston is able to
recount the everyday strategies and bodily practices that characterize insurgent
practice and (re)produce violent norms. However, due to the ambition of the
methodology, not all ethnography is similarly thick: his recounting of competing historical claims to a specific parcel of land is very persuasive, but his
accounting of the violence of evictions marshals little substantive evidence.

A major argument of Holston's is that citizenship is a practice and an
embodied phenomenon, yet his evidence for this is restricted to his present-day
ethnographic work. In other words, his historical research does not account
for the embodied experiences of past citizens. For instance, the first half of the
book – the historical context – engages the macro scale and elite policy formulations. It does not draw on historical memoirs or other textual sources produced
by Brazil's impoverished and racialized citizens. The historical archive on
which Holston draws is presented almost as if it represents the full reality of
the past. It is not clear if and how citizens have historically been mobilizing
and whether, or in what ways, they may have *also* been practicing a form of
embodied insurgent citizenship. Put differently, given that Holston's evidence
for citizenship experience and everyday practice is only of the *present*, there is
little to support his argument about the *novelty* of post-1970s 'insurgence' (cf.
Fischer, 2010). How do we know citizens historically were not practicing
insurgent citizenship?

Holston's positionality is partially, albeit not fully, elucidated throughout
the text. He acknowledges that he privileges these two communities because
of his relationships with them, but does not, beyond the preface, acknowledge
his relationship with Teresa Caldeira (his longtime partner) and the extent to
which this partnership (and her work in Lar Nacional and Jardim das
Camélias) have inevitably shaped the final product. Most importantly to us,
Holston does not elaborate on the potential challenges and/or advantages that
his positionality – as a white, English-speaking, cis-male American – presented
to him while interacting with his research subjects. We question to what extent
his positionality affects his depictions of 'the poor', which are for the most part
represented as an undifferentiated mass. While he documents the history of
slavery and colonization, there is little attention to how the contemporary

periphery is inhabited by, (re)produces, or even consumes *índios* (indigenous peoples) and other racialized identities. How do historically entrenched inter-sectional axes of difference continue to shape contemporary urbanization movements? Holston compellingly nods to gender differences in SABs and how female leadership centered concerns of health, education, recreation, and childcare, whereas male leaders focused almost exclusively on land rights. We would have appreciated greater methodological attention to these issues of intersectionality and differential experiences of being poor, and to the impact of interrelated processes of racialization, colonization, and patriarchy in shaping insurgent citizenship.

The question of whiteness and its effect on Holston's analysis is particularly timely at the current conjuncture, admittedly one decade after the book's pub-lication, when racialized police violence in Brazil is making global headlines. In the peripheries of Brazil's cities, military police and gang violence kill young black men at extreme rates, and have done so over the last few decades. Holston's story is not told from the experiences of these young black men, who are members of the Brazilian working or under-class. Instead, it is told from the perspective of constitutional citizenship – which he says *includes* indigenous and black peoples in its model – and from the experiences of the generalized insurgent subject. This focus on an undifferentiated working class is not uncommon in Brazilian citizenship, but this perspective is currently being trou-bled by Afro- and indigenous-Brazilian voices that upend assumptions of Brazil's racial democracy (cf. Vargas, 2006; Ferreira da Silva, 2009; Perry, 2013). Indeed, Jaime Amparo Alves (2018) has recently articulated a very dif-ferent conceptualization of insurgence from the spaces and experiences of black death in São Paulo's urban peripheries. Engagement with Holston's book, moving forward, should recognize the intersectional and differential experiences of being poor, particularly when the experiences of the periphery prove deadly for Brazil's darker-skinned 'citizens'.

Relatedly, *Insurgent Citizenship* is likely interpreted differently from the situated perspectives of those reading it. Holston claims to make an important intervention in theories of democracy and modernity by foregrounding Brazil's own constitutional and democratic development from the historically situated perspective of the country. He argues that Brazil's modernity is particular, just as American and French formulations are. Yet he still privileges the perspective of the northern reader, as he tells his story in explicit relation to North Atlantic formulations of citizenships and theories of democracy. Perhaps tellingly is how we, the authors of this chapter, responded differently to this tactic as a function of our respective positionalities. Carolyn, from Canada ('the North'), appreciated Holston's broad historical and **comparative urbanism** focus in lay-ing out key moments and shifts in policy throughout Brazil's history, and for being explicit about how his argument intervenes in hegemonic (read: northern) theory of modernity and democracy. Fernanda, from Brazil ('the South'), felt that Holston's analysis of these other countries diverted focus from key aspects of Brazil's historical development and marginalized other countries' experiences that might have been more appropriate for understanding Brazil. While these reflections are not mutually exclusive, they do expose how differently positioned readers might read the book and see its contributions to northern/southern theory.

Take-home lessons

The engagement and constructive critiques we have leveled here are developed from a space of significant respect for James Holston and his work. We believe that Holston's ambitious methodology offers much to guide new and emerging scholars, while also demonstrating some of the pitfalls of such ambition. In this final section we briefly articulate key take-home lessons we have absorbed from the book.

Holston conducts a historical and ethnographic accounting of citizenship in Brazil. By undertaking archival and secondary research, he provides a compelling account of the *longue durée* of land policy, constitutional citizenship, and distribution of rights. To undertake this work he engages with lawmakers' and politicians' speeches, different iterations of the Constitution and articles therein, official statistics, maps, and the secondary literature of historians. He then turns to ethnographic research of present-day contestations over land in the peripheries of São Paulo. Holston conducts participant observation of court cases and resident meetings, interviews with community residents and leaders, and discourse analysis of public documents written by the military police and narco traffic factions. In juxtaposing these forms of evidence, he is able to show how past ambiguity over land shapes present-day court contestations, and how these contestations also seek to interpret/recreate the past in ways beneficial to the claimant. Combining historical archival work and present-day ethnography also allows Holston to argue that insurgence is the result of historically entrenched marginalization.

His historical investigation demonstrates how and why urban peripheries have developed as spaces of marginalization, autoconstruction, and insurgence, while his ethnography demonstrates how this situation of urban peripherality has been central to claims-making and, indeed, a new democratic citizenship at the national scale. He extrapolates this process of insurgence to other southern **postcolonial cities,** arguing like Caldeira (2017) that autoconstruction in urban peripheries is the means and substance of struggle for rights to the city.

Yet this work also begs caution due to its ambitious nature. In trying to privilege a *longue durée* – from colonization in the fifteenth century to present-day narco traffic under democracy – Holston is not able to provide a full picture of different embodied citizenships throughout Brazil's history. Moreover, in combining historical investigation of elite and state policy with ethnographies of peripheral residents, Holston is primarily able to account only for the everyday citizenship practice of the *contemporary* moment, thus throwing into question the *novelty* of insurgence. Finally, we are cautious of what Holston leaves out – his lack of explicit reflexivity about his positionality makes it difficult to know how his situatedness has shaped the book's interpretations.

Studies with a similar methodological orientation could think of ethnography itself in its historical form: to think of the past as also always embodied, and to recognize the archive as legitimating only a particular version of the past, much as property claimants do in court. Holston's work is an important step forward in thinking of how to do this through an accountable, engaged, participant–observer methodology. We look forward to emerging research that carries this important project forward.

15

VISUALIZING LIQUID CITIES: ON MATTHEW GANDY'S *THE FABRIC OF SPACE*

CS Ponder and Sophie Webber

KEYWORDS: assemblage urbanism, comparative urbanism, infrastructure, more-than-human world/urban nature, postcolonial cities/subaltern cities

Water flows and dystopian modernities in six cities

In *The Fabric of Space,* Matthew Gandy (2014) grapples with the social and environmental transformations brought about by the tangled relationship between water and modernity. Structured chronologically, the book starts in Paris in the mid-nineteenth century, before traveling to Weimar Berlin, postcolonizing Lagos in the 1940s, Millennial Mumbai, contemporary Los Angeles, and a future, imagined, and flooded London. Taking original inspiration from the nineteenth-century photographer Félix Nadar's arresting images of the newly modernized spaces of Paris's sewer system, Gandy journeys to the five other cities in order to explore locally embedded cultural representations of water-centered urban environmental change. The book argues that despite the promises of modernity that have accompanied so-called improvements to urban water systems, the form that they take is not developmentally linear, singular, or predictable: responses to health crises have been riddled with failures, the prevention of flooding is unattainable in practice, and the provision of potable water to diverse urban populations remains inconsistent. Gandy also examines the modernization of urban water to consider changing state–society relations, including public health and hygiene norms, and the deepening marginalization of the – often racialized and informally housed – urban poor.

The book interlaces cross-disciplinary debates, ranging from climate science to environmental humanities, and an array of empirical sources, including participant observation, interviews, and representative visual culture and literature. As Gandy describes:

> During the course of my research I visited the Paris sewers and found a well-organized municipal spectacle; ... I swam in Berlin's lakes and felt the warmth of the sun and the cool shade of pine trees; I stepped across open drains in Lagos next to concrete surfaces festooned with faded posters; I noticed the maps and diagrams on the walls of engineering offices in Mumbai; ... I wandered along the concrete landscapes of the Los Angeles River; ... and I marvelled at the afternoon sun glinting on the steel-clad gates of the Thames Barrier. (2014: viii)

This quote represents the most explicit discussion of research methods in the text – where Gandy discusses what he actually *did* to assemble his research findings. Yet while a certain ethnographic sensibility is implied in this brief, poetic description of the book's method, the use of visual and literary culture is unquestionably its primary (and distinctive) mode of analysis. The book is punctuated by arresting accounts of high-modern architecture, stills from films, reprints of photographs and paintings expressing shifting public health and leisure norms, and descriptions of literary works concerned with the 'sound, smell, and even subtle cadence' of cities (2014: 18). Brief ethnographic observations, expert interviews, and archival and document analysis are supporting or supplementary methods.

Taking the fluidity of water as an analytical trope (as the 'fabric' of space), the book examines how water and its **infrastructure** produce uneven urban topographies and diverse socio-spatial relations. In the first substantive chapter, Gandy analyses the reconstruction of urban sewer infrastructure with the rebuilding of Haussmannite Paris starting in the 1850s. Using Nadar's photos, maps of the new sewer system, and Georges Seurat's 1884 painting *Bathers at Asnières*, Gandy suggests that the sewer infrastructure helped to rearrange relations between nature and society, and between the body and the city. These rearrangements displaced unwashed working-class bodies from the city center to the 'melancholic banlieue'. Next, Gandy takes us to Weimar Berlin where eco-socialist visions sought to connect the urban majority to public bathing lakes on the city's edge – not just for public health, but also for the machinic production of collective happiness. Taking a cue from its many visual, cinematic, and theatrical artists in residence, Gandy frames Berlin as the experimental city. He uses the artistic expression of the time, and particularly the film *Menschen am Sonntag* ('People on Sunday'; 1930), to explore shifting bodily norms and environmental politics.

The middle chapters leave the literary, performance, and visual arts behind to a large extent, however. Chapter 3 shifts to colonial Lagos, studying techno-modernist attempts to protect the city from mosquitoes and malaria in the 1940s. This reveals how water in the city – its lack or overabundance, and role in spreading disease – interacts with racialized segregation, increased exposure to disease, and limited welfare services. Yet Gandy observes that urban poverty and disease are rarely mentioned in the cultural representations of the time. In the fourth chapter, on Mumbai, Gandy uses expert interviews, analyses of reports, and the scholarly literature to argue that planners in the city seek the 'perfect synthesis between engineering science and urban modernity' (2014: 109) through flooding defenses and potable water provision. Contrary to the dreams of city planners, and their power-laden maps indicating piped water connections, the chapter demonstrates that universal service provision encounters colonial, caste, and class limits – turning modern-day Mumbai into a 'hydrological dystopia' where water flows are formative in reproducing striking inequalities.

We return to poetry and public arts in his chapter 5, where the enigmatic Los Angeles River is a portent of the fragmented city and contemporary imaginaries of ecological restoration. Along its highly channelized and concretized route, conservationists use nativist rhetoric to argue for an ecological return, while others use its concrete to document the city's exclusionary history. Finally, in the sixth chapter Gandy introduces us to a dystopian future where London is drowning, courtesy of J. G. Ballard's (1962) novel *The Drowned World* and scientific projections of future sea-level rise. Across a variety of science-fiction urbanisms and 'cli-fi' (climate science fiction), Gandy imagines the socio-spatial crises that this kind of environmental change might invite. Echoing the journey along the Los Angeles River, these techno-modernist attempts at flood control in London reveal glimpses of potentially more than just relations between society and nature in the city.

In this chapter we deconstruct Gandy's book in two ways. The following section situates the contribution in the context of recent debates in urban theory, particularly with respect to urban political ecology, **assemblage urbanism** versus political economy approaches to urbanism and urbanization, and multi-city comparisons spanning the global North and South. While these connections remain implicit, or understated, the book contains methodological and conceptual insights for these key debates. Second, the chapter focuses more explicitly on methods – questioning the 'fit' of the cultural representations that Gandy deploys with respect to the concerns of the book. Relative to methodological and representational norms in critical urban studies, *The Fabric of Space* is distinctive in its use of the literary, performance, and visual arts as a source of empirical material and inspiration. Gandy continually asks (2014: 221): 'Why has the engineering of modernity gone awry[?]', and why has it produced such 'persistent inequalities'? We ask, in turn, whether this strategy of analyzing cultural representation affords new insights into the production of social and environmental inequalities.

We conclude by reflecting on the politics of cultural representations amidst the globalizing urban water crisis.

Reassembling urban theory across cities

The book takes urban political ecology (UPE; see Heynen et al. 2006b) as its starting point. Two tenets of UPE are that social and natural urban space are mutually produced, and that these processes are unevenly realized across cities. These tenets are affirmed throughout the book. In the case of the Los Angeles River, for example, Gandy complicates the binary between a concretized, channelized, and highly engineered river and the romantic imaginary of ecological restoration to riparian zones. Instead, he asserts the syntheses of biophysical and cultural processes, or the 'innate hybridity' of urban space by considering the 'spontaneous nature' of weeds and vegetation that emerge despite the ostensibly barren, cement terrain. There exist no 'natural' riverine systems, he argues, only reinvented social and natural relations. Second, each chapter considers how the flows and governance of water re/produce sociospatial inequalities. The case of Mumbai is demonstrative: the disparities between the dream of modernizing the water system, and achieving universal provision and the harsh realities of unequal access between global elites and the urban poor, are productive of uneven urbanization. Where Mumbai has long striven toward a technically advanced network of water provision, sanitation, and sewers, the city has consistently failed to achieve these hydrological ambitions. Whether through access to piped water or exposure to flooding, the flow of water constitutes one of the principal axes of injustice in the city. The postcolonial, nation-building state is ambivalent here – sometimes further marginalizing its urban majority, and at other times seeking to extend formal water provision.

Unlike most work in UPE, however, *The Fabric of Space* is much less concerned with questioning processes of explicitly *capitalist* urbanization (cf. Brenner, 2009a). Gandy seeks instead to understand why the utopian promise of modernity itself has failed. Thus, rather than analyzing cities as products of and factors in capitalist value production, he focuses on the urban in its role as the primary spatiality of modernity. He builds on concepts such as 'decomposing' and 'multiple modernities' (Gandy, 2014: 223; see also Ferguson, 2006) in order to work against false hierarchies of cities according to where they are presumed to lie on an imagined singular and stagist path to development. This non-linearity and fracturing of modernity is also echoed in the ordering of the city chapters.

Again, contrary to another large stream of research in UPE, Gandy's analysis does not easily rely on assemblage-inspired approaches either (McFarlane, 2011a; 2011c). Gandy recognizes the difficulties inherent in rationalizing urban space through the modernization of water infrastructures, and that these efforts inevitably produce uneven 'geographies of failure and neglect' (2014: 5). He is also convinced that the **more-than-human world** of cities is crucial to any analysis of urbanism and changes to the urban form: these components 'should be woven into the analytical frame' (2014: 102). Yet in *The Fabric of Space* Gandy is reluctant to acknowledge non-human agency – there is very little focus on the materiality of nature, even of water. For Gandy, the unpredictable nature of providing and managing this 'uncooperative commodity' of water (cf. Bakker, 2003; Bakker and Bridge, 2006) does not necessarily imply the agency of non-humans.

Consider the case of attempts to control water, mosquitoes, and malaria in Lagos. Early twentieth-century efforts to protect Lagos and its inhabitants from malaria through policies of segregation and scientific racism did not fail due to some agential capacity of mosquitoes, as Timothy Mitchell (2002) has suggested of development failures in Egypt. Rather, Gandy attributes causality to the city being ultimately 'too large, too complex' to be 'reorganized at [the colonial authority's] will' (2014: 88). Additionally, the attempts of the Lagos-based British authorities to use quinine to protect its subjects were constrained by the fiscally conservative metropole. Soon after, the desire to eradicate malaria failed amidst growing ambivalence toward, and the eventual decline of, the colonial project in the region. Gandy seems at pains to reassert, relative to Mitchell (2002), the importance of social relations in understanding urban water provision and its public health effects. Accordingly, the continuing malarial prevalence in Lagos is not caused by 'mosquitoes [that] are "actors" in the sense of an undifferentiated causal network that downplays human sentience' (2014: 102). While nature is important for understanding urbanism in Lagos, Gandy foregrounds socio-spatial marginalization and governance failure. Similarly, in the case of Mumbai, Gandy suggests that the Indian state seems quite capable of exerting its control over the hydrological cycle – contra any suggestion that water has intrinsic intransigence and therefore agential capacity. Rather, the failure of water provision in the city is a result of the 'dynamics of urban growth [that] have long eluded the grasp of urban technocrats' (2014: 124).

Gandy therefore complicates theories of more-than-human agency in assembling the city, carefully highlighting the ways that **urban nature** should be incorporated, as well as pointing out the limits of such conceptualizations. Whereas debates between political economic and assemblage, actor–network, and posthumanist-inspired approaches to studying urban environments were once polarized (see Brenner et al., 2011), Gandy's approach represents something of a rapprochement. Indeed, in the wake of the book's publication, research in urban political ecology that experiments methodologically and conceptually with these two approaches has proliferated (e.g., Ranganathan, 2015).

The book also sits in relation to debates about methodological city selection and **comparative urbanism** and **postcolonial cities/subaltern cities**. Over the last decade, Jennifer Robinson (2011a; 2016) and Ananya Roy (2009) have demanded new geographies of urban theorizing, derived not from the paradigmatic cases like New York City or London, but from diverse – and frequently global Southern – cities. Gandy (2002) has extended, geographically, his focus on urban water from New York. Far from 'ordinary', however, his six cities are archetypes of distinctive urbanizations: Paris as the 'capital of the nineteenth century' and Los Angeles as the 'architectural citadel of "postmodern urbanism"' (Gandy 2014: 23), for example. In addition to seeking diversified cities as bases for urban theory, Robinson (2011a) argues for keeping all cities within a framework of a 'world of cities' in order to encourage comparison and theorization across global North and South. Gandy experiments with holding multiple studies together, putting six cities into conversation with one another, rather than privileging a single case. This methodological framework enables a consideration of 'a more polyvalent set of developments that effectively decenters existing narratives of urban change' (Gandy 2014: 23). Indeed, his aim in this six-city undertaking is not to perform a 'search for more obvious points of comparison' (2014: 24), but rather to use comparative elements as the basis for, and encouragement of, reflection on a broader set of themes through strikingly different lenses.

But there are analytical tradeoffs in abandoning the 'quasi-scientific' (Robinson, 2016: 3) comparison of structural similarities for 'occasional connec- tions or cross-cutting themes' (Gandy, 2014: 24) across cities held in a rather loose comparative embrace. Gandy presents readers with six wildly different lived realities as illustrative of fractured modernity. The cases all center on the 'evolving relations' between urban infrastructures built up over time, nature, and the urban imagination (2014: 2). Do these lived realities present them- selves as examples of, or variations on, a broader theory? Or are they theoretically generative 'singularities', as Robinson (2016: 13–14) demands of urban theory? Perhaps more importantly, are these city cases *equally* generative, or singular? Since each city case is granted its own chapter, along with its own political ecology of water problems, Gandy's analysis certainly does not perpetuate a developmental binary between cities of the global North or South. Paris, Berlin, Los Angeles, or London are not framed as the prototypical modern city. There is no 'catching-up' to do for anyone here; what exist instead are different expressions of, and elaborations on, the experience of modernity. And yet, the cases of Lagos and Mumbai stand out as cities negotiating socio-ecological crises rather than creatively experimenting with utopian urban futures as in Berlin, London, or Los Angeles. The result is to perpetuate tropes of the crisis-ridden postcolonial city and erode the visibility of imagined socio-ecological futures rooted in the global South.

Gandy recognizes the potential for connections between the cases, recalling in passing, for example, the colonial influence London held over Mumbai and Lagos, and suggesting that urban ecological design and nature-based flood mitigation have brought the LA River to the world. However, analytical link- ages between the six cities are rarely pursued. As a result, Gandy pays scant attention to inequitable colonial afterlives and relationalities that remain between London and Lagos, and London and Mumbai, even while these cities (and others in the book) remain variously entangled. These cases seem ripe for relational comparison – for highlighting colonialism, modernity, and urban water control as a relational process. Although this expansive technique of analyzing cities in parallel allows Gandy to examine how the socio-technological project of modernity unfolds along the same topological lines that power itself moves *within* these six cities, there are clear limits to his ability to reach *across* them, explicitly to connect and compare their experiences.

Engaging the visual and literary arts

Gandy uses an interdisciplinary approach to explore urban spatialities of hydro-social power. He reasons that if power is socially dispersed and at work potentially anywhere or even everywhere, then multiple methods of knowing and doing research are required to examine it. He argues that 'cultural representations of cities … enrich our understanding of urban environmental change [… and] provide insight into the interstitial spaces of the modern city' (2014: 18). Notably for Gandy this means taking the explanatory power of the humanities and visual culture seriously. The book uses photos, film, paintings, and literature as methodological artifacts in order to access the emotional and material sensuality of everyday life under six different modes of modernity.

What Gandy sacrifices for this ephemeral sense of 'being there', however, is the fine-grained empirics of participant-observation-style ethnography or the more positivist ability to generalize from systematic sources of data. This work forsakes the detailed documentation of everyday hydro-social survival strategies of the urban poor in the six cities, for example, in exchange for a more temporally and texturally inclusive analysis of the ways in which modernity has transformed urban socio-spatial relations, broadly speaking. To take the Parisian example, through Nadar's photographs readers are shown how the nineteenth-century technological innovation of flash photography shed light literally and figuratively on the city's newly modernized sewer system. Photos of the sewers were broadcast, leading the urban public to reconceptualize their shared imaginary of these underground tunnels. Walter Benjamin (1968: 80–81) describes the photographs as a formative moment in the 'new technical and social reality' of modernity: sewers were no longer perceived as feared spaces of abjection, but as modernized spaces of progress. Cultural practices with socio-spatial effects also developed on the basis of differentiated abilities to make use of the new urban plumbing system. Public bathing houses became increasingly rare, as the development of in-home, residential plumbing systems led to the effective privatization of bathing practices. This was a cause of deepening social stratification as unbathed, odiferous working-class bodies became an aberrant presence in Hausmann's new city. What this visual approach to understanding urban environmental change hides, however, is an account of what happened to the unwashed working classes in response to these changes – how they navigated their newly curtailed right to the city.

In Weimar Berlin, we are presented with a nascent, utopian vision of modernity by way of a silent movie. The film is an unscripted series of vignettes featuring everyday life in the city in the 'last "carefree" summer of the Weimar Republic' (2014: 77). Gandy describes the scene of a day trip from the city to the newly built public lakeside swimming facilities that were constructed in an effort to bring leisure back into urban life. Four Berliners (two couples) take public transportation to a lakeshore designed with time-efficient commuting in mind, in an effort to shorten the working day and increase quality leisure time. Gandy uses selected stills from the film to emphasize an emergent sensibility of the era – one that takes joy in bodily pleasures like eating, drinking, and sun bathing, as well as in the corporeal form of the body itself. Readers are shown that in Weimar Berlin, bodies are no longer meant only for laboring, hiding under voluminous clothes, or for bathing alone, but are themselves things to take pleasure in and from. In turn, the urban landscape reflects and sanctifies this changed status by enabling and provisioning publicly accessible leisure-time activities, like swimming, for the urban masses. In counterpoint to this narrative of 'corporeal liberation' however, Gandy emphasizes that a newfound emphasis on fit, happy, and playful bodies was not only emancipatory, but served to strengthen stereotypes regarding 'ideal body-types' and a militaristic emphasis on healthy bodies in the service of the nation.

In the Paris and Berlin chapters, Gandy foregrounds the ways that social relations are mediated by water, and brings shifting public-health norms and the biopolitical disciplining of bodies into urban studies. He produces an account of the way that water and its flows uncover the 'powerful link between the body and the built environment' (2014: 54). Yet, while his use of historical visual culture as empirical evidence allows us analytical entry into Haussmann's Paris and Weimar Berlin, we understand the socio-spatial changes that modernity has wrought only through these artists' impressions and Gandy's interpretations of them. We have no 'unperformed' sense of the ways in which these changes materially affected the rhythms or practices of everyday urban life either as a whole, or – importantly – for particularly impacted populations. At root here, then, are questions of the politics and power of representation. Across the Paris, Berlin, and Los Angeles and London cases, we read of (and see) diverse forms of artistic expression: independent and working-class films and vast public visual-art installations alongside Hollywood movie stills and the works of impressionist masters of the nineteenth century. But noticeable silences remain, demanding accountability for the gendered, classed, raced, and other perspectives that are left out when relying on western notions of artistic expression to inform our understanding of social difference in urban life.

Gandy also somewhat uncharacteristically eschews a heavy emphasis on visual and literary culture as explanatory analytical objects in his chapters on Lagos and Mumbai. In Lagos, Gandy is unable to access sufficiently illustrative empirical material from the literary or visual arts, frankly admitting to the absence of 'a distinctive Nigerian voice in relation to public health discourse' (2014: 100) operating within the public realm prior to mid-century. He speculates on the possible reasons for the dearth of Nigerian historical representation, ultimately characterizing the situation as a 'historiography of absence'. Though he briefly engages the work of two Nigerian novelists in the chapter, Cyprian Ekwensi and Chinua Achebe, Gandy cites the socio-cultural elitism of the 'burgeoning' Nigerian literary circles and their tendency to lean on 'drama [more] than realist fiction' (2014: 99) as reasons for the absence of explorations of urban poverty in the arts. This explanation evades the implications of his own positionality vis-à-vis Nigerian arts; it is after all his (westernized) judgment as to what constitutes relevant or legitimate cultural representations (Rose, 2001). Questions remain unanswered, then, regarding research design and the 'fit' between Lagos the other cities given Gandy's methodological commitment to analysis of visual culture and literature. This is especially the case if these absences risk reinforcing crisis narratives of Southern cities while overlooking indigenous forms of cultural representation.

There also remains the question of the political or analytical efficacy of cultural representation as method in periods of extreme socio-environmental inequality. It is in modern-day Mumbai, where he is most explicitly concerned with forms of socio-spatial polarization and its articulation with access to water and exposure to flood, that Gandy turns to expert interviews and participant observation in marginalized communities. While there are thriving cultural industries in Mumbai, these make little appearance. When taken together with the Lagos chapter, this suggests that the exposure of stark social and environmental inequalities is not well served by a methodological commitment to examine the visual and literary arts.

In the dystopian modernities of Los Angeles and London, Gandy's commitment to just socio-natural futures in cities is apparent. And in these two cities his engagement with cultural representation is again impressive, perhaps due to the plethora of visual art and literature in, on, and from these cities (although there is no detail about how authors and artists were selected for analysis). In Los Angeles, Gandy demands that our channelized rivers are deserving of environmental admiration, artistic analysis, and urban care. Drawing from the poem of Luis J. Rodriguez – 'This concrete river ... pouring over nightmares of wakefulness' (quoted in Gandy, 2014: 146) – he argues that the river is suggestive of the violence the city has wrought on its poor. Contemporary utopian visions for ecological restoration along the river erase the ways that artists have sought to document alternate histories of dispossession in the city. Moreover, these visions enact new dispossessions, overriding the river's function as a 'hidden world of refuge' (2014: 169), and ushering in opportunities for waterfront 'ecological gentrification'. In London, Gandy connects 'sci-fi' imaginaries of epic natural disasters producing urban destruction with socio-spatial analyses of contemporary flooding disasters to show that those most at risk of inundation in urban flood zones are, and always have been, the city's marginalized poor. 'The current environmental crisis', says Gandy, 'pose[s] grave threats ... if we do not imagine a better kind of human society, the outcome of current trends will intensify existing patterns of conflict and inequality' (2014: 213). He concludes: 'The science [of engineering water] is not mysterious, so that persistent inequalities must remain political in origin ... The upgrading of infrastructure networks ... can itself become a tool of governmentality that serves to sharpen and reinforce social inequalities' (2014: 221–222).

In Paris, Berlin, Los Angeles, and London, Gandy reveals that visual culture and literature can be revealing of the social relations and practices that constitute the urban as much as expert interviews or more traditional methods of social science inquiry. This method reaches its limit in Lagos and Mumbai. However, even if the explanatory power of visual art and literature may be limited in contexts of urgent political economic crises, Gandy himself is all too aware of what is at stake.

Conclusion

Matthew Gandy's exploration of the relations between water, public culture, and modernity in *The Fabric of Space* is a distinctive contribution to urban studies. Although his approach to understanding socio-ecological relations across six cities speaks to debates in urban political ecology, assemblage urbanism, and comparative urbanism, these references remain oblique. As a result, the book's exact contribution to these debates can be difficult to appreciate. His engagement with cultural and literary representations across the six cities is evocative of historical, contemporary, and future socio-ecological transformations while it also delinks conceptions of modernity with teleological notions of development. And yet the highly consequential methodological choices underpinning the book, notably concerning the selection of city cases and empirical materials, are unfortunately not subjects of explicit discussion or reflection. While Gandy takes care to maintain equality between the *experiences* of each of the cities in the book, the largely unacknowledged inconsistencies in *representation* across the city chapters – with respect to creativity, experimentation, and crisis – ultimately contribute to a degree of unevenness in methodological evidentiary, and interpretative, terms. Similarly, the breadth and reach of the analysis limit the ability of the book to explain across the city cases, with inter-urban connections left for readers to identify and draw out themselves. Indeed, the book leaves few crumbs for those who might wish to follow Gandy's approach as a model of research design and methodological innovation. In this context, one might say that the overarching goal of not just illuminating but gaining analytical leverage from a six-city investigation of the historical and contemporary roots and representations of socio-ecological crises was less than fully realized, giving more the appearance of suggestive juxtaposition than exacting comparison.

16

WRITING THE HETEROGENEOUS CITY: ON ABDOUMALIQ SIMONE'S *CITY LIFE FROM JAKARTA TO DAKAR*

Prajna Rao and Andre Comandon

KEYWORDS: comparative urbanism, everyday urbanism, infrastructure, postcolonial cities/subaltern urbanism, urban informality

AbdouMaliq Simone's city is dense with precarious potentials and uncertain possibilities that are assembled every day by its residents. In carefully compiling what those odds entail, he details how movements and interactions, intentionally and unintentionally, shape urban life and spaces. *City Life from Jakarta to Dakar* (2010) is a rich presentation from his continued engagement with cities in Africa and Southeast Asia over the last 40 years. His heterodox strategies for fieldwork and style of writing emerge out of a range of interactions, from deep involvement to ephemeral encounters with people and places in these cities. With an intention to reorient ways of seeing cities, he eschews conventions of comparison and replicability to infuse a fluidity into urban theorization that challenges, yet widens, our understanding of everyday urbanism.

Simone's work emerges from a critique of the international development and social scientific research that shapes narratives of cities across the global South in terms of deficiencies – of infrastructure, democracy, livelihoods, and

markets. His provocation is to shift from narratives of deficiencies to narratives of potentials. He is interested in what he calls the 'virtuality of the urban
poor', which exists within conditions of impoverishment, but is not fully actu-
alized within common understandings of what it means to be poor (Simone,
2010: 224). His critique of formal policy and planning interventions stems
from their failure to recognize and harness the potential of urban heterogeneity, in anticipation of a seemingly ordered future that is rarely ever fully
realized. Instead he argues in favor of exploring the messiness of a city that
allows itself 'to be messed with' by people to produce ambivalent results for
themselves and the city (2010: 210). 'What urban residents can do with each
other' is a recurring phrase, and it underscores Simone's intention of bringing
people and their capacities to the fore in urban theorizations. These capacities
include their intuitive, speculative, anticipatory, and experimental impulses
that are spawned, sustained, and even exploited in what he calls *intersections* –
shifting places, people, and practices that open multiple trajectories for individuals,
groups, and the city.

City Life from Jakarta to Dakar is Simone's perambulation through the
many cities shaping his career, with this book being one stop on his way to the
next destination. Read together with *For the City Yet to Come* and *Jakarta,
Drawing the City Near*, it becomes evident how he builds on concepts sketched
out in Africa to reiterate them in Jakarta. In this book, he draws on accumu-
lated observations of everyday urbanism, which he calls *cityness*, to develop
conceptual tools with which, he proffers, we may explore cities from Jakarta
to Dakar and beyond. Although his travels are across Africa and Southeast
Asia, he insists upon the applicability of his devices across the stubborn
North–South divide: 'the "destination" of this book is not for studies of specific
regions or development problems. Rather, it hopes to be a tool-box of ideas,
stories, and points of view applicable to making urban conditions everywhere
a little more creative and just' (Simone, 2010: xiv). He makes connections conceptualizing *peripheries* as spaces that are created by people and their relations
to the rest of the city rather than as a location, allowing him to navigate
between Bangkok and Paris, or jump from Brussels to Kinshasa.

Simone expands the scope of what can be studied in cities, grasping phenomena that are not easily measurable or observable with planned field
approaches. He uses what he calls an 'inventive method' (2010: 279), which
requires scratching below the surface meanings of what is observed and passed
on as accepted ways of looking into and at the city. A sense of the unexpected
in Simone's analysis emerges from reframing the density of urban networks as
essential to creating a version of the city that responds to its realities. The
reframing positively engages with the entangled relationships, economies, and
daily practices, exploring how they are so densely intertwined in a city that
separations between the formal and informal, adult and youth, citizen and
migrant, are no longer distinct. This inventiveness may be mistaken as creativity for the sake of creativity, or as an over-complication of what ought to be

simplified, but Simone is quite transparent about this methodology being a political project for making cities more just. Aligned with much scholarship in **postcolonial cities/subaltern urbanism**, his methodology reorients urban research to center its residents. It transforms them from passive recipients (of urban services) or victims (of exclusion) into active participants with their own social, economic, political, and religious agendas, which often exceed questions of survival. However, unlike the focus of most urban ethnographies on everyday lives in single cities, Simone uses inventive devices to discern relations of everyday lives in multiple contexts. In *black urbanism*, which is the final proposition of his book, he shows not just how connections travel, but also how lives of people themselves are transmitted across multiple contexts, with their own subjectivities and practices, to be transformed in myriad ways. This is the greatest achievement of the book: he offers analytical devices with which urban complexity across different cities may be grasped, without theoretically fixing it.

Reflecting his exploratory engagement with cities, Simone's method draws significantly from his collaborations with local institutions that have specific agendas for research and action within their contexts. These include his work with Muslim welfare social organizations in Abidjan and Accra, a professional theater group in Khartoum, and a spate of teaching and consulting assignments in universities, local government, and community development agencies across African cities. Often himself faced with the uncertainties of these jobs, he moved between diverse kinds of employment that shaped his relationship with these cities. For example, he entered Jakarta on invitation from the Urban Poor Consortium, a renowned local organization that advocates for the rights of the marginalized in the city. Though these organizations provided gateways for Simone to enter the cities for work, he neither necessarily shares their political positions nor allows them to define the scope of his investigations. His encounters and friendships with autonomists, communists, Sufi families, Islamic activists, artists, and urban residents inform the ways in which he sees, experiences, and writes about these cities (Burga, 2009).

From city to *cityness*: reframing urban interactions

With an intention to embrace urban complexity, Simone imagines everyday life through frames of conceptualization that retain an immediate connection to urban residents. Here, he teases out four key offerings – *cityness*, *periphery*, *intersections*, and *black urbanism* – also reiterating other concepts developed in previous works (*urban public* and *people as infrastructure*) and preluding his subsequent work on the *near-south* (Simone, 2014).

Echoing critical scholarship in urban studies (Amin and Thrift, 2002; Brenner and Schmid, 2015), Simone denies the possibility of cities as integrated entities, whose residents and activities are effectively coordinated under an overarching set of values, rules, and institutions. Instead, he calls for engaging with a heterogeneous *cityness* that 'really characterizes a city – its capacities to continuously reshape the ways in which people, places, materials, ideas, and affect are intersected – and is often the very thing that is left out of the larger analytical picture' (2010: 5). Citing the Ojuelegba district of Lagos (2010: 4), he illustrates how interacting regimes of official and customary order sustain highly productive operations that allow for day schools to turn into prayer meetings at night, right next to bars and discos; design consultancies that function as law offices in the day; and laundry soap, medicines, and votive candles sold right next to marijuana cigarettes. The intensity of urban operations belie the lines between binaries such that he is not convinced by any 'urban politics that focuses exclusively on defining who is included and who is excluded, who has rights and who doesn't, and who belongs and who doesn't ... [It] will always produce a situation that doesn't fit that calculation' (2010: 261).

Despite its fecundity, Simone observes how urban theorizations sideline *cityness* to the *periphery*. He discusses a range of 'peripheralizations', focusing on cities at the periphery of urban analysis, or on spaces, identities, and practices that have been left out of consideration – also pointing out how peripheries can spawn a resourcefulness and complexity that is perhaps 'even more convention-ally "urbanized" than the center' (2010: 160). He cites the example of peri-urban villages in the Shenzhen Municipality that came to house half of Shenzhen's 13 million residents, but whose rural status barred them from access to public amenities and housing. Improvisations therein of parking garages turning into classrooms, or alleyways into sites for health centers and nightclubs, allowed for a working of everyday life and night in imaginative ways, much like Ojuelegba. Unable to come up with alternatives of their own, the Shenzhen Municipality reduced the pace of its demolitions, implicitly recognizing the increased impor-tance of existing peripheries to the metropolitan system as a whole (2010: 44). Simone demonstrates how urban peripheries allow for vibrant, formidable economies that are linked to globalized networks, even as they are obfuscated by dominant discourses of informality and marginalization, and further excluded from conversations on economic growth.

The *intersection* is an analytical device for bringing differences into mani-fold relationships that produce unforeseen capacities and experiences, valuably extending what is thought to be possible. Movement within and between urban spaces generates these intersections, spawning an economy of anticipa-tion. Residents are constantly engaging in calculations to make a choice as to which intersection, which set of connections and movements, will open the most propitious future. In Kinshasa, people travel long distances to the market with nothing to sell or buy, hoping that opportunities will arise by virtue of just being present. The market becomes a focal point of the city because it is the one place where that possibility is open, and where divisions and conflicts can give way to change in the city. In a dysfunctional context with little predictability residents adapt to become more than human; they *become* the urban **infrastructure** – moving goods, services, and information for the city. In this role, they absorb the city's intense contradictions, which force them to live in separated realities. These persistent divisions and the lack of reliable institutions preclude their coming together, but produce the potential for a 'something else' or what Simone alludes to as 'a faint glimpse of an urban public': a heterogeneous assemblage of people, whose identities may clash but who still create a movement that is greater than their individual identities, without a sense of commonality (2010: 143–144).

Through a framing of *black urbanism*, Simone calls for attention to a mode of living by which urban residents from Jakarta to Dakar attempt to become persons who, despite their differentiated identities and spatialities, are able to think, reflect, and shape their existence productively. Black urbanism is about the ways in which colonialism, immigration, and movement shape residents' conditions of possibility, while not fully explaining people's determination to circumvent, subvert, and even transmute established norms and forms. Much like his other concepts, it breaks binaries without losing them: they are held proximate for productive use. In other words, he is not much occupied with how people are differentiated into the inside or outside, but with how they utilize their location of being 'aside'. From his own work with African entrepreneurs in Southeast Asia he uses this analytical device as 'a means of tying together the various situations and tactics that have been at work in the long history of African people moving out into and around a larger urban world' (2010: 268). Drawing lines between traders at Welcome House in Bangkok and workers from former West African colonies in Parisian banlieues, he demonstrates resonances in how they establish commerce and informational networks within interiorized common spaces that have been peripheralized from the city.

Using these four conceptual tools, Simone brings marginalization (of spaces, practices, economies, identities) to the fore, without framing it in terms of failings. He is more interested in how anxiety, anticipation, speculation, and experimentation, emerging from growing precarity, can be put to productive use by residents. He leaves matters of institutional interactions largely untouched, engages little with the histories of why particular urban configurations are the way they are, and avoids the imagination of a singular future in favor of multiple unknowable futures. His critique of uneven development and processes of capitalist circulation likely will leave political economists wanting a more thorough engagement with structures of economy and power, but Simone, like Ash Amin and Nigel Thrift (2002), Colin McFarlane (2011c), Edgar Pieterse (2011), and other relational theorists, finds political economy frameworks insufficient for understanding the heterogeneous city-in-flux. His active engagement with a 'politics of the possible' assumes marginalization as a given and urban futures as open and uncertain. Despite the explicit commitment to a more just city, he offers no paths or images of what that might look like, rendering his pursuit for equality ambiguous. In focusing on the potential of urban residents to shape their own lives, it could be argued that Simone concedes to those seeking to shift onto urban residents the responsibility of caring for themselves. Emphasizing places of dire need and the ways in which residents work around them, he draws out newer connections and potentials, without ever suggesting how these may lead to improved lives. Even though his own work in these cities has involved advocacy and policy consultations along with research practice, he offers no hints or suggestions for how these frames may be useful for institutional or tactical intervention.

From Jakarta to Dakar: transcending comparative boundaries

In order to conceptualize everyday life in cities Simone utilizes a methodology that deploys a relational framework, binding meticulous ethnographic observations with evocative writing. His relational framework centers on notions of mobility, circulations, and movement along and beyond streets, between various parts of the city, across various social relations and even countries. His ethnographic method mirrors that mobility, as he leaps between cities of Southeast Asia and Africa to draw novel connections. For example, in discussing Mayo district on the periphery of Khartoum, he shows how the everyday lives of refugee youths are intertwined with new forms of religion, language, morality, and faith, along with mobility and technology that enable skirmishes between the periphery and city, which also intersects with opportunities influenced by the Chinese domination of oil production, financial investments from the Arab world, and Asian imports en route to Douala. These intersections offer the refugees not only economic possibility, but also a sense of being part of the city. Simone uses a relational framework that engages with multiple places, spaces, and times to demonstrate how neighborhoods, rife with traumas experienced from elsewhere, generate possibilities of life-making and city-making that exceed what we know of urban transformations. Thus, the cities in the book are neither stable objects of comparison nor indicators of trending similarities or differences. Rather, they are working assumptions of having 'something to do with each other', along the lines of what Robinson (2016: 14) calls a generative comparison.

In another study, of inner-city renewal in Johannesburg, he combines a familiar analysis of developers' incentives and actions, empirical descriptions of relocation and redevelopment projects, and housing affordability to illuminate the complexity of the intersections between state initiatives and on-the-ground realities. He particularly highlights the tensions between state policy that enables specific types of redevelopment projects, and the operations of local NGOs and municipal agencies that often produce more disruption than relief to the lives of affected residents. He illustrates the limitations of grand interventions, which produce false choices between relocation and evasion for some urban residents, especially undocumented migrants, and steers attention toward their capacity to use diversionary tactics and networks to maintain precarious homes. As with most of his work, Simone only touches upon a critique of mainstream

economic development and urban policy, whether in reference to financialization of cities, the development of industrial corridors, or export processing
zones. He sees these as unimaginative abstractions that have little to do with a
majority of the city, even though they may be connected globally. Instead, he
concentrates his attention on the global reach of localized agglomerations as
Mayo, Central Johannesburg, the Kali Baru-Senen printing district in Jakarta,
or the Otigba Computer Village in Lagos. These rely on horizontal and vertical
intersections of histories, materials, investments, skills, and information, connecting these districts with other parts of the city, with suppliers in Asia, and
with financial markets globally.

Simone imagines 'a situation where Dakar, Lagos, Nairobi, Dubai, Bangkok,
and Jakarta ... are "neighbors" in a single metropolitan space, and what that
experience might be like for people who would live within it' (2010: 263). In
doing so, he seeks to connect creative practices of inhabitation, livelihoods,
spatial assembly, and social diversification that operate without adhering to
any formalized prescriptions, so that these may also be considered seriously in
analyses of global change.

Simone's fieldwork may be understood as an ethnography of, from, and
into the shadows. He digs deep into nooks and crevices of urban spaces and
human experience where few care to pay attention, and leaves no trail. His
insights and observations are rich, evocative, and convey his sense of *cityness*
in a way that is rarely achieved in urban studies. Describing a bus transport
center, he pays attention to the tangible and intangible circuitries of words,
money, effort, sentiment, favors, obligations, action, and information, highlighting how the bus shelter intersects with much more than transit markets in
the city. His vivid descriptions of spaces, connections, and practices are not
always anchored in specific times and locations, and verge on what may be
dismissed as anecdotal (in contrast to conventionally structured case studies).
His style of fieldwork is improvisational; representations are partial, and theorizations fluid. Fieldwork requires that vulnerable subjects be protected, and
his strategy of not leaving a trail is perhaps a conscious decision to engage
with heterogeneous activities without betraying their invisibility. Similarly, in
cases where his descriptions are more detailed, he implicates actors across the
il/legal divide, so as to mitigate any risk of exposure for any single group due
to this research. His interactions with various residents are mediated through
specific interpersonal dynamics, reflected in the ways he represents them. Even
though it is Simone's agenda to focus attention on the urban residents, it is not
very clear if they echo his version of their intentions. A conspicuous lack of
their representation makes it difficult to know if he speaks *with* or *for* while
writing *about* them. Simone uses his ethnographic material not so much
toward empirical ends, but to generate theory from everyday lives. In the production of urban theory, especially from daily practices which are provisional and
varied, the question of whose voice to represent (and how) becomes significant. However, he does not engage much with the relationship between the

researcher–researched or its representation, attending instead to the politics of intention and method of research. His ethnographic intentions are less about giving residents or his collaborators a 'voice', and more about engaging with them to widen prospects for research and practices that magnify the potential of *cityness*.

The other leg of Simone's methodology is his writing. *City Life* reads like a series of lectures that employ a meandering narrative with occasional nods to contemporary urban studies. His formulations draw insights from media studies, psychology, and cultural studies, and subaltern and postcolonial scholarship, deployed to the extent that they enrich his field-based theoriza-tions. He works on a vocabulary for cities composed of shifting aggregates and partialities. As Ackbar Abbas observes (UCHRI, 2015), Simone does not describe the city but de-scribes the city; he un-writes what is known to be the city to conjure another imagination, however elusive it may be. He engages with the ephemeral and the intangible as they intersect with the presumably stable, tangible aspects of urban environments, a messiness that often is approached as something to be tidied up or made invisible. His writing approach consciously works toward theorizing an ontology of a city that is incessantly reworking itself. In weaving his writing within a relational framework, he constructs frames to reimagine everyday urban practices, such that they can be observed across multiple contexts without presuming any permanence.

Simone's writing reflects a consciousness of how analytical categories are not only descriptive, but also performative. In other words, his work reiterates that research projects may not only constitute different perspectives of a single reality, but also enact different realities. Writing about cities in a particular way makes some realities more real than others. Treating reality not as a given but an enactment, Simone deploys his framework, fieldwork, and writing to enact a precarious urban that is rife with unpredictable potential. In doing so, he shifts the 'production of the urban' from an epistemological to an onto-logical project. He delves deeply into the lives of the 'urban majority', who are poor but not destitute; into self-built environments that are lumped as slums but are more than shelter; into everyday life that includes **urban informality** but involves more than practices of survival and resilience. He pushes beyond established ideas of poverty, risk, and informality to evoke provisional images of resource, anticipation, and creativity. He refrains from further stabilizing terms through which some of these spaces and practices are conventionally understood – slums, social capital, social networks – articulating a language to summon new relations while cognizant of the fragilities with which relation-alities are coproduced, cultivated, and even crushed. His explorations with language and writing are not merely an aesthetic indulgence; they seek to avoid nineteenth-century Euclidean preoccupations of fixing, demarcating, and separating the world into neat categories, experimenting with language that grasps the fleeting, distributed, multiplicitous, non-causal, chaotic flows

and connections that reflect the contemporary urban. Simone's written enactment of the provisional city contrasts significantly from other structured
academic writing on cities. He does not lay out the method legibly, nor does
he offer easy takeaways. Significant intellectual labor must be invested to grip
his writing, without which the book becomes less effective for those seeking a
quick read on cities from Jakarta to Dakar.

Beyond Dakar

In *City Life from Jakarta to Dakar*, Simone configures a methodology that ele-
vates studies of everyday lives from empirical particularities to studies that
generate meso-level theoretical frames for diverse urban contexts. He does so by
disaggregating parts and practices of differentiated cities in order to reassemble
them into a conceptual space for relational inter-urban comparisons. Such a rich
metropolitan space, composed of multiple cities with ever-transforming relations,
requires Simone's sustained engagement over a long period, uniquely positioning him
to produce a work of this scale and depth. However, his use of a relational framework, stretching across spaces, times, scales, identities, and materials, may be
useful to seek out unseen connections, draw unusual parallels, and evoke radical juxtapositions, producing more pluralistic comparative urban research. This
framework is especially useful when more conventional approaches of 'seeing
cities through elsewhere', restricted by seeking objective criteria for comparison
or embedded in singular space–time frames, are insufficient for comparing cities.
This is also the difficulty of working on cities relationally, however, treating
spaces, times, practices, and agents as always in relation to each other. If everything is related to everything, how we choose which relations to focus on, and
for what generative comparisons, requires a thorough and reflexive engagement
with research intentions and methodology.

Simone's use of relational frames inspires comparison of cities that have
seemingly no connection, on the basis of criteria that resist measurement, built
through an earnest engagement to observing everyday urban life. This can
inspire others, as when Garth Myers (2014) uses insights from Nairobi and
Cape Town to destabilize the narrative of inclusivity spearheading Hartford's
transit plan in Connecticut. Myers mobilizes *cityness* not only to highlight
similarities in conditions of marginalization in Kenya, South Africa, and the
United States but also to suggest a path forward. Simone's contributions
to **comparative urbanism** and **everyday urbanism** are reflected in how other
authors have evoked his work to emphasize the ability of urban residents to
(re)create cities through everyday actions (e.g., Amin, 2013; McFarlane,
2011c; Pieterse, 2011; Till, 2012). His conceptual frames also have inspired a
re-evaluation of African urbanism as productive of urban theory. Jose
Arguello et al. (2013) adopt his critiques of urban periphery to refocus studies
of African cities away from slums as the epitome of urban poverty, and toward
the productivity of inner-city neighborhoods. Mary Lawhon et al. (2014: 507)

highlight the possibilities in shifting language away from Africa's failings to 'reorient theory-making and stabilize a different image of the city – what it is (ontological difference), how it works (epistemological difference), whom it is for, and how it can be changed'. Whereas his empirical methods are improvised in ways that are difficult to replicate faithfully, they reinforce the need for keen attention to the messy, the fleeting, the material, and the immaterial in fieldwork. In this way, his methodology presents another opening for studying in and theorizing from the South, but in ways that can also be imagined for urban conditions elsewhere, including the North.

If urban theorization combines studying and writing as integral to creating the city, Simone's work reveals how cities can be recreated or reassembled with carefully improvised research methodologies. The making of the city, both in its form and in theory, are inseparable, with implications for how researchers and policymakers intervene in it. Simone's writing of the city releases ambiguous energies of urban heterogeneity that are simultaneously empowering and unsettling. His relational framework opens unseen connections, without laying out a path for how it might be replicated. Similarly, his improvised ethnographic investigations and inventive writing are particularly specific, emerging from his own experiences and subjectivities. His work may not offer any templates for conducting urban research, but it stimulates curiosity, provokes attention to the messy, and offers a variety of cues to studying cities with all their uncertainties and assiduous detail. *City Life from Jakarta to Dakar* is a fruitful testimony to how methodology – including the framing, fieldwork, and writing – is implicated within the politics of urban research, reminding the reader that a greater reflexivity toward all three is essential in rigorously constructing our cities, and their plural knowledges.

17

IN SEARCH OF ORDINARY 'ELSEWHERES' IN GLOBAL URBANISM: ON OLA SÖDERSTRÖM'S *CITIES IN RELATIONS*

Rachel Bok

KEYWORDS: comparative urbanism, global cities/ordinary cities, more-than-human world, neoliberal urbanism, postcolonial cities

Palermo is hardly an intuitive starting point for what would at first glance appear to be a comparison of the 'Southern' cities of Hanoi and Ouagadougou. But it was during his journeys to this city in the 1990s that the Swiss cultural geographer Ola Söderström began to see in Palermo traces of other European cities, such as Berlin and London, before shifting his sights to the global South to understand what a translocal, relational perspective might reveal about the variegated nature of global urban development. The result was a decade-long study spanning both continents and disciplinary terrains of urban studies – a testimony to the lived, demanding nature of transnational research. This nod to Palermo in the preface of a book about the porous worlds of Hanoi and Ouagadougou is a telling indicator of what lies in wait for readers: a glimpse into the extraordinary connections to elsewhere that cause us to see **ordinary cities** differently.

Ola Söderström's *Cities in Relations* (henceforth, *CiR*), published in 2014, appeared after the re-emergence of calls for empirical investigations into **comparative urbanism**. Söderström explicitly positions *CiR* as a methodological intervention that seeks to advance a *relational comparison* of Hanoi and Ouagadougou. It revolves around the central research question of how these two globalizing cities of the South have shaped, and been shaped by, their relations with elsewhere. Söderström's main argument is that a relational analysis of cities would require scholars to conceive of relations not merely as 'abstract conceptions', but as 'historical products', constructed through processes of power and grounded materially (2014: 3). This is couched in a deeper argument he makes for a more expansive, grounded conceptualization of globalization, opting for the French term *'mondialisation'* to convey the multitude of global interconnections that exceed the economic reductionism that he sees as characteristic of research on **global cities** and **neoliberal urbanism**.

This chapter critically evaluates Söderström's methodological exposition of relational comparison. *CiR* is a pioneering, monograph-length study in how to *practice* relational comparison. This itself is a significant achievement considering that the chorus of calls for relational comparison in urban studies has markedly outstripped empirical investigations thereof (but see Cook and Ward, 2012). Indeed, *CiR* illustrates how comparative urbanism necessarily is a theoretical–empirical project (Nijman, 2015). More than merely method or academic technique, *CiR* also reflects an aspiration, aligned with certain streams of comparativism and particular ethico-political concerns, for a more 'cosmopolitan' urban studies (Robinson, 2011a). Still, there remain several missed opportunities in Söderström's approach that, when examined more broadly, undercut its postcolonial agenda and reinforce the need for urban scholars to reflect more systematically on the purpose, practice, and politics of (relational) comparison.

In what follows I detail the mechanics and practicalities of Söderström's methodology of relational comparison, discuss the wider context of the 'renaissance' of comparative urbanism in urban studies, before critically assessing his methodology: that is, the value of using relations as the basis of comparison; the Deleuzian perspective that informs his methodological approach; and the question of his ethico-political commitments. I conclude by raising three questions surrounding the theoretical and methodological stakes of conducting relational comparison, and strategies for moving this method forward in urban studies.

Doing relational comparison

Söderström's methodology unfolds through an exploratory yet systematic comparison of the 'worlds of relations' of Hanoi and Ouagadougou. For him, a relational comparison 'takes relations, their evolution, form, intensity, and orientation as the elements of comparison' (2014: 3). He draws on geographical scholarship by Ash Amin, Doreen Massey, and Claude Raffestin, also paying homage to Gillian Hart (2002), reiterating that a relational geography must be attentive to power, historical trajectories, interplays between relationality and territoriality, and possibilities for transformation. His relational thinking is post-structuralist and Deleuzian, set in sharp contrast to what he considers the hierarchical and neostructuralist relationality of the Globalization and World Cities Research Network (https://www.lboro.ac.uk/gawc/) – a hint as to what guides his choice of cities.

Hanoi and Ouagadougou are capital cities in Southeast Asia and West Africa that reflect the unevenness of the globalizing South. Söderström views them as 'real laboratories' for observing how transnational relations might shape urban development, primarily because these cities were 'relation-poor' (i.e., more isolated and marginal) at certain points in Vietnam and Burkina Faso's histories before being 're-connected' to global flows in the 1990s – hence his decision to focus on the 1990–2010 timeframe (2014: 2). Both are former French colonies that maintain linkages with France and experienced rapid urbanization under the privatization of land ownership and economic deregulation in the 1990s. Each city has taken a distinct trajectory of globalization (Hanoi's more economic; Ouagadougou's more political), with different geopolitical orientations of cross-border relations (Hanoi with its Asian neighbors; Ouagadougou with African and European cities). Söderström's rationales for choosing Hanoi and Ouagadougou reflect a broader motivation to see from the South and challenge an anglophone metrocentricity (Bunnell and Maringanti, 2010) that frames **postcolonial cities** as insignificant by conventional global city metrics.

Söderström's attention to how their 'elsewheres' matter ensures that *CiR* is about more than (just) these two cities. There are hardly any interactions between Hanoi and Ouagadougou, at times creating the impression of two case studies stacked side by side, which prompts the much-needed question of what exactly it means to compare cities through their relations with elsewhere. Purposively transcending dominant themes in urban-policy mobilities scholarship, Söderström emphasizes three types of urban translocal and transnational relations: urban policies, in particular public space policy for its ostensibly more progressive ethos; urban architectural forms, investigating 16 newly built places in each city (buildings, public space, infrastructure); and urban practices and discourses, especially their mutually constitutive relationship with city dwellers' subjectivities. First, he compares the relations of Hanoi and Ouagadougou in terms of their type, intensity, and orientation, injecting specificity into otherwise vague invocations of relational analysis. Second, he compares the effects of these relations in different domains of urban development, pinning down the generative potential of relations. Third, he compares the timeframe of urban development in Hanoi and Ouagadougou from 1990 to 2010, tracing this temporality over long-term trajectories and short-term instances of policymaking to investigate past and present city relations in the making.

Söderström implements a mixed-methods approach that combines quantitative and qualitative methodologies. Drawing on previous collaborative research with teams based in Hanoi and Ouagadougou, statistical data were compiled from documents produced by international organizations (e.g., World Bank, KOF Swiss Economic Institute), national statistical offices, municipal offices, and existing studies (e.g., GaWC research). Using these data, he summarizes national-level trends in Vietnam (1945–2012) and Burkina Faso (1960–2012) in the form of a more traditional comparative study. Söderström examines flows of capital (foreign direct investment, remittances, development aid); people (population dynamics, tourism, student migration); and information (Internet access and cellphone subscriptions).

In terms of qualitative methods, Söderström relies on in-depth interviews (20 in Hanoi, 18 in Ouagadougou) with professionals involved in governing urban policy and built environments, including architects, municipal and national government officials, international organization staff, researchers, activists, and artists. He also uses 'object biography' to trace specific changes in urban development, focusing on urban forms (and the relations constituting their creation and usage) and using actor–network theory to explore the relationship between material forms and society (drawing on Guggenheim and Söderström, 2010). To uncover sites where different dimensions of urban development come together (investments, regulations, design processes, and user experiences), based on 'expert' interviews, he selects 16 objects (buildings, public spaces, parks) built during 1990–2010 in each of Hanoi and Ouagadougou as representative of change in that city. This is operationalized in two phases. First, he assesses the role of transnational relations in influencing object design, utilizing visual documentation (surveying photographs and architectural plans) and interviews with the relevant architects and their clients (30 in Hanoi, 49 in Ouagadougou). Second, he focuses on how these forms shape urban culture and subject-making, selecting eight objects in each city for which he undertook shorter interviews and participant observations with their users (73 in Hanoi, 64 in Ouagadougou). This brings a Latourian sensibility to bear on relational comparison by integrating the **more-than-human world** into the analysis, which Söderström sees as crucial to comprehending the coproduction of knowledge in processes such as architectural design.

Comparative urbanism redux: the promise of relationality?

The current enthusiasm for comparative urbanism has generated two Special Issues in the journal *Urban Geography* alone within the last decade (Nijman, 2007a; McFarlane and Robinson, 2012). A favored term to describe this surge of interest is 'renaissance'. Kevin Ward (2008) notes that research in this subfield peaked in the 1970s and 1980s before slowing in the early 1990s, cautioning that a comparative urbanism for the twenty-first century would need to retain past insights while challenging the taken-for-granted conceptualization of cities as territorially bounded units. This renaissance has generated a plurality rather than a consensus on the purposes and methodologies of comparison. Examples include Nick Clarke's (2012) actually existing comparative urbanism study of UK town-twinning partnerships; Jan Nijman's (2007b) systematic multiple individualizing comparisons framework for understanding Miami, Florida; scalar urban comparativism in Europe and North America (Boudreau et al., 2008; Glick Schiller, 2012); and Ian Cook and Kevin Ward's (2012) relational comparison of waterfront planning in Cleveland, Ohio.

Current thinking owes a great deal to Jennifer Robinson's (2011a; 2015) efforts to rework the conventions of comparison for a more 'cosmopolitan urban studies' (Robinson, 2006), clearly an inspiration for CiR. According to Robinson (2011b: 13), this has the potential to craft a 'revitalized urban comparativism that is more adequate to the task of thinking through a world of cities'. It would require reflecting more deeply on matters of methodology and theorization, but also conceiving more expansively of the existing ways whereby scholars view, categorize, and classify cities (Gough, 2012). There is undeniably a wider postcolonial angle here: Garth Myers (2014: 104) wields comparative thinking to reconsider 'the meaning of cityness and the roles, functions and shapes of urban areas, when accepted understandings for these derive from Euro-American contexts', resonating with the sort of deconstructive relational thinking that continually questions taken-for-granted relationships between knowledge, place, and power (Roy, 2016).

In this spirit, Ward (2010) argues that comparative urbanism should focus less on searching for similarities and differences between cities and more on deploying a relational comparison 'that uses different cities to pose questions of one another' (2010: 480). Following Hart's (2002: 297) conceptualization of relational space, he conceives of urban space and politics as relational and dynamically interconnected. Proponents of relational comparison (e.g., McFarlane, 2010; Robinson, 2011b; Jacobs, 2012a) commonly invoke Ward's (2010) framework, as does CiR. Yet Glick Schiller (2012) cautions that relational comparison runs the risk of overemphasizing horizontal networks of connection to the neglect of (hierarchical) power structures (but see Jacobs, 2012b).

Relational comparison has an obvious appeal; encouraging urban scholars to consider cities in a more open and flexible manner seems especially crucial in an age of global interconnection. Yet this begs the fundamental question of what makes a comparative methodology 'relational'. Jane Jacobs (2012a: 412) notes that relational thinking has been operationalized in rather different ways by urban scholars, indicative of its 'irreconcilable grammars of relationality'. Hart (2018: 372) similarly observes that different invocations of relationality in comparative urbanism can be 'quite incommensurate'. As an example, Hart notes that her approach to relational comparison is influenced by Massey, Coronil, and Lefebvre; Robinson draws on Lefebvre as well, but combines this with readings of Deleuze and Althusser; Roy's approach is more deconstructive. Yet Hart argues that they share an epistemological perspective: a principled wariness of grand theoretical overtures, a processual awareness of constitutive forces, and a profound skepticism of anglophone and Eurocentric thinking. In this wider context of debates on relational comparison that have yet to systematically confront these differences, I return to *CiR* to consider what is distinctive about relational comparison, the theoretical antecedents that have influenced Söderström's methodological framework, and how *CiR* ultimately falls short of its postcolonial ambitions.

Reflecting on *Cities in Relations*

Söderström (2014: 20) remarks that, with the exception of Hart's work, the current state of relational comparison is framed largely as a theoretical critique of traditional comparativism. Given the general lack of empirical engagement, *CiR* is valuable because Söderström provides a concrete definition of relational comparison *and* a practical methodological exposition of how it can be done. *CiR* thus offers a primer of sorts to studying city relations for others to build upon and refine. McFarlane and Robinson (2012) suggest that scholars will need to craft new methods and approaches to comparison in order to comprehend diverse urban experiences. Yet, by deploying largely traditional methods *CiR* makes relational comparison appear feasible, and can thus be considered a generative 'experiment' in relational comparative urbanism.

Söderström counters the critiques of fluidity and vagueness that are frequently levelled at relational approaches by proposing a comparative strategy that compares city relations via registers of intensity, domain, and orientation. This is a useful starting point to think about how to *differentiate* relations. In 'Transnational policy relations' (his chapter 3), he studies the role of foreign expertise in governing transnational master-planning and urban policy relations in Hanoi and Ouagadougou. He combines a longitudinal analysis of masterplans and policy documents with interviews with professionals to emphasize the historical specificity of these planning relations, particularly their postcolonial dimensions. This enables him to show that the two cities have forged qualitatively different policy relations that (continue to) shape their divergent trajectories of urban globalization and the range of historical influences at play. By documenting the variability of urban and national transitions to neoliberalism, he offers nuanced perspectives on such oft-invoked terms as globalization and neoliberal urbanism.

This methodological strategy of differentiating city relations enables Söderström to demonstrate how connections that are oriented toward different political stakes and outcomes 'often relate one city to many others' (2014: 64), drawing different combinations of cities into the same frame of analysis to make them commensurable. This pushes scholars to ask *which* relations matter, *when* in the city's development, and *why* this configuration of relations and cities was produced at this particular time. For Hanoi, the 'relations that matter' are market-centered – the sizeable property sector of Pacific Asia comes to mind – connecting it with cities in South Korea, Indonesia, and Japan. For Ouagadougou, meaningful diplomatic connections are established with North African, European, and Middle Eastern cities, culminating in the performative establishment of Ouaga 2000, a '"presidential" special zone' for partner countries to showcase these relations (2014: 82). Yet such diplomatic linkages are at times wielded in conflicting ways by competing scales (municipal and national) of Burkina Faso's state apparatus, leading Söderström to an analysis of how Ouagadougou's transnational relations also constitute a multiscalar 'battleground' between political interests. Tracing the cleavages and fault lines of translocal urban relations pushes scholars to re-evaluate urban spatialities by bringing a diversity of urban processes into the analysis, possibly also creating radically different relationships of comparison to those of a more conventional (territorial) comparison (Robinson, 2011b).

Söderström's approach to relationality is informed by Deleuzian thinking, which orientates his research design towards possibilities of difference, novelty, and transformation in urban life. This is framed as a critique of research in urban entrepreneurialism and neoliberal urbanism that searches principally for sameness rather than for difference. The ambition to conceptualize more-than-neoliberal policy relations influences his choice to focus on public space policy, which he regards as not typically neoliberal. Methodologically, Deleuze provides a topological perspective that involves surveying a repertoire of policy exchanges, including the actual travels of (human and more-than-human) actors and the more immaterial, imaginative circuits of circulation that might not have been part of the formal policymaking process (e.g., visits, citations). Söderström elaborates on this in his chapter 4 ('Public space policies on the move'), parsing the contradictions and tensions between relationality and territoriality in public space policymaking in Hanoi. He develops the concept of 'loose threads', denoting connections that exceed formal policymaking, to understand how policies are 'arrived at' rather than how they 'arrive from elsewhere' (Robinson, 2013b: 11).

Tracing loose threads unveils '*potential* policies within these different translocal connections before the choice and black-boxing of a specific solution' (Söderström, 2014: 97; emphasis added). He contrasts three types of translocal connections of public space policymaking: policy mobility (actual–formal); topological representations (discursive–material); and inter-referencing (discursive–imaginative). The variety of these loose threads is indicative of the range of perspectives that constitute imaginaries of public space in Hanoi – of what currently exists but also of what the city could become. This has the virtue of opening the black box of policymaking to unveil processes of negotiation, conflict, and paths not taken. Yet actual instances of power are strangely absent; this could have been addressed through interviews with users/citizens affected by the destruction of public space, not just with professionals. This neglect may derive from Söderström's desire to avoid the search for 'sameness' that he thinks plagues research on neoliberal urbanism. But it also brings to mind Glick Schiller's (2012) dissatisfaction with (Deleuzian) relational thinking for underemphasizing power hierarchies. Persistent trajectories of policymaking matter precisely because directionality can reflect power differences.

Söderström's Deleuzian perspective has other shortcomings. First, attention to (transformative) novelty needs to be balanced with attention to stability and persistence. For example, the question of why certain 'loose threads' are consistently discarded may be explained by institutional constraints and long-term policymaking regimes. Second, his conception of territory is thin, stemming from a general lack of engagement with theorists of territory and/or the state; even Deleuze and Guattari's corpus of work on (de)territorialization is strangely neglected. Söderström appears to use aspects of embeddedness and generativeness of policy relations in different domains of urban development as a proxy for territory and territoriality, claiming to 'look more precisely at the territorial aspect of these policies by focusing on how these relations generate the specific domain of policies for public space' (2014: 62). Yet McFarlane (2016: 172) notes that Söderström sets up a dualism between relationality and territoriality that risks 'undermin[ing] a nuanced sense of relationality in that it leaves us with an underspecified sense of territory as both relational and non-relational'.

Söderström explicitly situates CiR within the postcolonial critique of global cities research, in order to '"speak back" to mainstream urban studies' (2014: 175). In his concluding argument, inspired by John Friedmann (2007), Söderström makes the case for an 'assets-based politics of urban relatedness' (2014: 171): this would impel practitioners of urban governance to conceive of urban development strategies – and draw on intercity relations – that are more locally sensitive. Congruent with this is a politics (and ethos) of learning that would encourage practitioners to reflect more deeply on the appropriateness of models of urban growth for particular cities, as well as the careful cultivation of inter-urban relationships that would best suit the needs and ambitions of cities and their citizens. Söderström bemoans the destruction of Hanoi's distinctive social assets by professionals pursuing global city dreaming, while commending Ouagadougou's municipal strategy. In this view, Ouagadougou's weak global economic connections offer the unexpected silver lining of shielding the city from the aspirations plaguing Hanoi. Indeed, CiR ultimately advocates an approach to urban planning and translocal relationship-building that is sensitive to the needs of a city's citizens.

It is debatable whether CiR lives up to its postcolonial ambition. Söderström's choices of Hanoi and Ouagadougou go beyond the usual suspects of urban research and learning – while also raising Ouagadougou as a model of sorts – but the analysis falls short of a genuinely postcolonial critique with regards to the broader theory-cultures of its research design. McFarlane (2010: 737) relates this question of theory-cultures to the ethico-politics of comparison, which are 'fundamentally about … the epistemic and institutionalized relations of power between different scholarly and non-scholarly communities within and between different cultures of knowledge production'. The actors and authors Söderström selects to speak for Hanoi and Ouagadougou mean that *CiR* reiterates existing power relations. Interview quotes largely originate from the professionals with whom most of the in-depth interviews were conducted, and 'experts' also determined the sample of objects analyzed, reinforcing the elite-centric focus of policy mobility research (Bunnell and Marolt, 2014). Moreover, *CiR*'s aspiration to theorize back to mainstream urban studies is undercut by its conceptual architecture of European (largely francophone) theorists: Deleuze, Foucault, Latour, etc.

A second issue relates to who counts as a researcher. Söderström explains that *CiR* is a single-authored monograph because the relational comparison of Hanoi and Ouagadougou was only undertaken following initial collaborative research. In the preface, he acknowledges the support of bigger, presumably diverse research teams based in Hanoi and Ouagadougou (and Palermo), likening these efforts to a 'human science laboratory' wherein the labors of comparison were 'distributed across different sites and collectively constructed' (2014: xvi) – a telling metaphor that elides the inescapable complexities inherent to envisioning, coordinating, and undertaking comparative urbanism. Any meaningful transnational comparison necessarily entails collaborative, multicultural ventures and research networks (Myers, 2014). For a text that is so emphatic about its methodological purpose, it is oddly silent about the transnational circuits of labor that were integral to enabling this relational comparison. A relational comparison that is reflexive about matters of methodology and theory surely must reflect not just on the cases, but also on the interpersonal, power-laden relations through which researchers interact with each other to make comparison possible (e.g., divisions of labor, linguistic and cultural exchanges, and reliance on local interlocuters). Questions of who gets to speak on behalf of which cities, and in what manner, are questions of participation and authorization that constitute the 'complex cultural political economy of existing comparativism' (Jacobs, 2012a: 910).

Learning from *Cities in Relations*

There is much to learn from *CiR*, not just about strategies for undertaking relational comparison, but also about advancing urban studies more broadly. As a pioneering effort that sets out a unique and feasible methodological framework, *CiR* is invaluable for the sub-field of comparative urbanism. It also provides a fine-grained analysis of cities often considered marginal to global urbanization – an entry point into comparing cities in ways that might do justice to their complexity and diversity.

In concluding, this methodological excavation of *CiR* raises several questions for urban studies with respect to advancing comparative urban research. First, what is the purpose of comparative urbanism more generally and relational comparison in particular? Should it be to destabilize and surprise, overturning taken-for-granted assumptions? This is what Benedict Anderson (2016) has long advocated in deploying comparison as a discursive strategy, not unlike Robinson's (2011a) reflections on the politics of commensurability in comparison and Myers' (2014) provocative argument for making unexpected comparisons. Söderström's choice of Hanoi and Ouagadougou carries the risk that these cities will be bracketed off as 'incomparable' to, for example, northern cities. This, combined with *CiR*'s dependence on northern theoretical frameworks, such as policy mobility and geographies of architecture, results in a comparison that may reinforce rather than unsettle existing norms of commensurability. A counter-approach would have been to undertake a more extensive multi-site strategy that brings Hanoi and Ouagadougou directly into comparative conversation with northern cities, thereby working within but also across the heuristic of North–South relations.

Second, there is the question of how postcolonial theory and relational comparison are related. Postcolonial thinking has reinvigorated interest in urban comparison; some of the strongest advocates of relational comparison are postcolonial scholars. Among the range of postcolonial approaches present in urban studies, *CiR* draws most extensively on the **ordinary cities** critique to revisit arguments of modernity, development, and neoliberalism. But, as Jacobs (2012a: 904) asks, 'Does comparativism somehow better serve the postcolonial imagination?' A dialogue between postcolonial and non-postcolonial approaches to comparison might be useful in this regard.

Third, how might scholars *practically* integrate less visible relations of place, knowledge, and power into (relational) comparative research designs? Comparison is usually undertaken by large, multi-sited, and multicultural research teams, such as those with whom Söderström worked in Hanoi and Ouagadougou before writing *CiR*. These entail transnational divisions of labor, a translational politics of exchange, and decisions about authorship, authority, and language. Who was responsible for which tasks and why? How did researchers grapple with a range of local complexities while holding cities in comparison? While Söderström has little to say on this, in moving forward, scholars need to be more reflexive and open about how they have grappled with these complexities in methodological discussions about comparison. Tradeoffs will surely be made, but these should be viewed less as impediments to research design and more as opportunities to advance methodological and theoretical conversations about comparing cities. Conceived of more expansively and *ethically*, comparison is not just a method(ology), but a 'mode of thought that informs how urban theory is constituted' (McFarlane, 2010: 31). The critical reflections provoked by comparative urbanism are advancing urban studies, but these must be accompanied by methodological expositions that are reflexive about the structural relations through which knowledge of the urban is generated.

18

URBAN COMPARISON, QUANTIFIED: ON MICHAEL STORPER ET AL.'S *THE RISE AND FALL OF URBAN ECONOMIES*

Andre Comandon, Kenton Card and Joseph A. Daniels

KEYWORDS: agglomeration, comparative urbanism, uneven urban development, urban governance

The Rise and Fall of Urban Economies (2015) (henceforth *Rise and Fall*) seeks to elucidate how, of two of the world's most prosperous urban regions in 1970, one remained at the top and the other fell behind. In answering this question, Michael Storper collaborated with co-authors Thomas Kemeny, Naji Makarem, and Taner Osman to trace the diverging trajectories of the Bay Area and Los Angeles. *Rise and Fall* is an impressive achievement that mobilizes broad theoretical strands connected to the field of regional economic development to peel away the layers of explanation for the divergence between the two regions, evaluate the merits of each, and draw implications for regional development scholarship and policymaking.

Storper et al. develop an atypical approach to uncovering the factors and processes that they hypothesize caused the divergence. In addition to tracing the urban evolution of the two diverging metropolitan regions, the authors are concerned with the sources of these processes. To isolate the root cause, they examine the combination of exogenous and endogenous factors that fostered a cohesive institutional environment propitious to the growth and resilience of the new economy in the Bay Area while triggering a pattern of fragmentation that undermined the technology edge Los Angeles once possessed. They adopt a case study approach to identify non-linear, idiosyncratic events, also harnessing unwieldy data underlying this process. The individual pieces of evidence are weak as singular empirical refutations of theoretical predictions, if evaluated independently, but Storper et al.'s seductive narrative glues together disparate pieces into a compelling argument.

Taken together, *Rise and Fall* provides a model for harnessing collaborative analysis to synthesize a wide variety of data, undertaking detailed empirical analysis of 'exemplary' case studies in order to push the field of regional economic development in a new direction. Principally this takes the form of a 'myth-busting' motif: major theoretical reasons for divergence/convergence from a variety of perspectives are teed up and then critiqued, in order to illustrate why a synthetic approach is preferable. The ambitious scope of the study, combining multiple theoretical threads and abundant data, creates tradeoffs between quantitative (or formal hypothesis testing) analysis and more sociologically rich institutional analysis. The intentions of the authors are to uncover the roots of divergence: the factors that, beyond chance, sent the two regions down different growth and institutional paths. The analysis is more successful in explaining the (quantitative) realities of divergence between the two metropolitan regions than in revealing the institutional origins of such divergence, reflecting the relative strength of the two analytical frameworks. Institutional analysis requires depth and nuance not easily achieved in a monograph that already does so much to set up the investigation.

Rise and Fall complements and expands on Storper's earlier *Keys to the City* (2013; henceforth, *Keys*). Parallels between the two books are therefore useful in illuminating *Rise and Fall*'s methodological choices and highlighting the tradeoffs. However, *Rise and Fall* is undoubtedly an original contribution, and the collaboration seems to provide a bedrock for creative innovation and deep analysis. We therefore begin with a discussion of the role of collaboration in shaping the book.

Collaborative comparison

The process of collaborative research and writing is embedded throughout *Rise and Fall* but largely unaddressed therein. The authors reflect neither on their individual contributions nor on how their intellectual trajectories shaped the analysis. We think it is important to highlight that Storper was the chair of his co-authors' doctoral dissertations. Thomas Kemeny (graduated 2009) is a well-established scholar whose independent research has focused on the role of innovation and specialization, having collaborated with Storper on multiple prior occasions. Naji Makarem (graduated 2013) and Taner Osman (graduated 2015) completed doctoral theses on topics directly related to the subject matter of this book. Makarem undertook a comparative study of income divergence in the Bay Area and Southern California, focused on the socio-relational context embedded within the institutions of the two regions. Osman focused on the Bay Area and how the political geography of the region and its land use intersect to affect the locational decisions of high-technology firms. *Rise and Fall* goes beyond this prior work, exemplifying how close collaboration between advisor and advisees can make a substantial contribution to the field.

Storper et al. are explicit in their methodological choices. They eschew feeding variables into a statistical model to determine which are of greatest significance, in favor of 'rigorously organizing [their] case study with questions that draw from the findings of the large-scale empirical studies' (Storper et al., 2015: 15). Methodologically, the book aims to contribute to Edward Leamer's (2012) call for using knowledge steeped in detailed examination of empirical realities to improve econometric modeling and develop realistic behavioral assumptions. In this respect, the book is a continuation how *Keys* 'attempts to occupy a middle ground of respect for the technical workings of theory, although using mostly words and stories to communicate, with some numbers and models' (Storper, 2013: 8). The collaboration complements this narrative-based methodological approach with a fine-grained quantitative empirical examination, sutured together through a narrative strategy that makes the collaborative project greater than the sum of its individual contributions.

Rise and Fall is replete with original empirical analysis. The simplicity of its empirical analyses, presented as its main evidence, belies astounding preparatory work. The primary sources of data, the Integrated Public Use Microdata Series (IPUMS) and North American Industrial Classification System (NAICS), are 'off-the-shelf' datasets, but require considerable work to extract the relevant variables. IPUMS contains individual records (usually 1% or 5% of population) sampled to be representative at a scale small enough to study intra-regional variations. These data need to be meticulously cleaned, selected, and standardized to ensure consistency between regions and across decades. While the authors rely on simple comparison of means for most of their evidence, the data are structured so that the most salient measures can be used. This allows them, for example, to precisely adjust income in each region to account for housing costs, or to derive the skill composition of the workforce disaggregated by migration status. The NAICS classifies firms into groupings by economic sector, down to specific clusters (e.g., software publishing). This enables the authors to delve much deeper into the economic structure of the two regions than would be possible for a multi-metropolitan study. As they point out, the data are so detailed that keeping track of all the relevant dimensions for a great number of regions would be excessively taxing and unlikely to remain consistent.

These data are used to substantiate their argument that the nature of the divergence between Los Angeles and the Bay Area is driven by different patterns of specialization. Specialization, they argue, is not just about how concentrated activities are in the region, but also how leaders in key industries relate to each other. The authors draw from the work of Mark Granovetter (2005) on networks, among others, to develop the argument that the Los Angeles economy is more diverse and more fragmented, which results in the lack of synergy that the corporate networks of the Bay Area have fostered. The data used to corroborate this argument are the most original empirical contribution of the book. The team gathered the data from the US Securities and Exchange Commission's Form 10-K to develop representations of elite network infrastructures. These forms list the members of corporate boards of all large firms, enabling the authors to map overlaps in board membership across corporations. The end-product is a simple and intuitive way to visualize the specialization trajectories of Los Angeles and the Bay Area. Simply put, LA lacked the institutional networks to reproduce innovations and sharing of ideas between industries, often instead overwhelmed by a collective worldview in which LA was positioned as a 'low-road' competitor in a variety of siloed industries.

From convergence to divergence

Divergence is an issue for Storper et al., both because they see the literature that predicts convergence between regions as creating a convention that needs revision, and because it implies that some regions are at risk of falling further behind. The authors argue that divergence and convergence are not pre-given, but depend on a set of metropolitan factors that can be identified, and therefore addressed. To develop their argument, the authors begin with a critical examination of four theoretical strands – development theory, regional science and urban economics, new economic geography, and theories of institutions – asking how well models developed within those traditions can accommodate empirical realities presented in their data.

Storper and colleagues draw from each theoretical strand to scrutinize an extensive list of factors and associated variables, which they call the 'usual suspects' of regional development: the role of economic structure, employment and skill composition, demographics and migration, business cost and cost-of-living differences, and institutional infrastructure. Examining each theoretical framework in turn, they show how its most salient variables are insufficient to explain metropolitan divergence, arguing that they are symptomatic of the underlying process of divergence rather than illuminating the cause. The authors' aim is not to discredit the theoretical approaches but to pinpoint discrepancies and insufficiencies, thereby provoking researchers in each stream to come up with more robust explanations and tools.

Storper et al. assemble the research dealing with convergence under the umbrella of regional science and urban economics. Under a set of assumptions that emphasizes mobility, and differences in regional endowments of labor and capital, cost of living, and the cost of doing business, lead firms and people are predicted to relocate from expensive regions to cheaper ones, equalizing inter-metropolitan wages and prices and triggering convergence (Glaeser, 2008). The authors find the evidence to support this model inconsistent. Beyond the obvious discrepancy of the divergence in real income, the underlying causes (usually land regulations or amenities) hypothesized to explain divergence within this approach are not supported by the authors' data.

Development theory provides the foundation of Storper et al.'s primary ana-lytical comparative framework, but also important conceptual tools. Comparative analysis relies on having well-defined, bounded units of analysis, bounded by the nation state at the international scale in the case of development theory. For both international and regional research, scale and the degree to which one can compare the significance/magnitude of findings across units of different sizes are a concern. The authors argue that the comparative framework is better fitted to regional-scale analysis because it overcomes obstacles that limit cross-national comparisons (e.g., distinct legal and economic institutions). Yet regional 'boundaries' are not as clearly defined as national boundaries, muddling urban comparisons.

The authors proceed by defining 'region' in terms of an integrated economic market, wherein the prices of labor, land, and housing are similar when com-pared to areas outside the region, after accounting for differences in quality (2015: 230). This logic rests on two central underlying concepts: **agglom-eration** and the urban land nexus (Scott, 1980; Scott and Storper, 2015). Agglomeration refers to the process by which regions become specialized in certain tradeable sectors, as firms and people pursue the advantages of sharing infrastructure, public services, and the collective energy of a certain sector concentrated in an urban region. This co-location facilitates matching the most appropriate labor pool with employers, as well as learning through the dense informational networks that pervade cities (Duranton and Puga, 2004). The urban land nexus is the manifestation of agglomeration in space: the ways in which economic incentives, social–economic differentiation, and political con-straints influence how households and firms produce variegated urban spaces knit together by infrastructure. These two processes are critical to justifying the 'regional' unit of analysis, which the authors argue is best approximated by the Combined Statistical Area, but they also justify the structure of com-parison itself.

With the two regional units established, Storper et al. proceed to cast Los Angeles and the Bay Area into 'development clubs'. The notion of club, bor-rowed from development theory, provides the thrust for their differentiation of these metropolitan regions on the basis of 'quality' (2015: 18) or specialized comparative advantage and wages. Storper et al. show how Los Angeles and the Bay Area belonged to the same club in 1970, in terms of real income levels and levels of economic specialization, but since have diverged. In effect, they seek to show why and how Los Angeles followed a 'low-road' and the Bay Area a 'high-road' vision (2015: 139). The club metaphor supports the main thrust of their analysis, which argues that Los Angeles mis-identified its comparative advantage by trying to compete with cities that belonged to the club of land-abundant, low-cost regions. They argue that this stemmed from Los Angeles leaders' well-intentioned attempt to accommodate a growing low-to-middle-wage economy that attracted many new residents to the region. This vision clashed, however, with constraints imposed by a dense city within one of the wealthiest states in the country. This resulted in a fragmented economy: a mix of a high-value, high-technology economy and routine, lower-wage activities (such as logistics and transportation).

New economic geography provides the theoretical framework for explaining why industries thrive and grow despite pressures to move to cheaper regions. Like regional science and urban economics, it emphasizes that firms will locate based on seeking combinations of labor, capital, and (importantly) knowledge that best serve their productivity. These models have an element of mobility, constrained by the enhanced productivity that firms gain from co-location. The authors argue that agglomeration theory provides a more succinct explanation for *why* Los Angeles continues to be the leader in the entertainment industry, and Silicon Valley in computer technology. Yet the authors argue that the new economic geography falls short in explaining *how* these industries came to dominate within their respective regions, and *why* initial specialization evolved toward ever-higher value-added production in the Bay Area, but toward activities producing largely low- and middle-income jobs in Los Angeles.

The authors' use of *theories of institutions* is murkier. They suggest that this framework lacks the 'theoretical sophistication' to develop a coherent explanation for how the thousands of institutional decisions happening across a metropolitan region shape outcomes (2015: 238). At the same time, institutional theories provide the main analytical framework holding the argument of the book together. Storper et al. initially define institutions as 'rules of the game', consistent with the use of institutions in economics as a set of parameters that constrain individual decisions and solve collective action problems. But they greatly expand on that definition, mostly implicitly, to accommodate the role of different actors in shaping institutions and tracing the evolution of institutions within a cultural framework, in ways that are more consistent with historical and sociological approaches. We examine this in detail below.

Crafting a quantitative institutional narrative of regional development

Storper et al.'s institutional analysis weaves the sum of the evidence examined in the context of the four theoretical strands with the authors' original contribution in the form of a quantitatively informed institutional narrative. Their approach centers on how patterns of cooperation and conflict, arising within regional contexts, influence the ideas and institutional environments shaping how actors see themselves and their role in their respective metropolitan region. The authors adopt a constructivist epistemology, whereby normative world-views emerge from the socialization of actors within a particular context to play a critical role in sustaining the success or decline of a particular area. For example, the 'openness' of the Bay Area is a result of an institutional context that foments and spreads such thinking among actors. For Storper et al. this is the key to the Bay Area's success.

Rise and Fall argues that urban studies scholars and policymakers should integrate a concern for institutions, broadly defined, as essential to under-standing urban regional development. Yet the authors paradoxically focus less on institutions themselves (e.g., state or regional business associations) than on how participants behave and their output (policy documents and budgets). This creates gaps in their explanation as to the nature of institutions, the con-flicts embedded within them, and relationships among them. This generates a sharp difference between the quantitative backbone of the book and the depth of the institutional narrative deployed to consolidate interpretation of these data.

In focusing on the metropolitan region scale, Storper et al. avoid some of the shortcomings of the development literature. By keeping key sources of variation constant (e.g., legal and economic systems) they are better able to deal with institutional complexity than the often reductive analysis found in cross-national studies (Acemoglu et al., 2005). Yet their quantification of the comparative analysis requires them to operationalize institutions. This means finding variables that capture institutional differences. The authors make use of that strategy twice.

Following their analytical approach to the other theoretical strands, Storper et al. strive to highlight inconsistencies between what institutional theories would predict about the two regions and their empirical findings, focusing on regional budgets as a manifestation of these differences. Yet institutional theory does not yield the same kind of clean theoretical predictions as the other theories, yielding no clear hypothesis for the authors to scrutinize. Instead, they posit that the data 'require considerable interpretation' to inform how budgeting shapes divergence (Storper et al., 2015: 130). The share of the metropolitan budget devoted to public safety becomes an indicator of the lib-eral proclivities of the Bay Area. This is substantiated with data showing that the region spends a smaller share of its budget on crime than Los Angeles, even though crime is higher. Yet, this conclusion is dependent on interpreting the budget data in terms of a percentage share: the Bay Area spends close to $1,000 more per capita on public safety, creating a dissonance with this nar-rative (2015: 131, Table 6.2).

Much of their analysis rests on interpretation and contextualization. The leap between budgets and culture feels tenuous, and the narrative about the Bay Area's entrepreneurial environment is open to interpretation (Teitz, 2017). By privileging one approach, their argument fails to provide a more substantive analysis of institutions. In their assessment of each theoretical approach, the authors advocate for more systematic development and collection of data relevant for the kind of institutional analysis they conducted (Storper et al., 2015: 238). The claim that intuitionalist analysis lacks theoretical sophistication is directed toward a specific kind of institutional theory. In advancing this version of institutional theory, they seek to establish a method based on quantitatively testable hypotheses. For example, they advocate for a greater effort to collect data on the role, budget, and structure of different governmental organizations that operate in metropolitan regions. Yet, in their final account Storper et al. suggest that such an approach is insufficient.

Neatly recapitulating their book-length analysis in Chapter 9, the authors seek to capture the element of 'luck'. They highlight the growth of biotechnology in the two regions to demonstrate how the lack of integrative networks in Los Angeles led to a close-ended managerial style of growth that works well for single dominant firms but precludes the growth of the kind of vibrant and innovative cluster found in the Bay Area. They call this the *zeitgeist*, based on Paul Duguid's characterization of the Bay Area's 'open source culture' (Storper et al., 2015: 205). This description closely corresponds to the sociological notion of cognitive scripts, an analytical framework based on how people see themselves in relation to their environment and what they value. This leads to an explanation that grounds an identification of 'robust actors', who spearhead innovation into viable businesses, in the environment that sustains and multiplies those businesses. In other words, the zeitgeist of an 'open source culture' means that potential leaders in the Bay Area are much better placed to 'succeed' than those same leaders if they happened to be in Los Angeles.

The institutional narrative favored by Storper et al. privileges a self-contained analysis, however, that does attend to the broader historical structure within which those actors are working. The role of the state, for example, is largely removed in a research design that emphasizes controlling for larger structural factors as much as possible by picking regions within the same state in the same country. Yet institutions are in perpetual interactions across geographical scales, such that their impact is highly variegated based also on local-scale institutional structures. Put otherwise, the divergent models of industry formation in the Bay Area and Los Angeles should take more seriously how local political and business interests interacted with state and federal institutions to bolster their interest. Such an analysis would be more open to the possibility that factors at the state and federal level gave advantages to the Bay Area, factors that are not easily captured through a purely regional focus.

In neglecting a deeper engagement with the institutional history of the two regions, conflicts and their causes remain superficial; the role of power differentials in reinforcing institutions is obscured; and patterns of change and constancy are not drawn sharply enough into relief to identify critical factors or events. The result is an analysis that says less about the institutional development of these regions than it does about the current institutional status of the Bay Area and Los Angeles. In this regard, despite concerns for seeking the origins of divergence we often return to a view that remains rather presentist.

Disrupting the productivity paradigm

Rise and Fall concludes that San Francisco's higher overall real income not only insures that the region's entire income distribution is higher, but also enables everyone to benefit from increases in productivity. The critical mechanism in this argument is the notion of the multiplier effect, which Storper et al. argue is much higher in the specialized tech industry of the Bay Area than in the fragmented economy of Los Angeles. The multiplier effect quantifies how high-income jobs (producing goods and services for the global market) have local economic impact by contributing directly and indirectly to a region's overall prosperity, expanding the number of low- and middle-income jobs (localized goods and services).

The authors conclude that regional development focused on economic specialization in San Francisco was 'better for all'. This parallels the metaphors Peter Marcuse (2005) decries in allocating functions to cities that are appropriate to those concerned, but are assumed to benefit all urban residents. The authors go to great length to substantiate this link, asserting for example that San Francisco not only has higher average real wages, but also has higher wages at the low end of the income distribution. Yet the data are unclear on this last point. They show that real wages have increased much faster in San Francisco, adjusting for housing costs, but it is not clear whether other numbers included in the analysis are similarly adjusted. The differences between the two metropolitan regions also are not nearly as substantively significant at the lower end of the income distribution.

Furthermore, in asserting that 'the strictly local or neighborhood effect [on regional development] is very small' (2015: 231), Storper et al. neglect the dynamics of **uneven urban development**. The metropolitan scale of the data cannot account for the possibility that lower-income households are increasingly relegated to the urban peripheries, where costs, especially in terms of access to public goods and services, are highly uneven and difficult to adjust for. This is not to negate the overall finding of the book; even if we were to account for these differences, it may be that the Bay Area is indeed more equitably prosperous than Los Angeles. But in treating both metropolitan regions as uniform units of analysis, the tradeoffs between specialization and spatial and economic inequity are neglected.

This neglect of uneven urban development as a salient dimension for comparing the success of the two metropolitan regions, focusing instead on mean income as the metric for comparison, means that *Rise and Fall* cannot tackle the implications of broader regional income hierarchies. In the authors' account, divergence matters because Los Angeles missed an opportunity to be more like the Bay Area, making its residents worse off. Yet questions arise, for example, about the role of Los Angeles as a transportation and logistics hub, and as a major gateway and home for international (particularly undocumented) immigrants. From a utilitarian perspective, the tradeoffs between Los Angles as a higher-income region and its present configuration become muddled. We cannot know, for example, how those living in Los Angeles, and in the rest of the state, would fare if Los Angeles had become more specialized, relegating some of its core current functions to another location that provides lesser opportunities for occupational advancement.

Storper (2013: 228) gestures to issues linked to regional income hierarchy in *Keys*, noting that it is impossible for 'all city-regions to be at the top of the income hierarchy or stay there permanently'. Here, however, the lack of any relational comparison of the two metropolitan regions runs the danger of underplaying the degree to which their fates are tied. In focusing on the regions as self-contained units, it becomes difficult to tackle questions about the respective roles the cities play in the state economy and beyond. This traditional approach to **comparative urbanism** forecloses the possibility that the two regions are intimately linked in their destinies: that one region's choices may impact the other's trajectory. The focus on divergence also diverts from questions about the ability of high-wage specialization to address pressing issues of displacement, **urban governance**, and state violence.

Conclusion

Rise and Fall serves as a model for harnessing large-scale data analysis in a collaborative project, challenging widely held conventions in urban economic theory. The authors' detailed engagement with different theories and methodological approaches enables them to deepen the analytical thrust of quantitatively driven critical scholarship. At the same time, its tradeoffs are worth noting, particularly for junior scholars hoping to make a mark through collaboration.

Much like the politics of research collaboration, the politics embedded in the analysis and framing of the questions the authors explore is largely implicit, possibly for related reasons. *Rise and Fall* not only brings together distinct theoretical and methodological backgrounds, but presumably also brings together scholars with different politico-ethical commitments. The interpretation of data that is so crucial to developing the narrative of the book is embedded within a dynamic of implicit commitment to greater justice through increasing the income of all living in a region – a clear contrast with the ethico-political commitments to 'emancipatory alternatives' and to counter orthodoxy behind recent calls for a radical positivism (Wyly, 2011: 907). Perhaps a decision was made to strip this analysis as much as possible from such commitments so as not to betray the distinct positions of the co-authors, thereby presenting a unified narrative as a key strength of their analysis. We can only speculate about the give and take involved in this specific project, but it seems clear that researchers will have to judge carefully how much they are willing to compromise on their own commitments when embarking on a long-term collaborative project.

Storper et al.'s emphasis on the importance of interpretation, highlighting the oft-neglected possibility of casting data to fit a story, raises important questions about different perspectives. We appreciate the transparency with which they invite such further analysis, alternative explanations, and a more robust theorization of the region. Working with the empirical data gathered here, others could draw different conclusions and offer alternative narratives about the divergence and equity implications within these cities. For example, the analysis could be flipped to examine the grip that corporate elite networks have on regional development, and their role in perpetuating the exploitation of cheap labor and shaping policies that favor regional elites. This study also highlights the tradeoffs involved in pursuing a specific kind of method and/or theory. Our discussion of institutional analysis above, for example, emphasizes the importance of looking beyond what the data can tell. When working with an object as embedded in human interactions as institutions, especially the holistic definition Storper *et al.* ascribe to, new data sources can fill only some of the many gaps. This book shows that much can be achieved through careful data analysis and contextualization, but also shows what is left out in terms of historical and structural analysis.

In mixing narrative analysis with rigorous but simple quantitative data analysis Storper et al. craft an account that is highly approachable, and generative for quantitatively and qualitatively inclined readers alike. Furthermore, the authors provide a distinct contribution whose transparent methodological and theoretical choices are open to interrogation from other perspectives. All may not agree with the authors' conclusions – which many will see as sitting adjacent to mainstream or 'non-critical' approaches – but their spirit of holistic, myth-busting analysis and of collaborative knowledge production should be taken to heart by all critical urban scholars.

PART III
REFLECTIONS

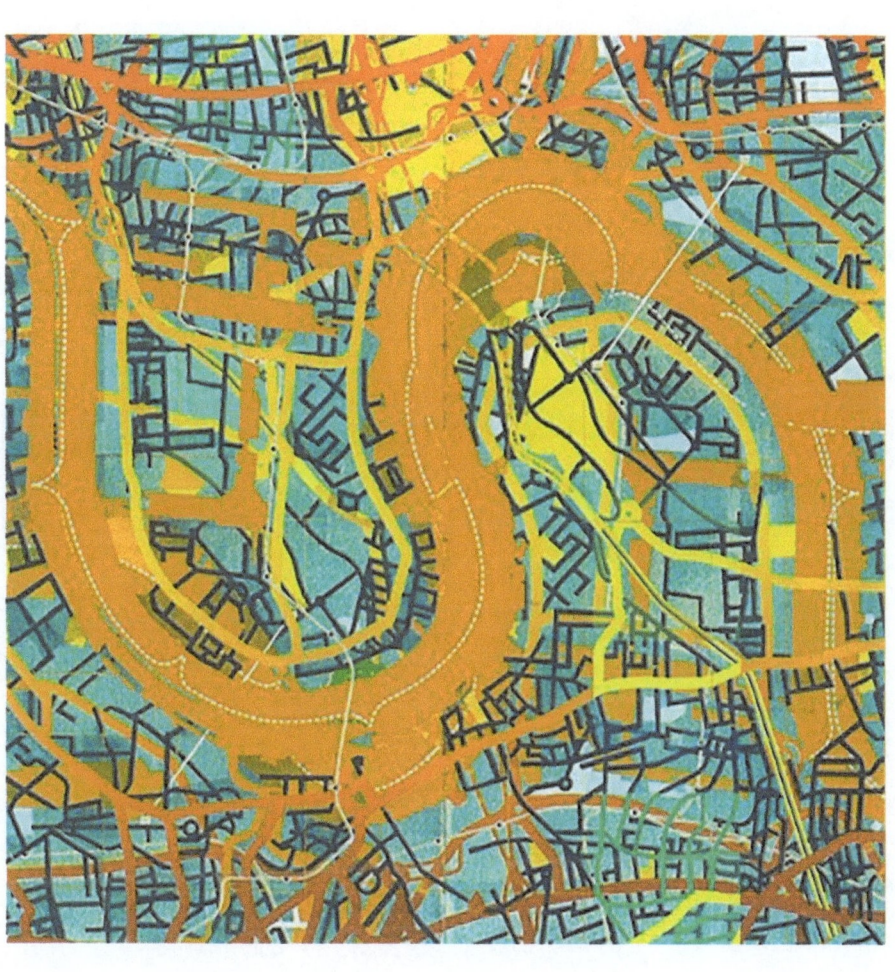

19

TURNING URBAN STUDIES INSIDE/OUT

Helga Leitner, Jamie Peck and Eric Sheppard

Introduction: practicing critical urban studies

Process and practice have been watchwords for this book, as they were for the collaborative seminar that preceded it. Along with our collaborators, we have been concerned to excavate and explicate generative modes and models of practice, in both creative research and constructive critique. The monographs that were the focus for Part II of the collection were each encountered, as we indicated in Chapter 3, not simply as 'finished' contributions but more as windows onto different forms of research practice. Specifically, they were each read for methodology and reverse-engineered as a means to uncover the underlying conditions and constitutive practices involved in their production; to find and position both the author and her research practices in the text; and to derive lessons and insights from this process in a manner attuned to the interests and concerns of researchers entering the field. Furthermore, in tracing the path from a collaborative seminar for graduate students to a published collection of essays, reflections, and keyword entries, we have sought in a parallel fashion to be transparent and reflexive about our own (shared) processes and practices.

In following this approach and in assembling this volume, we have sought to make two broad interventions into the field of critical urban studies. The first, and in a sense the most immediate and practical, has involved the somewhat unconventional construction of *Urban Studies Inside/Out* as a shareable resource or platform from which to build constructive engagements with research practice, documenting, codifying, and reflecting along the way.

This process began with the identification of monographs (appropriate) for close scrutiny and 'constructive deconstruction'. This was not quite a process of 'we begin with our favorite books', but that idea at least captures the spirit of selecting and then approaching these texts not with the aloof disposition of a 'distant' reviewer, or as targets for no-holds-barred critique, but from the perspective of fellow researchers learning the ropes. In itself this marked something of a break with the typical circumstances, habits of mind, and norms of engagement in graduate seminars, in which it is not unusual for 'set texts' to be treated quite mercilessly, or subjected to 'deficit critiques', on the basis of what they leave out or for approaches not taken. Instead, the monographs considered here were approached on the basis of a more positive and constructive disposition: more for their achievements rather than for alleged absences or deficits, achievements assessed in the first instance in light of the authors' own objectives and aspirations, taking due account of the circumstances of the book's germination and production. This meant beginning with, and developing an appreciation for, the 'inside story' of each book. For these reasons, the contributors to this collection were invited to exhaust the possibilities of 'internal' critique – attentive to authors' objectives, methods, and methodologies – before turning to external critique, and assessment of the books from different perspectives and vantage points. Even external critiques, it was emphasized, should reflect the empathetic stance of the fellow researcher, indeed a fellow member of the community of researchers; they should not be about taking pot-shots from the sidelines. This (more) constructive disposition additionally governed the subsequent ethos of evaluation and critique developed collectively by seminar participants and contributors to this volume.

Turning from the inside to the outside, *Urban Studies Inside/Out* also seeks to make a second and more expansive intervention, in relation to the field of critical urban studies more broadly. As we discussed in Chapter 1, this field of critical, interdisciplinary inquiry was substantively shaped in the last quarter of the twentieth century largely (although not exclusively) as a project of political economy. In its postmillennial form, the field of critical urban studies has been recalibrated and reconstructed in a host of ways, particularly in light of feminist critiques of productivism and essentialism, post-structuralist critiques of determinism and economism, and postcolonial critiques of developmentalism and Eurocentrism – each of which has spawned new research programs and new ways of seeing and engaging with the urban. None of these should be considered a one-to-one replacement (or substitute) for urban political economy, which itself has continued to evolve, not least in dialogue and debate with these critiques and alternatives. Undeniably, the field is more heterogeneous and heterodox than before, as a more diverse and variegated palimpsest-cum-mosaic of perspectives and practices. And rather than revolving, as it once arguably did, around a dominant center of gravity shaped by a closely related cluster of political economy approaches, the field now is more disparate, polyvocal, and polycentric, being structured around a series of axes of difference and debate. Tendentially more global, more cosmopolitan, and more pluralistic than before, this could be represented as a radical break or paradigm shift; one might also say that the field of critical urban studies is continuing to express, explore, and realize its underlying character as a radically open and heterodox project attuned to the difference that the urban makes, the difference that cities make. Heterodox fields are always subject to contestation, not only inevitably but quite properly so, but this is no reason for them to become minefields.

Critical urban studies can be said to be a field of diversity and difference, which in principle ought to be an asset. But there are no guarantees. Making the most of this asset, realizing its potential, is not something that should be expected to come naturally; it involves work. If the advances that are being made – on multiple fronts, and in a multitude of ways – are not combined with a parallel effort to reconstruct, and continue to work on, what we might call the field's 'communicative fabric' (including its codes of scholarly exchange, its conventions of knowledge production, and its culture of engaged coexistence), then there is a risk that diversity and difference could become quite the opposite of an asset: a source of rifts and ruptures. Pitted against these risks, there are those lines of constructive commonality, which connect rather than divide the research field/community of critical urban studies, that we identified in Chapter 3: first, the widespread recognition of cities as relational constructions, in terms of both their internal constitution and inter-urban positionality; second, the understanding that each reading of (or methodological approach to) the city is a partial one, and therefore necessarily positioned among other readings; and third, that there exists a shared, post-disciplinary lingo and lexicon, which builds upon rather than suppresses 'local' dialects and idioms. As such, it is a field that (re)makes itself through difference.

Something similar might be said, in principle, about methodological difference, although our sense is that the research community has more work to do truly to capitalize on the diversity of practices in the field. In Chapter 2, we made the argument that methodology – in the expansive sense of methodological practice, research design, and politics, rather than merely as a collection of tools – could be thought of as a terrain or meeting ground across which new kinds of conversations might be developed. More methodological transparency, more methodological reflexivity, more methodological talk, and an elevated level of methodological consciousness: all of these have the potential to open up new lines of conversation and new opportunities for mutual learning and enrichment. After all, there is more than one way to read, write, and represent the city, with each methodological vantage point being both partial and positional. Developing and deepening dialogical approaches to methodology, and to research practice and praxis, are necessary to each and every approach to critical urban studies, which after all bear the responsibility of positionality as well as a duty to both acknowledge and work with difference. It is in this spirit that we drew attention to four different clusters of methodological praxis: close encounters, as experientially rich modes of engagement; connectivities, as ways to recognize the constitutive character of network relations; comparison, as a means to draw out distinctive differences, recurrent patterns, and new insights across sites and situations; and conjuncture, as an invitation to deep contextualization and situational analysis – not as mere repositories of tools or mutually exclusive modes of inquiry, but as coexisting and overlapping approaches to the urban. Elevating the level of methodological consciousness, mutual recognition, and explicit engagement is not just a matter of bringing this heterogeneity to the surface; it is about capitalizing on heterogeneity, finding new combinations and conversations, and making more out of the sum of these parts.

Urban Studies Inside/Out is premised on a wager that there is much (still) to be gained from a concerted focus on research practice, craft, and methodology, not as a distraction from deep-seated ontological and theoretical differences, or as a means of papering over the cracks, but as a space of mutual learning across differences – in approach, emphasis, perspective, and positionality. Fundamentally, this is how the monographs examined in Part II of this collection were engaged, which in aggregate speak to at least some of the effervescent diversity present in the field, the conversations across which remain, to date, relatively underdeveloped. On reflection, we would be the first to acknowledge that the methodological and geographical diversity displayed in the collection of methodological commentaries in Part II – reflecting the happenstantial bundle of interests and concerns of those who joined the UBC/UCLA seminar – barely begins to capture the diversity actually existing in the field as a whole, some of which we signaled in Chapter 2, although we would hope that the present volume is recognized as a constructive start. It is in this spirit that, rather than presenting hard-and-fast conclusions from this experimental enterprise, we prefer to offer a series of openings – openings to a different kind of conversation in critical urban studies, focused not on fixed positions but on the potential of engaging across different and coexisting methodological pathways. Quite the opposite of anointing a singular methodological canon, this is a matter of exposing, explicating, and reflecting constructively on the practice and craft of urban research – learning from how it is done when it is done well – in a manner that is deliberative and dialogical, rather than adversarial or combative. 'Positively relational' is how this practice-oriented approach might be portrayed.

With this orientation in mind, this closing chapter seeks to look forward rather than backward. It is concerned with how we might get to a rather different kind of future in critical urban studies, departing from the contested present in a way that is focused more on opportunities than obstacles. We do this in sympathy with the argument of J.-K. Gibson-Graham (1996) that in order to act (and practice) differently we must first learn to think differently. In the remainder of this concluding chapter, we develop two themes. The first addresses the matter of starting from where we are, in the form of a commentary on the prevailing theory culture in critical urban studies. Second, we outline a case for the adoption of transformative research practices in the form of engaged pluralism and responsible knowledge production.

Unbounding urban theory cultures

The wide variety of socio-spatial theories and philosophies that critical social scientists have drawn on over the past 20 years, particularly in the anglophone academic literature, can feel quite mind-boggling, perhaps especially for emergent and early-career scholars. Many of these lurk in the background of the variety of urban theoretical approaches currently in use (see Chapter 1) – positivism, empiricism, structuralism, Marxism, feminism, postmodernism, post-structuralism, and postcolonialism, not to mention critical race and queer theory, intersectionality, and actor–network and assemblage theory. One way to pick your way through this theoretical minefield of 'isms' is to simply commit to one of them, to choose a 'lane', and then remain in it – a particular temptation in doctoral programs that do not push their students to read widely before alighting on a theoretical framework and thesis topic. This may feel efficient in the short term, but can often trigger problems down the road, if theoretical fashions and topical concerns suddenly shift (as they often do), or if the path initially chosen comes to feel too well trodden, leading to a predictable or otherwise familiar destination. What seems timely and even edgy at the beginning of your graduate program can feel out of date or stale by the time you finish. A third problem is that some of the high-profile debates between proponents of these various theoretical frameworks in urban studies have become increasingly entrenched and vitriolic over recent years: wagons are circled around one perspective, erecting walls by denigrating rivals. Such internecine conflicts, ironically between scholars who share critical perspectives and a desire to build more emancipatory alternatives, undermine attempts to realize such alternatives (one 'no', many 'yes'es). Yet, more disconcertingly, there may also be whiffs of personal ambition, career calculation, and even animus. For emergent scholars, enjoined to pick a side, or taking a side because this seems like a less risky course – thereby identifying with a particular scholarly community but finding themselves separated from others – this undermines any temptation to work creatively across such constructed intellectual boundaries.

From the perspective of the field as a whole, this can lead to balkanization, stifling of the creativity so often found in various forms of intersectional or boundary work, and fostering of a negative or counterproductive theory culture. There is a real danger that counter-punching debates leave behind less than they find – diminishing alternatives while missing opportunities to articulate their own position in positive terms, and contributing to a collective theory culture that is less than the sum of its parts. More positive theory cultures, in contrast, seek to make more out of differences (not less), rewarding 'net' contributions made on their own terms rather than points scored against another side. In other words, they foster positive-sum conditions, valuing constructive (and purposefully reconstructive) dispositions. This may well entail running out of one's lane, and developing new conversations and combinations, but even those who opt to stay in lane can do so in a way that makes the most of that position and perspective, rather than taking away from others. Lest this sounds like laissez-faire relativism, idealism, naiveté, or (worse still), complacency or apologism, recall that critical and heterodox enterprises must also be diverse enterprises: they often work at their best when diversity is leveraged as a strength. There is a role for vigorous critique on the 'inside' of such heterogeneous fields, needless to say, but something has been lost if tough, counter-punching critiques become ends in themselves, or if the scholarly terrain begins to feel like a minefield into which some are reluctant to tread.

Instead of approaching this minefield as a choice between various philosophical/ theoretical/methodological schools (Coke or Pepsi?), we focus here on how they overlap and potentially can complement one another. We advocate for a *both/and* rather than an *either/or* approach to urban research practice, one which involves figuring out how to create conversations across the boxes that competing perspectives tend to lock themselves into; Trevor Barnes and Eric Sheppard (2010) call this engaged pluralism. Of course, this is not always possible: the selection of urban theories, for example, is not like a box of chocolates. But keeping a lookout for commonalities and complementarities, rather than exacerbating differences, is simply more open-minded and forward-looking. After all, critical thinking should be all about continually *reflecting* on and reassessing what we, as researchers, have come to take for granted – not simply raising the drawbridge in the defense of hard-core beliefs. It should also contribute to an ultimately constructive culture of knowledge production.

The standard philosophical starting points for knowledge production are *ontology* (our belief about what exists in the world) and *epistemology* (how we can gain knowledge about that world). Epistemology then shapes choices of *methodology* – what we should do to gain that knowledge (the topic of this book). In classical western philosophy, two ontologies dominated the European Enlightenment (when societies sought to liberate themselves from religious dictates): *idealism* – the notion that the world depends on how humans perceive it; and *realism* – the notion that the world exists independently of human thought. From the mid-twentieth century, realism became reframed as *empiricism*: we can observe the world, meaning that knowledge production is based on observation (Popper, 1959). Further, a third major ontological tradition was formulated: *structuralism* – the view that what we can observe is shaped by deeper, unobservable structural forces that cannot be derived from empirical analysis (Dosse, 1998). After 1968, a new wave of critical French philosophers emerged who were highly critical of their Marxist forebears and Communist Party fellow travelers. Styling themselves post-structuralists, they provided a philosophical grounding for postmodernism, triggering a prolif-eration of post-prefixed approaches (Barnes, 1996). Post-structuralists rejected the notion that knowledge production starts with ontology, insisting that 'any ontology is itself grounded in an epistemology about how we know "what the world is like"' (Dixon and Jones, 1998: 250). This prompted an ontological turn in the critical social sciences. Following the argument that different epis-temologies can generate their own ontologies, theoretical debates increasingly focused on defending competing ontological claims. The post-2000 geographical scale debates were a case in point, unhelpfully framed as flat ontologies versus. scalar ontologies (Escobar, 2007; Leitner and Miller, 2007; Marston et al., 2005).

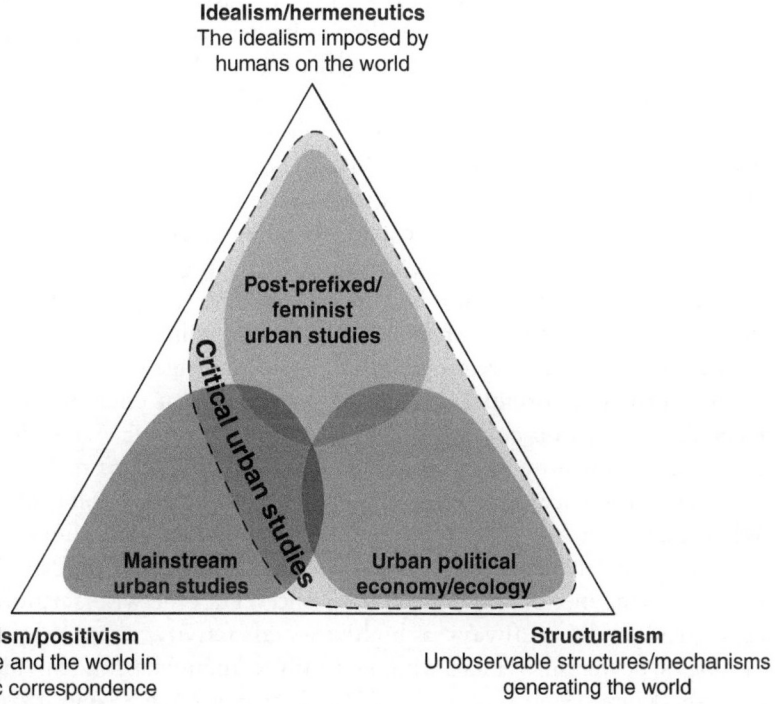

Figure 19.1   Polyvalent knowledge cultures

Source: authors; drawn by Matt Zubrowski, Cartographer, UCLA Department of Geography

When philosophers, and social scientists, turn to ontology, there is a distinct tendency for debates to become polarized (as was the case in the geographical scale debate, but see Jones et al., 2017). In the eighteenth century, British and French realist/empiricists fought it out with German idealists. In the nineteenth century, Marx advanced his materialism by seeking to knock down Hegelian idealism. In the post-prefixed era, these differences and planes of conflict have further multiplied. One way to push back against such polarization, mutual negation, and retreat into seemingly non-overlapping camps, is to position these perspectives in relation to one another, as an invitation into the intervening territories. This can be visualized as a knowledge production triangle, as depicted in Figure 19.1 (Sheppard, 2005).

Located at each apex of this triangle is one of the three classical modes of knowledge production of (pre-/post-prefixed) European philosophy, mid-twentieth-century style: idealism, empiricism, and structuralism. These are usually presented as mutually exclusive ideal types (summarized in Table 19.1). Yet, while such ideal types are grist for a philosophical argument, really existing knowledge production can never be confined to any one of these extremes. Consider logical empiricism (also known as positivism), which claimed that value-free explanations of the world can be derived from testing our theories against carefully made observations. This was wildly popular among philosophers of science (and social scientists) in the 1950s and 1960s, but by the 1970s even philosophers no longer bought this argument (Sheppard, 2014b). Indeed, when the great logical empiricist philosophers of the age gathered in a room at Cambridge University in 1946, they could not agree afterward whether they had observed Ludwig Wittgenstein threaten Karl Popper with a poker (Edmonds and Eidinow, 2002). Consider, for example, the science of climate change. Climatologists do not just collect objective data; their already existing theories of climate change shape what data they think are relevant, data that then tend to be used to reinforce rather than challenge those theories (Popper, 1959). Further, as Bruno Latour (2004) argues, what come to be framed as facts also depend on cultural norms and political power. Achieving scientific consensus about how to interpret the resulting data seems to be plagued by persistent differences of interpretation (hermeneutics trumping observation). While there is a broad (but not universal) consensus that climate change is anthropogenic, there are passionate differences of opinion about specific causal factors, forcing mechanisms, and consequences. Put otherwise, scientific knowledge production is always a highly social activity, shaped by scientists' ideologies, power differentials within scientific communities, and broader societal contexts (Kuhn, 1962; Livingstone, 2003; Longino, 2002; Shapin, 1996).

Visualizing these three competing traditions as apexes of a triangle creates space for every possible combination (also of methodologies of observation, interpretation, and theorization). Unlike philosophical ideal types, the research practices of really existing knowledge producers will be found somewhere within the space of the triangle (even those who claim to be located at one of the poles). Applying this to urban studies, we have filled the triangle in terms of the zones encompassed by mainstream urban studies on the one hand, and critical urban studies on the other. These spaces can be said to contain the principal 'belts' of theoretical discourse and debate in contemporary urban studies – spaces of scholarly interchange to which

Table 19.1   Three classical European modes of knowledge production

	Idealism	Empiricism	Structuralism
Ontology	The world humans perceive is determined by the meaning we give to it; it does not exist independently of that meaning	What exists in the world is independent of human perception	What humans perceive is shaped by underlying processes that account for the world we experience
Epistemology	Knowledge is gained through interpretation, to derive the meaning of what we think we see	Knowledge is gained by carefully observing the world and testing our knowledge against those observations	Knowledge is gained by theorizing how these underlying forces shape the world, and human understandings of it
Methodology	Hermeneutics and related interpretive tools, to gain an understanding of the meaningful world	Testing theories against observations, to explain how some observable phenomena cause others	Constructing coherent theoretical accounts of how the world works, which can explain observable events

Source: authors

research projects, designs, and programs are typically yoked (cf. Paige, 1999). In turn, within critical urban studies we have sketched out the epistemological and methodological range of urban political economy and postmillennial scholarship. Importantly, these zones overlap. The zones of overlap are important spaces, the location of boundary objects (Star, 1989; Bowker and Star, 2000), where boundary-transcending urban research can be pursued – zones for practicing engaged pluralism. Thinking about knowledge production through the lens of the triangle can be a prompt to consider the many commonalities between groups of researchers in terms of research practice, even when they rhetorically claim to be radically different from one another philosophically (e.g., about whether to start with global capitalism or individual intersectional positionalities). Even this is a bit misleading, however, as there may also be vital differences even *within* a particular approach. For example, structural Marxists like Louis Althusser (1967) insist that observation is not only irrelevant to knowledge production, but also downright counterproductive as it leads theorization down the wrong path. Yet other Marxists hew to various forms of critical realism that leave space for structural theorizing, while insisting that the validity of such theories also must be assessed in terms of their ability to account for the world itself (Bhaskar, 1975; Sayer, 1992).

Countervailing forces

Notwithstanding the possibilities of out-of-the-box thinking and engaged pluralism, at the time of writing, debates on urban theory remain rent with critique and counter-critique, misunderstanding and misrepresentation, and defensiveness and recrimination – notwithstanding the creative recombinations that, in principle, retain the capacity to inspire and catalyze research practice (including many of the books reviewed in Part II of this collection). Occasional calls for engaged pluralism in urban studies have yet to gain much traction (Brenner, 2018; Peake et al., 2018; van Meeteren et al., 2016). Some of this may simply reflect how academia works (Kuhn, 1962): the next generation's ideas face difficulties finding favor from the previous generation, now ruling the roost, who present themselves as defenders of their particular corner or section of turf. Yet these challenges have become increasingly intractable – reflecting a conjunctural moment in contemporary (anglophone) academia that itself ought to occasion reflection and reflexivity.

At the scale of the researcher, the intellectual culture of the humanities and social sciences values the lone scholar – someone whose contributions are conventionally judged, in the final analysis, by their sole-authored research. The lone-scholar culture is one in which positions are readily personalized, while critique too easily can become personal: when my published scholarship is critiqued, this is directed at me and my identity. Paradoxically, while critical scholars believe in the power of collective action and are dismissive of possessive individualism, their intellectual cultures are often plagued by exactly this kind of behavior. By contrast, the natural sciences now value a collective research and publishing culture with the vast bulk of articles having multiple authorship.

At the institutional scale, the neoliberalization of (anglophone) academic institutions incentivizes specialization, fast and quickly published scholarship, and competitive individualism – moving fast and breaking things (Mitchell, 2000). In conjunction with the intensification of various forms of social media discourse, the imposition of competitive metrics appears to be amplifying these conditions. Internalizing neoliberal norms of the responsible, competitive individual within the academy only reinforces the already existing institutional culture discussed above. Scholars located in southern institutions face additional challenges: lack of access to the means of research (books, journals, and large research grants), institutional environments that discourage basic research and/or foreclose critique, and conditions of work that force them to take second jobs or consulting contracts to make ends meet (Nyong'o, 2016).

Further, in an audit culture where our work is to be quantified and ranked (article and citation counts, funds raised, journal impact scores, and department and university league tables), with such 'outcome measures' increasingly driving institutional support for and validation (or discrediting) of research, short-termism and instrumentalism have become endemic. Work life increasingly invades family and personal time as we seek to keep up with the shifting goal-posts of institutional expectations, generating a stress that is harmful both to thinking and acting differently and to altruism (Mullings et al., 2016). Those making their way to the top of the rankings gain considerable political and cultural capital – and then are offered work contracts enabling them to stay at the top ('relief' from teaching, for example). Those acquiring this capital must defend it, with potential rivals seeking to undermine it. One consequence of this is that even when 'safe' discussion spaces are created in which flattened, engaged, boundary-crossing pluralism is possible, the publications stemming from such events (often mandated by funders) – having entered the public sphere – reiterate and even entrench these underlying conditions.

At the supra-institutional scale, other biases create hierarchies that are inimical to critical scholarship's inclination to question authority. Global scholarship is dominated by highly ranked institutions, whose critical scholars gain further power from this association. These institutions are overwhelmingly located in the North Atlantic realm and its white settler colonies, with English the lingua franca (Nettle and Romaine, 2002; Paasi, 2005; Rodríguez-Posé, 2004). Critical urban studies scholars located elsewhere face basic funding and linguistic barriers, which can only be overcome by kowtowing to the hegemonic norms of critical scholarship as defined in these northern institutions. To gain international recognition (and, frequently, increased salaries) they must publish in anglophone journals (ideally with high impact factors), so their research must conform to what is judged cutting-edge by those journal editors and referees.

If critical urban studies, not just as an academic field but as a research community, has been facing some challenging times of late, it must be recognized that many of the underlying causes are structural, circumstantial, and institutional, rather than individual. By the same token, it would be wrong to code all of the associated stresses and tensions solely in negative terms, or to frame them in nostalgic narratives of an urban studies tradition somehow 'lost'. They are also indicative, after all, of the business of transformative change, with disputes and dislocations being not only inevitable but also necessary to the achievement of real change, the breaking-down of old barriers, and the dismantling of pre-existing hierarchies. Debates themselves, and the airing of real differences, are certainly not the problem. There are reasons to be concerned, however, if this leads to estrangement and disengagement, if communication breaks down. Not all differences are reconcilable, of course, and difference itself is often generative. But calcified or hardened differences are something else, especially if this is associated with ruptures in mutual understanding and dialogue. It is for these reasons that we advocate moving toward a more plurally engaged urban studies, which in turn implies developing collective strategies that are robust in the face of the challenging conditions that we have sketched above. It is to this issue that we now turn.

Transforming research practices

Despite, or (perhaps better) because of the challenges, and particularly at this time of apparent intensification, we want to conclude by offering some suggestions about how to prioritize and normalize academic practices that reinforce a culture of engagement and collaborative scholarship across differences in urban research practice. We do so by briefly outlining two propositions. The first concerns the practices of engaged pluralism, while the second addresses the question of responsible knowledge (co)production.

Toward engaged pluralism within and beyond the academy

One aspirational template for breaking down intellectual fences is engaged pluralism (Barnes and Sheppard, 2010). Influenced by feminist and pluralist philosophy, engaged pluralism is about attending to and learning from different perspectives. The aspiration is creating an intellectual space where all voices of relevance to theorizing the urban are convened together for open-minded intellectual exchange, with an orientation toward learning from one another – ready and willing to change our view when others offer persuasive counter-arguments – instead of tenaciously defending a pre-existing position. Richard Bernstein argues that practicing engaged pluralism involves

> resolving that however much we are committed to our styles of thinking, we are willing to listen to others without denying or suppressing the otherness of the other ... The initial task is to grasp the other's position in the *strongest* possible light ... The other is not an adversary ... but a conversational partner. (1989: 15–17, italics in original)

This should be a 'round table' where all perspectives – Helen Longino (2002) calls these 'local epistemologies' – get an equal hearing, with space for both reason and passion. The goal is to critically interrogate, and as necessary deconstruct, any pre-existing claims for superior understanding and knowledge. Longino argues that any such monism likely was arrived at by the intentional or unintentional exclusion of other perspectives, and will be deconstructed when such other voices are taken seriously. It is not expected that the result of such an exchange need be consensus; interlocutors may agree to disagree, but still will come away from the conversation having learned from it. The real test would be: have you shifted your position as a result of the exchange? If not, you probably were not listening attentively and open-mindedly.

Of course, this is much easier said than done. Even when such conversations are convened with a shared goal, interlocutors arrive not just with different perspectives, but do so in the context of unequal social capital. This enables some (likely senior, anglophone, male scientists – 'the best and the brightest') to dominate the conversation, with others inclined to defer to their expertise.

Such domineering positionalities must necessarily be challenged for engaged pluralism to work. Since the powerful are positioned to enforce their notion of consensus on others, Iris Marion Young (1990; 1997; 2000: 49) argues that more voice be given to the least advantaged, transforming 'mere exclusion and opposition to the other into engaged antagonism within accepted rules'. Chantal Mouffe (1999) argues that rational argument only tends to reproduce pre-existing power relations, and thus that the goal of engaged pluralism requires agonistic (conflictual) exchange between participants.

Unequal power dynamics are even more pronounced if we extend knowledge production beyond the academy. Taking the perspectives and concerns of ordinary people and their understandings seriously, for example, through participatory action research, has the political potential to productively unsettle ivory-tower debates with an eye to interrogating their practical relevance. Urban residents develop their own understanding and practical frameworks, with an aim of improving their livelihood possibilities, which may be at best tangentially related to the debates and disputes in urban studies. While their understandings are not necessarily superior, neither should they be accorded dominance, extending the field of knowledge producers beyond the academy prompts urban scholars to retain sight of the 'so what?' question that German critical theorists called the *Verwertungszusammenhang*: what knowledge does and who it is for.

Enabling responsible cultures of knowledge production

During the past few decades there has been a rising tide of conversations and critical reflections on the current mode of conduct of research and science, from a variety of different groups and from different parts of the globe. They have highlighted the connections between knowledge production, power, and the need for a responsible ethic as the starting point, which according to Tariq Jazeel and Colin McFarlane should be 'seeking to unsettle and de stabilize the certitudes of knowledge and theory as it is produced' (2009: 118). While highlighting the partiality of all forms of knowledge, they recognize that there exists a knowledge hierarchy that privileges theoretical innovation over detailed empirical research: male over female and white over non-white voices, voices from the global North over those of the global South, academic over popular knowledge, etc. Much of the credit for exposing and challenging these hierarchies and proposing alternatives goes to the writings and actions of feminist scholars, including black feminists and scholars based in the global South, such as the Subaltern Studies Collective who brought postcolonial approaches to the northern academy. Together these different provocations have challenged dominant cultures of knowledge production while emphasizing the coproduction of knowledge with new modes *and tones* of academic debate, as well as more inclusive and co-equal research practices. This has stimulated conversations across disciplinary boundaries, the North–South divide, social differences, and between academics and social activists.

Which preconditions can facilitate such conversations and create space for the development of alternative modes of interaction? Every engagement with difference requires the development of and adherence to clear codes of conduct – how we talk/write about and with others. The need for codes of conduct has become very visible and urgent given some of the recent conversations among urban theorists, which have been dominated by combative and hurtful words and tones, and claims to superiority and inferiority, reifying and fortifying rather than deconstructing hierarchies. Practices such as posturing, combative language, and belittling the work of others seem to become particularly prominent when conversations transition to written documents. Co-organizers of a recent skirmish over theoretical commitments and perspectives related how verbal, face-to-face interactions were more likely to result in productive debates and negotiations across difference, only for this to break down when participants were asked to write out their thoughts for public consumption (Linda Peake, Darren Patrick, Raiyashree N. Reddy, Sue Ruddick, Gokboru Tanyildiz and Roza Tchoukaleyska et al., email 2018). We presume that this is because individuals may find it harder to denigrate others face to face, fearing that they might be called upon to justify their claims and behavior. By contrast, the written word – either on paper or the computer screen – does not shout back when you say outrageous things and belittle the contributions of colleagues. Debates of that sort resemble ping-pong games and rarely result in productive discussions that promote learning and further knowledge.

Such skirmishes can be avoided, however, by requiring participants in both verbal face-to-face and non-verbal communications, to 'check their egos at the door' and adhere to codes of conduct that prioritize being cognizant of and sensitive to the unequal power relations and dynamics in any public. But codes of conduct alone are not sufficient, because an underlying requirement is a willingness and commitment to listen and learn from the Other/other perspectives. Learning and listening to one another need not mean reaching agreement with the other, though. To the contrary: a good learning environment needs to make room for and allow for agonism.

Building relationships and learning to talk to each other take time for extended engagement – time that many academics either do not have or do not want to take. Negotiating across differences also requires spaces that facilitate such negotiations, ideally enabling face-to-face interactions, as we observed when we met at the White Mountain Research Center to turn seminar papers into this book. Mass conferences, now necessary stops on the circuit for ambitious academics to display themselves, clearly provide very little space–time for this kind of discussion and debate; they are not venues that lend themselves to such interactions. Recent innovations that seek to create such time–spaces include dialogic workshops, which assign priority to interactions and communication among participants, thus facilitating the coproduction of knowledge. Yet these are difficult to organize, and in their own way are exclusionary (in the sense that attendance must be limited).

Mutual learning is possible through open knowledge coproduction and research collaboration. While collaborative research and knowledge coproduction have long been a mainstay in the natural and life sciences, this has not been the case for the social sciences and humanities, which remain dominated by the lone-scholar model. It is only recently that we are seeing fledgling attempts systematically to move away from this model of knowledge production toward collaborative research extending across disciplinary boundaries and beyond the academy. For example, there is growing recognition that contemporary environmental problems require the combined efforts of different disciplines and an active dialogue with practitioners in the private and public sector as well as from civil society (van der Hel, 2016). Unpacking challenges and opportunities for tackling 'wicked problems' such as urban poverty and sustainability require similar forms of dialogue and collaboration. Recent research in applied health, for example, has prioritized the coproduction of knowledge, whereby users are considered active agents whose knowledge and experience receive equal consideration to that of professionals; users and professionals see their relations as reciprocal and their collaboration as mutually beneficial, resulting in superior knowledge that is translated into practice. This research also recognizes the need for an institutional infrastructure that encourages the participation of users and professionals in the coproduction of knowledge, in order to facilitate change (Heaton et al., 2016). Such collaborations with actors outside the academy (e.g., through participatory action research) not only make good on the responsibility of researchers to their research subjects, but also contribute to decolonizing the academy.

Similarly, collaboration that considers scholars from the global South as equal partners can have multiple benefits. It can contribute to destabilizing presumptive hierarchies between theoretical and place-based knowledge and may also promote more responsible knowledge production across the North–South divide. The dominant model underlying much of the urban research conducted in the global South by multilateral organizations and global consultancies located in the global North tends to assign to scholars in cities of the global South the role of empirical, place-based knowledge producers, with the theoretical frameworks for making sense of the empirics being supplied by scholars and professionals from the global North. Treating the empirical knowledge produced by scholars in the global South as co-equal with theoretical knowledge can challenge the heavy-handed imposition of northern urban theories onto southern cities, raising awareness that knowledge, ideas, and theoretical frameworks will (have to) change as they are transferred between North and South. Indeed, insights gained through research on southern cities can render new lenses of vision and understanding also for northern cities (and, of course, across other geographical lines of difference). Our own experiences of working between the global North and South have shown us that these benefits can be very real, but so are the challenges of negotiating across knowledge cultures and hierarchies, in both the academy and society at large.

Developing a responsible culture of knowledge production is difficult: strug-gling against current forms of engagement requires hard work, determination, and agreement on shared goals; it requires a willingness to learn from each other without having to achieve consensus; it requires time, to build relation-ships and coproduce knowledge; and it requires that we construct facilitating spaces and organizational infrastructures, including codes of conduct. It also requires negotiating the oftentimes-competing responsibilities of researchers: to research subjects and their communities, to the academy, and to those societies and places where our jobs and our research are located. Yet the payoffs – practicing a flexible, collaborative, open-minded, and diverse urban studies – are worth the effort. Our hope is that *Urban Studies Inside/Out*, and the collaborative practices that underpinned its construction, will be read as a constructive contribution to this objective.

PART IV
RESOURCES

KEYWORDS

Agglomeration
Assemblage urbanism
Comparative urbanism
Displacement/dispossession
Everyday urbanism/urban encounters
Financialization
Gentrification
Global cities/ordinary cities
The housing question
Infrastructure
More-than-human world/urban nature
Neoliberal urbanism
Planetery urbanism
Postcolonial cities/subaltern urbanism
Post-political city
Right to the city
Smart cities
Suburbanization
Uneven urban development
Urban citizenship
Urban commons
Urban governance
Urban (im)mobilities
Urban informality
Urban social movements
Urban sustainability and resilience

Agglomeration

CS Ponder

Agglomeration refers to the concentration of one or more economic activities in time and space to obtain benefits accruing from co-location. The concept is both a process and a noun. As a noun, it refers to the advantageous clustering of firms in a particular locality which nearly always occurs at the urban scale. As a process, agglomeration arises from firm-level calculations that these benefits outweigh the influence of other factors shaping the relative profitability of different locations (such as access to raw materials, to markets, and to labor). When these cost-saving benefits (agglomeration economies) are high enough, the economically rational decision is to co-locate. Agglomeration economies have two aspects. First, localization economies refer to the benefits of co-locating with firms engaged in closely related activities, because of the efficiencies generated through proximate inter-firm linkages and face-to-face communication with suppliers and competitors, and from local states keen to attract this economic sector (e.g., Silicon Valley). Second, agglomeration economies are the broader benefits of locating in any urban area irrespective of whether related firms co-locate there, such as access to transport and communications networks, to large consumer markets, to a large, well-trained, and diversified labor force, and to corporate services.

The study of agglomeration belongs to a larger school of thought in economic geography known as location theory, which seeks to explain the location of capitalist economic activities. Johann von Thünen (1966 [1826]) sought to explain the location of agricultural activities relative to an urban market, on the basis of how access to market shaped the ability of producers to pay land rent. Walter Christaller's (1966 [1933]) 'Central Place Theory' attempted to geometrically systematize and explain the existence and location of market towns of different sizes and with different mixes of retail goods. The economist Alfred Marshall (1920 [1890]) sought to explain the emergence of 'industrial districts' – a conceptual forerunner to agglomeration. He observed that physical proximity allows many small firms working in a single industry to flourish in a specific place, primarily by selling complementary products and services to one another ('horizontal and vertical specialization'). Historical examples include the Lancashire region of cotton and textile production, or the Midland region's dominance of ceramics, both in the UK.

Since the 1980s, agglomeration economies have become a prime explanation for the presence of cities, as they provide a convincing rationale for why economic activities concentrate in space. This theory of urbanization remains extremely influential among urban economists and related urban theorists (see Scott and Storper, 2015). In this view, capitalist cities are economic entities, whose existence is the result of firms taking advantage of agglomeration economies, supplemented by local states seeking to enhance those economies in order to incentivize local entrepreneurs and attract extra-local investment.

Agglomeration also circulates more broadly. **Global cities** are often defined by the particular activities that co-locate in them: transnational corporate head-quarters, corporate services, a stock market, and the like. Saskia Sassen (1991) measures the relative economic power of global cities based on various metrics that capture the presence and type of agglomerative activity co-locating therein. Richard Florida (2002) seeks to explain the economic prosperity of cities in terms of their ability to attract a 'creative class' who will then stimulate cutting-edge industrial clusters to underwrite that prosperity. Researchers studying the ongoing fragmentation of global capitalist production – global production networks – treat agglomeration as a dynamic, transnational mode of economic organization that shapes international divisions of labor and regional develop-ment possibilities (Coe et al., 2008). Marion Werner (2016) meanwhile is notable for her focus on the ways that agglomeration achieved through global production networks reflects and contributes to uneven development through-out the global economy.

Agglomeration remains an enduring and influential concept within urban theory, but has not gone without critique. For some time, urban theorists have debated whether the idea is sufficient to explain urbanization, or whether cities are more than the sum of these economic parts. Postcolonial urban theorists question whether it suffices to present agglomeration as a general theory of urbanization (e.g., Robinson and Roy, 2016). While recognizing the utility of agglomeration, they doubt whether it can adequately explain processes of urbanization outside of the Euro-American contexts in which the theory was developed, also highlighting a number of different concepts and processes such as **ordinary cities** and **urban informality**. By contrast, Scott and Storper (2015) insist that agglomeration, combined with the urban land nexus, can explain the existence of any city. As a result, agglomeration has become caught up in a larger epistemological debate about the purpose of urban theory and the implications of unequal power relations between the global North and the rest of the world, debates that become, and remain, embedded in the development of key concepts.

References

Christaller, W. (1966) [1933] *Central Places in Southern Germany*, translated by Carlisle W. Baskin. Englewood Cliffs, NJ: Prentice Hall.

Coe, N., P. Dicken and M. Hess (2008) 'Global production networks: realizing the potential', *Journal of Economic Geography,* 8(3): 271–295.

Florida, R. (2002) *The Rise of the Creative Class and How It's Transforming Work, Leisure, Community, and Everyday Life.* New York: Basic Books.

Marshall, A. (1920) [1890] *Principles of Economics*, 8th edition. London: Macmillan.

Robinson, J. and A. Roy (2016) 'Debate on global urbanisms and the nature of urban theory', *International Journal of Urban and Regional Research*, 40(1): 181–186.

Sassen, S. (1991) *The Global City: London, Tokyo, New York*. Princeton, NJ: Princeton University Press.

Scott, A. and M. Storper (2015) 'The nature of cities: the scope and limits of urban theory', *International Journal of Urban and Regional Research*, 39(1): 1–15.

Thünen, J. H. von (1966) [1826] *Von Thünen's Isolated State: An English edition of Der isolierte Staat by Johann Heinrich von Thünen*, translated by C. M. Watenberg, edited with an introduction by P. Hall. London: Pergamon Press.

Werner, M. (2016) 'Global production networks and uneven development: exploring geographies of devaluation, disinvestment, and exclusion', *Geography Compass*, 10(11): 457–469

Further reading

Saxenian, A. (2006) *The New Argonauts: Regional advantage in a global economy*. Cambridge, MA: Harvard University Press.

Assemblage Urbanism

Sophie Webber

Assemblage urbanism is both an approach to studying cities and an ontological claim about the nature of cities, one that extends agency to human and more-than-human actors; it is also relational, and process- and practice-oriented. In recognizing that agency is both widely and non-hierarchically distributed, assemblage urbanism embraces **more-than-human** actors, materials, natures, and technologies as formative in urban phenomena, thereby challenging modernist distinctions between nature and the city. Accordingly, the city is not a stable configuration, but a relational achievement that is enacted through collections of heterogeneous actors, both human and non-human. Urban assemblages are constantly in the making, in states of becoming. This implies that there is no singular city, but rather multiple urbanisms in states of ongoing assemblage, and that grasping the fluidity and multiplicity of these urbanisms requires deeply empirical investigations of more-than-human enactments. Assemblage urbanism often places itself in contrast to critical, structuralist approaches to the city that draw from Marxian political economy.

Theories and approaches to urban assemblage have two principal points of departure: Deleuze and Guattari's notion of *agencement* and Latour's actor–network theory (ANT). Translated from the French word *agencement*, Gilles Deleuze and Félix Guattari's (1986) rendering of assemblage refers to a 'constellation' of heterogeneous components, where alliances and alloys are key. This assemblage approach is concerned with both component parts and the agency of the assemblage, determined by interactions and relations. These assemblages are always provisional – constantly territorialized and deterritorialized – and therefore open up new possibilities. In contrast, urbanists who draw from Latourian ANT center radical relationality in the constitution of objects and processes, insisting on generalized symmetry between human and non-human actors. As Bruno Latour (2005: 72) describes it, the ANT project aims to 'extend the list and modify the shapes and figures of those assembled as participants' and to unpack how they 'act as a durable whole'. While both the *agencement*- and ANT-derived perspectives are suggestive of the production of urban injustices and inequalities, they tend to address these issues obliquely rather than presuming a priori the sources and sites of causation, or the loci and forms of power. In its focus on constant coming together and falling apart, Deleuze and Guattari's reading of assemblage points to the possibilities for assembling more just cities, and the labor and work that such alterities require. Latourian assemblages seek to inspire more participatory and democratic practices which recognize humans and non-humans as political actors.

Consider one illustrative example: Jane M. Jacobs (2006: 2) examines how the public residential highrise building form coheres by cataloguing the 'relational assemblages of human and non-humans that work together to "make" a building'. Jacobs does this by rescaling the public residential highrise as a 'thing' – on equal footing to small toys, or advanced capitalism – that is both made and unmade. In her investigation of two building events, Singaporean and British state-sponsored residential highrises, Jacobs traces the processes by which these 'things' are socially and materially 'stitched together', as buildings, as global, and as big. To do this, she looks to the inverse, to unravelling. In 1968 the Ronan Point tower in London, partly came apart: a gas explosion led to the collapse of one corner of the building, taking four lives. An inquiry into the cause found this to be a singular event – with blame not located with the pipes, the stove, its owner, its installers, their tools, or the constructors of the building. Instead, together, 'the building and its many makers become an emblematic point in the big story of the demise of the highrise as a sanctioned housing type in the West' (Jacobs, 2006: 20). In this building event, the public residential highrise lost its human and non-human authors, and 'shrunk back', subsequently falling out of favor in its public and municipal forms. Jacobs demonstrates that the highrise, as an urban form and function, is always incomplete and in process, its hanging-together requiring diverse socio-material allies.

For critics, assemblage urbanism is a politically and ontologically flat approach that erroneously dismisses uneven social relations and fails sufficiently to theorize capitalism and social and state power. Thus, Neil Brenner et al. (2011) appreciate the empirical and methodological contributions that assemblage approaches have made in urban studies, specifically in attending to the materialities of socio-natural relations in cities. However, they argue that the assemblage approach has limited explanatory power and fails to account for political economic contexts and institutions. In passing over an analysis of capitalism, assemblage approaches fall short in identifying the actors, forces, and processes necessary for social change. According to a (broadly Marxian) political economic consideration of the urban, assemblage approaches leave questions about how to challenge and change unjust urban social relations largely unaddressed.

Alongside debates concerning **comparative urbanism** and **postcolonial cities/subaltern urbanism**, assemblage approaches have initiated a new generation of urban studies over the last decade. This distributed, relational, multiplicative, and processual orientation and ontology have taken urban studies into socio-material sites, to consider diverse actors, and to find interstitial places for, and ways of, intervening politically. While disagreements between assemblage and political economic approaches to critical urbanism are unlikely to be resolved through declarative proclamations about the purpose and future of the field, adventurous and innovative empirical and theoretical research (e.g., Ranganathan, 2015) can begin to bring these two approaches together for insightful analyses of urban problematics and pathways towards social justice.

References

Brenner, N., D. Madden and D. Wachsmuth (2011) 'Assemblage urbanism and the challenges of critical urban theory', *City*, 15(2): 225–240.

Deleuze, G. and F. Guattari (1986) *A Thousand Plateaus*. Minneapolis: University of Minnesota Press.

Jacobs, J. M. (2006) 'A geography of big things', *Cultural Geographies*, 13: 1–27.

Latour, B. (2005) *Reassembling the Social: An introduction to actor–network theory*. Oxford: Clarendon.

Ranganathan, M. (2015) 'Storm drains as assemblages: the political ecology of flood risk in post-colonial Bangalore', *Antipode*, 47(5): 1300–1320.

Further reading

De Landa, M. (2006) *A New Philosophy of Society: Assemblage theory and social complexity*. London: Continuum Press.

Farias, I. and T. Bender, (2010) *Urban Assemblages*. London: Routledge.

McFarlane, C. (2011) 'Assemblage and critical urbanism', *City*, 15(2): 204-224.

Comparative Urbanism

Emma Colven

Comparative urbanism is simultaneously a methodological intervention, sub-field, and research agenda within urban studies, which prioritizes acts of comparison in order to produce knowledge about cities and urban processes. Comparison has a long history within urban studies. Emerging during the late 1960s and enjoying particular popularity during the 1970s within urban sociology and political science, early comparative research sought to identify similarities or difference between cities, generally treating these as units of analysis existing in isolation from one another. In contrast, 'relational comparison', which has emerged as part of a recent renaissance in comparative methodologies, prioritizes analyses that also account for the relationships between different urban processes and sites.

The earlier generation of comparative urban research can be broadly categorized as engaging in four common methodologies of comparison: individualizing, universalizing, variation finding, and encompassing (Tilly, 1984). *Individualizing* comparison uses case studies to implicitly or explicitly compare a particular city with more general theories and experiences. Thus Jan Nijman (2007) deploys 'multiple individualizing comparisons' between Miami, Amsterdam, Dublin, and Shanghai in order to examine Miami's status as a global city. Whereas *universalizing* comparison seeks to identify laws of explanation that hold true across contexts, *variation finding* compares cases in order to identify variations in general trends, typically relying on comparison between 'similar' cases. For example, Janet Abu-Lughod's (1999) comparative study of New York, Chicago, and Los Angeles sought to illuminate the differentiated impacts of the global economy across these sites. *Encompassing* comparison uses comparative analysis to examine potentially differentiating but overarching processes (such as globalization or capitalism) across different contexts. Unlike variation-finding comparison, this explains similarities or differences between cases as 'consequences of their relationships to the whole' (Tilly, 1984: 125). Illustrative of this mode is Saskia Sassen's (1991) global city thesis, which organized cities around the world into hierarchies, reflecting their positioning within global networks of capital and information.

These more empiricist modes of comparison largely fell out of favor during the 1990s, as postmodern and post-structural approaches gained traction (Ward, 2010). Yet, by the 2000s comparative urban research was experiencing renewed popularity. As comparative urbanism subsequently began to crystallize as a distinct sub-field of urban studies, 'relational comparison' emerged as an alternative methodological intervention. Ontologically distinct from earlier forms of comparison, relational inter-urban research draws on relational and embedded theorizations of space developed by geographers such as Doreen Massey to examine 'how different cities are implicated in each other's past, present and future' (Ward, 2010: 480).

This re-emergence of interest in comparative urban research can be attributed to two major developments. First, debates during the late twentieth century concerning globalization promoted a growing awareness of the interconnectedness of different people and places within a globalizing world. Largely focusing on economic processes, scholars undertook wide-ranging comparative analyses to examine the connections between cities as nodes within broader networks. For example, **global cities** scholarship compared cities around the world according to their economic function within the global economy. Significantly, this included peripheral cities performing 'global city functions', such as coordinating business and financial services or global investments. This literature thus demonstrated the productive potential of bringing a diverse set of cities into comparative perspective.

The second key development was the 'southern turn' in critical urban studies, which gained prominence in the early 2000s in the form of postcolonial critiques of mainstream urban studies. Proponents of a southern turn, noting that urban theory has largely been drawn from empirical observations made in cities of the global North, argue that such theory may possess only limited analytical currency in other geographical contexts. In *Ordinary Cities*, Jennifer Robinson (2006) critiques the global cities literature for perpetuating a developmentalist thinking that privileges cities of the global North (such as Chicago and Los Angeles) as norms for comparison, while obscuring others from view. For example, she argues that the literature's narrow economic focus effectively renders a large number of cities irrelevant to the global economy, thereby excluding them from analysis. She makes a case for treating all cities as potential sites from which to build theory, rather than restricting this to a select few 'world' cities. This challenges comparative urbanism to broaden its comparative approach, by utilizing new locales as bases for comparison to develop new theoretical insights. This emergent wave of comparative urban research also constitutes a research agenda, one concerned with provincializing 'northern' urban theories that are presumed to have global purchase (see also **global cities/ ordinary cities**). By generating provocative critiques of mainstream urban theory and seeking to redefine comparative urbanism, this scholarship has prompted much debate. While some scholars celebrate attempts to destabilize enduring categories and theorizations, others warn that this may come at the expense of producing generalizable theories. These vibrant debates illustrate that, far from a singular approach to urban studies, comparative urbanism is characterized by a diverse set of methodological and ontological approaches.

References

Abu-Lughod, J. (1999) *New York, Chicago, Los Angeles: America's global cities*. Minnesota: University of Minnesota Press.

Nijman, J. (2007) 'Place-particularity and deep analogies: a comparative essay on Miami's rise as a world city', *Urban Geography*, 28(1): 92–107.

Robinson, J. (2006) *Ordinary Cities: Between modernity and development*. London: Routledge.

Sassen, S. (1991) *The Global City: New York, London, Tokyo*. Princeton, NJ: Princeton University Press.

Tilly, C. (1984) *Big Structures, Large Processes, Huge Comparisons*. New York: Russell Sage Foundation.

Ward, K. (2010) 'Towards a relational comparative approach to the study of cities', *Progress in Human Geography*, 34(4): 471–487.

Further reading

Kantor, P. and H. Savitch (2005) 'How to study comparative urban development politics: a research note', *International Journal of Urban and Regional Research*, 29(1): 135-151.

McFarlane, C. (2010) 'The comparative city: knowledge, learning, urbanism', *International Journal of Urban and Regional Research*, 34(4): 725-742.

Peck, J. (2015) 'Cities beyond compare?', *Regional Studies*, 49(1): 160-182.

Pickvance, C. (1986) 'Comparative urban analysis and assumptions about causality', *International Journal of Urban and Regional Research*, 10(2): 162-184.

Displacement/Dispossession

Fernanda Jahn-Verri

Displacement refers to the removal of human and more-than-human actants from locations they inhabit, as a result of processes compelling such reloca- tions. In rural areas, for example, displacement can affect animals, plants, minerals, and human populations, triggered by such events as deforestation, infrastructure development, and **planetary urbanization**. In urban studies, scholarship tends to focus on the social impacts of displacement, usually refer- ring to the dislocation of individuals and communities from the land they occupy and its consequences. Displacement can imply both the act of moving out and the state of being removed from. The former is glossed as 'voluntary', as in the case of those bought out during **gentrification**; the latter is 'involun- tary', also understood as processes of forced eviction. Whereas voluntary displacement is presumed to be part and parcel of urban change, as land is converted to a higher rental use by means of the land market, involuntary displacement is usually driven by a variety of environmental, political, cultural, and economic processes, including natural disasters, civil wars, urban renewal, and the exertion of eminent domain.

Understanding urban land transformations in terms of 'voluntary' displace- ment is a long-standing tradition in mainstream urban theory, dating back to the Chicago school. In the 1960s and 1970s urban scholars were cautious when associating gentrification with displaced communities, but in the 1980s gentrification scholars coined 'gentrification-led displacement' to highlight the negative outcomes of this form of neighborhood change. More recently, the focus has turned to the social justice implications of displacement. According to David Harvey (2003: 145), new urban land enclosures and revitalization initiatives are core capitalist expansion strategies driven by mechanisms of 'accumulation by dispossession'. Not only are people displaced, but also the land they occupied is commonly enclosed and appropriated for use by the private and public sectors. According to Ananya Roy (2017), private property discourses are used to legitimate confiscating the land from the poor, even expelling them from the city as a whole. Highlighting its racialized dimensions, she terms this racial banishment.

Theoretical and empirical research seeking to understand neighborhood change and displacement in North American and European cities has recently been challenged, on the grounds that it is insufficient to understand removals outside the global North. Tom Gillespie (2016) contends that accumulation by dispossession cannot fully explain displacement in cities like Accra where, instead of being incorporated into circuits of capital as labor or consumers, the poor are completely expelled from **urban commons**. They are excluded from urbanity itself, with removals implying not only a loss of property but also, significantly, of personhood and **urban citizenship.** Such displacement also is argued to be incomplete: residents resist displacement, also performing alternative livelihood practices that exceed it. In the case of Jakarta, for instance, displacement in 'illegal' *kampungs* is confronted in two ways by informal tenants: defying **dispossession,** 'but also working to re-constitute informal livelihoods and living spaces that exceed capitalist social and economic relations' (Leitner and Sheppard, 2018: 438).

Raquel Rolnik (2013) and others argue that slum clearance and reconstruction programs also control who is accorded **rights to the city,** highlighting how state-led actions shape displacement and dispossession. In Rio de Janeiro, in preparation for the 2016 Olympic Games, residents of urban *favelas* were targeted for forced evictions. In New Orleans, Hurricane Katrina triggered a state of exception that enabled social cleansing, with the number of occupied affordable housing units in the metropolitan area falling from 11,000 to 2,300 (Adams et al., 2009: 8). In India, scholars note that removals initiated by state and judiciary authorities, on the grounds of preserving aesthetic norms or 'public interest', hide the much more perverse practice of expelling certain 'kinds' of citizens from the city. Indeed, questioning the apparent neutrality of legal, market, and planning mechanisms, Oren Yiftachel (2017: para 10) describes displacement in contemporary cities as 'a surface expression of urban coloniality'.

Recently, scholars have been emphasizing the importance of understanding the exclusionary outcomes of such urban transformation actions, going beyond highlighting how these processes occur, to examine their consequences: how such practices might represent a violation of human rights and rights to the city. With housing a constitutional right in many of the places where entire communities are currently being dislocated, or threatened with removal, it is important for researchers to pay attention to ways of contesting it. For example, scholarship on commoning, and on urban social movements that seek to disrupt the apparatus of private property, might help challenge and disrupt both the political discourses that denigrate urban informality and the discriminatory logics of property law that legitimate dispossession.

References

Adams, V., T. Van Hattum and D. English (2009) 'Chronic disaster syndrome: displacement, disaster capitalism, and the eviction of the poor from New Orleans', *American Ethnologist,* 36(4): 615–636.

Gillespie, T. (2016) 'Accumulation by urban dispossession: struggles over urban space in Accra, Ghana', *Transactions of the Institute of British Geographers,* 41(1): 66–77.

Harvey, D. (2003) *The New Imperialism.* Oxford: Oxford University Press.

Leitner, H. and E. Sheppard (2018) 'From Kampungs to Condos? Contested accumulations through displacement in Jakarta', *Environment and Planning A: Economy and Space,* 50(2): 437–456.

Rolnik, R. (2013) 'Megaeventos: Direito à moradia em cidades à venda', in A. Jennings (ed.) *Brasil em Jogo: O que Fica da Copa e das Olimpíadas?* ['Megaevents: the right to housing in cities for sale', in *Brazil at Stake: What is left of the World Cup and Olympics*.] São Paulo: Boitempo Editorial, pp. 65–70.

Roy, A. (2017) 'Dis/possessive collectivism: Property and personhood at city's end', *Geoforum*, 80: A1–A11.

Yiftachel, O. (2017) 'Displaceability – a Southeastern Perspective on the Remaking of Urban Citizenship'. DRAN/MIT: New Directions in Displacement Research, 2. Available from http://mitdisplacement.org/symposium-oren-yiftachel.

Further reading

Bhan, G. (2009) '"This is no longer the city I once knew": evictions, the urban poor and the right to the city in millennial Delhi', *Environment and Urbanization*, 21(1): 127–142.

Blomley, N. (2008) 'Enclosure, common right and the property of the poor', *Social & Legal Studies*, 17(3): 311–331.

Ghertner, A. (2011) *Rule by Aesthetics: World-class city making in Delhi*. Hoboken, NJ: Wiley-Blackwell.

Roy, A. (2019) 'Racial banishment. Keywords in radical geography', *Antipode at* 50, 227–230.

Everyday Urbanism/Urban Encounters

Helga Leitner and Samuel Nowak

The notion of **everyday urbanism** draws attention to the often-overlooked micro spaces and spheres of everyday life in cities. The term was coined by architects and planners in the book *Everyday Urbanism* (Chase et al., 1999), which focuses on the construction of Los Angeles' vernacular landscapes such as neighborhood spaces, parks, and alleys. They argue that these spaces are produced through the everyday practices of residents, who should be accorded a central role in the design of the spaces in which they live and work. Whereas architects and planners have deployed everyday urbanism quite widely as a normative concept, many other scholars have conceptualized and undertaken empirical research on everyday urbanism, while not always calling it that. In *The Death and Life of Great American Cities* (1992), Jane Jacobs writes about the importance of neighborhood spaces for the vitality of cities. More recently, inspired by the writings of French philosophers on the practices of everyday life, urban scholars have drawn attention to the importance of the everyday in understanding how people work, dwell, recreate, gain access to health care and education, and more generally live together, thrive, and survive, in the process producing urban micro spaces.

Urbanists have examined different spheres of everyday urban life, especially with respect to poor people and neighborhoods in cities of the global South. Asef Bayat argues that social change is not only driven by **urban social movements** and collective action, but also by ordinary people, who contest, produce, and transform urban life and spaces through their everyday actions. He characterizes this as the 'quiet encroachment of the ordinary', defined as the 'silent, protracted, but pervasive advancement of the ordinary people on the propertied, powerful, or the public, in order to survive and improve their lives' (2013: 46). AbdouMaliq Simone (2014) narrates the city and its transformations through a large and diverse cast of actors – animating their uncertainties and difficulties, predilections and improvisations, negotiations and speculations, their experiences of violence, inventiveness, and creativity, the incrementalism of change, and the dense social networks and collaborations that they mobilize to secure livelihoods. Similarly, Colin McFarlane and Jonathan Silver (2017) examine how poor residents in Kampala both cope with challenges of life in the city and escape poverty through their everyday practices. They stress, however, that these practices need to be seen in relation to the unequal city and how state spaces create different conditions of possibility for individuals and groups. Most often employing ethnographic methods, this body of work foregrounds everyday practices and **urban encounters** as a mode of understanding urban processes.

Encounters with others are central to the lived experience of the urban everyday. Cities across the globe have long been sites where people of different social backgrounds and identities are thrown together. Indeed, inhabiting and moving through contemporary cities usually means coming into contact with socially different others – at work, in the neighborhood, and in public spaces. Research on urban encounters interrogates what happens in these encounters, especially with racially and ethnically different others (Valentine, 2008). Gordon Allport's contact hypothesis (1954), which states that under certain preconditions face-to-face contact has the potential to dismantle prejudice towards the Other, has been extremely influential in planning circles, with city governments introducing and supporting initiatives promoting face-to-face contact with immigrants such as cultural festivals and community programs. Yet a number of studies show that face-to-face encounters do not necessarily erode prejudices or transform negative attitudes toward the Other; certain types and spaces of encounter, especially fleeting encounters in public spaces, may re-inscribe rather than transform such attitudes (Matejskova and Leitner, 2011). Ruth Fincher et al. (2019) present four cases of encounters with difference in different spheres of urban life that catalyze new ways of living in difference in the urban everyday, suggesting that these can only be realized under conditions of equality (one of Allport's preconditions). These studies highlight how past encounters impinge on the present, and how the wider geographical and historical contexts in which cities are embedded shape encounters across difference.

As concepts and approaches, everyday urbanism and urban encounters suggest an ontology that makes the quotidian spaces of city life, and their ceaseless interactions, central to contemporary urban studies. From this perspective, encounters with difference in the manifold spaces of urban life are a way of building knowledge about everyday urbanism.

References

Allport, G. W. (1954) *The Nature of Prejudice*. Cambridge, MA: Perseus Books.

Bayat, A. (2013) *Life as Politics: How ordinary people change the Middle East*, 2nd edition. Stanford, CA: Stanford University Press.

Chase, J., M. Crawford and J. Kaliski (1999) *Everyday Urbanism*. New York: Crown Publishing.

Fincher, R., K. Iveson, H. Leitner and V. Preston (2019) *Everyday Equalities: Making multicultures in settler colonial cities*. Minneapolis: University of Minnesota Press.

Jacobs, J. (1992) *The Death and Life of Great American Cities*. New York: Vintage Books.

Matejskova, T. and H. Leitner (2011) 'Urban encounters with difference: the contact hypothesis and immigrant integration projects in Berlin', *Social and Cultural Geography*, 12(7): 717–741.

McFarlane, C. and J. Silver (2017) 'Navigating the city: dialectics of everyday urbanism', *Transactions of the Institute of British Geographers,* 42(3): 458–471.

Simone, A. (2014) *Jakarta, Drawing the City Near.* Minneapolis: University of Minnesota Press.

Valentine, G. (2008) 'Living with difference: reflections on geographies of encounters', *Progress in Human Geography,* 32(2): 323–337.

Further reading

Darling, J. and H. F. Wilson (eds) (2016) *Encountering the City: Urban encounters from Accra to New York.* Aldershot: Ashgate.

De Certeau, M. (2011) *The Practice of Everyday Life.* Los Angeles: University of California Press.

Financialization

Joseph A. Daniels

Financialization describes the historical intensification of financial markets and their intermediaries in socio-economic life. The financialization literature was catalyzed by contributions from Greta Krippner (2011) who, following Giovanni Arrighi's understanding of financialization as a recurrent stage of capitalism, set about providing empirical confirmation of its contemporary manifestation. She highlights the growth of the financial industry and the increasing involvement of non-financial firms in financial markets. Financialization involves an array of socio-technical practices including credit ratings, securitization, a shareholder-value orientation, and risk management that introduce new economic logics, metrics, and rationalities. These trigger structural and relational transformations ranging from macro-processes of global capitalism to the intimacies of everyday life.

In urban studies, financialization is mobilized to interrogate the role of finance in real-estate markets, infrastructures, and **urban governance**. Financialization became an explanatory buzzword following the 2008 US subprime mortgage crisis (Aalbers, 2016), but urban scholarly interest in financialization long precedes this moment. In the 1970s Henri Lefebvre predicted that there might come a time when finance would dominate the production of urban space. In the 1980s David Harvey speculated that capital would reach its full financial form when land could be treated as a 'pure financial asset'. Subprime mortgage markets enabled firms like GM, by way of its retail banking subsidiary GMAC (now Ally), to treat urban space as merely another financial asset. Contemporary treatments of financialization in urban studies remain indebted to these interventions, drawing on them for proto-conceptualizations of financialization.

Three approaches to financialization dominate contemporary urban studies. The first focuses on financial dynamics *within* cities. This research has contributed significantly to understanding the constitutive role of urban space in the 'unfolding' of the global financial crisis. It follows efforts by financial actors to carve up the city into a series of revenue-producing components that are convertible into financial assets, including urban real estate, transit systems, utilities, and urban redevelopment projects. Taking specific instruments, policies, or funding mechanisms (e.g., subprime mortgages; Aalbers 2016) as analytical objects, this approach confirms Harvey's speculation regarding capital's tendency toward treating urban land as a 'pure financial asset'.

A second approach, influenced by the marketization literature, draws on the **more-than-human** sensibilities of actor–network theory. Here, the differential financialization of urban space is explained as a 'power struggle' between calculative agencies within competing actor–networks (David and Halbert, 2014). In this view, agency is not restricted to a city's human agents (developers);

more-than-human actants – buildings, land, financial spreadsheets, and invest-ment models of discounted cash-flow – also shape outcomes. Within the Mexico City metropolitan region, Louise David and Ludovic Halbert (2014) demonstrate that transnational financial investors concentrated on peripheral property markets, because local property developers could lock them out of the Federal District's property markets. They did this by keeping the latter markets opaque, strategically restricting development data, such as rental yields, to close-knit communities of ready-to-invest financial and political insiders. This excluded international investors, who require standardized metrics and formu-las to make decisions about risk 'transparent'. Here different 'algorithms' for investment location decisions among financial and non-financial actor–networks in Mexico City shape the extension of, or resistance to, processes of financializa-tion. Such research has identified how the iterative use of more-than-human financial metrics and devices can shape urban development trajectories.

The third line of research, instigated by Rachel Weber's (2010) institutional analyses of Chicago, focuses on financialization, urban governance, and the state. Taking municipal financing seriously – its entanglement in credit-rating agencies, municipal bond markets, and financial product innovation – shifts the analytical gaze from the financialization *of* the city to financialization as mode of governance *through* the city. Work by Philip Ashton et al. (2016) on infrastructure lease contracts arranged by the City of Chicago exemplifies this approach. The City of Chicago, by selling the income produced from parking meters to a financial investor, acquired novel financial expertise in creating a 'new' financial asset and short-term profits. Yet this also entangled the city in new management practices to ensure the long-term viability of parking meters as financial assets. This can lock a city into certain infrastructural forms, as investors' contracts prevent alterations that negatively impact the financial value of their assets. In short, the city becomes the risk manager for financial actors, instituting a form of urban financial discipline.

Financialization scholarship has renewed interest in (urban) finance, through a diversity of approaches that draw attention to its multidimensional forms. In urban studies, the focus has quickly moved from how financialization acts on the urban to how it co-evolves with urbanization processes. Scholarship on comparative urban research of the real-estate–financial nexus has proposed that financialization in the global South pre-dates, and is more intense than, its northern arrival (Aitken, 2015). This suggests that the theoretical and empirical bias toward the North Atlantic is misplaced, opening space for critical analysis of the relational and temporal constitution of financialization across North and South. Additionally, researchers are turning toward questions of financializa-tion-as-state-strategy and its implications for the local state as a site of politics or democracy. In this historical conjuncture of finance-led accumulation, with emergent forms of austerity and **neoliberal urbanism** becoming colonized by financial actors, instruments, and logics (Peck and Whiteside, 2016), engagement with financialization is increasingly critical within urban studies.

References

Aalbers, M. (2016) *The Financialization of Housing*. New York: Routledge.

Aitken, R. (2015) *Fringe Finance: Crossing and contesting the borders of global capital*. New York: Routledge.

Ashton, P., M. Doussard and R. Weber (2016) 'Reconstituting the state: city powers and exposures in Chicago's infrastructure leases', *Urban Studies*, 53(7): 1384–1400.

David, L. and L. Halbert (2014) 'Finance capital, actor–network theory and the struggle over calculative agencies in the business property markets of Mexico City Metropolitan Region', *Regional Studies*, 48(3): 516–529.

Krippner, G. (2011) *Capitalizing on Crisis*. Cambridge, MA: Harvard University Press.

Peck, J. and H. Whiteside (2016) 'Financializing Detroit', *Economic Geography*, 82(3): 235–268.

Weber, R. (2010) 'Selling city futures: the financialization of urban redevelopment policy', *Economic Geography*, 86(3): 251–274.

Further reading

Arrighi, G. (1994) *The Long Twentieth Century*. London: Verso.

French, S., A. Leyshon and T. Wainwright (2011) 'Financializing space, spacing financialization', *Progress in Human Geography*, 35(6): 798–819.

Harvey, D. (2006) [1982] *The Limits to Capital*. London: Verso.

Gentrification

Devra Waldman

Gentrification refers to a socio-spatial and economic process whereby older, often formerly industrial working-class areas in central cities are redeveloped by individual homeowners and private capital, transforming them into mixed-use environments geared toward the middle class. Gentrification includes redevelopment of working-class housing, new retail outlets, warehouses mutating into trendy office spaces, refashioned waterfront landscapes, and newly built townhomes or high-rise apartments. A common consequence of gentrification is **displacement** of the working class and urban poor, who no longer can afford the increased rent, housing, and living costs triggered by gentrification.

Ruth Glass coined gentrification in 1964, describing changes in London where working-class neighborhoods were being invaded and rehabilitated by middle-classhouseholds. Many argue that gentrification emerged in large metropolitan areas facing deindustrialization in the 1950s, but gentrification already was underway in New York City, New Orleans, Charleston, and Washington in the 1930s, and even can be read into Baron Haussmann's creation of Paris's nineteenth-century boulevards (Smith, 1996).

From the 1980s to the mid-1990s, gentrification scholarship debated contrasting production-based and consumption-based explanations. Production-driven theories explain gentrification as the consequence of the geographically uneven investment of capital: the historical devaluation of specific locations through disinvestment eventually makes them attractive for new rounds of investment. A prime example is Neil Smith's rent gap theory: he argued that gentrification becomes a profitable neighborhood investment when ground rents earned by the current land use are sufficiently below those that would accrue to gentrified land uses (i.e., retail, restaurant, middle-class housing, etc.). Production-based theoretical perspectives are critiqued for difficulties in measuring the rent gap, but also for an economic determinism that privileges economic rationalities and the state over individual actions.

Consumption-based theories focus on the gentrifiers. David Ley argues that shifting industrial and occupational structures in advanced capitalist cities created an expanding professionalized middle class that drives gentrification. Consumption-driven explanations highlight how these groups are drawn to central city environments to express countercultural identities, the role of gender (through increased single-women households and dual-earner relationships), and the role of gentrification aesthetics in creating environments with distinct cultural and artistic themes (e.g., loft spaces). These theories are critiqued for ignoring how broader political economic structures shape gentrification, but also because focusing on middle-class gentrifiers, sometimes conceptualized as 'urban pioneers', masks gentrification's polarizing effects. In this view, consumption-based approaches can justify privileging the middle class, construct urban poor residents as unwelcome or out of place, and rationalize middle-class colonization of working-class neighborhoods (Smith, 1996).

From the mid- to late 1990s, gentrification scholarship moved beyond this production/consumption binary. Issues of class largely remained central, but many focused on the cultural politics of new middle-class groups, while situating their analysis in the context of broader structures. For example, Pierre Bourdieu was utilized to explore notions of habitus expressed by middle-class gentrifiers, how these become valorized by politicians, developers, and policy elites, and how they are reproduced at larger scales for wealthy groups looking to enhance the economic value of central cities (Zukin, 2010). Others worked to intersect class with other axes of difference, such as gender, sexual identity, and race. Some highlighted how gentrification often triggers the banishment of certain racialized groups. Additionally, some have investigated the complicated politics of how black middle-class gentrifiers protect spaces from white middle-class control, while simultaneously excluding the most vulnerable residents (often poor and racialized populations) in these areas (Boyd, 2005).

Most recently, gentrification scholars have turned to focus on how gentrification intersects with globalization, neoliberalism, and the role of the state, and on the local particularities that emerge. This seeks to tease out the variegated manifestations of gentrification across the globe. Some scholars argue that gentrification is associated with states governed by neoliberal strategies, and with cities that are connected into broader circuits of global capital (Smith, 2002). This has triggered considerable debate. Some assert that neoliberal urban practices driving gentrification constitute a new form of colonialism, as gentrification practices are exported from northern cities to the global South. These practices privilege whiteness and wealth, universalize neoliberal urban governance, and disadvantage marginalized residents (Atkinson and Bridge, 2005). Others argue that deploying the term gentrification in southern **postcolonial cities** obscures the distinctiveness of land development, displacement, tenure regimes, and planning in those cities, by comparison to Euro-American cities where the term was coined (Ghertner, 2014).

While approached through various theoretical perspectives, necessitating diverse methodological approaches, gentrification remains of central importance for understanding the relationships between urban land use changes, the politics of exclusion and displacement, the role of state and private actors, as well as contestations of these processes.

References

Atkinson, R. and G. Bridge (eds) (2005) *Gentrification in a Global Context*. London: Routledge.

Boyd, M. (2005) 'The downside of racial uplift: meaning of gentrification in an African American neighborhood', *City & Society*, 17(2): 265–288.

Ghertner, A. (2014) 'India's urban revolution: geographies of displacement beyond gentrification', *Environment and Planning A*, 46(7): 1554–1571.

Ley, D. (1996) *The New Middle Class and the Remaking of the Central City.* Oxford: Oxford University Press.

Smith, N. (1996) *The New Urban Frontier: Gentrification and the revanchist city.* New York: Routledge.

Smith, N. (2002) 'New globalism, new urbanism: gentrification as global urban strategy', *Antipode,* 34(3): 427–450.

Zukin, S. (2010) 'Gentrification as market and place', in J. Brown-Saracino (ed.) *The Gentrification Debates: A reader.* London: Routledge, pp. 37–44.

Further reading

Lees, L., T. Slater and E. Wyly (eds) (2013) *Gentrification.* London: Routledge.

Slater, T. (2006) 'The eviction of critical perspectives from gentrification research', *International Journal of Urban and Regional Research,* 30(4): 737-757.

Smith, N. (1987) 'Gentrification and the rent gap', *Annals of the Association of American Geographers,* 77(3): 462-465.

Zukin, S. (1989) *Loft Living: Culture and capital in urban change.* New Brunswick, NJ: Rutgers University Press.

Global Cities/Ordinary Cities

Nafis Hasan

Global cities has replaced the analytical term world city, proposed in the 1980s by John Friedmann (1986) to highlight the central functions performed by cities within the globalizing dimensions of contemporary urbanization. 'World city' came to be seen as inadequate to describe the relational, interconnected transactions of finance and investment *among* world cities. **Global cities** references major urban centers that have transcended their respective national urban systems, articulating localized economic, demographic, and socio-cultural processes with a broader, globalized configuration of capitalist cities.

Friedmann (1986), focusing on the international division of labor in the context of the crisis in the North American industrial world, conceptualized the emergence of world cities (in the US and European 'core', except for São Paulo and Singapore) as part of an urban order imposed by global capitalism. In his view, cities' spatial and class composition and demographics depend on their hierarchical position vis-à-vis the needs of global capitalism. Saskia Sassen popularized global cities, focusing more on the concrete, grounded processes shaping globalization while giving them more agency with respect to globalizing capitalism. For her, global cities (New York, London, and Tokyo) are sites that control the global production of commodities, specialized services, and financial innovation – but they are also are sites where low-wage immigrant labor concentrates to support these activities. She subsequently expanded the scale at which these practices take shape, highlighting new connections between cities and supranational organizations (Sassen, 2001 [1991]).

The first generation of global-cities research focused on the attributes of a global city (e.g., a stock market, transnational corporate headquarters, immigrant labor). Since 2000 this has been supplemented by research, particularly by the Globalization and World Cities Research Network (GaWC), tracing cities' positionality within global inter-urban corporate networks, also using this to rank them as alpha, beta, or gamma global cities. GaWC concludes that London and New York are highest ranked in terms of 'global network connectivity', with London–New York the most intense of all 'global city dyads'. It also argues that a global economy dominated by these networks triggers inequitable and unsustainable consumption patterns (Beaverstock et al., 2000).

Together, the 1970s crisis of North Atlantic Fordism, an emergent new international division of labor led by transnational corporations, and the 1980s and 1997 Third World debt crises rapidly reshaped the contours of globalizing capitalism and its cities. This was supplemented by the rise of new information and communication technologies and the increasingly territorial, dispersed nature of commodity production (Brenner and Keil, 2006). In this context, neo-Marxist urbanists analyzing the capitalist character of modern urbanization sought to embed cities within a macro geographical context. Resonating with this was the influence of world-system theory, teasing out the global connections that linked capitalist prosperity in already industrialized countries and their cities with Third World underdevelopment and dependency, and with class formation, arguing for a more systematic, reflexive analysis of the global parameters of capitalism in both historical and contemporary contexts.

'Ordinary cities' was coined to expand the investigation of 'globalizing cities' to all cities; in the global North and South, both wealthier and poorer cities are globalizing, and thus articulated within global-forms of capitalism (Marcuse and van Kempen, 2000). Ash Amin and Stephen Graham (1997) stressed the ordinariness within all cities. Arguing against global-cities scholarship, Jennifer Robinson (2006) proposed ordinary cities as a frame for positing that cities in the global South also are central to the global economy; this flattened ontology treats all cities as ordinary and global, in differentiated ways. The ordinary-cities approach connects with **postcolonial cities**, drawing on postcolonial critiques that call for an engagement with experiences and scholarship outside the west. This seeks to refute western notions of modernity and development that align the idea of the 'modern' primarily with western cities, from which they supposedly diffuse to 'backward' and 'non-modern' places. It also challenges political economic theorizations, stressing the significance of the cultural politics of urban space.

More recent scholarship looks more closely at the divergent pathways of global and globalizing city formation: the diversity of processes and region-specific patterns through globalization articulates with urban restructuring. In this view, cities in China, Brazil, Africa, and the Middle East globalize differently. This focuses on the new centralities and marginalities that crystallize within global urban networks, emerging forms of regulation and governance, variegated socio-political contestations, and more-than-economic connectivities linking cities with one another (Ren and Keil, 2018). One empirical impetus for this is the recognition that certain countries in the global South (particularly the BRICS) have emerged as economic superpowers in the last decade. The increasingly intensified digitization of urban life and mega-city expansion also are transforming global urban spaces. The restructuring of the world economy in the wake of the 2008 global financial crisis provides a further context for conceptually rethinking globalizing cities. Recently, space is additionally being created to critically engage between the scholarship on global and on ordinary cities (van Meeteren et al., 2016).

References

Amin, A. and S. Graham (1997) 'The ordinary city', *Transactions of the Institute of British Geographers*, 22(4): 411–429.

Beaverstock, J., R. G. Smith and P. J. Taylor (2000) 'World-city network: a new metageography?', *Annals of the Association of American Geographers*, 90(1): 123–134.

Brenner, N. and R. Keil (eds) (2006) *The Global Cities Reader*. New York: Psychology Press.

Friedmann, J. (1986) 'The world city hypothesis', *Development and Change*, 17(1): 69–83.

Marcuse, P. and R. van Kempen (eds) (2000) *Globalizing Cities: A new spatial order?* Oxford: Blackwell.

Ren, X. and R. Keil (eds) (2018) *The Globalizing Cities Reader*. Abingdon: Routledge.

Robinson, J. (2006) *Ordinary Cities: Between modernity and development*. London: Routledge.

Sassen, S. (2001) [1991] *The Global City: New York, London, Tokyo*, 2nd edition. Princeton, NJ: Princeton University Press.

van Meeteren, M., B. Derudder and D. Bassens (2016) 'Can the straw man speak? An engagement with postcolonial critiques of "global cities research"', *Dialogues in Human Geography*, 6(3): 247–267.

Further reading

Taylor, P. J. and B. Derudder (2015) *World City Network: A global urban analysis*. London: Routledge.

The Housing Question

Tom Howard

The **housing question** is a *problématique* for interpreting the causes, effects, and political salience of housing crises. Its name is derived from three epony-mous pamphlets written by Friedrich Engels between 1872 and 1873, which addressed the deplorable state of working-class housing in Western Europe during the Industrial Revolution. Rather than analyzing housing as an iso-lated, discrete phenomenon, Engels insisted it must be understood in relation to broader structures of social domination and capital accumulation. Alongside a de facto reliance on Marxian understandings of capitalism, this relational emphasis distinguishes scholarship on the housing question from the field of housing research more generally.

Engels' pamphlets on the housing question were written as critiques of hous-ing reforms advanced by liberal and anarchist contemporaries, whom he accused of treating housing misery as distinctive from class oppression. For Engels (1973: 318), landlord 'overreach' and housing decrepitude were instead among the 'innumerable *smaller* secondary evils' caused by the exploitation of labor by capital (emphasis in original). Following Marx, Engels asserted that value is only created through human labor: insofar as rent is an exchange of pre-existing value (qua money commodities), exploitative landlord practices were therefore a subordinate concern to the enforced need to sell one's labor power. Even if the class power of rentiers was undermined by expanding pro-letarian homeownership – as advocated by the followers of French anarchist Pierre-Joseph Proudhon – Engels argued that deterioration and shortages would persist in working-class housing markets due to structural forces pushing wages down to subsistence levels. Accordingly, he proposed that housing crises could not be resolved through reforms which bolstered private property rights and fueled land markets, but only by abolishing capitalism itself.

To illustrate this position, Engels examined how housing conditions structure, and are structured by, several larger social phenomena. Four of these have been particularly influential in the subsequent literature on the housing question: processes of value-production and circulation; underlying structures of social power; the socio-spatial dynamics of capitalist urbanization; and processes of class struggle.

As a primary focal point in European housing debates, rent extraction like-wise predominated Engels' discussion of housing and economic value. But housing figures more centrally in processes of value-production and circula-tion than Engels could have anticipated from 1870s Germany. Investment in housing was pivotal to numerous historical regimes of accumulation, as in the case of North American **suburbanization** under Fordism, where housing growth underwrote economic growth by creating and stimulating markets for consumer goods (Madden and Marcuse, 2016). Under late **neoliberal urbanism**, credit borrowed against home equity has been a vital demand-side stimulus for economic growth, driving up effective demand among consumers (Aalbers and Christophers, 2014). Alongside other fixed **infrastructures** of urban development, housing also plays a crucial role in absorbing capital surpluses, storing value, and forestalling devaluation during moments of overaccumulation in productive sectors (Aalbers and Christophers, 2014). Expansion of credit markets under **financialization** has only accelerated such flows. Such movements illustrate how housing constitutes a key element of what David Harvey (1985) calls the secondary circuit of capital, itself crucial to the circulation, reproduction, and realization of capitalist value more broadly. Specifying the role of housing in value-production and circulation remains a central focus for writing on the housing question (Aalbers and Christophers, 2014).

Questions of value-production point toward underlying structures of social power. As Engels observed, labor's vulnerability to the demands of capital drives working-class housing insecurity. Among others, however, Susan Saegert (2016) has argued that Engels glosses over the differential housing insecurity of women, who remain disproportionately burdened with the additional responsibility of unwaged, socially reproductive household labor. Moreover, class phenomena articulate with, and are structured by, axes of social difference tied to race, gender, sexual orientation, (dis)ability, citizenship, age, and the like. Intersections between these structures of domination differentiate how particular social groups are exposed to housing insecurity. Lower wages for women, immigrants, and racialized minorities, for instance, translate into increased vulnerability to price fluctuations in housing markets; such groups are also more likely to suffer the predations of tenant harassment, eviction, **dispossession,** and displacement through rental conversions or public housing privatization (Madden and Marcuse, 2016: 98–104).

Such uneven geographies of risk and insecurity shape the socio-spatial dynamic of not only capital accumulation, but also urbanization more broadly. In an analysis salutary to the literature on **gentrification**, Engels (1973: 319) presciently observed that explosive urban growth rates gave 'an artificial and enormously increasing value' to land in working-class neighbourhoods, which 'pushed workers out of the centre of towns towards the outskirts'. From this vantage point, the housing inequalities of a given urban land nexus cannot be resolved through market-led solutions – on both the supply and demand sides – but 'merely shifted elsewhere' (1973: 368; cf. Smith, 1996). Contemporary writing on the housing question is concerned with determining how oppressive power structures in housing, both including and exceeding class, shape these uneven geographies (Madden and Marcuse, 2016; Saegert, 2016).

Engels was not just concerned that market-led approaches would reorganize instead of resolving housing crises. He was also concerned that working-class homeownership would demobilize class struggle by giving proletarians a stake in upholding capitalism. Contemporary scholars have echoed this argument and demonstrated how homeownership programs have historically worked as a 'bulwark against communism', insofar as they increase dependency on wage labor and undercut class solidarity (Aalbers and Christophers, 2014: 385; cf. Madden and Marcuse, 2016: 74–82). But not all struggles for housing are aimed at securing such provisions. Several **urban social movements** have incorporated housing decommodification, common ownership, and non-market housing as bases for a **right to the city**. While Engels may have worried that such initiatives fragment and undermine revolutionary class struggles, others have probed how political conflicts over housing can be generalized into broader anti-capitalist movements (Madden and Marcuse, 2016; Saegert, 2016). Posing matters of inequality and deprivation in terms of the housing question is, from this position, not only a matter of grasping how housing misery is 'embedded in the structures of class society' (Madden and Marcuse, 2016: 6), but also, and more importantly, an attempt to determine how these structures can be undone.

References

Aalbers, M. and B. Christophers (2014) 'Centering housing in political economy', *Housing, Theory & Society*, 31(4): 373–394.

Engels, F. (1973) 'The housing question', in *Marx & Engels Collected Works*, volume 23. London: Lawrence and Wishart, pp. 317–391.

Harvey, D. (1985) *The Urbanization of Capital: Studies in the history and theory of capitalist urbanization*. Oxford: Blackwell.

Madden, D. and P. Marcuse (2016) *In Defense of Housing*. London: Verso.

Saegert, S. (2016) 'Re-reading "the housing questions" in light of the foreclosure crisis', *ACME*, 13(3): 659–678.

Smith, N. (1996) *The New Urban Frontier: Gentrification and the revanchist city*. London: Routledge.

Further reading

Berry, M. (1981) 'Posing the housing question in Australia: Elements of a theoretical framework for a Marxist analysis of housing', *Antipode*, 13(1): 3–14.

Bond, P. (1995) 'Urban social movements, the housing question, and development discourses in South Africa', in D. Moore and G. Schmitz (eds) *Debating Development Discourse: Institutional and popular perspectives*. New York: Macmillan, pp. 149–177.

Hodkinson, S. (2012) 'The return of the housing question', *Ephemera*, 11(4): 423–444.

Murphy, E. and N. Hourani (eds) (2013) *The Housing Question: Tensions, continuities, and contingencies in the modern city*. Burlington, VT: Ashgate.

Infrastructure

Tanya Matthan

Infrastructure is popularly understood as the networks that enable the movement of goods and services critical to the functioning of societies. Often equated with 'public works', the term has conventionally referred to systems of transportation, water supply, energy, and communications, seen as hallmarks of development. Critical urban studies, however, conceptualizes infrastructure not simply as a thing or a system, but as a complex socio-technical *process* that differentially enables and disables flows of people, materials, and information within and across cities (Graham and McFarlane, 2015). Scholars also have expanded the concept to reference both 'hard' technologies and 'soft' cultural, political, and economic institutions, including people themselves. Ranging from high-speed rail networks and electrical grids to biometric identity cards and financial instruments, infrastructures are sites of capitalist production and state-building, spaces of environmental transformation, and mediators of power relations (McFarlane and Rutherford, 2008). Employing infrastructure as both a conceptual tool and an object of inquiry, scholars ask: Who can(not) travel? Where does water (not) flow? Why are roads (not) built there?

Studies of infrastructure can be traced back to the mid-twentieth century, when historians of technology drew attention to the 'invisible city' – circuits of wires, cables, and pipes supporting urban landscapes. Further, they highlight the co-constitution of social and technical systems, comprising physical artifacts like transformers and transmission lines, and institutions such as manufacturing firms and investment banks. Within the disciplines of geography and architecture, however, the focus was on the design of specific material objects, rather than processes of connection and maintenance (Graham and Marvin, 2001). Grounded in presumptions of technological rationality and the apolitical rationalities of service provision, infrastructures were viewed as the domain of engineers and planners. Further, infrastructures appeared opaque, a taken-for-granted background, often 'black-boxed' by city dwellers (in the global North) for whom they seemed universal, coming into view only upon breakdown. However, as Susan Leigh Star notes, 'Study a city and neglect its sewers and power supplies (as many have), and you miss essential aspects of distributional justice and planning power' (1999: 379).

Studies of infrastructure burgeoned in the context of the historical disintegration of the 'modern infrastructural ideal' (Graham and Marvin, 2001). Between the 1850s and 1960s, many cities in the global North witnessed the creation of centralized networks to deliver dependable services of heat, light, and mobility across the metropolis, constituting the planned and cohesive city.

Toward the end of the twentieth century, however, this ideal was undermined, most powerfully through processes of neoliberalization, but also in light of feminist, environmentalist, and postcolonial critiques of the inherent inequities and biases of infrastructure. Existing urban infrastructures began to decay and collapse, as maintenance stagnated and public infrastructures experienced privatization and **financialization**. Infrastructural development came to be centered on creating premium spaces, such as hub airports and investment enclaves to serve the needs of global elites. Yet, as scholars researching **post-colonial cities** point out, the trajectory of this ideal has been different in the global South, where infrastructure remains a never-quite-realized aspiration; the fabric of these (but also western) cities has always been differentiated (McFarlane and Rutherford, 2008).

Recently, scholars of infrastructure draw conceptually from actor–network theory and **assemblage urbanism**, emphasizing the relationality of infrastructural networks. For example, while a highway might be a working infrastructure to an automobile owner, it is a topic of concern to a construction worker and a potential difficulty for a pedestrian (Star, 1999); it may be mundane and/or monumental to different groups. Crucially, these systems of connection and disconnection shape **urban (im)mobilities** through the organization of movements and barriers. Moreover, theorists emphasize the vitality of **more-than-human** aspects of infrastructure, whereby the material and biophysical properties of, say, electrical cables and water shape the working of infrastructural systems in significant ways.

Studying experiences of building, maintaining, and using infrastructures offers a productive lens into the nature and politics of **everyday urbanism**, from the ways in which socio-technical systems are brought into being to their imbrication in processes of exclusion and contestation. Thus Nikhil Anand (2011) argues, in navigating Mumbai's water supply network, that differently positioned actors (slum dwellers, engineers, brokers) must mobilize 'pressure' (technical, biophysical, political). While this unequally structured hydraulic infrastructure leaves many of the city's poorer inhabitants outside its fold, residents still manage to access water – by petitioning politicians, and clandestinely connecting to the system through illegal pumps and wells. By marshaling technical (pipes and plumbers) and social resources (patrons and handlers) to procure water, they assert their **right to the city**.

As both 'things' and relations between 'things', infrastructures constitute the material base and backdrop of urban life (Larkin, 2013). Diverse objects have been labeled infrastructures – from technological systems to accounting practices and webs of sociality – and each analyzed in distinct ways. This plurality of artifacts and approaches to urban infrastructure in the current historical moment has produced a generative flux across geography and allied disciplines, bringing to light interconnected aspects of infrastructural networks that both sustain and undermine contemporary urbanism.

References

Anand, N. (2011) 'Pressure: the politechnics of water supply in Mumbai', *Cultural Anthropology*, 26(4): 542–564.

Graham, S. and S. Marvin (2001) *Splintering Urbanism: Networked infrastructures, technological mobilities and the urban condition*. London: Routledge.

Graham, S. and C. McFarlane (eds) (2015) *Infrastructural Lives: Urban infrastructure in context*. London: Routledge.

Larkin, B. (2013) 'The politics and poetics of infrastructure'. *Annual Review of Anthropology*, 42: 327–343.

McFarlane, C. and J. Rutherford (2008) 'Political infrastructures: governing and experiencing the fabric of the city', *International Journal of Urban and Regional Research*, 32(2): 363–374.

Star, S. L. (1999) 'The ethnography of infrastructure', *American Behavioral Scientist*, 43(3): 377–391.

Further reading

Anand, N., A. Gupta and H. Appel (eds) (2018) *The Promise of Infrastructure*. Durham, NC: Duke University Press.

Kaika, M. and E. Swyngedouw (2000) 'Fetishizing the modern city: the phantasmagoria of urban technological networks', *International Journal of Urban and Regional Research*, 24(1): 120-138.

Simone, A. (2004) 'People as infrastructure: intersecting fragments in Johannesburg', *Public Culture*, 16(3): 407-429.

More-Than-Human World/Urban Nature

Hudson Spivey

The **more-than-human world** and **urban nature** are concepts denoting the non-human organisms, materials, and processes that both comprise 'the city' as a physical form and which are enrolled into the socio-material process of urbanizing space. Both terms indicate a theoretical, methodological, and analytical sensibility toward urban research that avoids rigid ontological distinctions between the so-called 'natural' and 'human' domains. Scholarship in this vein attends to the complex entanglements between human bodies, artifacts, imaginaries, and the material entities and processes that sustain and exceed them. Urban nature is an expansive category, ranging from the bio-geophysical context of city settlements, including the local climate, vegetation, and wildlife communities, to urban green spaces like gardens and parks. More-than-human approaches to urban research emphasize the abiding interconnections between the human and non-human worlds, such that even supposedly human-made artifacts in the urban built environment – including **infrastructures** like roads, power grids, and storm water and sewerage systems – are permeated and sustained by non-human organisms and forces.

Since the 1980s, scholarship on nature–society relations across the humanities and social sciences has revolutionized dominant conceptions of the relationship between human social systems and the non-human environment. Prominent sub-fields engaging with urban themes, including environmental history, urban geography, and urban political ecology, have explored the implications of this reconceptualization for the analysis of urban environments. This has generated a variety of lexical innovations that attempt to transcend the limits of the modernist imagination, including 'second nature' (Smith, 1984; Cronon, 1991) and 'socio-ecology' (Heynen et al., 2006), which emphasize the dialectical ways through which humans and the more-than-human world shape and permeate one another. In an early intervention, Neil Smith (1984) used the Marxian concept of 'second nature' to argue that human production systems do not eliminate 'first nature' (or nature in its raw state) – but rather transform it. Nature in the city is thus best conceptualized as a form of 'second nature' – a *produced* nature – that has both biophysical properties and human-imposed characteristics. Water running from a tap, for instance, is both a biophysical entity tied to the global water cycle and a social product, in that human labor, technology, and expertise are required to build and operate the systems that transport the water from source to sink.

Literary scholars and urban historians were some of the first to challenge the prejudice that the city was a space without nature. Raymond Williams' (1973) *The Country and the City* revealed how urban areas were stitched to their rural hinterlands through networks of labor and material production.

Urban scholars have examined how cultural representations of urban nature and 'urban imaginaries' (Gandy, 2014) have transformed over time, as well as how such imaginaries continue to inform the evolution of the city's built form and its broader ecological relations. In his environmental history of Chicago, William Cronon (1991) showed how the growing metropolis depended on the enrollment of vast more-than-human forces (like prairie soil, grain, timber reserves, and the bodies of livestock) into purportedly 'human' systems of capital accumulation. Historical and cultural approaches to urban nature have remained a mainstay among both historians and geographers, and include studies of urban sanitation, water infrastructure (Gandy, 2014), and natural disaster.

Critical urban theorists have innovated a variety of novel concepts and approaches for analyzing environmental processes and conflicts in urban settings. Such studies use the tools of critical social theory not only to explain urban socio-natural configurations, but also to generate strategies for their progressive transformation. Approaches in environmental justice (EJ) and urban political ecology (UPE) examine the impacts of uneven geographic development on the coproduction of urban socio-natures and inequality. UPE draws on Marx's theory of social metabolism and Smith's (1984) early study of the capitalist production of 'second nature' to analyze how unequal power relations in cities 'produce socio-environmental conditions that are both enabling, for powerful individuals and groups, and disabling, for marginalized individuals and groups' (Heynen et al., 2006: 10). Heynen et al.'s agenda-setting collection includes studies examining the social production of urban hunger, the political economy of lawns, and the politics of water distribution and provision in South Africa. Using political ecology's traditional sensitivity toward the role of political economic forces in shaping access to environmental resources and amenities, UPE pushes urban scholars to explore how questions of social and economic justice in the city are also fundamentally ecological questions.

Recent approaches of **assemblage urbanism** have moved beyond Marxian political economy and instead draw inspiration from a range of 'post-humanist' ontologies, including Deleuze and Guattari's assemblage theory and Latour's actor–network theory. These non-dualistic ontologies enable scholars to explore the liveliness of animals and even inanimate objects in urban environments, emphasizing how the agency of organisms and inorganic materials can resist or upend human ambitions for mastery. Unlike UPE, these object-oriented approaches refuse to grant analytical preference to social structures, like class, race, or gender, as determining factors behind urban socio-ecological inequality, and often displace the 'human' as the proper subject of an urban ecological politics. Instead, they examine how political possibilities in the city encompass a broader field of relations between humans and non-humans, such that 'urban liveability involves civic associations and attachments forged in and through more-than-human relations' (Hinchliffe and Whatmore, 2006: 124).

In their study of raptors and water voles in contemporary Birmingham, UK, Steve Hinchliffe and Sarah Whatmore (2006) challenge urban scholars to move beyond merely analyzing urban environments toward actively transforming cities to increase the potential for human–non-human encounters and collaborations.

As urban areas across the planet face growing threats from climate change, research on urban nature has also examined a variety of approaches for promoting **urban sustainability and resilience**. Potential strategies range from policy mechanisms for low-carbon transitions to urban design innovations like green buildings and collective urban farming. Increasingly, planners, urbanists, and urban citizens are recognizing the complex feedbacks between urban environments and the global environment, and are seeking urban designs and policies that account for how cities are embedded in the more-than-human world.

References

Cronon, W. (1991) *Nature's Metropolis: Chicago and the Great West*. New York: W.W. Norton & Company.

Gandy, M. (2014) *The Fabric of Space: Water, modernity, and the urban imagination*. Cambridge, MA: MIT Press.

Heynen, N., M. Kaika and E. Swyngedouw (eds) (2006) *In the Nature of Cities: Urban political ecology and the politics of urban metabolism*. New York: Routledge.

Hinchliffe, S. and S. Whatmore (2006) 'Living cities: towards a politics of conviviality', *Science as Culture*, 15(2): 123–138.

Smith, N. (1984) *Uneven Development: Nature, capital, and the production of space*. Athens, GA: University of Georgia Press.

Williams, R. (1973) *The Country and the City*. New York: Oxford University Press.

Further reading

Braun, B. (2005) 'Environmental issues: writing a more-than-human urban geography', *Progress in Human Geography*, 29(5): 635–650.

Greenhough, B. (2014) 'More-than-human-geographies', in R. Lee et al. (eds) *The Sage Handbook of Progress in Human Geography*. London: Sage, pp. 94–119.

Neoliberal Urbanism

CS Ponder

Neoliberal urbanism fuses two long-standing objects of analysis in urban studies: neoliberalism, as a mode of 'entrepreneurial' governance and set of relations rooted in free-market ideologies; and urbanism 'as a way of life', which understands the socio-spatiality of cities as the major nexus through which people experience modernity. Research into neoliberal urbanism provides a critique and analysis of neoliberalism as the currently hegemonic mode of organizing economy, nature, and society, within which cities are understood to occupy key nodal positions. As a critique of neoliberalism and as an approach to urban research, it starts from the premise that contemporary processes of urbanization have become foundational to methods of neoliberal capital accumulation. It emphasizes how the production of the city is now driven by market-based, profit-seeking projects such as the redevelopment of ports or city centers into luxury waterfront or downtown residential and consumer spaces. The results of the ensuing intra-urban competition between cities for such entrepreneurial development projects are expressed through popular metrics like the Global Cities Index – rankings that themselves have intensified jockeying between urban areas for higher positions in the hierarchical network of world cities. Meanwhile, research focused on tracking the socio-spatial repercussions of such entrepreneurial development projects on urban life has shown that outcomes typically include the displacement of lower-income, gendered, and/or minority populations from key areas of the city. **Gentrification** has thus become a major lens through which the social impacts of neoliberal urbanism are studied.

Within the analytical framework of neoliberal urbanism, cities are seen not only as sites of 'actually existing' neoliberalism (Brenner and Theodore, 2002), but also as likely locations for social contestations against neoliberal projects and policies (Leitner et al., 2007). Researchers working in this vein conceive of neoliberalism as a dynamic, multiscalar ideological and political economic project, and contend that a processual and context-specific understanding of neoliber*alization* is necessary to understanding neoliberalism as it is practiced on the ground in real-life situations. This approach to analyzing neoliberalism emerged in the early 2000s in response to critiques of totalizing conceptions of neoliberalism (e.g., Brenner and Theodore, 2002). Aihwa Ong (2006) and others (e.g., Robinson, 2011) suggest, however, that while the research agenda of neoliberal urbanism now usefully focuses on multiscalar processes, theorizations from an empirically narrow sample of sites, almost completely drawn from the global North, are still a mainstay of the project, weakening the explanatory power of the concept. This has triggered research examining globally variegated forms of neoliberal urbanism (e.g., Karaman, 2013).

In the past decade, a related research stream has become concerned with what is termed 'austerity urbanism', which investigates consequences for cities of the even deeper retrenchment of the state in the aftermath of the 2008–2010 global financial crisis. Here researchers are finding that many cities are increasingly unable to afford **infrastructure** and service provisions as previous decades of neoliberalization are compounded by the post-crisis revocation of federal support and tax revenues. In turn, this has engendered the mobilization of urban activist groups seeking to contest the conditions of post-crisis austerity (Mayer, 2013). Austerity-inspired urban social justice movements deeply opposed to the continued hegemony of neoliberalism include the Occupy Wall Street movement (2011), Los Indignados in Spain (2011), and the Black Lives Matter movement (2013–). Mass urban protests against austerity have repeatedly taken place in cities across Europe and North and South America since 2011.

Methodologically speaking, research on neoliberal urbanism is dominated by case study approaches. However, debates within the field suggest that theoretical saturation has been reached regarding the amount of new knowledge that can be gained from elucidating neoliberal urbanism through single case studies (e.g., Peck, 2015). The focus thus has begun to shift to **comparative urbanism**, but questions remain regarding how to make comparisons in ways that are theoretically productive rather than taxonomic. Relational comparison is increasingly considered to be particularly useful in terms of knowledge production.

There has also been an epistemological debate regarding how research into neoliberal urbanism should understand the city itself: as a bounded settlement pattern relationally connected to macro-processes and contexts (cf. Hackworth, 2007), as an assemblage of human and non-human actants and agents (cf. Ong, 2006), or as part of a world-wide process of urbanization without any spatially bounded limits, as put forth by conceptualizations of **planetary urbanization**. Choices also abound regarding which sites, perspectives, and geographies are the most appropriate for investigation and theory construction, including whether to 'study-up' and examine the actions and logics of neoliberal power-brokers, as for example in the literature on policy mobilities, or to consider contestations from below (Leitner et al., 2007).

References

Brenner, N. and N. Theodore (2002) 'Cities and the geographies of "actually existing neoliberalism"', *Antipode,* 34(3): 349–379.

Hackworth, J. (2007) *The Neoliberal City: Governance, ideology, and development in American urbanism.* Ithaca, NY: Cornell University Press.

Karaman, O. (2013) 'Urban neoliberalism with Islamic characteristics', *Urban Studies,* 50(13): 3412–3427.

Leitner, H., E. Sheppard, K. Sziarto and A. Maringanti (2007) 'Contested urban futures: decentering neoliberalism', in H. Leitner, J. Peck and E. Sheppard (eds) *Contesting Neoliberalism: Urban frontiers*. New York: Guilford Press, pp. 1–25.

Mayer, M. (2013) 'First world urban activism', *City*, 17(1): 5–19.

Ong, A. (2006) 'Neoliberalism as a mobile technology', *Transactions of the Institute of British Geographers*, 32(1): 3–8.

Peck, J. (2015) 'Cities beyond compare?', *Regional Studies*, 49(1): 160–182.

Robinson, J. (2011) '2010 Urban geography plenary lecture – the travels of urban neoliberalism: taking stock of the internationalization of urban theory', *Urban Geography*, 32(8): 1087–1109.

Further reading

Harvey, D. (1989) 'From managerialism to entrepreneurialism: the transformation in urban governance in late capitalism', *Geografiska Annaler: Series B, Human Geography*, 71(1): 3–17.

Wirth, L. (1938) 'Urbanism as a way of life', *American Journal of Sociology*, 44(1): 1–24.

Planetary Urbanization

Mikael Omstedt

Planetary urbanization denotes the claim that processes of urbanization have escaped the bounded scale of 'the city', extending to that of the planet (Brenner and Schmid, 2015). Arguing that it is no longer meaningful to contrast an urban inside with a rural outside, proponents of this concept contend that there is now a continuous 'urban fabric' that unevenly stretches across the entire planet – an explosion of urbanization shaped by twenty-first-century capitalism. Even the seemingly most remote landscapes, from the Himalayas and Antarctica to the Amazon and the Pacific Ocean, are bound up with processes of connectivity, energy extraction, and water and food supply that sustain global urban life. This implies abandoning any conceptualization of the urban as contained by the extent of the built environment, in favor of examining the extra-local processes that sustain such landscapes.

This theoretical agenda seeks to systematically rethink the categories of urban studies, expanding on French urban theorist Henri Lefebvre's speculations on the transition into a completely 'urban society': he dubbed this the urban revolution. Planetary urbanization has been advanced by Neil Brenner and Christian Schmid, together with Brenner's associates in the Urban Theory Lab at Harvard University. They push beyond David Harvey's (1996) call to turn attention from 'the city as a thing' to 'urbanization as a process', arguing that the city, urban studies' traditional theoretical category, must be replaced. Dismissing the search for new urban typologies that more fully capture a new kind of city (e.g., edge city or in between city) as inadequate, Brenner and Schmid suggest that the field should come to terms with the urban as 'a multiscalar *process* of sociospatial transformation' (2015: 165, emphasis in original), rather than as a universal form, a settlement type, or a bounded spatial unit. In this view, urbanization involves three moments: (i) *concentrated urbanization* – the agglomerations within which people and capital cluster; (ii) *extended urbanization* – the extra-local 'operational landscapes' that support agglomeration with construction materials, energy, food, and water; and (iii) *differentiated urbanization* – the ongoing creative destruction and uneven development of both these agglomerations and their operational landscapes. Andy Merrifield (2013) argues that planetary urbanization also is a deeply political process, since urbanization is essentially about the creation of social interrelations through the assembling of people. He argues that when the urban fabric stretches across space, this breaks down separations between peoples and enables their unification in a 'politics of the encounter', in turn opening up opportunities for large-scale emancipatory change.

Methodologically, the concept of planetary urbanization seeks to overcome the 'methodological cityism' seen as characterizing urban studies to date – whereby the city is analytically privileged as the object of analysis, whereas the 'non-city' is downplayed regardless of its actual significance for urban processes (Angelo and Wachsmuth, 2015). This formulation poses its own methodological challenges: the question of where urban scholars should ground their research becomes acute if the city is no longer a privileged site. The Urban Theory Lab has deployed large-scale visualizations of global flows and human environmental footprints to illustrate the planetary extension of urban processes. Infrastructures of connectivity and material flows are a central object of such research, combined with utilizing more conventional case study methods to interrogate the role of ostensibly 'rural' locations as nodes within these vast urban operational landscapes.

At a moment when political economic urban theory is in question, the proposal that planetary urbanization offers a new epistemological framework to counter the fragmentation of critical urban studies has been criticized for offering a totalizing grand narrative that simultaneously obscures socio-spatial difference and upgrades Eurocentric universalization to the planetary scale (Peake et al., 2018). In particular, the notion of 'urban theory without an outside' has been accused of overstretching the concept of the urban while ignoring capitalist urbanization's constitutive other, and critics have expressed concern that such a meta-framework, primarily seeking to critique established understandings of global urbanism, offers little to guide political intervention in the form of everyday urban practice. Furthermore, while agreeing with taking a relational approach to conceptualizing the urban, others contend that the city should remain a focus of analysis, in continual dialectical tension with such wider processes (Davidson and Iveson, 2015).

Through the influence of its proponents, planetary urbanization has rapidly become one of the most contentious and widely debated formulations in contemporary urban studies. Notwithstanding the various criticisms, it does provide a language to bring what is going on beyond the city into urban scholarship. It deconstructs a rural–urban binary that appears increasingly irrelevant in a world of global connections, while methodologically emphasizing the importance of multi-sited research for tracking the interconnectivities of an ever-extending urban fabric.

References

Angelo, H. and D. Wachsmuth (2015) 'Urbanizing urban political ecology: a critique of methodological cityism', *International Journal of Urban and Regional Research*, 39(1): 16–27.

Brenner, N. and C. Schmid (2015) 'Towards a new epistemology of the urban?', *City*, 19(2–3): 151–182.

Davidson, M. and K. Iveson (2015) 'Beyond city limits: a conceptual and defense of "the city" as an anchoring concept for critical urban theory', *City*, 19(5): 646–664.

Harvey, D. (1996) 'Cities or urbanization?', *City*, 1(1–2): 38–61.

Merrifield, A. (2013) 'The urban question under planetary urbanization', *International Journal of Urban and Regional Research*, 37(3): 909–922.

Peake, L., D. Patrick, R. N. Reddy, G. Tanyildiz, S. Ruddick and R. Choukaleyska (eds) (2018) Special Issue: 'Planetary urbanization', *Environment and Planning D*, 36(3): 373–610.

Further reading

Arboleda, M. (2016) 'In the nature of the non-city: expanded infrastructural networks and the political ecology of planetary urbanization', *Antipode*, 48(2): 233–251.

Brenner, N. (ed.) (2014) *Implosions/Explosions: Towards a study of planetary urbanization*. Berlin: Jovis Verlag.

Lefebvre, H. (2003) *The Urban Revolution*. Minneapolis: University of Minnesota Press.

Postcolonial Cities/Subaltern Urbanism

Prajna Rao

Postcolonial cities broadly refers to cities whose contemporary conditions continue to be affected by their historical encounters with European colonialism. There are varied and contentious interpretations of postcolonial cities, which are loosely separable into two predominant strands of inquiry. The first examines postcolonial cities as empirical analytical *objects*: urban sites where recently independent nations worked toward cultivating a new identity. For instance, Abidin Kusno (1998) focuses on the vibrant contestations over the production of built forms, art, architecture, cultural symbols, and identities in Jakarta, reflecting upon how Indonesians – predominantly its Jakarta-based national elites – engaged in dialogue with their colonial (and sometimes precolonial) past. The same strand also includes scholarship that vehemently rejects definitions of the postcolonial as 'once-colonized', arguing how, for example, Mumbai (periphery) and London (metropole) cannot be disentangled from one another; they were and continue to be irrevocably entwined by their histories (King, 1990). The second strand of inquiry deviates from treating postcolonial cities as urban sites belonging to a particular space and time. Here, postcolonial cities function as a conceptual *frame* that demands a rethinking of the fundamental terms by which knowledge about cities is constructed and represented. This strand challenges universalized theorizations of the city drawn from specific, observed experiences of select Euro-American cities, arguing that lesser known geographies, practices, and processes must also be examined to achieve a richer understanding of the urban.

This second strand, currently more influential, draws its original critique from the Subaltern Studies Group (SSG) of South Asian scholars that emerged in the 1980s. The SSG critiqued an excessive focus in South Asian history on elite politics oriented toward the Euro-American west, drawing attention instead to what Gramsci called the *subaltern*: people at the margins of hegemonic structures of society and study. Extending this critique to urban studies, **subaltern urbanism** generally denotes research and practice that prioritizes those spaces, subjects, and processes that are marginalized in dominant urban narratives. In postcolonial urban studies, the subaltern primarily constitutes the urban poor who, although exploited, exercise forms of economic and political agency that go beyond questions of survival, also shaping urban environments. Rejecting Weberian ideas of an autonomous and rule-bound state, subaltern urbanism works to reveal more flexible, porous, and appropriable practices of state machinery. It demonstrates how, albeit under exploitative and contingent conditions, subalterns pursue negotiable political relations with local bureaucracies, enabling them to access **rights to the city**: shelter, livelihoods, and opportunity. Methodologically, subaltern urbanism encourages empirical investigations of everyday life over grander urban narratives. While some consider such studies as simply observed detail, a host of postcolonial scholars including AbdouMaliq Simone (2010) and Solomon Benjamin (2008) have demonstrated how subaltern urbanism, by exploring diverse urban subjects, spaces, and conditions, also can be generative of theory.

In a similar spirit, the frame of postcolonial cities seeks to explore newer sites for theory making, often misunderstood as located only within the formerly colonized global South (postcolony). Rather, these are any sites that offer distinctive experiences that are generative of alternative productive and provocative theoretical frameworks for other cities across the stubborn North–South divide. Insights from researching Jakarta, Kolkata, and Cape Town, for example, may be applied for an alternative interpretation of New York and Berlin. Indeed, New York and Berlin also can be studied through the postcolonial cities frame, paying critical attention to their histories of involvement with colonialism and how those legacies are reworked into contemporary city-making. Coll Thrush (2007) offers such a postcolonial account of contemporary Seattle, by attending to how the histories of dispossession and displacement of Native populations have always been intertwined with their labor of survival, resistance, endurance, and activism, building the city to its current experience. Simone (2010) details how the everyday interface for an urban majority in Kinshasa is deeply affected by colonial reconfigurations of tenure, property, government, infrastructure, and urban form, in addition to social constructs of morality, identities, and privilege.

Some scholars critique the theoretical framing of postcolonial cities for muddling coherent theories of the urban with empirical variation, rather than offering robust alternative theorizations; others argue that the inexorable logic of globalization has triggered a convergence of metropolitan urban forms, implying that the historical influences of colonial empires are no longer relevant for understanding the contemporary city. Proponents of *postcolonial cities* defend the frame, not only for its attention to the crucial role that historical trajectories play in globalization/urbanization, but also for shifting the study of cities beyond an implicitly northern framework dominated by a standardized understanding of the urban economy and its associated nexus of locations, land uses, and human interactions (Roy, 2015) (cf. Yeoh, 2001; *International Journal of Urban and Regional Research*, 2016).

Notwithstanding uncertainty about whether it will endure as a fruitful category, the concept of postcolonial cities undoubtedly has offered critical urban studies a reorientation of old histories and new geographies, vantage points, subjects, methodologies, practices, and spaces, toward more plural ways of understanding and representing the urban.

References

Benjamin, S. (2008) 'Occupancy urbanism: radicalizing politics and economy beyond policy and programs', *International Journal of Urban and Regional Research*, 32(3): 719–729.

International Journal of Urban and Regional Research (2016) 'Intervention: global urbanism and the nature of urban theory', 40(1): 164–246.

King, A. D. (1990) *Urbanism, Colonialism, and the World-Economy: Cultural and spatial foundations of the world urban system.* London: Routledge & Kegan Paul.

Kusno, A. (1998) 'Beyond the postcolonial: architecture and political cultures in Indonesia', *Public Culture,* 10(3): 549–575.

Roy, A. (2015) 'Who's afraid of postcolonial theory?', *International Journal of Urban and Regional Research,* 40(1): 200–209.

Simone, A. (2010) *City Life from Dakar to Jakarta.* London: Routledge.

Thrush, C. (2007) *Native Seattle: Histories from the crossing-over place.* Seattle: University of Washington Press.

Yeoh, B. S. (2001) 'Postcolonial cities', *Progress in Human Geography,* 25(3): 456–468.

Further reading

Chatterjee, P. (2004) *The Politics of the Governed: Reflections on popular politics in most of the world.* New York: Columbia University Press.

Gramsci, A. (1971) *Selections from the Prison Notebooks 1929-1935,* translated by Q. Hoare and G. N. Smith. New York: International Publishers.

Post-Political City

Joe Penny

The term **post-political city** diagnoses a condition in which the collective political possibilities presented to people in cities by politicians and bureaucrats, through formal institutionalized decision-making channels, are narrowed in the name of economic exigency qua political necessity, and suggests that 'properly' political imaginations, movements, and subjectivities are required to break from business-as-usual urban policymaking.

Proponents of this frame base their arguments on the ontological distinction that post-foundational theorists make between 'politics' and 'the political'. In *Dis-agreement*, Jacques Rancière (1999), a widely cited theorist of 'post-politics' despite never using the term, distinguishes 'the political' from what is usually associated with politics, including the actions of parliaments and judiciaries, the work of civil servants and local bureaucrats, and the everyday machinations of policymaking. He suggests that none of these activities are political. Rather, they are part of a 'police order'.

By 'police order', Rancière is not referring narrowly to 'the cops'. Instead, he is pointing to a diffuse set of social practices through which a consensus about social givens is realized. The 'police order' denotes a society's taken-for-granted configuration of perception and meaning in which certain discourses, rationalities, and arguments are articulated, heard, and understood, and from which certain policies and programs are legitimized and normalized.

In contrast, 'the political' is reserved for actions and events that rupture the 'police order', fundamentally disrupting its foundational assumptions. In contrast to arguments or conflicts over specific technical measures, policy instruments, and their effects, political actions call into question the underlying and unspoken boundaries separating what is and is not a sensible political or policy option. Politics, in short, is a particular occurrence – a moment of *dissensus* that breaks a consensus.

Inspired by this distinction, urban scholars have mobilized the post-political city concept to critique the democratic and political deficits of **urban governance**, particularly under **neoliberal urbanism**. Erik Swyngedouw (2005), who coined the term post-political city, locates the contemporary constitution of the post-political condition in new forms of collaborative governance-beyond-the-state, 'which give a much greater role in policy-making, administration and implementation to private economic actors on the one hand and to parts of civil society on the other' (2005: 1992). Typically composed of unelected partnerships of expert actors, these spaces of urban govern*ance* have largely replaced or bypassed the rules and procedures of (at least somewhat more) accountable representative govern*ment* in liberal democracies. Going against those lauding these technologies as empowering, democracy enhancing, and effective, Swyngedouw suggests that the work of such governance is to purposefully remove politics from decision-making in favor of a managerial and profit-maximizing consensus.

Following Swyngedouw, processes of collaborative governance have come under scrutiny from a post-political city perspective for their depoliticizing consequences. Across a range of urban policy issues, from major infrastructure projects (Hilbrandt, 2017) to the installation of a small recreational facility in a park (Paddison, 2009), a growing body of scholarship demonstrates that, while the inclusionary and consensual thrust of collaborative governance is widely extolled, the time for and terms of debate in these supposedly democratic spaces is becoming evermore tightly circumscribed. This facilitates the smooth progress of market priorities, not withstanding deepening ecological, economic, and political crises. An illustrative example can be found in Emma Ormerod and Gordon MacLeod's (2018) account of housing regeneration in Gateshead, an industrial town in northeastern England, following the global financial crisis. They demonstrate how a program of housing market renewal was pursued through a depoliticizing partnership of unelected actors working outside of representative governmental structures. This partnership relied heavily on expert consultants and participatory planning to construct a narrow consensus for, and outflank disagreement and dissensus against, what amounted to a profit-maximizing program of land privatization.

Far from being an outlier, the Gateshead experience is repeatedly echoed in the critical urban studies literature. In case after case, state-sponsored programs promoted as collaborative governance are reduced to the realpolitik of increasingly managerial, technical, and even coercive modes of policymaking in pursuit of competitive, global, secure, and sustainable cities (Davidson and Iveson, 2015), despite the often violently exclusionary effects on those subjected to/participating in them.

The analytical purchase of the post-political city is clear in the scholarly output it has inspired over the past decade. Yet, it is not without its discontents. Critics of the term contend that the distinction between 'policing' and 'politics' is too simplistic a binary to capture the messy realities of struggle in cities, unduly privileging the revolutionary over the incremental, and risking a debilitating 'all or nothing' analysis of social change.

Perhaps one way to address this concern is to emphasize the incomplete nature of the post-political city. From this perspective, one might point to *processes* of post-politicization where the post-political city symbolizes an age-old, yet ultimately unrealizable, elite project to govern unchallenged. Less a dystopian present or future foreclosed, the post-political city warns of a tendency that city dwellers must continue to frustrate.

References

Davidson, M. and K. Iveson (2015) 'Recovering the politics of the city: from the "post-political city" to a "method of equality" for critical urban geography', *Progress in Human Geography*, 39(5): 534–559.

Hilbrandt, H. (2017) 'Insurgent participation: consensus and contestation in planning the redevelopment of Berlin-Tempelhof airport', *Urban Geography*, 38(4): 537–556.

Ormerod, E. and G. MacLeod (2018) 'Beyond consensus and conflict in housing governance: returning to the local state', *Planning Theory* (online first, http://journals.sagepub.com/doi/full/10.1177/1473095218790988).

Paddison, R. (2009) 'Some reflections on the limitations to public participation in the post-political city', *L'Espace Politique*, 8(2).

Rancière, J. (1999) *Dis-agreement: Politics and philosophy*. Minneapolis: University of Minnesota Press.

Swyngedouw, E. (2005) 'Governance innovation and the citizen: the Janus face of governance-beyond-the-state', *Urban Studies*, 42(11): 1991–2006.

Further reading

Driscoll Derickson, K. (2017) 'Taking account of the "part of those that have no part"', *Urban Studies*, 54(1): 44–48.

Mitchell, D., K. Attoh and L. Staeheli (2015) 'Whose city? What politics? Contentious and non-contentious spaces on Colorado's Front Range', *Urban Studies*, 52(14): 2633–2648.

Right to the City

Hudson Spivey

The **right to the city**, a concept first advanced by French Marxist theorist Henri Lefebvre, is a claim to enlarge the bounds of urban democracy by giving all urban inhabitants the ability to access and shape the urban environment and, by doing so, also shape themselves. This would include 'the right to information, the rights to use of multiple services, and the right of users to make known their ideas on the space and time of their activities in urban areas; it would also cover the right to the use of the center' (Lefebvre, 1991: 34). Henri Lefebvre first elaborated the concept of 'the Right to the City' in a 1967 essay of the same title, and later expanded upon it in *The Urban Revolution* (2003 [1970]), which he wrote in the wake of the urban uprisings of 1968. For Lefebvre (2003 [1970]), the urban character of these uprisings signaled that the terrain of anti-capitalist political struggle had emerged from the factory floor to engulf all parts of the city, regardless of class position. This signaled a widespread desire among the urban masses for a greater command over the space-making processes that shaped their day-to-day lives. Anticipating this unrest, Lefebvre (1996 [1967]: 158) wrote that: 'the right to the city is like a cry and a demand ... [that] can only be formulated as a transformed and renewed right to urban life.'

Lefebvre's concept became the object of renewed scholarly attention in the late 1990s following the wave of neoliberalization and massive disinvestment in public services that further undermined the livelihoods of urban inhabitants in the global North and South. Urban theorists seized on the right to the city as a concise formulation of the variety of emergent social movements contesting **gentrification, displacement, urban immobility**, the lack of housing and critical infrastructure, and dwindling public space in the city. According to David Harvey (2003: 941), the right to the city spans beyond traditional campaigns for distributional justice and 'is not merely a right of access to what the property speculators and state planners define'. It functions, rather, as a right to shape actively the social, political, cultural contexts, and built environment of the city in a way that fulfills not only the urban denizens' basic needs, but also their social, political, and aesthetic aspirations. Struggles against evictions, the lack of affordable housing, the criminalization of the poor and immigrant communities, and the promotion of mega-projects can be configured as broader movements to reappropriate urban space for the city's marginalized inhabitants.

For Peter Marcuse (2009: 185), materializing the right to the city constitutes 'the ultimate purpose of critical theory'. It is both a utopian, aspirational claim to an ideal city – sometimes post-capitalist, always just – and a normative prescription for an urban politics that foregrounds public participation in the allocation, development, and governance of the city. In recent years, it has been deployed by both scholars and urban activists for its challenge to the fiscal retrenchment and austerity of **neoliberal urbanism**. While urban theorists continue to debate the scope and relevance of Lefebvre's original concept, the right to the city has become a rallying cry for numerous social movements led by marginalized urban populations in cities throughout the global North and South. Tenants' rights organizations like Abahlali baseMjondolo in South Africa and the Right to the City Alliance in the United States have campaigned against evictions and for the right to public housing. These and other **urban social movements** aim to transform prevailing **urban governance** norms to align with radical democratic principles, and seek to guarantee access to basic amenities, such as food, shelter, water, and sanitation, for all inhabitants of the city.

Numerous citizen-led activist groups and urban social movements attest to the continued political relevance of the claim for a right to the city across the global North and South. The Right to the City Alliance is a US-based non-profit organization that focuses primarily on empowering marginalized communities in the struggle to prevent gentrification and secure affordable housing for low-income residents. The 'participatory budgeting' developed in Porto Alegre, Brazil, also developed out of a concern with equity and social justice in a city where a third of the population lacked adequate access to urban amenities like clean water, sanitation, and electricity. Despite the evident mobilizing power of the phrase, the increasing adoption among NGOs and government agencies of the 'right to the city' – to the extent of even enshrining it in federal law in Brazil's City Statute – risks domesticating the radical anti-capitalist implications of Lefebvre's original formulation to fit within prevailing neoliberal governance norms (De Souza, 2010).

Recent debates have questioned both theoretical and practical obstacles to realizing the right to the city in practice. Mark Purcell (2002) argues that Lefebvre's original vision held that any urban inhabitant, or *citadin*, should be granted the ability to make decisions about the appropriation, distribution, and use of urban space. If taken literally, this would not discriminate between urban citizens from different national origins and would therefore 'confront national citizenship as the dominant basis for political membership' (2002: 103). Purcell raises questions about the scalar limits to the right to shape the city: if land reform in Oaxaca would impact immigration from Mexico to Los Angeles, should urban citizens of Los Angeles be allowed to influence Oaxacan land policies? Given such complex geographies of human and capital mobility in the twenty-first century, Purcell argues that the struggle to achieve the right to the city will ultimately hinge on how the city is defined in spatial and scalar terms. Without a clear definition of the limits to **urban citizenship** – and in the absence of any clear geographic boundaries to the city in an age of **planetary urbanization** – the right to the city faces real practical obstacles. While it functions well as a motivating platform for mobilizing the city's disenfranchised residents, there is still a risk of its being reduced to a mere 'right to housing' or 'right to amenities' without challenging the broader political economic context of the contemporary urban world.

References

De Souza, M. (2010) 'Which right to which city? In defense of political-strategic clarity', *Interface: A Journal for and about Social Movements,* 2(1): 315–333.

Harvey, D. (2003) 'The right to the city', *International Journal of Urban and Regional Research,* 27(4): 939–941.

Lefebvre, H. (1991) 'Les illusions de la modernité', in I. Ramoney, J. Decornoy and Ch. Brie (eds) La ville partout et partout en crise, Manière de voir, 13. Paris: Le Monde diplomatique.

Lefebvre, H. (1996 [1967]) 'The right to the city', in E. Kofman and E. Lebas (eds) *Writings on Cities*. London: Blackwell, pp. 63–184.

Lefebvre, H. (2003 [1970]) *The Urban Revolution*. Minneapolis: University of Minnesota Press.

Marcuse, P. (2009) 'From critical urban theory to the right to the city', *City,* 13(2–3): 185–197.

Purcell, M. (2002) 'Excavating Lefebvre: The right to the city and its urban politics of the inhabitant', *GeoJournal,* 58(2–3): 99–108.

Further reading

Harvey, D. (2008) 'The right to the city', New Left Review, NS 53: 23–40.

Mitchell, D. (2003) The Right to the City: Social justice and the fight for public space. New York: Guilford Press.

Smart Cities

Nafis Hasan

Smart cities are places where information and communications technology (ICT) is combined with infrastructure, architecture, everyday objects, and people to address social, economic, and environmental problems. ICT is seen as a means for creating effective public policy to raise productivity and competitiveness of city government and businesses, as well as to enable the real-time control of urban utilities and services, along with the enforcement of public safety and security.

Smart cities first appeared in the mid-1990s in the United States, in a 'self-congratulatory way' (Hollands, 2008), essentially by naming existing cities endowed with the aforementioned characteristics as 'smart'. Outside the United States, Adelaide in Australia and Cyberjaya and Putrajaya in Malaysia were also labeled smart as they employed ICT to automate the operation of municipal functions. A revival of smart cities in 2008 was spearheaded by corporations that linked technological smartness to economic and sustainable development (Söderström et al., 2014). For instance, IBM's Intelligent Operations Center for Smarter Cities, a technological system that can 'accurately gather, analyze and act on information about city-systems and services', has been adopted by city governments around the world. Unlike the post hoc naming of cities as smart, the global spread of smart cities has given rise to greenfield urbanism and start-up city plans (Kennedy and Sood, 2016). Dholera in India, Songdo in Korea, and Masdar in the United Arab Emirates are some recent examples.

Accelerating technological innovation has been associated with a burgeoning discourse of smart cities, often fusing corporate and market logics with digital futurism. Smartphones, the mobile applications industry, open government data, 'big data', open-source hardware, and free networks are now being seen to offer the potential for producing real-time information that becomes a basis for decision-making, beyond the centralized mainframe paradigm of corporations like IBM and Cisco. Commentators are now marveling at the potential for residents to engage in the reciprocal 'smartening' of their cities, by participating in the 'smartphone software ecosystem'. Governments have latched onto these ideas of corporate-led, technology-centered development along with participation by citizens. For instance, when the national government of India launched the $7 billon Smart City Mission in 2015, state governments across the country engaged more than 30 global technology-consulting firms to draft their respective visions, while the national government solicited the responses of some 2.5 million people on a dedicated web platform.

In the urban studies field, the smart-city movement is typically viewed in one of two ways: as the manifestation of aspirational urban visions characteristic of a particular historical and geographical moment; or as the subject of critiques skeptical of its vague commitments to inclusion, its techno-centric and elitist ambitions, and its apparent indifference to social injustice. The former usage appeared in the early 1990s in the United States in conjunction with the idea of a 'technopolis', in which scientific knowledge was mobilized in support of innovation-rich economic growth and improved social amenities (Hall, 1995). Drawing on management, organizational, and communication theories, the idea of technopolis was predicated on corporate internationalization and market integration, as some cities were seen to be well placed to reap benefits from this form of capitalism. Subsequently, some urban economists and economic geographers, particularly in the United States and Europe, have presented smart cities as engines for economic growth – combining high rates of employment, human capital, and workforce productivity with lifestyle amenities (Shapiro, 2006), albeit with lower doses of technological futurism than in other parts of the smart-cities literature. In more recent years, the smart-city formula has been increasingly linked to the idea of global connectivity and to opportunities for economic development related to intercity trade. In this context, the attraction of foreign direct investment is identified as a key component of smart-city development, as cities seek favorable positions within global networks. Finally, there is a strand of smart-city discourse that derives from engineering, where 'intelligent cities' mobilize networked infrastructures as a means to realize social, environmental, and cultural development objectives.

In their critiques of smart cities as elitist, techno-centric visions of urban development, some urban studies scholars counter with a humanist discourse in which the smartness of a city should be less about reinventing governance as a means to succeed in the digital age and more about social learning, education, social capital development, environmental sustainability, and engaging the body politic (Eger, 2000; Hollands, 2008). This alternative perspective is informed by a critique of mainstream smart-city initiatives in which the avowed goals of improving the quality of urban life through the interaction of technology and knowledge-building processes is but a smokescreen for the merger of business competitiveness with social well-being. Here, the smart city serves as a label for pursuing the agenda for **neoliberal urbanism,** with deleterious consequences for social justice. These critiques have been joined by new lines of research from urban studies scholars outside the west, where smart-city programs have been problematized as a new type of greenfield urban development. In India, for example, these developments have been reworking the political economy of land, initiating new geographies of economic activities and logics of exception, while serving as catalysts for the privatization of urban governance (Kennedy and Sood, 2016). Similarly, critical research has traced how real-estate speculation in the post-Asian financial crisis period was critical to the making of Songdo City in South Korea.

References

Eger, J. M. (2000) 'Smart communities becoming smart is not so much about developing technology as about engaging the body politic to reinvent governance in the digital age', *Urban Land*, 60(1): 50–55.

Hall, P. (1995) *Technopolis: High-technology industry and regional development in Southern California*. Berkeley: University of California Press.

Hollands, R. G. (2008) 'Will the real smart city please stand up? Intelligent, progressive or entrepreneurial?', *City*, 12(3): 303–320.

Kennedy, L. and A. Sood (2016) 'Greenfield development as tabula rasa', *Economic & Political Weekly*, 51(17): 41–49.

Shapiro, J. (2006) 'Smart cities: quality of life, productivity, and the growth effects of human capital', *Review of Economics and Statistics*, 88(2): 324–335.

Söderström, O., T. Paasche and F. Klauser (2014) 'Smart cities as corporate storytelling', *City*, 18(3): 307–320.

Further reading

Datta, A. (2015) 'New urban utopias of postcolonial India: "entrepreneurial urbanization" in Dholera smart city, Gujarat', *Dialogues in Human Geography*, 5(1): 3–22.

Deakin, M. (2013) *Smart Cities: Governing, modelling and analyzing the transition*. New York: Routledge.

Kitchin, R. (2015) 'Making sense of smart cities: addressing present shortcomings', *Cambridge Journal of Regions, Economy and Society*, 8(1): 131–136.

Townsend, A. (2013) *Smart Cities: Big data, civic hackers, and the quest for a new utopia*. New York: W. W. Norton.

Suburbanization

Tom Howard

Suburbanization refers to processes of non-central city development and spatial expansion. It implies the production of new spatialities distinctive from dominant conceptions of both 'rural' and 'urban' space. The global diversity of suburban landscapes, however, belies any claim to the existence of an essential social pattern or built form that can be characterized as definitively 'suburban'. Moreover, the social content and cultural meanings associated with urbanity, suburbanity, and rurality vary across time and space. Suburbanization is therefore an inherently relational concept, referencing developmental processes that mediate between historically and geographically specific constructions of city and countryside.

Reflecting the inward-facing gaze of urban studies in the global North, anglophone research has largely theorized suburbanization from the vantage point of North American and European case studies (Keil, 2013). While recent scholarship has considered a broader range of sites, most notably in **postcolonial cities** (Wu and Phelps, 2011), theories of suburbanization have consistently worked around a series of coherent themes. Four salient and enduring themes in this literature are: the political economic causes and consequences of suburbanization; the relationship between suburbanization and social identity; suburbanization and **urban governance**; and the question of specifying 'suburban' space in the context of the broader socio-spatial fabric.

Suburbanization is recursively linked to the development of capitalist economies, both shaping and being shaped by contextual regimes of accumulation. Dispersions of working-class populations to peripheral districts, for instance, served as a disciplinary check on militant, labor-based **urban social movements** in nineteenth-century industrial cities. Conversely, the formation of dispersed residential districts was itself enabled by the spatial disaggregation of work and family life wrought by the rise of factory-led **agglomeration** economies and parallel disintegration of household-based production (Walker, 1981). The class fragmentations of this spatial division of labor have a gendered dimension, as modern suburbanization has entailed and fostered separations between a masculinized domain of paid labor and feminized spaces of domesticity and unpaid household labor (Hayden, 2003). Beyond labor relations, suburban development has itself been a driver of capitalist accumulation processes. After World War II, mass suburbanization in Western Europe and North America underwrote Fordist growth cycles both by absorbing capital surpluses and by stimulating demand for consumer goods. More recently, following economic reforms that have increased reliance on domestic consumption and property development, suburban development has been identified as a key component of the Chinese growth model (Wu and Phelps, 2011).

Questions of social identity loom large in these political economic processes. Particularly in North America, the parallel emergence of widespread suburbanization and cultures of mass consumption has created enduring associations between the two, where post-war suburbs popularly connote conservative values of homeownership, conformity, consumerism, and heteronormative standards of domesticity centered on the nuclear family (Beauregard, 2006). Like other constructions of community identity, however, such identities are founded on a series of constitutive exclusions. Restrictive mortgage-lending rules, redlining, and racially coded legal covenants effectively excluded many non-white populations from the formative stages of the USA's post-war suburbanization. Elsewhere, the state-directed concentration of high-density public housing and large migrant populations in France's suburbanized banlieues has, amidst the retreat of mass production since the 1970s, constructed these sites as segregated zones of racialized poverty (cf. Ebner et al., Chapter 7). Recent revisionist histories furthermore highlight how presumptions of coherent or essential suburban identities are undercut by persistent, if muted, forms of internalized difference and conflict (Kruse and Sugrue, 2006). While constructions of social and spatial distance from other aspects of city life shape certain shared patterns of **everyday urbanism** for suburbanites – alienation and anomie serving as classical concerns – suburbanization processes articulate with patterns of social integration and disintegration in ways that vary, sometimes dramatically, across different historical and geographical contexts.

The socio-spatial transformations entailed by suburbanization are molded by cognate urban governance structures. Supportive planning protocols, legal standards, and credit-granting institutions shape the conditions of possibility for suburbanization as a large-scale phenomenon. Substantial public subsidies for supportive **infrastructures** – roads, electrical grids, sanitation lines, and public institutions – also play an integral role. As pro-development coalitions and urban growth machines struggle to secure these provisions from various state institutions, suburbanization is characterized by a continuous rescaling of governance architectures through processes of secession, annexation, and amalgamation (Walker, 1981). Cleavages in jurisdictional authority between cities and their suburbs can fuel political struggles over who is responsible for funding and maintaining extensive infrastructure networks. Planning authorities furthermore struggle to provide services such as mass public transit to many suburbs, as their socio-spatial organization often makes such provisions prohibitively expensive. For advocates of **urban sustainability and resilience,** the automobile dependencies and infrastructural inefficiencies enforced by such landscapes undermine the long-term viability of mainstream suburbanization models (Keil, 2013).

Under the competitive imperatives of **neoliberal urbanism,** restless dynamics of **uneven urban development** have produced variegated landscapes that often diverge from the presumed homogeneity of suburbanism in its classic form(s). The growth of mixed-use and higher-density developments on urban peripheries has called into question the spatial referents typically associated with suburbia, spawning new landscapes across which the conventional demarcations of center and margin are not so clearly legible. Since the 1990s, several neologisms have been coined to describe these new spaces: exurbs, edge cities, technoburbs, boomburbs, exopoles, metroburbs, and so on. The umbrella term 'post-suburbia' has recently been deployed to account for the polyvalent, heterogeneous character of contemporary developments on urban peripheries (Wu and Phelps, 2011). Some have also argued that patterns of built-form homogeneity and social polarization associated with **gentrification** have led to the 'suburbanization' of conventionally 'urban' districts (Keil, 2013). Perhaps the most substantial challenge for suburban studies, however, lies in the penumbrae of formal, informal, and semi-formal developments associated with postcolonial cities in the global South. As (sub)urban theorists struggle to explain and typify the changing peripheries of cities in the global North, the exclusion of these sites from formal theories of suburbanization poses a challenge yet to be systemically addressed.

References

Beauregard, R. (2006) *When America Became Suburban*. Minneapolis: University of Minnesota Press.

Hayden, D. (2003) *Building Suburbia: Green fields and urban growth, 1820–2000*. New York: Pantheon.

Keil, R. (2013) 'Welcome to the suburban revolution', in R. Keil (ed.) *Suburban Constellations*. Berlin: JOVIS, pp. 8–17.

Kruse, K. and T. J. Sugrue (eds) (2006) *The New Suburban History*. Chicago: University of Chicago Press.

Walker, R. (1981) 'A theory of suburbanization: capitalism and the construction of urban space in the United States', in M. Dear and A. J. Scott (eds) *Urbanization and Planning in Capitalist Society*. New York: Methuen, pp. 383–429.

Wu, F. and N. A. Phelps (eds) (2011) *International Perspectives on Suburbanization: A post-suburban world?* New York: Palgrave Macmillan.

Further reading

Fishman, R. (1987) *Bourgeois Utopias: The rise and fall of suburbia*. New York: Basic Books.

Keil, R. (2017) *Suburban Planet: Making the world urban from the outside in*. Cambridge: Polity.

Knox, P. L. (2008) *Metroburbia, USA*. New Brunswick, NJ: Rutgers University Press.

Mace, A. (2013) *City Suburbs: Placing suburbia in a post-suburban world*. New York: Routledge.

Uneven Urban Development

Andre Comandon

Uneven development is a concept of Marxian and Trotskyist origin deployed in critical investigations of socio-economic inequality. In its initial formulation, it emphasized the contradictions that emerged from the interdependence of countries pursuing economic development through the exportation and expansion of exploitative capitalist social relations. Geographers like David Harvey, Doreen Massey, and Neil Smith elaborated on the spatial and scalar dynamics of capitalism and drew attention to the relational (more than local) constitution of so-called 'urban problems'. **Uneven urban development** seeks to make sense of the diverse processes by which capital is endlessly mobilized to take advantage of unequal land use values, labor qualities, and social conditions, giving rise to differentiated urban spaces. It is manifest, for example, in the contradictory coexistence of informal and formal modes of urban development in slums or the rush of speculative capital investments in neglected, but securitized, older downtowns.

David Harvey's work, beginning with *The Limits to Capital*, was instrumental in spurring the reformulation of uneven development. Working across scales from the local to the transnational, he maintained that geographical differentiation – the inequalities tied to the nature of land – is a product of processes of capital accumulation rather than a given (1982: 416). This insight pointed to the potential for firms to exploit gaps in cost and access between places, within and outside the location where capital is produced, to alleviate over-accumulation. When faced with a crisis due to over-accumulation of capacity, firms must devalue and abandon capital, triggering a localized crisis. However, through the financial sector, firms can restart the cycle of accumulation in a location more fitted to their use and with greater institutional backing.

In linking the spatial organization of work and employment to uneven development, Doreen Massey (2004) did much to expand on how the uneven distribution of economic functions defines the relation between places. The location of headquarters in London, for example, established the city as a node for decision-making that not only influenced the decision of other firms to locate their headquarters there, but also meant that other cities became subordinate in the functions they performed. This translates to unequal social relations. The concentration of highly paid professionals in London necessarily required high concentrations of low-wage service workers in the peripheries of the city and a network of precarious labor outside the region and the country to perform subsidiary tasks. 'Development' in one place is duly combined with the 'underdevelopment' of others.

Neil Smith's (1982) elaboration of the concept of uneven spatial development involved the integration of his idea of the rent gap in order to theorize how unevenness in cities fits within the broader circulation of capital and all manner of social struggles. Rent gap theory is based on the premise that the longevity of urban development necessarily creates gaps between the potential rents that can be extracted from a given parcel and the actual rents over time. When that gap is large enough, an area is primed for redevelopment. Smith's work duly represents a foundational contribution to the theorization of **gentrification**.

Uneven urban development is an evolving concept. The changing landscape of capitalism requires periodic revisions and adaptations, a process reflected in the intellectual projects engaging with this theory. Smith, for example, initially focused on differences between inner city and suburbs. However, **agglomeration** economies producing large capital surpluses and globalized capital movements have substantially complicated this process in cities from San Francisco to Shenzhen and Johannesburg. The movement of capital is no longer restricted to internal considerations, but takes on added layers as corporations consider the full portfolio of international land values in making their decisions.

Uneven urban development implies a particular approach to studying empirical ramifications. It privileges social relations and power struggles embedded in the built environment, in institutional forms, and in patterned social relations. It shares some commonalties with formulations in orthodox economics, but uneven development deviates from frameworks that assume equilibrium conditions (Clark, 1988; Sheppard, 2016). It effectively shifts the focus from supposed 'deviations' from equilibrium conditions to instead emphasize the connections between processes driving growth on the one hand and crisis on the other, where the central concern is with unequal social relations. Events like the 2008 mortgage crisis can be interpreted in these terms, shaped as they clearly were by the shifting geographies of financial power, followed by the aftermath of bailouts and bank consolidations. The constitutively connected other sides of the crisis are traced through the geographies of risk and economic dislocation, which heaped the burdens of adjustment on vulnerable households and most acutely those whose homes were foreclosed.

Extant approaches to uneven urban development have their limits, however. Research focused on the social structure of cities has underlined the need for more nuanced explorations of the racialized and gendered facets of uneven development, for instance, relating to issues like displacement (Slater, 2017). In principle, the theoretical framework seems to be flexible enough that it can accommodate these and other revisions and adaptations, while retaining its relevance for understanding the inherently uneven nature of urban development.

References

Clark, E. (1988) 'The rent gap and transformation of the built environment: case studies in Malmö 1860–1985', *Geografiska Annaler, Series B: Human Geography*, 70(2): 241–254.

Harvey, D. (1982) *The Limits to Capital*. London: Verso.

Massey, D. (2004) 'Uneven development: social change and spatial divisions of labor', in T. J. Barnes, J. Peck, E. Sheppard and A. Tickell (eds) *Reading Economic Geography*. Malden, MA: Blackwell.

Sheppard, E. (2016) *Limits to Globalization: Disruptive geographies of capitalist development*. Oxford: Oxford University Press.

Slater, T. (2017) 'Planetary rent gaps', *Antipode*, 49(1): 114–137.

Smith, N. (1982) 'Gentrification and uneven development', *Economic Geography*, 58(2): 139–155.

Further reading

Massey, D. (1984) *Spatial Divisions of Labour*. London: Macmillan.

Peck, J. (2016) 'Uneven regional development', in D. Richardson, N. Castree, M. F. Goodchild, A. Kobayashi, W. Liu and R. A. Marston (eds) *The Wiley-AAG International Encyclopedia of Geography*.Oxford: Wiley-Blackwell, 13 pp., https://onlinelibrary.wiley.com/doi/full/10.1002/9781118786352.wbieg0721.

Smith, N. (2008) [1984] *Uneven Development: Nature, capital, and the production of space*, 3rd edition. Athens: University of Georgia Press.

Storper, M., T. Kemeny, N. Makarem and T. Osman (2015) *The Rise and Fall of Urban Economies: Lessons from San Francisco and Los Angeles*. Stanford, CA: Stanford Business Books.

Urban Citizenship

Kyle Loewen

Urban citizenship refers to the role of cities in practicing citizenship through processes like claims-making and the formation of publics. The urban is a significant site, space, and scale for investigating citizenship for a number of reasons. First, citizenship is commonly associated with nation states that grant rights and responsibilities. Urban citizenship disrupts this conflation by calling attention to the role of cities in regulating the boundaries of group membership (Varsanyi, 2006). Second, while political theory considers citizenship in abstract terms, research on urban citizenship focuses on the production and practice of citizenship in concrete settings and situations (Secor, 2004). The idea of urban citizenship therefore identifies the city as a strategic site for researching citizenship formations while destabilizing formal conceptions of citizenship.

The conceptual boundaries of urban citizenship are fluid because the idea of citizenship itself has been subject to deconstruction and reformulation. On the one hand, scholars have challenged universal theorizations of citizenship by arguing that non-citizenship is constitutive of the definition and practice of citizenship itself (Isin, 2002). Without this outside, citizenship and group membership have no meaning. A second approach explores the others or outsides of citizenship in order to locate and describe alternative citizenship formations, including everyday, ordinary, and insurgent citizenships (Holston, 2009). It is within this second approach that the urban citizenship literature has uniquely focused on the formation of citizenship within the production of urban space, rather than concentrating on its formal boundaries. There are connections here to **urban informality** and **everyday urbanism**.

Effective claims-making on the part of urban subjects requires a foundation of some kind. When citizenship is considered as a legal status, legal regimes that differentiate between citizens and multiple kinds of non-citizens provide this basis not only for citizens to claim rights and resources, but also for governments to exclude non-citizens from these same benefits. Scholars of urban citizenship have argued that in addition to law, the city itself can become a resource to make and contest claims (see **right to the city**). Ana Secor's (2004) research on Kurdish migrant women in Istanbul is exemplary in this regard. Tracing the contestations of citizenship in migrant women's everyday spatial practices, Secor recounts the story of how a Kurdish woman, Inci, 'became political' after years of living in Istanbul but remaining silent about her Kurdish identity. Inci states:

> Last year I was wearing traditional Kurdish clothes and one week I walked around like that ... They stopped me on the street and asked 'what country are you from?' I said 'I am from this country, this land, but I am a Kurd and because of this I wear the clothes of a Kurdish woman.' (2004: 363)

Secor's interpretation is that Inci is positioning herself as a citizen by claiming her Kurdish culture within an urban community that is otherwise hostile to her identity. Significantly, the street itself provides the material basis for Inci's claim and becomes the place where she can confront a hostile public. In this example, the urban community becomes the group toward and within which claims are made, and the city becomes the site for staking these claims.

In addition to making claims on and through urban space, scholars have highlighted how cities and publics are constructed through practices of citizenship, such as dialogue, disagreement, protest, and participation. Demonstrating this process of public formation, Helga Leitner and Christopher Strunk (2014) characterize the work of immigrant advocacy in Washington, DC as an assemblage. They show how a diverse set of urban actors construct models of insurgent citizenship that challenge mainstream criteria of group membership. Focusing on struggles over local policies prohibiting day laborers from gathering on street corners, this research traces how religious communities, unions, national worker-center networks, and concerned local residents come together to fight anti-immigrant policies. The authors argue that, through the work of advocacy, this assemblage of insurgent citizens is able to coalesce in the absence of any formal alliance or even a shared set of strategic goals. This example demonstrates how practices of urban citizenship can bring together novel coalitions of actors, sometimes forming antagonistic publics around shared concerns with social justice.

The city and the production of urban space are crucial for understanding the materialization of citizenship: the city becomes an object to claim; the production of urban space becomes a resource for making claims and contestations around these processes of production through struggle over new communities. In dealing with this fluidity of citizenship, urban scholars have looked beyond formal definitions to consider the complex ways that multiple processes and practices interact to produce subjects, acts, and sites of citizenship. These endeavors are critical, but it is important that they begin to consider the limits of 'citizenship' itself. There is a risk that theorizing all political action as citizenship may inadvertently obscure political formations that refuse or exceed its boundaries (De Genova, 2010). Ironically, such an effect would reinstate the universalizing drive of 'citizenship' that this research has long critiqued.

References

De Genova, N. (2010) 'The queer politics of migration: reflections on "illegality" and "incorrigibility"', *Studies in Social Justice*, 4(2): 101–126.

Holston, J. (2009) *Insurgent Citizenship: Disjunctions of democracy and modernity in Brazil*. Princeton, NJ: Princeton University Press.

Isin, E. (2002) *Being Political: Genealogies of citizenship*. Minneapolis: University of Minnesota Press.

Leitner, H. and C. Strunk (2014) 'Assembling insurgent citizenship: immigrant advocacy struggles in the Washington DC Metropolitan Area', *Urban Geography*, 35(7): 943–964.

Secor, A. (2004) '"There is an Istanbul that belongs to me": citizenship, space, and identity in the city', *Annals of the Association of American Geographers*, 94(2): 352–368.

Varsanyi, M. (2006) 'Interrogating "urban citizenship" vis-à-vis undocumented migration', *Citizenship Studies*, 10(2): 229–249.

Further reading

Baubock, R. (2003) 'Reinventing urban citizenship', *Citizenship Studies*, 7(2): 139–160.

Urban Commons

Kenton Card

Urban commons are objects linked to the practice of commoning, which can be defined as the collective reclamation, utilization, and/or management of urban environments. In recent years, the framework of urban commons has come to enjoy widespread currency, especially among radical scholars and activists, where it is often taken as an indicator of incipient alternatives to **neoliberal urbanism**. In the context of the ongoing privatization of nature and state assets, various types of urban commons have been ascribed, in oppositional terms, by the collective control of the basic necessities of life and subsistence, often through forms of de-commodification and non-commodification, in various degrees of separation from the dominant ethos of capitalism. These forms of urban commoning include alternative modes of governance, typically at the local scale, of natural and urban resources, land, housing, food, mobility, industry, education, and so forth.

A genealogy of urban commons can be said to run between Karl Marx, Garrett Hardin, and Elinor Ostrom, extending to new practices of enclosure and contemporary forms of urbanization. In the first volume of *Capital* (1990: 874), Marx wrote a history of English common land prior to the historical moment of 'conquest, enslavement, robbery, murder, in short, force' that ultimately led to a 'separation between the workers and the ownership of the conditions for the realization of their labour'. As farmers were removed from the land, they were violently separated from the natural endowment for food production and livelihood. 'Primitive accumulation', Marx wrote, is 'nothing else than the historical process of divorcing the producer from the means of production' (1990: 874–875). It describes the moment and process of enclosing common lands via the deployment of contracts guaranteeing property rights for ownership, which simultaneously undermined the bases for autonomous subsistence, forcing farmers into wage–labor relations. Marx points to the short-lived Paris Commune of 1871 as an important instance of the rupturing of these capitalist relations, a dictatorship of the proletariat enabling workers to create a direct democracy and the withering-away of the state.

As much as the commons has formed a centerpiece of Marxist praxis, it has also functioned as a foil for liberal economic thought. Liberal economists commonly cite Garrett Hardin's (1968) 'Tragedy of the commons' to illustrate the problems of open land access and to make the case for property rights as an essential ingredient in efficient markets. Hardin argued that common lands lead to overuse, as in the example of overgrazing in open fields. 'Each herdsman', Hardin (1968: 1244) writes, 'seeks to maximize his gain.' Private property rights are consequently perceived to be the panacea for incipient tragedies of the commons, mitigating tendencies for over-usage by means of the ability of owners to self-regulate and to exclude others. While the tragedy trope remains central to liberal economics, it is widely viewed with skepticism. In *Governing the Commons*, Elinor Ostrom (1990) challenged Hardin's argument by demonstrating empirically how common resources are often highly organized and protected from depletion by users. Concurrent to Ostrom's research on the management of natural resource commons, there has been extensive work on non-natural, urban, technical, and digital resources.

Marx's notion of primitive accumulation has been recuperated by the Midnight Notes Collective in their work on the 'new enclosures', a new round of attacks on the commons through strategies like privatization in the context of the global dominance of neoliberal capitalism. The new enclosures amount to a 'large-scale reorganization of the accumulation process, [which] uproot[s] workers from the terrain on which their organizational power has been built' (Midnight Notes Collective, 1990: 3). They take several forms – stripping people from means of subsistence and land due to debt, exacerbating labor mobility, the collapse of socialism, and challenging reproduction. In the context of an intensification of urbanization on a global scale, the new enclosures are seen here as a response to polymorphous mobilization of people's power, for instance, squatters occupying buildings under threat of speculative development, or the indigenous autonomous movement of the Zapatistas in Mexico.

Radical scholars and activists have increasingly mobilized the concept of the urban commons as a key component in postcapitalist politics (Gibson-Graham, 2006), challenging liberal property rights theory and practices of commodification, enclosure, and privatization in the context of accelerated urbanization. Cities are seen here as a vital site of power, production, and radical dissent. Whereas rural resource commons were classically built on close, often multigenerational community relationships, urbanization presents new challenges for the commons because dense urban populations are often *not* constituted in intimate communal relations, but in high concentrations of unrelated peoples, demanding new methods of forging solidarity among strangers over time (Huron, 2015). For example, community gardens often are collectives of strangers who develop closer bonds through the collective process of planting, weeding, and harvesting. In this context, commoning defines the social practice of coproducing, co-appropriating, and co-management. This might include the creation of a material thing, such as a community garden, its separation from conventional 'market' or 'state' control, or its ongoing maintenance or management through collective means. Since city centers contain some of the largest concentrations of wealth and power, land – among other resources – will be highly sought after. Commoning strategies are primarily organized along 'horizontal' lines, which some have questioned on the grounds of their apparently limited scalability in the face of global challenges.

Urban commons are sometimes presumed to be entirely inclusive spaces, in contrast to the exclusive nature of privately owned or more formally governed spaces. However, the balance between inclusivity and exclusivity can often be ambiguous in relation to phenomena such as housing, in which some degree of exclusion applies. The question of temporality is also perplexing: an urban common at one moment may not be so at another, such as in the case of an urban park (a 'private' or 'state' resource when fenced in, controlled, purchased, and common when appropriated for open access and utilization for all), challenging phenomenological claims to property. Thus, urban commons may not *be* so indefinitely, but may shift between common, state, and private conditions or modes of governance at different times, just as they may take different forms in different places. Some argue that commoning even includes protests and other instantaneous acts of commonality, which can reconfigure spaces, imaginaries, and strategies. The objects of urban commons and practices of commoning, their inclusiveness and exclusiveness, temporality, hierarchical relations, and navigation of market dynamics and state structures therefore present a number of open questions for the next generation of urban scholars.

References

Gibson-Graham, J.-K. (2006) *A Postcapitalist Politics*. Minneapolis: University of Minnesota Press.

Hardin, G. (1968) 'The tragedy of the commons', *Journal of Natural Resources Policy Research*, 1(3): 243–253.

Huron, A. (2015) 'Working with strangers in saturated space: reclaiming and maintaining the urban commons', *Antipode*, 47(4): 963–979.

Marx, K. (1990) *Capital*, Volume 1. Harmondsworth: Penguin.

Midnight Notes Collective (1990) 'The new enclosures', *Midnight Notes*, 10: 1–9.

Ostrom, E. (1990) *Governing the Commons: The evolution of institutions for collective action*. New York: Cambridge University Press.

Further reading

Akuno, K. and A. Nangwaya (2017) *Jackson Rising: The struggle for economic democracy and black self-determination in Jackson, Mississippi*. Quebec: Daraja Press.

Card, K. (forthcoming) 'Contradictions of housing commons: between middle class and anarchist models in Berlin', in D. Ozkan and G. Baykal (eds) *Commoning the City: Empirical perspectives on urban ecology, economics, and ethics*. London: Routledge.

Harney, S. M. and F. Moten (2013) *The Undercommons: Fugitive planning and black study*. New York: Minor Compositions.

Linebaugh, P. (2014) *Stop, Thief! The commons, enclosures, and resistance*. Oakland, CA: PM Press.

Urban Governance

Dimitar Anguelov

Urban governance, as opposed to urban government, refers to the networked relations between government and private sector actors (and occasionally civil society groups) involved in the generation and implementation of public policies in cities or metropolitan regions. This form of cooperation, generally referred to as public–private partnership, emerged in the context of state restructuring in the 1970s, and marks a shift from systems of *government* based on hierarchical state bureaucratic administration to systems of *governance* based on the horizontal coordination of a diverse field of actors and networks (Jessop, 2002). In the policy arena, practitioners, political elites, and advocacy groups have promoted urban governance as increasing stakeholder participation and empowering communities in the governance process. However, in practice this process is highly selective and has tended to privilege the interests, demands, and imaginaries of powerful business and political elites. Globally circulating 'good governance' models, promoting 'best practices' enjoin local governments to implement increasingly entrepreneurial development policies. Such policies tend to stress economic growth and prioritize economic efficiency rather than engage civil society or address socio-economic inequalities.

The urban governance literature emerged in the United States and Western Europe following the crisis of Keynesianism–Fordism, as greater responsibility in the provision of public services and infrastructure was downloaded to city governments amidst (national) state fiscal retrenchment: 'rollback neoliberalism'. In this context of state restructuring, urban regime theorists in the United States examined the ways local governments draw on private resources and actors to facilitate accumulation and growth. In other words, the capacity to govern was produced through coalition building between governments and interest groups (Stone, 1993). This literature introduced typologies of urban regimes (e.g., corporate, progressive, caretaker), based on the characteristics of the local governing coalition. Because of its focus on local political micro spaces, urban regime theory tended to neglect the influence of macro political economic structures and dynamics. In contrast, urban regulation theoretical approaches examined the macro relations between state regulation and capitalist accumulation, neglecting local political conditions and power dynamics. Regulationist accounts were thus critiqued for 'reading off' local governance configurations from macro political economic changes (Jones, 1998).

In navigating between the micro and macro levels of analysis, geographic accounts since the 1990s have posited urban governance in the neoliberal era as a dynamic process of state rescaling. Here, the urban represents the scale at and through which states organize and manage social and economic activities, and where local actors, institutions, and spaces differentially contest and reorganize this process, with geographically variegated outcomes (Brenner and Theodore, 2003; see **neoliberal urbanism**). Such work draws on a range of theoretical perspectives, from political economy to governmentality. Political economy approaches examine the relationships between government institutions, policies, stakeholders, and citizens. In the context of increasing inter-urban competition for investments, they show how quasi-public agencies with reduced democratic oversight leverage local assets and provide public subsidies to attract private investments. Similarly, in the context of reduced state welfare support, they highlight the shift from 'welfare to workfare', where market-oriented welfare provision is enacted through locally experimental programs for work activation and employability.

Governmentality approaches examine the relationship between government rationalities, policies, and the technologies of government through which state power is secured and government objectives are achieved. Under neoliberalism, they highlight the increasing deployment of 'evidence-based' planning and policies that utilize calculative methods to evaluate and monitor the performance of government subjects and spaces, enrolling them into governmental networks to promote neoliberal subjectivities of individual responsibility and entrepreneurialism. For example, the allocation of central state funds for local economic development is subject to competitive bidding processes based on performance and efficiency criteria. This output-centered governance deploys business knowledge and expertise (in quasi-public agencies) to define, implement, and monitor government programs, outflanking democratic input and supervision (MacKinnon, 2000).

Since the 1980s, global consultancies and multilateral policy banks such as the World Bank have propagated neoliberal 'good governance' models in developing countries, aimed at addressing governance 'failures' by limiting government, privatizing public goods and services, and expanding market relations. These governance models are predominantly derived from western urban contexts, premised on market liberalism. Given historical differences in institutional legacies, political cultures, and state–society relations, critical urban scholars have questioned the validity of these models for postcolonial cities, asking what governance models the postcolony can generate instead (see **postcolonial cities** and **urban informality**). For example, the World Bank's attempts to institutionalize Public–private partnerships for infrastructure financing in Indonesia have yielded hybrid configurations ('public–public partnerships') where city and state-owned enterprises participate as private parties in contractual relationships with the public sector, challenging neoliberal dictums that the state's role should be limited to regulatory functions. Beyond this critique of mainstream neoliberal urban governance, critical scholarship has also sought to expand the scope of investigation to consider the contribution of local grassroots and informal practices to urban governance and development (Parnell and Oldfield, 2017).

References

Brenner, N. and N. Theodore (2003) *Spaces of Neoliberalism: Urban restructuring in North America and Western Europe*. Oxford: Wiley-Blackwell.

Jessop, B. (2002) 'Liberalism, neoliberalism, and urban governance: a state–theoretical perspective', *Antipode*, 34(3): 452–472.

Jones, M. (1998) 'Spatial selectivity of the state? The regulationist enigma and local struggles over economic governance', *Environment and Planning A*, 29: 831–864.

MacKinnon, D. (2000) 'Managerialism, governmentality and the state: a neo-Foucauldian approach to local economic governance', *Political Geography*, 19(3): 293–314.

Parnell, S. and S. Oldfield (eds) (2017) *The Routledge Handbook on Cities of the Global South*. London: Routledge.

Stone, C. (1993) 'Urban regimes and the capacity to govern: a political economy approach', *Journal of Urban Affairs*, 15(1): 1–28.

Further reading

Lauria, M. (ed.) (1997) *Reconstructing Urban Regime Theory: Regulating urban politics in a global economy*. London: Sage.

Rhodes, R. A. W. (1996) 'The new governance: governing without government', *Political Studies*, 44(4): 652-667.

Urban (Im)mobilities

Samuel Nowak

Mobility describes the movement of a person, object, or idea across space. As a core geographical concept and wide-reaching empirical phenomenon, mobility appears at multiple spatial and temporal scales, from intercontinental migration to the daily commute. Within urban studies, explanations and understandings of mobility have focused primarily on rural-to-urban migration, inter-urban movement at the transnational, national, and regional scales (e.g., suburbanization), and especially intra-urban mobility and its associated infrastructure – sidewalks, roads, freeways, heavy/light rail, airports, etc. The term **urban mobilities**, therefore, denotes a plurality of movements that are intertwined with other urban processes. Mobilities in the plural also recognize that mobility is always situated in dialectical relation to immobilities: mobility and immobility are not simply opposites, but rather each constitutes and is contained within the other. In other words, the mobility of some people, capital, or ideas is dependent upon or productive of the immobility of others (Massey, 1991). While the so-called 'new mobilities paradigm' (Sheller and Urry, 2006) currently dominates discussion of (im)mobility, urban studies has a long engagement with the concept, taking on different conceptual meanings and empirical foci in different eras. In particular, three (im)mobilities have captured the attention of critical urbanists: urban transportation (people), uneven urban development (capital), and urban policy mobilities (ideas).

During the 1960s and 1970s, research on urban mobilities largely concentrated on where people moved within the city, why, and by what mode of travel. In particular, anglophone scholarship in urban studies focused on the wide-ranging impacts of the automobile on a wide range of urban processes including land use change, gender discrimination, urban sustainability, racial segregation, and economic inequality. 'The system of automobility', as sociologist John Urry (2004) later called it, is the cumulative spatial impact of automobiles, automobile manufacturing, and road networks on the urban form, as well as the cultural hegemony of the automobile in everyday life. In North American cities, the rise of automobility facilitated suburbanization, provided much greater personal mobility, and generated enormous economic growth. It also produced its own set of social and ecological pressures, such as white flight and racial segregation, traffic congestion, increased greenhouse gas emissions, and disinvestment in public transit. Thus, as a system of **urban (im)mobilities**, automobility intersects with and shapes a range of consequential urban social and environmental processes.

Throughout the late 1970s and 1980s, as critical urban studies became strongly influenced by Marxist theory, the (im)mobilities of capital circuits played a central role in political economic analyses of the production of urban space under capitalism. Capital has a contradictory imperative to be both mobile and fixed in place. The see-saw of investment and disinvestment enabled by this fixity of capital in the urban landscape is a central component in the production of **uneven urban development**. As David Harvey writes, 'uneven geographical investments in transport systems feed further uneven geographical developments. Behind this lies a fundamental contradiction between fixity and movement within the theory of capital accumulation in space and time' (2006: 101). Roads, for instance, provide the capacity for commodity circulation, the movement of laborers from the home to the place of production and back again, and the connection of spatially separated commodities, labor, markets, and points of production. The circulation of capital, therefore, requires infrastructural systems such as roads to allow for mobility of material objects, yet because of their spatially bounded nature, these systems are often destroyed or repurposed in order to allow for further rounds of capital circulation (Harvey, 2006).

More recently, urban theorists have been captivated by mobile ideas – urban policies, expertise, best practices, and techniques of governance. Inspired by scholarship on the politics of mobility (Massey, 1991), the literature on urban policy mobilities works to understand the circulation and mutation of policies as they move across cities and global networks. This literature distinguishes itself from traditional political science models of policy diffusion, emphasizing that policies are never redeployed in their 'pre-packaged' form (Peck and Theodore, 2015). Rather, they mutate as they move and are re-territorialized elsewhere. It is in this sense that urban policy mobilities are also concerned with the mobility/fixity dialectic of urbanism. While we live in a context of 'fast policy' transfer (Peck and Theodore, 2015), mobility is only ever a half-truth. Policies are also associated with certain places (e.g., the Porto Alegre model of participatory budgeting). As policymakers attempt to adopt one of these models to their own city, mobile policies are mediated and transformed through varying institutional power structures, geographical contexts, and socio-spatial positionalities (Sheppard, 2002).

In sum, the (im)mobility dialectic is deeply intertwined with urban processes at multiple spatial scales. Whether focused on people, capital, or policies, it is an analytic that enables an understanding of the urban as both fixed and mobile, territorial and relational, local and global. This wide-ranging purchase of the (im)mobilities dialectic is both its greatest strength and its greatest weakness. To understand everything as mobile diminishes the theoretical purchase of the concept and risks positioning it as the primary spatiality, ignoring how it intersects with other geographical concepts such as scale, place, space, networks, and socio-spatial positionality (Sheppard, 2002). Such conceptual considerations aside, however, urban studies' long-standing engagement with urban (im)mobilities demonstrates that it will remain a focus of research into the future.

References

Harvey, D. (2006) *Spaces of Global Capitalism*. New York: Verso.

Massey, D. (1991) 'A global sense of place', *Marxism Today*, 35(6): 24–29.

Peck, J. and N. Theodore (2015) *Fast Policy: Experimental statecraft at the thresholds of neoliberalism*. Minneapolis: University of Minnesota Press.

Sheller, M. and J. Urry (2006) 'The new mobilities paradigm', *Environment and Planning A*, 38(2): 207–226.

Sheppard, E. (2002) 'The spaces and times of globalization: place, scale, networks, and positionality', *Economic Geography*, 78(3): 307–330.

Urry, J. (2004) 'The "system" of automobility', *Theory, Culture & Society*, 21(4–5): 25–39.

Further reading

Cidell, J. and D. Prytherch (eds) (2015) *Transport, Mobility, and the Production of Urban Space*. New York: Routledge.

Cresswell, T. (2010) 'Towards a politics of mobility', *Environment and Planning D: Society and Space*, 28(1): 17-31.

Giuliano, G. and S. Hanson (eds) (2017) *The Geography of Urban Transportation*, 4th edition. New York: Guilford Press.

Kwan, M.-P. and T. Schwanen (2016) 'Geographies of mobility', *Annals of the American Association of Geographers*, 106(2): 243-256.

Urban Informality

Dimitar Anguelov

Urban informality encompasses a set of spaces, economic activities, and peoples (e.g., street vendors, squatters, slum dwellers) that are seen to exist outside the domain of state-sanctioned or 'formal' economic sectors, based on the capitalist relations of waged labor and private property. Such spaces, commonly labeled as 'slum' (or *favela*, *bidonville*, *kampung*), have long been inscribed as poor, marginalized, violent, and unsanitary, but more recently have been read as spaces of entrepreneurial potential, unencumbered by the state bureaucratic apparatus. Against accounts that have shaped mainstream (and popular) imaginaries, discourses, and policies, critical scholarship has sought to challenge the essentializing categories that distinguish the formal from the informal. Instead, it is posited that urban informality is an organizing logic of state power, foregrounding the power structures, interests, and practices that produce social and spatial difference.

The notion of informality emerged in the writings of Chicago school sociologists during the 1950s and 1960s, who tended to view the marginality of urban immigrants as an outcome of their culture: a 'culture of poverty' distinct from that of 'blasé' urbanites segmented into socio-economic positions. A similar binary distinction can be found in the work of William Arthur Lewis, whose dual-sector model of economic development saw unproductive labor from the subsistence sector (based on agricultural or petty capitalist activity) transitioning into the wage-based capitalist sector, driving productivity and growth in the process. Writing mostly on Latin America in the 1970s, dependency theorists likewise recognized that informal workers and spaces were integral to the capitalist city, seeing informality as distinct from, but structurally dependent on, the formal capitalist sector (AlSayyad, 2004).

Since the 1970s, cities of the postcolony have witnessed an explosion of spaces of informality amidst rapid urbanization and global economic restructuring. In this conjuncture, Hernando De Soto (1989) advances the free-market nostrum of minimal state intervention, portraying slum dwellers in Peru as entrepreneurs whose potential for wealth accumulation can be unleashed through the legalization of their property assets, enabling them to participate in the formal market. Kate Meagher (1995) challenges such market-oriented interpretations of informality. In the context of neoliberal structural-adjustment programming, she argues that informalization in Africa results from a process of global restructuring, where the state produces informality by removing the institutional supports for labor in order to secure (and widen) opportunities for capital accumulation. This can be seen as a particular articulation of **neoliberal urbanism**.

By challenging these structuralist narratives, which tend to present the urban poor as passive and marginalized, others have identified diverse forms of agency in the everyday lives and struggles of 'informal' urban residents. Asef Bayat (1997: 57) suggests it is through street politics – the 'quiet encroachment of the ordinary' – that 'informal people' are able to voice dissent and make appropriations (see **everyday urbanism**). Such accounts provide important insights into the political openings for social transformation available to the urban poor. However, by viewing informality as a generalized urban condition or as a way of life, it is arguable that these too reproduce a dualist contrast with a legalized, legible, and formal capitalist order (Roy, 2012).

More recent work on cities of the postcolony has sought to destabilize this enduring binary. Ananya Roy argues for a differentiation *within* informality, highlighting both elite and poor forms of informality where 'fully capitalized domains of property are no more legal than are squatter settlements and shantytowns' (2012: 5). By examining the process of informalization she highlights the active construction of the categories 'formal' and 'informal'. In contrast to Meagher, Roy argues that informalization is not simply an outcome of state policy or an object of regulation; rather, it is a practice of planning – a 'mode of the production of space'.

The production of space through planning also produces social difference, reflecting complex political struggles beyond economic and class dynamics. Oren Yiftachel conceives informality in terms of 'gray spaces' – those positioned 'between the "whiteness" of legality/approval/safety and the "blackness" of eviction/destruction/death' into which the state unevenly and partially incorporates marginalized spaces and populations, such as Bedouin Arabs or temporary labor migrants (Yiftachel, 2009: 89). Such gray spaces are not confined to the urban fringe but also 'exist at the privileged edges, those which straddle the "high" boundaries of the power system, exempted from strict legal compliance' (2009: 92).

Attention to the power structures and interests inherent in the practice of planning unsettles the notion of informality as a bounded empirical phenomenon, bringing into view the epistemologies of urban planning: how and by whom informality is theorized has implications for planning and its outcomes. Understood as process (informalization) and epistemology, urban informality offers a lens through which to interrogate and challenge hegemonic norms, practices, and interests that lie behind the production of spatial and social differences. Urban theorists can examine such processes across geographical contexts, extending beyond the realm of formalized capitalist relations and opening up potential for more progressive planning praxis.

References

AlSayyad, N. (2004) 'Urban informality as a "new" way of life', in A. Roy and N. AlSayyad (eds) *Urban Informality: Transnational perspectives from the Middle East, Latin America and South Asia*. Lanham, MD: Lexington Books, pp. 7–30.

Bayat, A. (1997) 'Un-civil society: the politics of the "informal people"', *Third World Quarterly,* 18(1): 53–72.

De Soto, H. (1989) *The Other Path: The invisible revolution in the Third World.* New York: Harper & Row.

Meagher, K. (1995) 'Crisis, informalization and the urban informal sector in Sub-Saharan Africa', *Development and Change,* 26(2): 259–284.

Roy, A. (2012) 'Urban informality: the production of space and practice of planning', in R. Crane and R. Weber (eds) *The Oxford Handbook of Urban Planning.* Oxford: Oxford University Press, pp. 691–706.

Yiftachel, O. (2009) 'Theoretical notes on "gray cities": the coming of urban apartheid?', *Planning Theory,* 8(1): 88–100.

Further reading

Pearlman, J. (1977) *The Myth of Marginality.* Berkeley: University of California Press.

Roy, A. (2005) 'Urban informality: towards an epistemology of planning', *Journal of the American Planning Association,* 71(2): 147-158.

Varley, A. (2013) 'Postcolonialising informality?', *Environment and Planning D: Society and Space,* 31: 4-22.

Watson, V. (2009) 'Seeing from the South: refocusing urban planning on the globe's central urban issues', *Urban Studies,* 46(11): 2259-2275.

Urban Social Movements

Nina Ebner

Urban social movement (USM) refers to both the ways in which the city – its governance structures, built environment, and social fabric – becomes the object of social activism, and how it functions as a platform for many forms of social and political action which extend through (and past) contestation located in urban space. In the first register, 'USMs of the city' include fights for squatters' rights, living wage campaigns, and movements for enhanced access to public space. In the second, 'USMs in and through the city' include struggles against capitalism, globalization, and immigrants' rights movements. USM research argues that cities are important sites for altering 'hegemonic power relations in urbanized societies, making broad claims for rights and justice, and building and mobilizing solidarities' (Miller and Nicholls, 2013: 452). Theoretical and empirical paradigm shifts in urban studies and in social movement theory – such as evolving conceptions of what constitutes 'the urban' or 'social movement', and how to theorize space – have fashioned the concept's genealogy. Over time, USM researchers have asked two primary questions: What is the role of social movements in the transformation of cities and urban governance? And what is the role of the urban, in shaping social movements?

An early, and enduring, conception of USM refers to collective mobilization for social, political, and environmental change in cities. 'USMs of the city' may include protests against urban renewal resulting in displacement of less-well-off residents, and movements for enhanced access to public goods and public space. Since the 1970s, researchers have examined how USMs have contributed to the creation of more livable and democratic cities for inhabitants. Not primarily concerned with understanding forms of contestation located in spheres of production, or solely focused on class struggles, researchers have studied how protest strategies help transform urban economic, political, and social institutions. Manuel Castells (1983), an influential contributor to USM scholarship, conceptualized USMs as movements that framed their campaigns around issues of collective consumption, targeting the local state (identified as responsible for the uneven provision of public resources).

USM research also explores how urbanity shapes the form (and spatiality) of political and social action. 'USMs in and through the city' describe movements where the urban is not the primary problematic, but a key organizational locus in larger multiscalar organizing efforts. USMs target evolving forms of governance, and challenge corporate development and the commodification of public space (Leitner et al., 2007). Since the 1990s, USM scholars have documented how cities function as key nodes for larger processes of neoliberal restructuring, and therefore also as spaces where resistance against hegemonic projects can emerge. Research in this tradition examines the ways in which multiple spatialities – place, scale, space, and network – are co-implicated in the imaginaries, and practices, of USMs.

Conterminously, another strand of USM research has developed inspired by the Right to the City movement, largely informed by Henri Lefebvre's (2003 [1970]) conception of **right to the city**, which invokes a call for the collective reclamation of urban space. In this tradition, the urban is both the site of struggle and the means of struggle, neither a passive object to fight over, nor a static platform on which multiscalar politics is performed. From struggles by public housing residents to reclaim their neighborhoods in New Orleans, to city dwellers in Rio de Janeiro resisting eviction in the lead-up to the 2014 World Cup, Right to the City movements worldwide have demanded a transformed access to urban space, and the freedom to determine collective urban futures.

In recent years, USM scholarship has flourished in Latin American, African, and Asian cities, with scholars advocating for the development, and incorporation, of more nuanced theoretical and methodological approaches in order to fully understand the trajectories of USMs that do not fit neatly within hegemonic explanatory frameworks applicable in North American and European cities (Roy and AlSayyad, 2004). Drawing on post-structural, de/postcolonial, and feminist methodological frameworks (among others), they highlight the importance of **everyday urbanism**, **urban citizenship**, and **urban informality** through an examination of contestation in the unexpected, liminal spaces of everyday life, and they draw attention to USMs as more than organized moments of collective action. For example, Salwa Ismail's (2006) research with residents of informal housing communities in Cairo demonstrates how the infrastructure for collective change can be found in everyday interactions, and in relations of exchange and solidarity, located in neighborhood mosques and marketplaces.

Finally, USM researchers continue to address a number of ongoing concerns: in particular, how to translate between everyday politics, and the need to build broad social movements for structural change. Recent scholarship inspired by **planetary urbanization** opens up new potentials, and perhaps pitfalls, for investigating USMs. If, as this methodological orientation suggests, all forms of socio-spatial organization are an extension of the urban, it is not clear what the continued significance of the urban might be for understanding contemporary social movements.

References

Castells, M. (1983) *The City and the Grassroots: A cross-cultural theory of urban social movements*. Berkeley: University of California Press.

Ismail, S. (2006) *Political Life in Cairo's New Quarters: Encountering the everyday state*. Minneapolis: University of Minnesota Press.

Lefebvre, H. (2003) [1970] *The Urban Revolution*. Minneapolis: University of Minnesota Press.

Leitner, H., J. Peck and E. Sheppard (eds) (2007) *Contesting Neoliberalism: Urban frontiers*. New York: Guilford Press.

Miller, B. and W. Nicholls (2013) 'Social movements in urban society: the city as a space of politicization', *Urban Geography* 34(4): 452–473.

Roy, A. and N. AlSayyad (eds) (2004) *Urban Informality: Transnational perspectives from the Middle East, Latin America, and South Asia*. Lanham, MD: Lexington Books

Further reading

Bayat, A. (2004) *Life as Politics: How ordinary people change the Middle East.* Amsterdam: Amsterdam University Press.

Harvey, D. (2012) *Rebel Cities: From the right to the city to the urban revolution.* New York: Verso.

Holston, J. (2008) *Insurgent Citizenship: Disjunctions of democracy and modernity in Brazil.* Princeton, NJ: Princeton University Press.

Merrifield, A. (2013) *The Politics of the Encounter: Urban theory and protest under planetary urbanization.* Athens, GA: University of Georgia Press.

Urban Sustainability and Resilience

Sophie Webber

Urban sustainability and resilience are policy formulations that seek to manage the relations between cities and environmental processes and changes. The relationship between the two ideas is vague: some use the terms interchangeably, others suggest that each is a component part of the other. Nonetheless, there are important conceptual differences. Urban sustainability is concerned with equilibrium and balance – between economic, social, and environmental concerns, and between current and future needs in cities. In contrast, urban resilience seeks to create cities and citizens that are able to withstand and transform in the face of uncertain threats and disruptions. The notions of urban sustainability and urban resilience both reflect a growing global consensus that urbanization is a principal cause of environmental damage and that cities are places of extreme vulnerability to a variety of shocks and stresses, but also that cities (and urban leaders) are properly in the forefront of innovatory efforts to tackle the challenges of environmental change. Despite these different emphases and orientations, the two ideas share important features as approaches to urban environmental intervention: first, the understanding that cities are currently neither sustainable nor resilient, but there are real and practical opportunities to make them so; and, second, the assumption that such interventions are best programmed in partnership with private and non-governmental actors, international institutions, and through horizontal city networks (Bulkeley, 2005).

The idea of sustainability emerged in the 1970s, diagnosing an ecological crisis caused by intensified urbanization and economic development. Sustainability was originally a radical vision that identified environmental problems as political, economic, and ethical rather than simply technical. But this has since been unevenly supplanted by a reformist and technocratic agenda for sustainable development, as popularized by the United Nations World Commission on Environment and Development (WCED). In the words of the WCED's Brundtland Commission (1987), sustainable development is that which 'meets the needs of the present without compromising the ability of future generations to meet their own needs'. Since this time, sustainability has exhibited two broad forms: a weak approach that makes tradeoffs between economic, social, and environmental pillars; and a strong approach that hierarchically nests economic processes within society, and in turn the environment. Weak sustainability asserts the substitutability of natural and human capitals, but strong sustainability does not, thereby positing ultimate environmental limits. Sustainability has become an important domain of **urban governance**, extending out to multilateral interventions as it has been cemented into international regimes as well as urban plans and policies since the 1990s.

Some critics argue that urban sustainability is merely a tool of **neoliberal urbanism**. Aidan While et al. (2004) argue that sustainability has become another vehicle through which cities have pursued entrepreneurial and managerial strategies of urban governance by means of a partial inclusion of environmental concerns as a temporary compromise between diverse city constituents in the context of political and environmental change. Sustainability is also used to legitimate particular forms of urban development, many of which intensify social, environmental, and economic inequalities across and within cities. Indeed, a growing body of research about eco-**gentrification** finds that urban sustainability projects can produce a dynamic where greening efforts displace low-income residents for upscale developments (Checker, 2011). As a result, some have concluded that urban sustainability projects ultimately prioritize economic over environmental objectives, allowing both to override social justice ambitions.

The concept of resilience has become prominent across a range of academic disciplines and practices, including engineering, psychology, national security, and global environmental change. Although the origins of the concept are contested, they are frequently traced to the work of ecologist C. S. 'Buzz' Holling, who argued that ecosystems do not have equilibria but are better defined as in flux, with multiple stable states. Resilience duly references the ability of ecosystems to maintain function amidst perturbations. Building on this conceptualization of ecosystems, resilience has subsequently been applied to a wide range of dynamic, complex, and adaptive socio-ecological systems, including cities. Notwithstanding the popularity of the idea of urban resilience in contemporary urban policy and research, there remain underlying tensions, including: the basic questions of what constitutes the urban and whether (urban) systems can achieve equilibrium; whether resilience represents a normative goal, and whether cities ought to adapt to specific challenges or seek to position themselves to be broadly adaptable to future threats (Meerow et al., 2016).

Ideas of urban resilience are founded on notions of flexible adaptation and risk management, leading critics to decry its affinities with neoliberal urbanism. Kate Derickson (2018) argues that urban resilience displaces questions about how to reduce vulnerabilities, obscuring the underlying, structural causes of the conditions to which cities and their residents have become 'vulnerable', and to which they must now be resilient. Instead, urban resilience focuses on adapting to and withstanding future uncertainties, including catastrophic threats, in the process effectively accepting the imperative to react to economic, environmental, and other risks.

Underlying critiques of urban sustainability and urban resilience are a recognition that the vagueness of both terms enables their co-optation within a range of mainstream urban governance agendas, often with negative effects for urban social, spatial, and environmental justice. Several urban environmental researchers have suggested that these agendas might be recuperated so as to focus on 'properly political' (rather than technical) urban governance questions (Derickson, 2018). Such a political position might focus on emergent socio-ecological commons, or making demands about when, where, for whom, and with what social and spatial effects urban resilience or sustainability is directed.

References

Brundtland Commission (1987) *Our Common Future: Report of the World Commission on Environment and Development.* New York: United Nations.

Bulkeley, H. (2005) 'Reconfiguring environmental governance: towards a politics of scales and networks', *Political Geography,* 24(8): 875–902.

Checker, M. (2011) 'Wiped out by the "greenwave": environmental gentrification and the paradoxical politics of urban sustainability', *City and Society,* 23(2): 210–229.

Derickson, K. (2018) 'Urban geography III: anthropocene urbanism', *Progress in Human Geography,* 42(3): 425–435.

Meerow, S., J. P. Newell and M. Stults (2016) 'Defining urban resilience: a review', *Landscape and Urban Planning,* 147(1): 38–49.

While, A., A. E. G. Jonas and D. C. Gibbs (2004) 'The environment and the entrepreneurial city: searching for the urban "sustainability fix" in Leeds and Manchester', *International Journal of Urban and Regional Research,* 28(3): 549–569.

Further reading

Hodson, M. and S. Marvin (2017) 'Intensifying or transforming sustainable cities? Fragmented logics of urban environmentalism', *Local Environment,* 22(1): 8–22.

BIBLIOGRAPHY

Aalbers, M. B. and B. Christophers (2014) 'Centring housing in political economy', *Housing, Theory and Society*, 31(4): 373–394.

Acemoglu, D., S. Johnson and J. A. Robinson (2005) 'Institutions as a fundamental cause of long-run growth', in P. Aghion and S. Durlauf (eds) *Handbook of Economic Growth*. Amsterdam: North-Holland, pp. 385–472.

Agnew, J. A. (1994) 'The territorial trap: the geographical assumptions of international relations theory', *Review of International Political Economy*, 1: 53–80.

Ahmed, S. (2004) 'Collective feelings – or, the impressions left by Others', *Theory, Culture and Society*, 21: 25–42.

Alonso, W. (1960) 'A theory of the urban land market', *Papers in Regional Science*, 6: 149–157.

Althusser, L. (1967) 'Contradiction and overdetermination', *New Left Review*, 41: 15–35.

Alves, J. A. (2018) *The Anti-Black City: Police terror and Black urban life in Brazil*. Minneapolis: University of Minnesota Press.

Amin, A. (2013) 'Surviving the turbulent future', *Environment and Planning D: Society and Space*, 31: 140–156.

Amin, A. and N. Thrift (2002) *Cities: Reimagining the urban*. Cambridge, UK: Polity.

Amin, A. and N. Thrift (2017) *Seeing Like a City*. Cambridge, UK: Polity.

Anand, N. (2011) 'Pressure: the politechnics of water supply in Mumbai', *Cultural Anthropology*, 26(4): 542–564.

Anand, N. (2017) *Hydraulic City: Water and the infrastructures of citizenship in Mumbai*. Durham, NC: Duke University Press.

Anand, N., A. Gupta and H. Appel (2018) *The Promise of Infrastructure*. Durham, NC: Duke University Press.

Anderson, B. (2016) 'Frameworks of comparison', *London Review of Books*, 38(2): 15–18.

Anderson, B. and C. McFarlane (2011) 'Assemblage and geography', *Area*, 43: 124–127.

Anderson, E. (1999) *Code of the Street: Decency, violence, and the moral life of the inner city*. New York: W. W. Norton.

Anderson, E. (2002) 'The ideologically driven critique', *American Journal of Sociology*, 107(6): 1533–1550.

Anderson, L. (2006) 'Analytic autoethnography', *Journal of Contemporary Ethnography*, 35(4): 373–395.

Angelo, H. and D. Wachsmuth (2015) 'Urbanizing urban political ecology: a critique of methodological cityism', *International Journal of Urban and Regional Research*, 39(1): 16–27.

Appadurai, A. (2001) 'Deep democracy: urban governmentality and the horizon of politics', *Environment and Urbanization*, 13(2): 23–43.

Arguello, J. E. M., R. Grant, M. Oteng-Ababio and B. Ayele (2013) 'Downgrading – an overlooked reality in African cities: reflections from an indigenous neighborhood of Accra, Ghana', *Applied Geography*, 36: 23–30.

Bair, J. and M. Werner (2011) 'Commodity chains and the uneven geographies of global capitalism: a disarticulations perspective', *Environment and Planning A*, 43(5): 988–997.

Baker, T. and P. McGuirk (2017) 'Assemblage thinking as methodology: commitments and practices for critical policy research', *Territory, Politics, Governance*, 5(4): 425–442.

Bakker, K. (2003) *An Uncooperative Commodity: Privatizing water in England and Wales*. Oxford: Oxford University Press.

Bakker, K. and G. Bridge (2006) 'Material worlds? Resource geographies and the "matter of nature"', *Progress in Human Geography*, 30(1): 5–27.

Barnes, T. J. (1996) *Logics of Dislocation: Models, metaphors, and meanings of economic space*. New York: Guilford Press.

Barnes, T. J. (2007) '"Not only … but also": quantitative and critical geography', *Professional Geographer*, 61: 1–9.

Barnes, T. J. and E. Sheppard (2010) '"Nothing includes everything": towards engaged pluralism in Anglophone economic geography', *Progress in Human Geography*, 34(1): 193–214.

Barnes, T. J., J. Peck, E. Sheppard and A. Tickell (2007) 'Methods matter: transformations in economic geography', in A. Tickell, E. Sheppard, J. Peck and T. J. Barnes (eds) *Politics and Practice in Economic Geography*. London: Sage, pp. 1–24.

Barnett, C. (2005) 'The consolations of "neoliberalism"', *Geoforum*, 36(1): 7–12.

Barthes, R. (1972) *Mythologies*. New York: Hill and Wang.

Bayat, A. (2000) 'From "dangerous classes" to "quiet rebels": Politics of the urban subaltern in the global south', *International Sociology*, 15(3): 533–557.

Beauregard, R. (1986) 'The chaos and complexity of gentrification', in N. Smith and P. Williams (eds) *Gentrification and the City*. London: Allen and Unwin, pp. 35–55.

Beauregard, R. (1993) *Voices of Decline: The postwar fate of American cities*. New York: Routledge.

Beauregard R. (2003) 'City of superlatives', *City and Community*, 2(3): 183–199.

Beauregard, R. (2006) 'Review of *New State Spaces*', *Urban Affairs Review*, 41(3): 416–418.

Benjamin, S. (2008) 'Occupancy urbanism: radicalizing politics and economy beyond policy and programs', *International Journal of Urban and Regional Research*, 32(3): 719–729.

Benjamin, W. (1968) 'Paris, capital of the nineteenth century', *New Left Review*, 48: 77–88.

Bernstein, R. J. (1989) 'Pragmatism, pluralism and the healing of wounds', *Proceedings and Addresses of the American Philosophical Association*, 63(1): 5–18.

Berry, B. J. L. and J. D. Kasarda (1977) *Contemporary Urban Ecology*. New York: Macmillan.

Berry, B. J. L. and A. Pred (1965) *Central Place Studies: A bibliography of theory and applications*. Philadelphia: Regional Science Research Institute.

Bhaskar, R. (1975) *A Realist Theory of Science*. Brighton: Harvester.

Björkman, L. (2015) *Pipe Politics, Contested Waters: Embedded infrastructures of Millennial Mumbai*. Durham, NC: Duke University Press.

Björkman, L. (2017) 'Infrastructure as method', Unpublished supplementary chapter in *Pipe Politics, Contested Waters: Embedded infrastructures of millennial Mumbai*, https://www.dukeupress.edu/Assets/PubMaterials/978-0-8223-5969-2_602.pdf (accessed April 16, 2019).

Björkman, L. and S. Campion (2016) 'It's local staff who keep Mumbai's water flowing in the face of systematic planning violations done in the name of world-class city making', http://eprints.lse.ac.uk/id/eprint/74796 (accessed September 22, 2017).

Blok, A. and I. Farías (eds) (2016) *Urban Cosmopolitics: Agencements, assemblies, atmospheres*. London: Routledge.

Blomley, N. (2004) *Unsettling the City: Urban land and the politics of property*. New York: Routledge.

Bondi, L. (1999) 'Gender, class, and gentrification: enriching the debate', *Environment and Planning D: Society and Space*, 17(3): 261–282.

Boudreau, J.-A., P. Hammel, B. Jouve and R. Keil (2008) 'New state spaces in Canada: metropolitanization in Montreal and Toronto compared', *Urban Geography*, 28(1): 30–53.

Bourdieu, P. (1980) *The Logic of Practice*. Stanford: Stanford University Press.

Bourdieu, P. (1993) *The Weight of the World: Social suffering in contemporary society*. Stanford: Stanford University Press.

Bourgois, P. (1995) *In Search of Respect: Selling crack in El Barrio*, 2nd edition. New York: Cambridge University Press.

Bourgois, P. and E. Dunlap (1993) 'Exorcising sex-for-crack prostitution: an ethnographic perspective from Harlem', in M. Ratner (ed.) *Crack Pipe as Pimp*. New York: Lexington Books, pp. 97–132.

Bowker, G. C. and S. L. Star (2000) *Sorting Things Out: Classification and its consequences*. Cambridge, MA: MIT Press.

Braun, B. (2005) 'Environmental issues: writing a more-than-human urban geography', *Progress in Human Geography*, 29(5): 635–650.

Brenner, N. (1998) 'Between fixity and motion: accumulation, territorial organization and the historical geography of spatial scales', *Environment and Planning D: Society and Space*, 16(4): 459–481.

Brenner, N. (1999a) 'Beyond state-centrism? Space, territoriality, and geographical scale in globalization studies', *Theory and Society*, 28(1): 39–78.

Brenner, N. (1999b) 'Globalisation as reterritorialisation: the re-scaling of urban governance in the European Union', *Urban Studies*, 36(3): 431–451.

Brenner, N. (2000) 'The urban question as a scale question: reflections on Henri Lefebvre, urban theory and the politics of scale', *International Journal of Urban and Regional Research*, 24(2): 361–378.

Brenner, N. (2001) 'The limits to scale? Methodological reflections on scalar structuration', *Progress in Human Geography*, 25(4): 591–614.

Brenner, N. (2004) *New State Spaces: Urban Governance and the Rescaling of Statehood*. New York: Oxford University Press.

Brenner, N. (2009a) 'What is critical urban theory?', *City*, 13(2–3): 198–207.

Brenner, N. (2009b) 'Open questions on state rescaling', *Cambridge Journal of Regions, Economy and Society*, 2(1): 123–139.

Brenner, N. (2014) 'Introduction: urban theory without an outside', in N. Brenner (ed.) *Implosions–Explosions: Towards a study of planetary urbanization*. Berlin: Jovis Verlag, pp. 14–35.

Brenner, N. (2018) 'Debating planetary urbanization: for an engaged pluralism', *Environment and Planning D: Society and Space*, 36(3): 570–590.

Brenner, N. and C. Schmid (2015) 'Towards a new epistemology of the urban?', *City*, 19(2–3): 151–182.

Brenner, N., J. Peck and N. Theodore (2010) 'Variegated neoliberalization: geographies, modalities, pathways', *Global Networks*, 10(2): 182–222.

Brenner, N., D. J. Madden and D. Wachsmuth (2011) 'Assemblage urbanism and the challenges of critical urban theory', *City*, 15(2): 225–240.

Brenner, N., P. Marcuse and M. Mayer (eds) (2012) *Cities for People, Not for Profit: Critical urban theory and the right to the city*. London: Routledge.

Brown, G. (2008) 'Urban (homo) sexualities: ordinary cities and ordinary sexualities', *Geography Compass*, 2(4): 1215–1231.

Brown, M. and L. Knopp (2014) 'The birth of the (gay) clinic', *Health and Place*, 28(1): 99–108.

Bulkeley, H. and M. Betsill (2005) 'Rethinking sustainable cities: multilevel governance and the "urban" politics of climate change', *Environmental Politics*, 14: 42–63.

Bunnell, T. (2015) 'Antecedent cities and inter-referencing effects: learning from and extending beyond critiques of neoliberalisation', *Urban Studies*, 52: 1983–2000.

Bunnell, T. (2016) *From World City to the World in One City: Liverpool through Malay lives*. London: Wiley-Blackwell.

Bunnell, T. and A. Maringanti (2010) 'Practising urban and regional research beyond metrocentricity', *International Journal of Urban and Regional Research*, 34(2): 415–420.

Bunnell, T. and P. Marolt (2014) 'Commentary: cities and their grassroutes', *Environment and Planning D: Society and Space*, 32(3): 381–385.

Burawoy, M. (1998) 'The extended case method', *Sociological Theory*, 16(1): 4–33.

Burawoy, M., A. Burton, A. A. Ferguson, K. J. Fox, J. Gamson, L. Hurst, N. G. Julius, C. Kurzman, L. Salzinger, J. Schiffman and S. Ui (1991) *Ethnography Unbound: Power and resistance in the modern metropolis*. Berkeley: University of California Press.

Burawoy, M., J. A. Blum, G. Sheba, G. Zsuzsa Gille, T. Gowan, L. Haney, M. Klawiter, S. H. Lopez, S. Ó. Riain and M. Thayer (2000) *Global Ethnography: Forces, connections and imaginations in a postmodern world*. Berkeley: University of California Press.

Burga, H. F. (2009) 'An interview with AbdouMaliq Simone', *Berkeley Planning Journal*, 22(1): 163–173.

Butler, J. (2002) *Gender Trouble*. London: Routledge.

Cahill, C. (2006) '"At risk?" The fed up honeys re-present the gentrification of the Lower East Side', *Women's Studies Quarterly*, 34(1/2): 334–363.

Caldeira, T. P. (2000) *City of Walls: Crime, segregation, and citizenship in Sao Paulo*. Berkeley: University of California Press.

Caldeira, T. P. (2017) 'Peripheral urbanization: autoconstruction, transversal logics, and politics in cities of the global south', *Environment and Planning D: Society and Space*, 35(1): 3–20.

Callon, M. (1984) 'Some elements of a sociology of translation: domestication of the scallops and the fishermen of St. Brieu Bay', *Sociological Review*, 32(1): 196–233.

Cartier, C. (2018) 'From "special zones" to cities and city-regions in China', in J. Doucette and B.-G. Park (eds) *Developmentalist Cities? Interrogating urban developmentalism in East Asia*. Leiden: Brill, pp. 196–218.

Castells, M. (1977) [1974] *The Urban Question: A Marxist approach*. London: Edward Arnold.

Chakrabarty, D. (2000) *Provincializing Europe*. Princeton, NJ: Princeton University Press.

Chan, K. W. (2007) 'Misconceptions and complexities in the study of China's cities: definitions, statistics, and implications', *Eurasian Geography and Economics*, 48(4): 383–412.

Christophers, B. (2019) 'Putting financialisation in its financial context: transformations in local government-led urban development in post-financial crisis England', *Transactions of the Institute of British Geographers*, 44(3): 571–586.

Chuang, J. (2014) 'China's rural land politics: bureaucratic absorption and the muting of rightful resistance', *China Quarterly*, 219: 649–669.

Clarke, J. (2014) 'Conjunctures, crises, and cultures: valuing Stuart Hall', *Focaal*, 70: 113–122.

Clarke, N. (2012) 'Actually existing comparative urbanism: imitation and cosmopolitanism in North–South interurban partnerships', *Urban Geography*, 33(6): 796–815.

Clifford, J. and G. E. Marcus (eds) (1986) *Writing Culture: The poetics and politics of ethnography*. Berkeley: University of California Press.

Colven, E. (2018) 'Navigating the waters of flood mitigation in Jakarta: promoting and contesting expert knowledges', PhD dissertation, Department of Geography, UCLA.

Cook, I. R. and K. Ward (2012) 'Relational comparisons: the assembling of Cleveland's waterfront plan', *Urban Geography*, 33(6): 774–795.

Cox, K. (2009) 'Review of New State Spaces', *American Journal of Sociology*, 115(3): 931–933.

Cronon, W. (1991) *Nature's Metropolis: Chicago and the great West*. New York: W. W. Norton.

Dahmann, N., D. Featherstone, W. Larner, E. Swyngedouw, F. Dufaux, S. Lehman-Frisch and M. Dikeç (2012) 'Reading Mustafa Dikeç's *Badlands of the Republic: Space, Politics and Urban Policy*', *Political Geography*, 31(5): 324–333.

Davidson, M. and K. Iveson (2015) 'Beyond city limits', *City*, 19: 646–664.

Davies, J. S. and I. Blanco (2017) 'Austerity urbanism: patterns of neo-liberalisation and resistance in six cities of Spain and the UK', *Environment and Planning A*, 49(7): 1517–1536.

Davis, M. (2006) 'Fear and money in Dubai', *New Left Review*, 41: 47–68.

Davis, M. (2010) 'Who will build the ark?', *New Left Review*, 61: 29–46.

Dear, M. (2000) *The Postmodern Urban Condition*. Oxford: Blackwell.

Dear, M. and J. D. Dishman (eds) (2001) *From Chicago to LA: Making sense of urban theory*. Thousand Oaks, CA: Sage.

Deeb, L. and J. Winegar (2012) 'Anthropologies of Arab-majority societies', *Annual Review of Anthropology*, 41: 537–558.

DeLanda, M. (2006) *A New Philosophy of Society: Assamblage theory and social complexity*. London: Continuum.

Deleuze, G. and F. Guattari (1987) *A Thousand Plateaus: Capitalism and schizophrenia*. Minneapolis: University of Minnesota Press.

Denzin, N. K. (1978) *The Research Act: A theoretical introduction to sociological methods*. New York: McGraw-Hill.

Dépelteau, F. (2013) 'What is the direction of the "relational turn"?', in C. Powell and F. Dépelteau (eds) *Conceptualizing Relational Sociology: Ontological and theoretical issues*. Berlin: Springer, pp. 163–185.

Derickson, K. D. (2015) 'Urban geography I: locating urban theory in the "urban age"', *Progress in Human Geography*, 39(5): 647–657.

Dikeç, M. (2007) *Badlands of the Republic: Space, politics and urban policy*. Malden, MA: Blackwell.

Dikeç, M. (2012) 'Space as a mode of political thinking', *Geoforum*, 43(4): 669–676.

Dirlik, A. (1997) *The Postcolonial Aura*. Boulder, CO: Westview.

Dittmer, J. (2010) 'Textual and discourse analysis', in D. DeLyser, S. Herbert, S. Aitken, M. Crang and L. McDowell (eds) *Sage Handbook of Qualitative Geography*. Thousand Oaks, CA: Sage, pp. 274–286.

Dixon, D. and J. P. Jones III (1998) 'My dinner with Derrida, or spatial analysis and poststructuralism do lunch', *Environment and Planning A*, 30(2): 247–260.

Doderer, Y. P. (2011) 'LGBTQs in the city, queering urban space', *International Journal of Urban and Regional Research*, 35(2): 431–436.

Dosse, F. (1998) *A History of Structuralism*. Minneapolis: University of Minnesota Press.

Duncan, J. S. (1990) *The City as Text: The politics of landscape interpretation in the Kandyan Kingdom*. Cambridge, UK: Cambridge University Press.

Duneier, M. (1999) *Sidewalk*. New York: Farrer, Straus and Giroux.

Duneier, M., P. Kasinitz and A. Murphy (eds) (2014) *The Urban Ethnography Reader*. Oxford: Oxford University Press.

Duranton, G. and D. Puga (2004) 'Micro-foundations of urban agglomeration economies', in V. Henderson and J.-F. Thisse (eds) *Handbook of Regional and Urban Economics*, volume 4. Amsterdam: Elsevier, pp. 2063–2117.

Edensor, T. and M. Jayne (eds) (2012) *Urban Theory Beyond the West: A world of cities*. London: Routledge.

Edmonds, D. and J. Eidinow (2002) *Wittgenstein's Poker: The story of a ten-minute argument between two great philosophers.* New York: HarperCollins.

Elwood, S., V. Lawson and S. Nowak (2015) 'Middle-class poverty politics: making place, making people', *Annals of the Association of American Geographers*, 105(1): 123–143.

Engels, F. (1872) *The Housing Question*. New York: International Publishers.

England, K. (1994) 'Getting personal: reflexivity, positionality and feminist research', *Professional Geographer*, 46(1): 80–89.

Escobar, A. (2007) 'The "ontological turn" in social theory: A commentary on "Human geography without scale", by Sallie Marston, John Paul Jones II and Keith Woodward', *Transactions of the Insititute of British Geographers*, 32(1): 106–111.

Fairbanks, R. P., II, (2009) *How It Works: Recovering citizens in post-welfare Philadelphia*. Chicago: University of Chicago Press.

Fairbanks, R. P., II, (2011a) '"Bodies is what makes it work": statecraft and urban informality in the Philadelphia recovery house movement', *Ethnography*, 12(1): 12–39.

Fairbanks, R. P., II, (2011b) 'The politics of urban informality in Philadelphia's recovery house movement', *Urban Studies*, 48(12): 2555–2570.

Fairbanks, R. P., II, (2012) 'On theory and method: critical ethnographic approaches to urban regulatory restructuring', *Urban Geography*, 33(4): 545–565.

Fairclough, N. (1995) *Critical Discourse Analysis*. Boston, MA: Addison-Wesley.

Fairclough, N. (2013) *Critical Discourse Analysis: The critical study of language*. London: Routledge.

Farías, I. (2011) 'The politics of urban assemblages', *City*, 15(3-4): 365–374.

Farías, I. (2012) 'Introduction: decentering the object of urban studies', in I. Farías and T. Bender (eds) *Urban Assemblages: How actor–network theory changes urban studies.* London: Routledge, pp. 1–24.

Farías, I. and T. Bender (eds) (2012) *Urban Assemblages: How Actor–network Theory Changes Urban Studies*. London: Routledge.

Ferguson, J. (2006) *Global Shadows: Africa in the neoliberal world order*. Durham, NC: Duke University Press.

Ferreira da Silva, D. (2009) 'No-bodies: law, raciality and violence', *Griffith Law Review*, 18(2): 212–236.

Fincher, R., K. Iveson, H. Leitner and V. Preston (2019) *Everyday Equalities: Making Multicultures in Settler Colonial Cities*. Minneapolis: University of Minnesota Press.

Fischer, B. (2010) 'Histories and Anthropologies of Citizenship by James Holston', *American Anthropologist*, 112(1): 154–156.

Friedmann, J. (1986) 'The world city hypothesis', *Development and Change*, 17(1): 69–83.

Friedmann, J. (2007) 'The wealth of cities: towards an assets-based development of newly urbanizing regions', *Development and Change*, 38(6): 987–998.

Fu, Q. and N. Lin (2014) 'The weaknesses of civic territorial organizations: civic engagement and homeowners' associations in urban China', *International Journal of Urban and Regional Research*, 38(6): 2309–2327.

Gandy, M. (2002) *Concrete and Clay: Reworking nature in New York City.* Cambridge, MA: MIT Press.

Gandy, M. (2008) 'Landscapes of disaster: water, modernity and urban fragmentation in Mumbai', *Environment and Planning A*, 40(1): 108–130.

Gandy, M. (2014) *The Fabric of Space: Water, modernity, and the urban imagination.* Cambridge, MA: MIT Press.

Ganti, T. (2014) 'Neoliberalism', *Annual Review of Anthropology*, 43: 89–104.

Garbin, D. and P. Millington (2012) 'Territorial stigma and the politics of resistance in a Parisian banlieue: La Courneuve and beyond', *Urban Studies*, 49(10): 2067–2083.

Geertz, C. (1973) *The Interpretation of Cultures: Selected essays.* New York: Basic Books.

Ghertner, A. (2015a) *Rule by Aesthetics: World-class city making in Delhi.* Oxford: Oxford University Press.

Ghertner, A. (2015b) 'Why gentrification theory fails in "much of the world"', *City*, 19(4): 552–563.

Gibson-Graham, J.-K. (1996) *The End of Capitalism (As We Knew It).* Oxford: Blackwell.

Gidwani, V. (2013) 'Value struggles: waste work and urban ecology in Delhi', in A. Rademacher and K. Sivaramakrishnan (eds) *Ecologies of Urbanism in India: Metropolitan civility and sustainability.* Hong Kong: Hong Kong University Press, pp. 169–200.

Gieryn, T. F. (2002) 'Three truth-spots', *Journal of the History of the Behavioral Sciences*, 38(1): 113–132.

Gieryn, T. F. (2006) 'City as truth-spot: laboratories and field-sites in urban studies', *Social Studies of Science*, 36(1): 5–38.

Glaeser, E. L. (2008) *Cities, Agglomeration, and Spatial Equilibrium.* Oxford: Oxford University Press.

Glick Schiller, N. (2012) 'A comparative relative perspective on the relationships between migrants and cities', *Urban Geography*, 33(6): 879–903.

Goffman, A. (2014) *On the Run.* Chicago: University of Chicago Press.

Goldman, M. (2011) 'Speculative urbanism and the making of the next world city', *International Journal of Urban and Regional Research*, 35(3): 555–581.

Goode, J. G. and J. Maskovsky (2001) *The New Poverty Studies: The ethnography of power, politics and impoverished people in the United States.* New York: NYU Press.

Goodwin, M. and J. Painter (1996) 'Local governance, the crises of Fordism and the changing geographies of regulation', *Transactions of the Institute of British Geographers*, 21(4): 635–648.

Goodwin-White, J. (2018) '"Go West, young woman?" The geography of the gender wage gap through the great recession', *Economic Geography*, 94: 331–354.

Goonewardena, K. (2018) 'Planetary urbanization and totality', *Environment and Planning D: Society and Space*, 36(3): 456–473.

Gough, K. (2012) 'Reflections on conducting urban comparison', *Urban Geography*, 33(6): 866–878.

Graham, S. and S. Marvin (2001) *Splintering Urbanism: Networked infrastructures, technological mobilities and the urban condition.* London: Routledge.

Graham, S. and C. McFarlane (eds) (2014) *Infrastructural Lives: Urban infrastructure in context*. London: Routledge.

Graham, S., R. Desai and C. McFarlane (2015) 'Water wars in Mumbai', in J. Law (ed.) *Power, Action and Belief: A new sociology of knowledge*. London: Routledge, pp. 196–223.

Granovetter, M. (2005) 'The impact of social structure on economic outcomes', *Journal of Economic Perspectives*, 19(1): 33–50.

Gray, M. and A. Barford (2018) 'The depths of the cuts: the uneven geography of local government austerity', *Cambridge Journal of Regions, Economy and Society*, 11(3): 541–563.

Grossberg, L. (1996) 'On postmodernism and articulation: an interview with Stuart Hall', in D. Morley and K.-H. Chen (eds) *Stuart Hall: Critical dialogues*. London: Routledge, pp. 131–150.

Grossberg, L. (2015) 'Learning from Stuart Hall, following the path with heart', *Cultural Studies*, 29(1): 3–11.

Guggenheim, M. and O. Söderström (eds) (2010) *Re-shaping Cities: How global mobility transforms architecture and urban form*. London: Routledge.

Gündoğdu, A. (2018) 'Disagreeing with Rancière: speech, violence, and the ambiguous subjects of politics', *Polity*, 49(2): 188–219.

Guo, X. (2001) 'Land expropriation and rural conflicts in China', *China Quarterly*, 166: 422–439.

Gupta, A. and J. Ferguson (eds) (1997) *Anthropological Locations: Boundaries and grounds of a field science*. Berkeley: University of California Press.

Hackworth, J. and N. Smith (2001) 'The changing state of gentrification', *Tijdschrift voor Economische en Sociale Geografie*, 92(4): 464–477.

Haila, A. (1990) 'The theory of land rent at the crossroads', *Environment and Planning D: Society and Space*, 8(3): 275–296.

Haila, A. (2015) *Urban Land Rent: Singapore as a property state*. Hoboken, NJ: Wiley.

Hall, S. (1986) 'Gramsci's relevance for the study of race and ethnicity', *Journal of Communication Inquiry*, 10(2): 5–27.

Hall, S. and D. Massey (2010) 'Interpreting the crisis', *Soundings*, 44: 57–71.

Harding, A. and T. Blokland (eds) (2014) *Urban Theory: A critical introduction to power, cities and urbanism in the 21st century*. Thousand Oaks, CA: Sage.

Harrison, J. and M. Hoyler (2018) *Doing Global Urban Research*. Thousand Oaks, CA: Sage.

Hart, G. (2002) *Disabling Globalization: Places of power in post-apartheid South Africa*. Berkeley: University of California Press.

Hart, G. (2018) 'Relational comparison revisited: Marxist postcolonial geographies in practice', *Progress in Human Geography*, 42(3): 371–394.

Harvey, D. (1969) *Explanation in Geography*. London: Edward Arnold.

Harvey, D. (1972) 'Revolutionary and counter-revolutionary theory in geography and the problem of ghetto formation', *Antipode*, 6: 1–13.

Harvey, D. (1973) *Social Justice and the City*. London: Edward Arnold.

Harvey, D. (1989) 'From managerialism to entrepreneurialism: the transformation in urban governance in late capitalism', *Geografiska Annaler B: Human Geography*, 71(1): 3–17.

Harvey, D. (1996) *Justice, Nature and the Geography of Difference*. Oxford: Blackwell.

Harvey, P. and H. Knox (2015) *Roads: An anthropology of infrastructure and expertise*. Ithaca, NY: Cornell University Press.

Hastings, A. (2014) 'Discourse and linguistic analysis', in K. Ward (ed.) *Researching the City*. London: Sage, pp. 85–98.

He, S. and F. Wu (2005) 'Property-led redevelopment in post-reform China: a case study of Xintiandi redevelopment project in Shanghai', *Journal of Urban Affairs*, 27(1): 1–23.

Heaton, J., J. Day and N. Britten (2016) 'Collaborative research and the co-production of knowledge for practice: an illustrative case study', *Implementation Science*, 11(20), https://doi.org/10.1186/s13012-016-0383-9.

Herbert, S. (2000) 'For ethnography', *Progress in Human Geography*, 24(4): 550–568.

Herrle, P., J. Fokdal and D. Ipsen (2014) *Beyond Urbanism: Urban(izing) villages and the mega-urban landscape in the Pearl River Delta in China*. Münster: LIT Verlag.

Hesse-Biber, S. N. and P. Leavy (2010) *The Practice of Qualitative Research*, 2nd edition. London: Sage.

Heynen, N. C., M. Kaika and E. Swyngedouw (eds) (2006a) *The Nature of Cities: Urban political ecology and the politics of urban metabolism*. London: Routledge.

Heynen, N., M. Kaika and E. Swyngedouw (2006b) 'Urban political ecology', in N. Heynen, M. Kaika and E. Swyngedouw (eds) *The Nature of Cities: Urban political ecology and the politics of urban metabolism*. London: Routledge, pp. 1–20.

Hidalgo Martinez, M. and C. Cartier (2017) 'City as province in China: the territorial urbanization of Chongqing', *Eurasian Geography and Economics*, 58(2): 201–230.

Hinkley, S. (2017) 'Structurally adjusting: narratives of fiscal crisis in four US cities', *Urban Studies*, 54(9): 2123–2138.

Holston, J. (2008) *Insurgent Citizenship: Disjunctions of democracy and modernity in Brazil*. Princeton, NJ: Princeton University Press.

Hsing, Y.-T. (2010) *The Great Urban Transformation: Politics of land and property in China*. New York: Oxford University Press.

Ismail, S. (2006) *Political Life in Cairo's New Quarters*. Minneapolis: University of Minnesota Press.

Jacobs, J. M. (2012a) 'Commentary – comparing comparative urbanisms', *Urban Geography*, 33(6): 904–914.

Jacobs, J. M. (2012b) 'Urban geographies I: still thinking cities relationally', *Progress in Human Geography*, 36(3): 412–422.

Jayne, M. and K. Ward (eds) (2016) *Urban Theory: New critical perspectives*. London: Taylor & Francis.

Jazeel, T. and C. McFarlane (2009) 'The limits of responsibility: a postcolonial politics of academic knowledge production', *Transactions of the Institute of British Geographers*, 35(1): 109–124.

Jessop, B. (1990) *State Theory: Putting the capitalist state in its place*. Cambridge: Polity.

Jessop, B. (1997) 'A neo-Gramscian approach to the regulation of urban regimes: accumulation strategies, hegemonic projects, and governance', in M. Lauria (ed.) *Reconstructing Urban Regime Theory*. London: Sage, pp. 51–73.

Jessop, B. and N.-L. Sum (2010) 'Critical discourse analysis, cultural political economy, and economic crisis', in R. de Cillia, H. Gruber, M. Kryzanowski and F. Menz (eds) *Discourse–Politics–Identity*. Tübingen: Stauffenburg, pp. 95–103.

Jonas, A. and D. Wilson (eds) (1997) *The Urban Growth Machine*. New York: SUNY Press.

Jones, J. P., H. Leitner, S. A. Marston and E. Sheppard (2017) 'Neil Smith's scale', *Antipode*, 49: 138–152.

Jones, M. (1997) 'Spatial selectivity of the state? The regulationist enigma and local struggles over economic governance', *Environment and Planning A*, 29(5): 831–864.

Kaika, M. (2005) *City of Flows: Modernity, nature, and the city*. London: Routledge.

Kanna, A. (2011) *Dubai: The city as corporation*. Minneapolis: University of Minnesota Press.

Katsikis, N. (2018) 'Visualizing the planetary urban', in J. Harrison and M. Hoyler (eds) *Doing Global Urban Research*. Thousand Oaks, CA: Sage, pp. 12–33.

Katz, C. (1994) 'Playing the field: questions of fieldwork in geography', *Professional Geographer*, 46(1): 67–72.

Katz, C. (2001) 'On the grounds of globalization: a topography for feminist political engagement', *Signs: Journal of Women in Culture and Society*, 26(4): 1213–1234.

Katz, M. B. (1996) *In the Shadow of the Poorhouse: A social history of welfare in America*. New York: Basic Books.

Kern, L. (2010) *Sex and the Revitalized City: Gender, condominium development, and urban citizenship*. Vancouver: UBC Press.

Kern, L. and H. McLean (2017) 'Undecidability and the urban: feminist pathways through urban political economy', *ACME*, 16: 405–426.

King, A. D. (1990) *Urbanism, Colonialism and the World-Economy: Cultural and spatial foundations of the world urban system*. London: Routledge.

Kirksey, S. E. and S. Helmreich (2010) 'The emergence of multispecies ethnography', *Cultural Anthropology*, 25(4): 545–576.

Kirkpatrick, L. O. and M. P. Smith (2011) 'The infrastructural limits to growth: rethinking the urban growth machine in times of fiscal crisis', *International Journal of Urban and Regional Research*, 35(3): 477–503.

Kitchin, R. (2014) 'The real-time city? Big data and smart urbanism', *GeoJournal*, 79: 1–14.

Kitchin, R. (2016) 'The ethics of smart cities and urban science', *Philosophical Transactions of the Royal Society A*, 374(2083): 1–15.

Knox, P. and P. J. Taylor (1995) *World Cities in a World-System*. Cambridge: Cambridge University Press.

Koivisto, J. and M. Lahtinen (2012) 'Conjuncture, politico-historical', *Historical Materialism*, 20(1): 267–277.

Kooy, M. and K. Bakker (2008) 'Technologies of government: constituting sub-jectivities, spaces, and infrastructures in colonial and contemporary Jakarta', *International Journal of Urban and Regional Research*, 32: 375–391.

Krätke, S., K. Wildner and S. Lanz (2014) *Transnationalism and Urbanism*. New York: Routledge.

Kristeva, J. (1982) *Powers of Horror: An essay on abjection*. New York: Columbia University Press.

Kuhn, T. S. (1962) *The Structure of Scientific Revolutions*. Chicago: University of Chicago Press.

Kurtz, H., H. Leitner, E. Sheppard and R. McMaster (2001) 'Neighborhood environmental inventories on the internet: Creating a new kind of community resource for Phillips neighborhood', *CURA Reporter*, XXXI(2): 20–26.

Larkin, B. (2013) 'The politics and poetics of infrastructure', *Annual Review of Anthropology*, 42: 327–343.

Latour, B. (1993) *We Have Never Been Modern*. Cambridge, MA: Harvard University Press.

Latour, B. (2004) 'Why has critique run out of steam? From matters of fact to matters of concern', *Critical Inquiry*, 30(1): 25–28.

Latour, B. (2005) *Reassembling the Social: An introduction to actor–network-theory*. Oxford: Oxford University Press.

Latour, B. (2016) '*Onus Orbis Terrarum*: about a possible shift in the definition of sovereignty', *Millennium*, 44(3): 305–320.

Law, J. (1996) 'On the methods of long-distance control: vessels, navigation and the Portuguese route to India', in J. Law (ed.) *Power, Action and Belief: A new sociology of knowledge?* London: Routledge and Kegan Paul, pp. 234–263.

Lawhon, M., H. Ernstson and J. Silver (2014) 'Provincializing urban political ecology: towards a situated UPE through African urbanism', *Antipode*, 46(2): 497–516.

Leamer, E. (2012) *The Craft of Economics: Lessons from the Heckscher-Ohlin framework*. Cambridge, MA: MIT Press.

Lees, L. (2003) '"New" urban geography and the ethnographic void', *Progress in Human Geography*, 27(1): 107–113.

Lees, L. (2004) 'Urban geography: discourse analysis and urban research', *Progress in Human Geography*, 28(1): 101–107.

Lees, L., T. Slater and E. Wyly (2007) *Gentrification*. New York: Routledge.

Lefebvre, H. (1991) *The Production of Space*. Oxford: Blackwell.

Lefebvre, H. (2003) [1970] *The Urban Revolution*. Minneapolis: University of Minnesota Press.

Le Galès, P. (2006) 'New state space in Western Europe?', *International Journal of Urban and Regional Research*, 30(3): 717–721.

Leitner, H. (1990) 'Cities in pursuit of economic growth: the local state as entrepreneur', *Political Geography Quarterly*, 9(2): 146–170.

Leitner, H. (2004) 'The politics of scale and networks of spatial connectivity: transnational interurban networks and the rescaling of political governance in Europe', in E. Sheppard and R. McMaster (eds) *Scale and Geographic Inquiry: Nature, society and method*. Oxford: Blackwell, pp. 236–255.

Leitner, H. (2012) 'Spaces of encounters: immigration, race, class, and the politics of belonging in small-town America', *Annals of the American Association of Geographers*, 102: 828–846.

Leitner, H. and B. Miller (2007) 'Scale and the limitations of ontological debate: a commentary on Marston, Jones and Woodward', *Transactions of the Institute of British Geographers*, 32(1): 116–125.

Leitner, H. and E. Sheppard (2003) 'Unbounding critical geographic research on cities: the 1990s and beyond', *Urban Geography*, 24(6): 510–528.

Leitner, H. and E. Sheppard (2016) 'Provincializing critical urban theory: extending the ecosystem of possibilities', *International Journal of Urban and Regional Research*, 40(1): 228–235.

Leitner, H. and E. Sheppard (2018) 'From Kampungs to condos? Contested accumulations through displacment in Jakarta', *Environment and Planning A*, 50(2): 437–456.

Leitner, H., C. Pavlik and E. Sheppard (2002) 'Networks, governance and the politics of scale: inter-urban networks and the European Union', in A. Herod and M. Wright (eds) *Geographies of Power: Placing scale*. Oxford: Blackwell, pp. 274–303.

Leitner, H., J. Peck and E. Sheppard (eds) (2007) *Contesting Neoliberalism: Urban frontiers*. New York: Guilford Press.

Lim, K. F. (2018) 'Researching state rescaling in China: methodological reflections', *Area Development and Policy*, 3(2): 170–184.

Lin, G. C. (2002) 'The growth and structural change of Chinese cities: a contextual and geographic analysis', *Cities*, 19(5): 299–316.

Lin, G. C. (2007) 'Reproducing spaces of Chinese urbanisation: new city-based and land-centred urban transformation', *Urban Studies*, 44(9): 1827–1855.

Livingstone, D. N. (2003) *Putting Science in its Place: Geographies of scientific knowledge*. Chicago: University of Chicago Press.

Longino, H. (2002) *The Fate of Knowledge*. Princeton, NJ: Princeton University Press.

Low, S. (2000) *On the Plaza: The politics of public space and culture*. Austin: University of Texas Press.

Low, S. and D. Lawrence-Zuñiga (2003) *The Anthropology of Space and Place*. Oxford: Blackwell.

MacKinnon, D. and K. D. Derickson (2012) 'From resilience to resourcefulness: a critique of resilience policy and activism', *Progress in Human Geography*, 37(2): 253–270.

MacKinnon, D. and J. Shaw (2010) 'New state spaces, agency and scale: devolution and the regionalisation of transport governance in Scotland', *Antipode*, 42(5): 1226–1252.

Maldonado-Torres, N. (2007) 'On the coloniality of being', *Cultural Studies*, 21(2–3): 240–270.

Marcuse, P. (2005) '"The city" as perverse metaphor', *City*, 9(2): 247–254.

Marston, S. A., J. P. Jones III and K. Woodward (2005) 'Human geography without scale', *Transactions of the Institute of British Geographers*, 30(4): 416–432.

Martin, D. (2003) '"Place-framing" as place-making: constituting a neighbor-hood for organizing and activism', *Annals of the Association of American Geographers*, 93(3): 730–750.

Martin, D. (2006) 'Review of *New State Spaces*', *Economic Geography*, 82(1): 113–114.

Marvin, S., A. Luque-Ayala and C. McFarlane (eds) (2015) *Smart Urbanism: Utopian vision or false dawn?* London: Routledge.

Massey, D. (1991) 'A global sense of place', *Marxism Today*, June: 24–29.

Massey, D. (2007) *World City*. Cambridge: Polity.

Matthews, P. (2010) 'The persistence of pathological discourses in urban regeneration policy', *Housing, Theory and Society*, 27(3): 221–240.

Matthews, S., J. Detwiler and L. Burton (2005) 'Geo-ethnography: coupling geographic information analysis techniques with ethnographic methods in research', *Cartographica*, 40(4): 75–90.

McCabe, C. (2007) 'An interview with Stuart Hall', *Critical Quarterly*, 50(1–2): 12–42.

McCann, E. (2002) 'The cultural politics of local economic development: meaning-making, place-making, and the urban policy process', *Geoforum*, 33(3): 385–398.

McCann, E. and K. Ward (eds) (2011) *Mobile Urbanism: Cities and policy-making in the global age*. Minneapolis: University of Minnesota Press.

McCann, E. and K. Ward (2012) 'Assembling urbanism: following policies and "studying through" the sites and situations of policy making', *Environment and Planning A*, 44(1): 42–51.

McFarlane, C. (2010) 'The comparative city: knowledge, learning, urbanism', *International Journal of Urban and Regional Research*, 34(4): 725–742.

McFarlane, C. (2011a) 'Assemblage and critical urbanism', *City*, 15(2): 204–224.

McFarlane, C. (2011b) 'On context: assemblage, political economy and structure', *City*, 15(3–4): 375–388.

McFarlane, C. (2011c) 'The city as assemblage: dwelling and urban space', *Environment and Planning D: Society and Space*, 29(4): 649–671.

McFarlane, C. (2012) 'Rethinking informality: politics, crisis, and the city', *Planning Theory and Practice*, 13(1): 89–108.

McFarlane, C. (2016) 'Comparing relational urbanism', *City*, 20(1): 171–173.

McFarlane, C. and J. Robinson (2012) 'Introduction – experiments in comparative urbanism', *Urban Geography*, 33(6): 765–773.

McKittrick, K. (2006) *Demonic Grounds: Black women and the cartographies of struggle*. Minneapolis: University of Minnesota Press.

McMichael, P. (1990) 'Incorporating comparison within a world-historical perspective: an alternative comparative method', *American Sociological Review*, 55(5): 385–397.

Meyer-Clement, E. (2016) 'The great urban leap? On the local political economy of rural urbanisation in China', *Journal of Current Chinese Affairs*, 45(1): 109–139.

Middleton, J. (2011) '"I'm on autopilot, I just follow the route": exploring the habits, routines, and decision-making practices of everyday urban mobilities', *Environment and Planning A*, 43(12): 2857–2877.

Mill, J. S. (1843) *A System of Logic, Ratiocinative and Inductive: Being a connected view of the principles of evidence, and methods of scientific investigation*. West Strand: John W. Parker.

Miraftab, F. (2009) 'Insurgent planning: situating radical planning in the global south', *Planning Theory*, 8(1): 32–50.

Mitchell, J. C. (1983) 'Case and situational analysis', *Sociological Review*, 31(2): 187–211.

Mitchell, K. (2000) 'The value of academic labor', *Environment and Planning A*, 32(10): 1713–1718.

Mitchell, T. (2002) *Rule of Experts: Egypt, techno-politics, modernity*. Berkeley: University of California Press.

Molotch, H. (1976) 'The city as a growth machine: toward a political economy of place', *American Journal of Sociology*, 82(2): 309–332.

Mouffe, C. (1999) 'Deliberative democracy or agonistic pluralism?', *Social Research*, 66: 745–758.

Mullings, B., L. Peake and K. Parizeau (2016) 'Cultivating an ethic of wellness in Geography', *Canadian Geographer*, 60(2): 161–167.

Myers, G. (2014) 'From expected to unexpected comparisons: changing the flows of ideas about cities in a postcolonial urban world', *Singapore Journal of Tropical Geography*, 35(1): 104–118.

Nagar, R. (2014) *Muddying the Waters: Coauthoring feminisms across scholarship and activism*. Champaign: University of Illinois Press.

Nagurney, A. (2013) *Network Economics: A variational inequality approach*. Berlin: Springer.

Nettle, D. and S. Romaine (2002) *Vanishing Voices: The extinction of the world's languages*. Oxford: Oxford University Press.

Newman, K. (1999) *No Shame in My Game: The working poor in the inner city*. New York: Knopf.

Nijman, J. (2007a) 'Introduction – comparative urbanism', *Urban Geography*, 28(1): 1–6.

Nijman, J. (2007b) 'Place-particularity and "deep analogies": a comparative essay on Miami's rise as a world city', *Urban Geography*, 28(1): 92–107.

Nijman, J. (2015) 'The theoretical imperative of comparative urbanism: a commentary on "Cities beyond Compare?" by Jamie Peck', *Regional Studies*, 49(1): 183–186.

Nimmo, R. (2011) 'Actor–network theory and methodology: social research in a more-than-human world', *Methodological Innovations Online*, 6: 108–119.

Nyong'o, P. A. (2016) 'Basic research and its challenges in East Africa', https://items.ssrc.org/basic-research-and-its-challenges-in-east-africa/ (accessed February 22, 2019).

O'Connor, A. (2001) *Poverty Knowledge: Social science, social policy, and the poor in twentieth-century US history*. Princeton, NJ: Princeton University Press.

Oldfield, S. and Z. Patel (2016) 'Engaging geographies: negotiating positionality and building relevance', *South African Geographical Journal*, 98(3): 505–514.

Ollman, B. (2003) *Dance of the Dialectic*. Urbana: University of Illinois Press.

Ong, A. (1999) *Flexible Citizenship: The cultural logics of transnationality*. Durham, NC: Duke University Press.

Ong, A. (2006) *Neoliberalism as Exception: Mutations in citizenship and sovereignty*. Durham, NC: Duke University Press.

Ong, A. and A. Roy (eds) (2011) *Worlding Cities: Asian experiments and the art of being global*. Chichester: Wiley-Blackwell.

Oosterlynck, S. and S. González (2013) '"Don't waste a crisis": opening up the city yet again for neoliberal experimentation', *International Journal of Urban and Regional Research*, 37(3): 1075–1082.

Paasi, A. (2005) 'Globalization, academic capitalism, and the uneven geographies of international journal publishing spaces', *Environment and Planning A*, 37(5): 769–789.

Paige, J. M. (1999) 'Conjuncture, comparison, and conditional theory in macrosocial inquiry', *American Journal of Sociology*, 105(3): 781–800.

Pannell, C. W. (2002) 'China's continuing urban transition', *Environment and Planning A*, 34(9): 1571–1589.

Parker, B. (2011) 'Material matters: gender and the city', *Geography Compass*, 5(6): 433–447.

Parker, B. (2016) 'Feminist forays in the city: imbalance and intervention in urban research methods', *Antipode*, 48(5): 1337–1358.

Parker, S. (2015) *Urban Theory and the Urban Experience: Encountering the city*. London: Routledge.

Parnell, S. and J. Robinson (2012) '(Re)theorizing cities from the Global South: looking beyond neoliberalism', *Urban Geography*, 33(4): 593–617.

Patel, Z., S. Greyling, S. Parnell and G. Pirie (2015) 'Co-producing urban knowledge: experimenting with alternatives to "best practice" for Cape Town, South Africa', *International Development Planning Review*, 37(2): 187–203.

Peake, L. (2016) 'The twenty-first-century quest for feminism and the global urban', *International Journal of Urban and Regional Research*, 40(1): 219–227.

Peake, L. and M. Rieker (eds) (2013) *Rethinking Feminist Interventions into the Urban*. London: Routledge.

Peake, L., D. Patrick, R. N. Reddy, G. S. Tanyildiz, S. Ruddick and R. Tchoukaleyska (2018) 'Placing planetary urbanization in other fields of vision', *Environment and Planning D: Society and Space*, 36(3): 374–386.

Peck, J. (1995) 'Moving and shaking: business elites, state localism and urban privatism', *Progress in Human Geography*, 19(1): 16–46.

Peck, J. (2012) 'Austerity urbanism: American cities under extreme economy', *City*, 16(6): 626–655.

Peck, J. (2013) 'Explaining (with) neoliberalism', *Territory, Politics, Governance*, 1(2): 132–157.

Peck, J. (2014) 'Entrepreneurial urbanism: between uncommon sense and dull compulsion', *Geografiska Annaler B: Human Geography*, 96(4): 396–401.

Peck, J. (2015) 'Cities beyond compare?', *Regional Studies*, 49(1): 160–182.

Peck, J. (2017a) 'Transatlantic city, part 1: conjunctural urbanism', *Urban Studies*, 54(1): 4–30.

Peck, J. (2017b) 'Transatlantic city, part 2: late entrepreneurialism', *Urban Studies*, 54(2): 327–363.

Peck, J. and N. Theodore (2007) 'Variegated capitalism', *Progress in Human Geography*, 31(6): 731–772.

Peck, J. and N. Theodore (2012) 'Follow the policy: a distended case approach', *Environment and Planning A*, 44: 21–30.

Peck, J. and N. Theodore (2015) *Fast Policy: Experimental statecraft at the thresholds of neoliberalism*. Minneapolis: University of Minnesota Press.

Peck, J. and H. Whiteside (2016) 'Financializing Detroit', *Economic Geography*, 92(3): 235–268.

Peck, J., N. Theodore and N. Brenner (2013) 'Neoliberal urbanism redux?', *International Journal of Urban and Regional Research*, 37(3): 1091–1099.

Perry, K.-K. Y. (2013) *Black Women Against the Land Grab: The fight for racial justice in Brazil*. Minneapolis: University of Minnesota Press.

Pieterse, E. (2011) 'Grasping the unknowable: coming to grips with African urbanisms', *Social Dynamics*, 37(1): 5–23.

Plumwood, V. (1994) *Feminism and the Mastery of Nature*. New York: Routledge.

Polanyi, K. (2001) *The Great Transformation*, 2nd edition. Boston, MA: Beacon Press.

Popper, K. (1959) *The Logic of Scientific Discovery*. New York: Basic Books.

Pratt, G. (2002) 'Collaborating across our differences', *Gender, Place and Culture*, 9(2): 195–200.

Pulido, L. (2000) 'Rethinking environmental racism: white privilege and urban development in Southern California', *Annals of the Association of American Geographers*, 90(1): 12–40.

Pulido, L. (2006) *Black, Brown, Yellow and Left: Radical activism in Los Angeles*. Berkeley: University of California Press.

Pulido, L. and J. De Lara (2018) 'Reimagining "justice" in environmental justice: radical ecologies, decolonial thought, and the Black radical tradition', *Environment and Planning E: Nature and Space*, 1(1): 76–98.

Qian, Z. (2013) 'Master plan, plan adjustment and urban development reality under China's market transition: a case study of Nanjing', *Cities*, 30(1): 77–88.

Rademacher, A. (2015) 'Urban political ecology', *Annual Review of Anthropology*, 44: 137–152.

Rademacher, A. and K. Sivaramakrishnan (eds) (2013) *Ecologies of Urbanism in India: Metropolitan civility and sustainability*. Hong Kong: Hong Kong University Press.

Ragin, C. C. (1987) *The Comparative Method: Moving beyond qualitative and quantitative strategies*. Berkeley: University of California Press.

Ranganathan, M. (2015) 'Storm drains as assemblages: the political ecology of flood risk in post-colonial Bangalore', *Antipode*, 47(5): 1300–1320.

Rao, V. (2006) 'Slum as theory: the South/Asian city and globalization', *International Journal of Urban and Regional Research*, 30(1): 225–232.

Read, B. L. (2003) 'Democratizing the neighbourhood? New private housing and home-owner self-organization in urban China', *China Journal*, 49: 31–59.

Ren, X. (2011) *Building Globalization: Transnational architecture production in urban China*. Chicago: University of Chicago Press.

Ren, X. (2018) 'From Chicago to China and India: studying the city in the twenty-first century', *Annual Review of Sociology*, 44: 497–513.

Rithmire, M. (2013) 'Land politics and local state capacities: the political economy of urban change in China', *China Quarterly*, 216: 872–895.

Robbins, P. (2004) *Political Ecology: A critical introduction*. Oxford: Blackwell.

Robinson, J. (2006) *Ordinary Cities: Between modernity and development*. London: Routledge.

Robinson, J. (2010) 'The travels of urban neoliberalism: taking stock of the internationalization of urban theory', *Urban Geography*, 32(8): 1087–1109.

Robinson, J. (2011a) 'Cities in a world of cities: the comparative gesture', *International Journal of Urban and Regional Research*, 35(1): 1–23.

Robinson, J. (2011b) 'Comparisons: colonial or cosmopolitan?', *Singapore Journal of Tropical Geography*, 32: 125–140.

Robinson, J. (2013a) 'The urban now: theorising cities beyond the new', *European Journal of Cultural Studies*, 16(6): 659–677.

Robinson, J. (2013b) '"Arriving at" urban policies/the urban: traces of elsewhere in making city futures', in O. Söderström, S. Randeria, D. Ruedin, G. D'Amato and F. Panese (eds) *Critical Mobilities*. Lausanne: EPFL Press, pp. 1–28.

Robinson, J. (2014) 'Introduction to a virtual issue on comparative urbanism', *International Journal of Urban and Regional Research*, doi:10.1111/1468-2427.12171.

Robinson, J. (2015) 'Comparative urbanism: new geographies and cultures of theorizing the urban', *International Journal of Urban and Regional Research*, 40(1): 187–199.

Robinson, J. (2016) 'Thinking cities through elsewhere: comparative tactics for a more global urban studies', *Progress in Human Geography*, 40(1): 3–29.

Rocheleau, D., B. Thomas-Slayter and E. Wangari (eds) (2013) *Feminist Political Ecology: Global issues and local experience*. London: Routledge.

Rodan, G. (2012) 'Consultative authoritarianism and regime change analysis: implications of the Singapore case', in R. Robison (ed.) *Routledge Handbook of Southeast Asian Politics*. London: Routledge, pp. 120–134.

Rodríguez-Posé, A. (2004) 'On English as a vehicle to preserve geographical diversity', *Progress in Human Geography*, 20(1): 1–4.

Roman, L. G. (2015) 'Conjunctural thinking – "pessimism of the intellect, optimism of the will": Lawrence Grossberg remembers Stuart Hall', *Discourse*, 36(2): 185–199.

Rose, D. (1984) 'Rethinking gentrification: beyond the uneven development of Marxist urban theory', *Environment and Planning D: Society and Space*, 2(1): 47–74.

Rose, G. (2001) *Visual Methodologies: An introduction to the interpretation of visual materials*. Thousand Oaks, CA: Sage.

Rose, G. (2007) *Visual Methodologies: An introduction to the interpretation of visual materials*, 2nd edition. London: Sage.

Roy, A. (2003a) *City Requiem, Calcutta: Gender and the politics of poverty*. Minneapolis: University of Minnesota Press.

Roy, A. (2003b) 'Paradigms of propertied citizenship: transnational techniques of analysis', *Urban Affairs Review*, 38(4): 463–491.

Roy, A. (2005) 'Urban informality: toward an epistemology of planning', *Journal of the American Planning Association*, 71(2): 147–158.

Roy, A. (2009) 'The 21st-century metropolis: new geographies of theory', *Regional Studies*, 43(6): 819–830.

Roy, A. (2011) 'Slumdog cities: rethinking subaltern urbanism', *International Journal of Urban and Regional Research*, 35(2): 223–238.

Roy, A. (2014) 'Slum-free cities of the Asian century: postcolonial government and the project of inclusive growth', *Singapore Journal of Tropical Geography*, 35(1): 136–150.

Roy, A. (2016) 'Who's afraid of postcolonial theory?', *International Journal of Urban and Regional Research*, 40(1): 200–209.

Roy, A. (2017) 'Dis/possessive collectivism: property and personhood at city's end', *Geoforum*, 80(1): 1–11.

Ruming, K. (2009) 'Following the actors: mobilising an actor–network theory methodology in geography', *Australian Geographer*, 40(4): 451–469.

Rydin, Y. (1998) 'The enabling local state and urban development: resources, rhetoric and planning in East London', *Urban Studies*, 35(2): 175–191.

Saegert, S. (2016) 'Rereading "The Housing Question" in light of the foreclosure crisis', *ACME*, 15(3): 659–678.

Sangtin Writers Collective and R. Nagar (2006) *Playing with Fire: Feminist thought and activism through seven lives in India*. Minneapolis: University of Minnesota Press.

Sargeson, S. (2011) 'The politics of land development in urbanizing China', *China Journal*, 66: 145–152.

Sargeson, S. (2013) 'Violence as development: land expropriation and China's urbanization', *Journal of Peasant Studies*, 40(6): 1063–1085.

Sassen, S. (1991) *Global City*. Princeton, NJ: Princeton University Press.

Saunders, P. (1981) *Social Theory and the Urban Question*. London: Hutchinson.

Sayer, A. (1985) 'The difference that space makes', in D. Gregory and J. Urry (eds) *Social Relations and Spatial Structures*. London: Macmillan, pp. 49–66.

Sayer, A. (1992) *Method in Social Science: A realist approach*, 2nd edition. London: Routledge.

Sayer, A. (2000) *Realism and Social Science*. Thousand Oaks, CA: Sage.

Sayer, A. (2001) 'For a critical cultural political economy', *Antipode*, 33(4): 687–708.

Schütte, S. (2014) 'Living with patriarchy and poverty: women's agency and the spatialities of gender relations in Afghanistan', *Gender, Place and Culture*, 21(9): 1176–1192.

Scott, A. J. (1980) *The Urban Land Nexus and the State*. London: Pion.

Scott, A. J. and E. W. Soja (eds) (1998) *The City: Los Angeles and urban theory at the end of the twentieth century*. Berkeley: University of California Press.

Scott, A. J. and M. Storper (2015) 'The nature of cities: the scope and limits of urban theory', *International Journal of Urban and Regional Research*, 39(1): 1–15.

Scott, J. (2017) *Social Network Analysis*. Thousand Oaks, CA: Sage.

Shapin, S. (1996) *The Scientific Revolution*. Chicago: University of Chicago Press.

Shatkin, G. (2014) 'Contesting the Indian city: global visions and the politics of the local', *International Journal of Urban and Regional Research*, 38(1): 1–13.

Shelton, T., M. Zook and A. Wiig (2015) 'The "actually existing smart city"', *Cambridge Journal of Regions, Economy and Society*, 8: 13–25.

Shen, J. (2007) 'Scale, state and the city: urban transformation in post-reform China', *Habitat International*, 31(3–4): 303–316.

Sheppard, E. (1995) 'Dissenting from spatial analysis', *Urban Geography*, 16(4): 283–303.

Sheppard, E. (2001) 'Quantitative geography: representations, practices, and possibilities', *Environment and Planning D: Society and Space*, 19(5): 535–554.

Sheppard, E. (2005) 'Knowledge production through critical GIS: genealogy and prospects', *Cartographica*, 40(1): 5–21.

Sheppard, E. (2008) 'Geographic dialectics?', *Environment and Planning A*, 40(11): 2603–2612.

Sheppard, E. (2014a) 'Globalizing capitalism and southern urbanization', in S. Parnell and S. Oldfield (eds) *The Routledge Handbook on Cities of the Global South*. London: Routledge, pp. 143–154.

Sheppard, E. (2014b) 'We have never been positivist', *Urban Geography*, 35(5): 636–644.

Sheppard, E. (2016) *Limits to Globalization: Disruptive geographies of capitalist development*. Oxford: Oxford University Press.

Sheppard, E. (2019) 'Globalizing capitalism's raggedy fringes: thinking through Jakarta', *Area Development and Policy*, 4(1): 1–27.

Sheppard, E., H. Leitner and A. Maringanti (2013) 'Provincializing global urbanism: a manifesto', *Urban Geography*, 34(7): 893–900.

Sheppard, E., V. Gidwani, M. Goldman, H. Leitner, A. Roy and A. Maringanti (2015) 'Introduction: urban revolutions in the age of global urbanism', *Urban Studies*, 52(11): 1947–1961.

Short, J. R. (2014) *Urban Theory: A critical assessment*. London: Macmillan.

Silver, C. and N. Fielding (2008) 'Using computer packages in qualitative research', in C. Willig and W. Stainton-Rogers (eds) *The Sage Handbook of Qualitative Research in Psychology*. London: Sage, pp. 334–351.

Simone, A. (2001) 'On the worlding of African cities', *African Studies Review*, 44(1): 15–41.

Simone, A. (2004a) *For the City Yet to Come: Changing African life in four cities*. Durham, NC: Duke University Press.

Simone, A. (2004b) 'People as infrastructure: intersecting fragments in Johannesburg', *Public Culture*, 16(3): 407–429.

Simone, A. (2010) *City Life from Dakar to Jakarta*. London: Routledge.

Simone, A. (2014) *Jakarta, Drawing the City Near*. Minneapolis: University of Minnesota Press.

Sin, C. H. (2002) 'The quest for a balanced ethnic mix: Singapore's ethnic quota policy examined', *Urban Studies*, 39(8): 1347–1374.

Slack, J. D. (1996) 'The theory and method of articulation in cultural studies', in D. Morley and K.-H. Chen (eds) *Stuart Hall: Critical dialogues*. London: Routledge, pp. 112–127.

Slater, T. (2006) 'The eviction of critical perspectives from gentrification research', *International Journal of Urban and Regional Research*, 30(4): 737–757.

Smart, A. and G. C. S. Lin (2007) 'Local capitalisms, local citizenship and translocality: rescaling from below in the Pearl River Delta region, China', *International Journal of Urban and Regional Research*, 31(2): 380–302.

Smith, D. A. and M. Timberlake (1995) 'Conceptualising and mapping the structure of the world system's city system', *Urban Studies*, 32(2): 287–302.

Smith, M. P. (2005) 'Transnational urbanism revisited', *Journal of Ethnic and Migration Studies*, 31(2): 235–244.

Smith, M. P. and M. Bakker (2008) *Citizenship Across Borders: The political transnationalism of El Migrante*. Ithaca, NY: Cornell University Press.

Smith, M. P. and L. E. Guarnizo (eds) (1998) *Transnationalism from Below*. New Brunswick, NJ: Transaction Publishers.

Smith, N. (1992) 'Geography, difference and the politics of scale', in J. Doherty, E. Graham and M. Malek (eds) *Postmodernism and the Social Sciences*. New York: St. Martin's Press, pp. 57–79.

Smith, N. (1996) *The New Urban Frontier: Gentrification and the revanchist city*. New York: Routledge.

Smith, N. (2000) 'What happened to class?', *Environment and Planning A*, 32(6): 1011–1032.

Smith, N. (2002) 'New globalism, new urbanism: gentrification as global urban strategy', *Antipode*, 34(3): 427–450.

Söderström, O. (2014) *Cities in Relations: Trajectories of urban development in Hanoi and Ouagadougou*. Chichester: Wiley-Blackwell.

Soja, E. W. (1989) *Postmodern Geographies: The reassertion of space in critical social theory*. London: Verso.

Soja, E. W. (1996) *Thirdspace: Journeys to Los Angeles and other real-and-imagined places*. Oxford: Blackwell.

Soja, E. W. (2000) *Postmetropolis: Critical studies of cities and regions*. Oxford: Blackwell.

Song, Y., M. Y. Wang and X. Lei (2016) 'Following the money: corruption, conflict, and the winners and losers of suburban land acquisition in China', *Geographical Research*, 54(1): 86–102.

Staeheli, L. A., P. Ehrkamp, H. Leitner and C. R. Nagel (2012) 'Dreaming the ordinary: daily life and the complex geographies of citizenship', *Progress in Human Geography*, 36(5): 628–644.

Star, S. L. (1989) 'The structure of ill-structured solutions: heterogeneous problem-solving, boundary objects and distributed artificial intelligence', in M. Huhns and L. Gasser (eds) *Distributed Artificial Intelligence 2*. Menlo Park, CA: Morgan Kauffmann, pp. 37–54.

Star, S. L. (1999) 'The ethnography of infrastructure', *American Behavioral Scientist*, 43(3): 377–391.

Stoker, G. and K. Mossberger (1994) 'Urban regime theory in comparative perspective', *Environment and Planning C: Government and Policy*, 12(2): 195–212.

Stone, C. N. (1993) 'Urban regimes and the capacity to govern: a political economy approach', *Journal of Urban Affairs*, 15(1): 1–28.

Storper, M. (2013) *Keys to the City*. Princeton, NJ: Princeton University Press.

Storper, M. and A. J. Scott (2016) 'Current debates in urban theory: a critical assessment', *Urban Studies*, 53(6): 1114–1136.

Storper, M., T. Kemeny, N. Makarem and T. Osman (2015) *The Rise and Fall of Urban Economies: Lessons from San Francisco and Los Angeles*. Stanford, CA: Stanford University Press.

Swanson, G. E. (1971) 'Frameworks for comparative research: structural anthropology and the theory of action', in I. Vallier (ed.) *Comparative Methods in Sociology: Essays on trends and applications*. Berkeley: University of California Press, pp. 141–202.

Swyngedouw, E. (1997) 'Neither global nor local: "glocalization" and the politics of scale', in K. Cox (ed.) *Spaces of Globalization*. New York: Guilford Press, pp. 137–166.

Swyngedouw, E. (2007) 'Impossible "sustainability" and the postpolitical condition', in R. Krueger and D. Gibbs (eds) *The Sustainable Development Paradox: Urban political economy in the United States and Europe*. New York: Guilford Press, pp. 13–40.

Swyngedouw, E. (2018) 'Insurgent citizens and the spectral return of the political in the postpolitical city', *City and Society*, 30(2), https://doi.org/10.1111/ciso.12175.

Swyngedouw, E. and N. C. Heynen (2003) 'Urban political ecology, justice and the politics of scale', *Antipode*, 35(5): 898–918.

Tang, B. (2015) '"Not rural but not urban": community governance in China's urban villages', *China Quarterly*, 223: 724–744.

Taylor, P. J. and G. Csomós (2012) 'Cities as control and command centres: analysis and interpretation', *Cities*, 29(6): 408–411.

Taylor, P. J. and B. Derudder (2015) *World City Network: A global urban analysis*. London: Routledge.

Teitz, M. B. (2017) 'The rise and fall of urban economies: lessons from San Francisco and Los Angeles: review', *Journal of the American Planning Association*, 83(4): 415–415.

Theodore, N. (2015) 'Generative work: day labourers' Freirean praxis', *Urban Studies*, 52(11): 2035–2050.

Theodore, N. and J. Peck (2012) 'Framing neoliberal urbanism: translating "common sense" urban policy across the OECD zone', *European Urban and Regional Studies*, 19(1): 20–41.

Thrift, N. (2008) *Non-Representational Theory: Space, politics, affect*. London: Routledge.

Till, K. (2012) 'Wounded cities: memory-work and a place-based ethics of care', *Political Geography*, 31(1): 3–14.

Tilly, C. (1984) *Big Structures, Large Processes, Huge Comparisons*. New York: Russell Sage Foundation.

Timberlake, M. (1985) *Urbanization in the World-Economy*. New York: Academic Press.

Tomba, L. (2012) 'Awakening the god of Earth: land, place and classes in urbanizing Guangdong', in B. Carrillo and D. S. G. Goodman (eds) *China's Peasants and Workers: Changing class identities*. Cheltenham: Edward Elgar, pp. 40–61.

Tomba, L. (2017) 'Finding China's urban: bargained land conversions, local assemblages, and fragmented urbanization', in V. Shue and P. M. Thornton (eds) *To Govern China: Evolving practices of power*. Cambridge: Cambridge University Press, pp. 203–228.

Tonkiss, F. (2011) 'Template urbanism: four points about assemblage', *City*, 15(5): 584–588.

UCHRI (University of California Humanities Research Institute) (2015) 'Abdoumaliq Simone entangled cties' [video file]. Retrieved from: https://www.youtube.com/watch?v=CmInDcuHqSk.

Valentine, G. and T. Skelton (2003) 'Finding oneself, losing oneself: the lesbian and gay "scene" as a paradoxical space', *International Journal of Urban and Regional Research*, 27(4): 849–866.

van der Hel, S. (2016) 'New science for global sustainability? The institutionalisation of knowledge production in Future Earth', *Environmental Science and Policy*, 61(July): 165–175.

van Meeteren, M., B. Derudder and D. Bassens (2016) 'Can the straw man speak? An engagement with postcolonial critiques of "global cities research"', *Dialogues in Human Geography*, 6(1): 247–267.

Vanolo, A. (2017) *City Branding: The ghostly politics of representation in globalising cities*. London: Routledge.

Vargas, J. H. C. (2006) 'When a favela dared to become a gated community: the politics of race and urban space in Rio de Janeiro', *Latin American Perspectives*, 33(4): 49–81.

Varley, A. (2013) 'Feminist perspectives on urban poverty: de-essentialising difference', in L. Peake and M. Rieker (eds) *Rethinking Feminist Interventions into the Urban*. London: Routledge, pp. 139–155.

Vora, N. (2013) *Impossible Citizens: Dubai's Indian diaspora*. Durham, NC: Duke University Press.

Wacquant, L. (2002) 'Review symposium – scrutinizing the street: poverty, morality, and the pitfalls of urban ethnography', *American Journal of Sociology*, 107(6): 1468–1528.

Wai Wong, S. (2015) 'Urbanization as a process of state building: local governance reforms in China', *International Journal of Urban and Regional Research*, 39(5): 912–926.

Walker, R. (2015) 'Building a better theory of the urban: a response to 'Towards a new epistemology of the urban?''', *City*, 19(2–3): 183–191.

Walks, A. (2006) 'Review of New State Spaces', *Annals of the Association of American Geographers*, 96(1): 227–229.

Wallace, D. and R. Wallace (1998) *A Plague on your Houses: How New York was burned down and national public health crumbled*. London: Verso.

Wallace, R. and K. McCarthy (2007) 'The unstable public health ecology of the New York Metropolitan Region: implications for accelerated national spread of emerging infection', *Environment and Planning A*, 39(5): 1181–1192.

Ward, K. (2008) 'Editorial – toward a comparative (re)turn in urban studies? Some reflections', *Urban Geography*, 29(5): 405–410.

Ward, K. (2010) 'Towards a relational comparative approach to the study of cities', *Progress in Human Geography*, 34(4): 471–487.

Warde, A. (1991) 'Gentrification as consumption: issues of class and gender', *Environment and Planning D: Society and Space*, 9(2): 223–232.

Watson, V. (2009) 'Seeing from the South: refocusing urban planning on the globe's central urban issues', *Urban Studies*, 45(11): 2259–2275.

Wekerle, G. R. (2005) 'Domesticating the neoliberal city: invisible genders and the politics of place', in W. Harcourt and A. Escobar (eds) *Women and the Politics of Place*. Boston, MA: Kumarian Press, pp. 86–99.

Werner, M., K. Strauss, B. Parker, R. Orzeck, K. Derickson and A. Bonds (2017) 'Feminist political economy in geography: why now, what is different, and what for?', *Geoforum*, 79(1): 1–4.

Wheeler, J. O., Y. Aoyama and B. Warf (eds) (2000) *Cities in the Telecommunications Age: The fracturing of geographies*. London: Routledge.

While, A., A. Jonas and D. Gibbs (2004) 'The environment and the entrepreneurial city: searching for the urban "sustainability fix" in Manchester and Leeds', *International Journal of Urban and Regional Research*, 28(3): 549–569.

Willis, P. (1977) *Learning to Labour: How working-class kids get working-class jobs*. Aldershot: Gower.

Wilson, D. (2014) 'Logics and legacies of positivist urban geography', *Urban Geography*, 35(5): 633–635.

Wilson, W. J. and A. Chaddha (2009) 'The role of theory in ethnographic research', *Ethnography*, 10(4): 549–564.

Wolch, J. R. and G. DeVerteuil (2001) 'New landscapes of urban poverty management', in J. May and N. Thrift (eds) *Timespace: Geographies of temporality*. London: Routledge, pp. 149–169.

Woods, C. (1998) *Development Arrested*. London: Verso.

Woods, C. (2017) *Development Drowned and Reborn: The blues and Bourbon restorations in post-Katrina New Orleans*. Athens, GA: University of Georgia Press.

Wu, F. (2018) 'Planning centrality, market instruments: governing Chinese urban transformation under state entrepreneurialism', *Urban Studies*, 55(7): 1383–1399.

Wyly, E. (2009) 'Strategic positivism', *Professional Geographer*, 61(3): 310–322.

Wyly, E. (2011) 'Positively radical', *International Journal of Urban and Regional Research*, 35(5): 889–912.

Wyly, E., K. Newman, A. Schafran and E. Lee (2010) 'Displacing New York', *Environment and Planning A*, 42(11): 2601–2623.

Yeh, E. T., K. J. O'Brien and J. Ye (2013) 'Rural politics in contemporary China', *Journal of Peasant Studies*, 40(6): 915–928.

Yiftachel, O. (2009) 'Critical theory and "gray space": mobilization of the colonized', *City*, 13(2–3): 246–263.

Young, I. M. (1990) *Justice and the Politics of Difference*. Princeton, NJ: Princeton University Press.

Young, I. M. (1997) *Intersecting Voices: Dilemmas of gender, political philosophy, and policy*. Princeton, NJ: Princeton University Press.

Young, I. M. (2000) *Inclusion and Democracy*. Oxford: Oxford University Press.

Zeiderman, A. (2018) 'Beyond the enclave of urban theory', *International Journal of Urban and Regional Research*, 42(6): 1114–1126.

Zhang, J. (2013) 'Marketization beyond neoliberalization: a neo-Polanyian perspective on China's transition to a market economy', *Environment and Planning A*, 45(7): 1605–1024.

Zhang, Y. and K. Fang (2004) 'Is history repeating itself? From urban renewal in the United States to inner-city redevelopment in China', *Journal of Planning Education and Research*, 23(3): 286–298.

Zukin, S. (1980) 'A decade of the new urban sociology', *Theory and Society*, 9(4): 575–601.

INDEX

actor–network methodologies, 30–1
Actor–Network Theory (ANT), 7, 18, 251, 279
agglomeration, 216, 220, **248**, 284, 299, 303
Agnew, John, 34
Amin, Ash, 7, 9, 54
Anderson, Elijah, 25
anglocentrism, 208, 211, 239, 299
Anguelov, Dimitar, xi, 82, 122, 311, 317
Anthropological Locations (Gupta and Ferguson), 26–7
assemblage urbanism, 18, 31, 91, 92, 94, 188, **251**, 276
audit culture, 238
austerity, 42, 264, 282
autoconstruction, 176, 178, 184
autogestion, 103–4

Badlands of the Republic (Dikeç), 56, 63–4, 101–11
Bair, Jennifer, 80
Baker, Tom, 31
banlieues, 64, 101–2, 111(n1), 300
  uprisings, 104–5, 108
Bay Area, 216–25
Beauregard, Robert, 24, 72
Beijing, 166, 169, 170–1
Berlin, 36, 66, 187, 288
  Weimar, 66, 187, 193, 195
Bernstein, Richard, 240
Berry, Brian, 14
Bhagidari, 83–6
binary thinking, 23, 78, 149
biopolitics, 193
Björkman, Lisa, 31, 63, 91
  Pipe Politics, Contested Waters 56, 63, 91–100
bodies, 25, 193
  see also embodied practices
Bogota, Colombia, 31
Bok, Rachel, xi, 206
boundary objects, 237–8

boundary work, 233
boundary zone, 134, 136, 138–9, 142
Bourgois, Philippe, 28, 143
  In Search of Respect, 56, 65, 143–53
branding, city, 24
Brazil, 66, 175–84, 294
Brenner, Neil, 8, 102, 122
  New State Spaces, 42, 56, 64, 122–32
Burawoy, Michael, 26, 39, 139–40, 168

Card, Kenton, xi, 112, 154, 216, 308
case studies, 23, 25, 28, 34, 38–40
  distended case method, 32
  extended case method, 26, 32, 38, 138, 168
Castells, Manuel, 6–7, 320
Chicago school, 14, 257, 317
China, 65, 166–73
Cities (Amin and Thrift), 54
Cities in Relations (Söderström), 36, 57, 67, 206–15
citizenship, urban, 71, 82, 84, 101, 104, 154, 163, 175–7, 258, **305**
  see also right to the city
City (journal), 50
city branding, *see* branding, city
City Life from Jakarta to Dakar (Simone), 57, 66, 196–205
cityism, methodological, 9, 127, 130–1, 284
cityness, 9, 198–9, 202, 204, 210
class
  and gentrification, 266–7
  and housing question, 272–4
  in India, 84–6, 97
  in urban political economy, 72
  and migration, 119
climate change, 17, 236, 280
close encounter methodologies, 23, 43, 232
  in the field, 25

close engagements, 23–4, 28
close readings, 23–4
co-authorship, 51–4, 217–18, 225, 243
collaboration, 51–4, 217–18
colonialism, 15, 200, 267, 287–8
Colven, Emma, xi, 82, 91, 254
Comandon, Andre, xi–xii, 101, 154,
    196, 216, 302
commons, urban, 257, **308**
commoning, 258, 308–10
comparative urbanism, 33–7, 122, 143,
    175, 186, 196, 206–7, 216, **254**
  and city selection, 190
  and cultural practices, 145
  and everyday life, 204
  and meso-level analysis, 125
  and methodology, 23, 214–15
  and norms of comparison, 23, 36, 255
  and positionality, 183
  and relationality, 209–10, 225
comparison, relational
  and comparative urbanism, 254
  and dialectics, 35
  methodology, 207–15
  and postcolonialism, 191–2
conduct, codes of, 51, 242
conjunctural methodologies, 23, 38–43
connectivity-based methodologies, 8, 10
*Contesting Neoliberalism: Urban
    frontiers* (Leitner et al.), xix
'context of context', 22, 126
Copenhagen, Denmark, 124
crack economy, 144–51
critical realism, 22, 125, 237
critical-race theory, 10, 13, 233
critique, cultures of, 54, 234, 238
cultural political economy, *see* political
    economy, cultural
cultural production theory, 144, 153
cultural turn, 11
'culture of poverty', 144, 317

Dakar, Senegal, 66, 196–205
Daniels, Joseph A., xii, 122, 154,
    216, 263
Davidson, Mark, 9
decline, discourses of, 24
deconstruction, constructive 54–62, 230
  see also reverse engineering
deductive approaches, 47–8
Delhi, India, 63, 82–90

Deleuze, Gilles, 18, 212, 251
deSouza, Allan, xvi, 1, 69, 227, 245
development theory, 220
difference, social, 12, 193, 273, 318
Dikeç, Mustafa, 24, 64, 101–11
  Badlands of the Republic, 56, 63–4,
      101–11
disarticulation, 80
discourse, 11–12
discourse analysis, 24–5, 64, 102, 105–8
  Foucauldian vs. Marxist modes, 120–1
  and Gramsci, 111 (n2)
  limitations of, 110–11
displacement, 165, 175, **257**
  and aesthetic politics, 88–9
  and Chinese urbanization, 166
  and gentrification, 266–7, 281
  and the housing question, 273
  and postcolonialism, 288
  and the right to the city, 293
  in São Paulo, 177, 179
dispossession, 168, 194, **257**, 273, 288
divergence, 67, 216–17, 219–20,
    224–5
Dubai: The City as Corporation
    (Kanna), 57, 64, 112–21
Dubai, UAE, 27, 112–21
Duncan, James, 24
dystopia, 188, 194

Ebner, Nina, xii, 101, 320
ecological modernism, 18
  urban economics, 10, 164, 219, 221
  see also political economy, urban
embodied practices, 11, 153, 181–5
  see also bodies
empiricism, 234–37
encounters, urban, 23, 175, 177,
    196, **260**
engaged pluralism, 233–4, 237–8, 240–1
Engels, Friedrich, 156, 158, 163, 272–4
English, as lingua franca, 239
entrepreneurial urbanism, 5, 115, 126,
    127, 212
  development, 42, 124, 281, 311
  governance, 4, 281, 324
  see also neoliberal urbanism
environmental change, 186, 243, 323–4
environmental justice, *see* justice
epistemology, 8, 9, 21, 222, 234–7
  'local epistemologies', 240

ethico-political commitment, 8, 11, 89, 110, 207, 225
  see also research ethics
ethnic segregation, 143
ethnography
  and archival work, 184
  and assemblage urbanism, 92, 94
  in boundary zones, 136
  and close encounters in the field, 25
  critical, 64, 141
  and everyday urbanism, 202
  geo-ethnography, 27, 32
  and interpretative techniques, 113
  institutional, 83
  multi-sited, 27
  multi-species, 27
  and political economy, 153
  and reflexivity, 139, 168
  and theory, 26
  and urban poverty, 137–8
  see also interviews as method *and*
    participant observation
Eurocentrism, 43, 49, 92, 211, 230
  see also anglocentrism
Everyday Equalities (Fincher et al.), 37
everyday urbanism, 91, 112, 133, 143–4, 196, 204, **260**
  and biopolitics, 135
  cityness, 197
  and citizenship, 305
  encounters, 261
  and gender, 73–6
  and gentrification, 78–9
  and infrastructure, 93–5
  and mobilities, 314
  practices, 11, 149, 182, 203
  and social movements, 321
  and the subaltern, 288
  and visual culture, 192
extended case method, 23, 32, 35, 38, 47, 138, 168
  see also case studies
external critique, 59–60, 230 (*see also* internal critique)

Fabric of Space, The (Gandy), 56, 66, 186–95
Fairbanks, Robert, 25, 26, 64–5, 133
  How It Works, 25, 41, 56, 64–5, 133–42
Farías, Ignacio, 7–8

feminism, 58, 230, 241
feminist geography, 11–13
  methodology, 23, 29–30, 71, 78, 144
  theory, 10, 28–9, 43, 57, 74, 79, 240
  urban studies, 63, 72–3, 149, 235
Ferguson, James, 26–7
financialization, 154, 155, **263**, 273, 276
financial crises
  Asian financial crisis, 160
  global financial crisis (2008), 42, 155, 173, 263, 270, 291
fiscal crisis (1970), 143
floods, 186, 188–9, 191, 194
Fordism, 4, 123, 269, 272, 311
Foucault, Michel, 24, 74, 106, 120, 134
France, 64, 101–10, 124, 208, 300

Gandy, Matthew, 36, 186
  The Fabric of Space, 56, 66, 186–95
gender, 12
  division of labor, 299
  and gentrification, 63, 71–8, 266
  silencing, 140
  violence, 150–1
genealogical analysis, 65, 154, 178–9, 161–4
genealogy, critical, 56, 67, 155, 157–8
generalization, 25, 47, 128, 131, 171
gentrification, 257, **266**
  and exclusion, 78–9
  and gender, 63, 71–8, 266
  and neoliberal urbanism, 281
  and rent gap theory, 303
  and resistance, 294
  and the state, 85
  theories of, 72
  see also displacement/dispossession
Germany, 33, 66, 124–5, 187, 193, 272
Ghertner, D. Asher, 27, 56, 63, 82
  Rule by Aesthetics, 56, 63, 82–90
Gibson-Graham, J-K., 232
Gieryn, Thomas, 14
global cities, 5, 15, 206–7, 249, 255, **269**
  see also world city
global financial crisis (2008), 42, 155, 173, 263, 270, 291
Globalization and World Cities Research Network (GaWC), 208, 269
glocalization, 126
Goffman, Alice, 54

governance, urban, 71, 112, 122, 133,
  154, 165, 216, 224, **311**
  aesthetic dimensions of, 84, 90
  and financialization, 263
  and gentrification, 267
  and governmentality, 74
  and land, 155
  meso-level comparison, 125–6
  multiscalar methodologies, 126–7
  and the post-political city, 290
  and poverty, 137
  and the right to the city, 293
  and smart cities, 297
  and the state, 123–4, 167
  and sustainability, 323
governmentality, 56, 74, 89–90, 135,
  138, 312
Graham, Stephen, 19
  Splintering Urbanism, 19
gray spaces, 318
Great Urban Transformation, The
  (Hsing), 56, 65, 165–74
grounded theory, 30
growth coalitions, urban, 126, 174, 300
growth machine, 4, 126, 300
Grossberg, Lawrence, 41
Guangzhou, China, 169, 172
Gündoğdu, Ayten 109–110
Gupta, Akhil, 26–7

Habermas, Jürgen, 12
Haila, Anne, 65, 154
  Urban Land Rent, 56, 65, 154–64
Hall, Stuart, 39
Hanoi, Vietnam, 36, 67, 206–15
Hardin, Garrett, 308–9
Harlan, Tyler, xii, 165
Harlem, New York City, 28, 65,
  143–52
Hart, Gillian, 35, 208, 210–11
Harvey, David, 6, 22, 257, 263, 273,
  284, 293, 302, 315
Hasan, Nafis Aziz, xii, 112, 269, 296
Herbert, Steven, 25
heterodoxy, 51, 196, 231, 234
heterogeneity, 174, 197, 205, 232
Holston, James, 27, 66, 175–8
  Insurgent Citizenship, 57, 66, 175–85
homeownership, 74, 77, 160–1, 272–4
housing question, the, 65, 154,
  156, 159, 163, **272**

Howard, Tom, xii, 133, 143, 272, 299
Hsing, You-tien, 65, 165–74
  The Great Urban Transformation, 56,
  65, 165–74
How It Works (Fairbanks), 25, 41, 56,
  64–5, 133–142
hukou system, 169
humanities, 192
hybridity, 189

idealism, 234–7
identity, cultural, 10, 115, 118,
  146, 305
immobilities, 293, 314
  see also mobilities, urban
incommensurability, 145, 152
India, 84, 91–9, 190, 258, 297, 296
individualism, 238
inductive approaches, 47–8
informality, urban, 82, 133, 143, 147–8,
  196, 203, **317**
  and access to infrastructure, 93,
  and agglomeration, 249
  conceptualizations of, 140–1
  and citizenship, 305
  and displacement, 258
  and governance, 86, 312
  and uneven urban development, 302
information and communications
  technologies (ICTs), 269, 296
In Search of Respect (Bourgois), 56, 65,
  143–53
infrastructure, 19, 91–2, 95–6, 186–7,
  196, **275**
  and agglomeration, 220
  and (im)mobilities, 314
  as method, 93–4, 97–9
  and the more-than-human, 278
  people as, 199
  and smart cities, 296
  and suburbanization, 300
  and urban governance, 311
institutional analysis, 221–3, 217
institutional history, 155, 157, 159–60,
  162, 223
institutional theories, 57, 221–3
Insurgent Citizenship (Holston), 57, 66,
  175–85
interdisciplinarity, 15, 50, 192
  see also postdisciplinarity
internal critique, xix, 59–60, 62, 230

International Journal of Urban and Regional Research (journal), 50
intersectionality, 12, 29, 66, 183, 233
interviews, as method, 52, 64, 73–7, 83, 117–18, 135, 150–1, 160, 170–3, 209
see also ethnography
Italy, 124–5
Iveson, Kurt, 9

Jacobs, Jane M., 210, 215, 252, 260
Jahn-Verri, Fernanda, xiii, 143, 175, 257
Jakarta, 27, 66, 197–8, 202, 258, 287
Jakarta, Drawing the City Near (Simone), 54
Jazeel, Tariq, 241
jíbaro identity, *see* identity, cultural
justice
   environmental, 17, 18, 27, 279, 324
   social, 12, 73–4, 79–80, 257, 294, 306, 324

Kandy, Sri Lanka, 24
Kanna, Ahmed, 27, 64, 112–21
   Dubai: The City as Corporation, 57, 64, 112–21
Kemeny, Thomas, 217
   The Rise and Fall of Urban Economies, 57, 216–26
Kern, Leslie, 63, 71–81
   Sex and the Revitalized City, 57, 63, 71–81
Keynesianism, 123–4, 311
keywords, in urban studies, 54, 67–8
knowledge production, 11, 13, 15, 22, 26, 31, 81, 152, 233, 236–7
   coproduction, 24, 28–9, 52, 209, 243
   cultures of, 234–5, 241–4
   lone scholar model, 238, 243
   philosophical premises, contrasting 234–7

Lagos, 36, 186, 188, 190–4, 199, 202
land, urban, 8, 65, 155, 165, 167, 173, 257, 263, 267
   and rent theory, 56, 154–6, 158, 161, 164
   nexus, 220, 249, 273
   see also Haila, Anne
Latour, Bruno, 18, 236, 251
Lawhon, Mary, 18, 204–5
Lefebvre, Henri, 115, 155, 263, 293

Leitner, Helga, xiii, xvii–xx, 3, 14, 21, 45, 229, 260
limit cases, 145, 153
listening, 242
literary analysis, 56, 66, 115, 187, 192–3, 278
local states, *see* state, local
Loewen, Kyle, xiii, 71, 305
London, UK, 8, 29, 188, 191, 194–5, 252, 266, 287, 302
   see also global cities
Longino, Helen, 240
Los Angeles, USA, 16, 188–9, 191, 194, 216–25
Los Angeles school, 14, 49

Makarem, Naji, 216, 217
   The Rise and Fall of Urban Economies, 57, 216–26
Maktoum, 113–20
marginality, urban, 142, 152, 317
Marvin, Simon, 19
Marx, Karl, 17, 158, 308
Marxism, 4, 238, 314
Massey, Doreen, 8, 29, 302
materiality, 17, 92, 95, 99, 190
Matthan, Tanya, xiii, 91, 275
McCann, Eugene, 31
McFarlane, Colin, 19, 31, 98, 211, 213–14, 241, 260
McGuirk, Pauline, 31
McMichael, Philip, 35
Melbourne, Australia, 13
meso-level analysis, 125–6, 128–32
metabolism, 17, 279
methodological cityism, 9, 127, 130, 284
methodological nationalism, 35, 108, 123, 130–1
methodological pluralism, 43, 50, 61–2
methods, research, 56–7
   mixed, 21, 63, 168, 209
   multi, 21, 119–20
   multi-sited, 65, 168–9
   pluralism, 43, 50, 61–2
   see also ethnography; qualitative/ quantitative analysis
mid-level concepts, 15, 26, 38–9, 48, 57, 66, 126
mid-level theories, 47, 64, 125
   see also meso-level analysis
Midnight Notes Collective, 309

Mill, John Stuart, 34
mobilities, urban, 31–2, 276, 314–15
  see also immobilities
modernity, 36, 66, 145, 148, 178, 183,
  186, 189, 191–3
monism, 50, 240
more-than-human, 16–20, 91, 186,
  190, 206, 209, 276, **278**
  agency, 95, 190, 263–4,
  and assemblage urbanism, 251
multiplier effect, 224
multiscalar analysis, 64, 107, 108, 122,
  123, 126–9, 181–2, 281
  see also scale
Mumbai, India, 36, 63, 91–99,
  186–95, 276

Nagar, Richa, 28
Nanjing, China, 169
nationalism, methodological, see
  methodological nationalism
nature, urban, 186, 190, **278**
neoliberalism, 80, 114, 121, 281, 311
neoliberalization, 20, 56, 103, 238, 276,
neoliberal urbanism, 71, 112, 119, 133,
  154, 206, **281**
  alternatives to, 308
  and contestation, 119, 294
  critique of, 212
  and globalization, 207
  and informalization, 317
  and land rent theory, 155
  and the post–political city, 290
  and poverty management, 138
  and smart cities, 297
  and suburbanization, 300
  and sustainability, 324
  see also austerity and entrepreneurial
    urbanism
Netherlands, the, 125
network analysis, 30, 32, 33, 57
New State Spaces (Brenner), 42, 56, 64,
  122–32
New York City, USA, 65, 146
  see also global cities; Harlem
Nigeria, see Lagos
non-representational theory, 7, 25
northern theory, 16, 183
  see also southern theory
Nowak, Samuel, xiii, 133, 143,
  260, 314

object biography, 209
Oldfield, Sophie, 29
Ollman, Bertil, 40
Omstedt, Mikael, xiii, 71, 122, 284
Ong, Aihwa, 80
On the Run (Goffman), 54
ontology, 105, 234–6, 270
oral histories, 95, 146
ordinary cities, 175, 177, 206, 249, 255, **269**
Ordinary Cities (Robinson), 15, 36, 255
orientalism, 116
Osman, Taner, 217
  The Rise and Fall of Urban
    Economies,
    57, 216–26
Ostrom, Elinor, 308–9
Ouagadougou, Burkina Faso, 36, 67,
  206–15

Palermo, Italy, 206
Paris, 186–7, 191–3,
  Commune, 308
  see also global cities
Park, Jaehyeon, xiv, 165
Park, Robert, 14
partial readings of the urban, 43, 50,
  202, 231
participant observation
  and actor–network methodologies, 30
  critiques/limitations of, 26, 113
  and distended case method, 32
  and extended case method, 138
  and the informal economy, 144
  see also ethnography
participatory action research, 21, 23, 29,
  61, 241, 243
participatory research, 66
Patel, Zarina, 29
patriarchy, 66, 121, 150, 183
Peck, Jamie, xiv, xvii–xx, 3, 21, 32,
  45, 229
Penny, Joe, xiv, 101, 290
performativity, 7, 24, 25, 31
  see also non–representational theory
Philadelphia, USA, 26, 64, 133–8
Pipe Politics, Contested Waters
  (Björkman), 56, 63, 91–100
place
  and agglomeration, 248
  -based analyses, 33, 34,
  -based knowledge, 93, 243

and ethnographic fieldwork, 26, 114
global sense of, 29, 35
-making practices, 105, 108
'out of place', 83, 267
see also gentrification
planetary urbanization, 8–9, 122, 127,
   130–1, **284**
planning, urban, 92, 213, 318
pluralism, methodological, *see* methods,
   research
Polanyi, Karl, 167
policy mobilities, 31, 32, 314, 315
political ecology, urban, 17, 189, 278–9
political economy, urban, 3–6, 230–1, 235
   culturalist critiques of, 11
   and feminist urbanism, 72
   and genealogical analysis, 154
   methodologies, 22
   and the more-than-human, 17
Polanyian, 165, 167
Ponder, CS, xiv, 186, 248, 281
Porto Alegre, Brazil, 37, 294, 315
positionality, 43, 58, 65, 231, 315
   social, 26, 28, 29, 88, 119, 139, 142,
      152, 171, 181, 182
   spatio-temporal, 23, 31, 38, 269
   see also reflexivity
positivism, 22, 225, 235, 236
post-disciplinarity, 50, 231
   see also interdisciplinarity
post-political city, 101, 102, **290**
postcolonial cities, 82, 91, 92, 133, 143,
   175, 186, 190, 196, 206, **287**
   and assemblage urbanism, 252
   and Euro-American theory, 92, 141, 208
   and gentrification, 267
   and informality, 16
   and infrastructure, 276
   and insurgent citizenship, 184
   North–South comparisons, 145
   and ordinary cities, 270
   and subaltern agency, 198
   see also subaltern urbanism
postcolonial critiques, 140, 144, 213,
   230, 255, 276
   see also southern theory
postcolonial theory, 14, 15, 56, 90,
   140–1, 215
postmodern theory, 4, 14, 235, 254
post-structuralism, 10, 12, 18, 23, 24,
   25, 230, 233, 235, 254

poverty, 64, 83, 84, 133–40, 143
power
   corporate/financial, 5, 249, 303, 309
   discursive/representational, 11, 12,
      31, 108
   differentials in ethnographic practice,
      23, 29, 65, 137, 139–40, 142
   state, 5, 107, 124, 128, 167, 317
   territorial, 167, 170, 171
practice, *see* research practice
primitive accumulation, 308–9
privatization, 308
Prouse, Carolyn, xiv, 175
provincializing urban theory, 7, 15, 18,
   49, 255
Puerto Rico, 146, 148
Pulido, Laura, 17–18

qualitative methods, 21, 25, 27, 28, 30,
   32, 33, 34, 40–1, 47
quantitative methods, 22, 30, 32–3, 47,
   67, 172, 217, 221
   quantizing, 28
queer theory, 10, 13

race, 12, 13, 147, 257
   see also whiteness *and* white privilege
Ragin, Charles 33–4
Rancière, Jacques, 83, 87, 89, 104, 106,
   103, 290
Rao, Prajna, xiv, 82, 196, 287
reading for method, 18, 48, 58, 59, 60,
   61, 231
   see also reverse engineering
realism, 234
realism, critical, 22, 125, 237
reflexive social science
   and comparative analysis, 214–15
   and constructive deconstruction, 60
   and discourse analysis, 105
   and ethics, 28
   and ethnographic practice, 23, 137,
      139–42
   and the extended case study, 38, 168
   and knowledge production, 238
   and situated knowledge, 30
   and theorization, 38, 40, 47, 137,
      171, 174
regimes, urban, 4, 311
regional policy, 124, 127, 216, 217,
   221, 222, 224

regulation theory, 5, 135, 138, 141, 142
relational comparison, *see* comparison, relational
relationality, 29–30, 49, 131, 208, 210, 212–13, 232
relational turn, 30
rent gap, 266, 303
replication, 66, 106, 164, 205
representation, politics of, 24–5, 28, 144, 152
    see also non-representational theory
research ethics, 17, 24, 28, 241–2
    see also positionality
research practices, xvii–xvix, 229–31
    both/an approach to, 234
    and collaboration, 20
    engaged pluralism, 234, 240
    induction vs. deduction, 47
    as iterative process, 26
    and knowledge production, 234–7
    principles of, 45
    reading for, 46, 55, 57–60,
    relation to theory, 22
    and responsibility, 241
    see also reading for method *and* reverse engineering
resilience, urban, 18, 280, 300, **323**
    see also sustainability, urban
resistance, urban, 86, 90, 92, 109, 149, 162, 166, 288, 323
    see also social movements, urban
responsibility, 52, 53, 231, 243
    see also *research ethics*
reverse engineering, xviii–xix, 54, 60, 229
    see also reading for method
revitalization, 79, 257
right to the city, 101, 104, 154, 163, 165, 170, 175, 274, **293**, 321
Rise and Fall of Urban Economies, The (Storper, Kemeny, Makarem and Osman), 57, 216–26
risk management, 263, 324
Robinson, Jennifer, 15, 36–7, 61, 190–1, 210, 255, 270
    Ordinary Cities, 15, 36, 255
Roy, Ananya, 140, 149, 163, 190, 257, 318
Rule by Aesthetics (Ghertner), 56, 63, 82–90
Ruming, Kristian, 30

San Francisco, USA, 34, 224
Sangtin Writers Collective, 29
São Paulo, Brazil, 66, 175–84
saturation, methodological, 65, 168, 171, 172
Saunders, Peter, 7
Sayer, Andrew, 11–12, 22
scale, geographical, 30, 33, 35, 38, 41–2, 56, 64, 65
    debates, 235
    politics of, 130
    theories of, 126
    see also multiscalar analysis
Schmid, Christian, 8, 9, 122, 284
science and technology studies, 19, 56
Scott, Allen, 8–9
Secor, Ana, 305–6
segregation, ethnic, 144, 177, 179, 188, 190, 314
settler colonial theory, 10
Sex and the Revitalized City (Kern), 57, 63, 71–81
Shanghai, China, 169
Shenzhen, China, 172, 199
Sheppard, Eric, xiv–xv, xvii–xx, 3, 8, 21, 45, 229
Simone, AbdouMaliq, 9–10, 54, 196
    City Life from Jakarta to Dakar, 57, 66, 196–205
    Jakarta, Drawing the City Near, 54
Singapore, 65, 154–64, 252, 269
smart cities, 7, **296**
smart urbanism, 19
Smith, Michael Peter, 32
Smith, Neil, 72, 266, 278, 302, 303
social justice, *see* justice, social
social movements, urban, 101, 154, 165, 175, 260, **320**
    in the aftermath of 2008 crisis, 282
    in Brazil, 176–80
    in China, 166
    and the commons, 308–10
    and ethnography, 162
    and housing, 274
    and the right to the city, 293–4
    and uprisings, 108
social network analysis, 30
socio-ecological transformation, 195
Söderström, Ola, 36, 67, 206
    Cities in Relations, 36, 57, 67, 206–15

southern theory, 14–16, 37, 184, 255
  see also northern theory
Spivey, Hudson, xv, 91, 112, 278, 293
Splintering Urbanism (Graham and
    Marvin), 19
state, the
  and biopolitics, 134
  and development, 42, 159–60,
      166, 172
  and gentrification, 85, 267
  and informality, 317–18
  and land ownership, 65, 154, 155–6
  and local power, 167
  and neoliberalism, 282
  and repression, 24, 103
  regulation theory, 135, 140
  and resistance from below, 104
  and scale, 126–7
  and social movements, 180
  and urban governance, 82, 107,
      123–4, 311–12
Storper, Michael, 8–9, 216–26
  *The Rise and Fall of Urban
    Economies*, 57, 216–26
structural adjustment, 317
structuralism, 234–7
subaltern urbanism, 16, 102, 143, 149,
    196, 198, 252, **287**
suburbanization, 272, **299**, 314
suburban studies, 299–301
sustainability, urban, 27, 112, 116, 280,
    300, 314, 323–5
  see also urban resilience
Sydney, Australia, 13, 30
symbolic capital, 147

technolopolis, 297
temporalilty, 36, 208, 310
Theodore, Nik, 32
theory cultures, urban, 145, 233–4
Thrift, Nigel, 7, 9, 25, 54, 200
Tilly, Charles, 34, 254
tone, of critique, 17, 26, 46, 61, 230,
    233–4, 238, 242
  see also critique, cultures of
Toronto, Canada, 13, 71
translocal connections, 32, 212
Tokyo, Japan, 15, 36, 269
  see also global cities
triangulation, 25, 56, 168–9, 174

UBC/UCLA graduate seminar, xvi,
    xvii–xviii, 46, 51–4, 242
uneven urban development, 49, 91, 122,
    143, 175, 216, **302**
  and agglomeration, 249
  and comparison, 224
  and 'contour lines', 148
  and infrastructure, 92, 189
  and neoliberal urbanism, 300
  and planetary urbanization, 284
  and postwar urban policy, 123, 127
  and segregation, 179
United Kingdom, 124–5, 248, 280
United States, 4, 64, 119, 294, 296–7,
    300, 311
universalism, 15, 43, 50, 144
urban, the
  conceptualizations, 6–10, 27, 49, 50,
      122, 203, 284–5
  lived experience of, *see* experience,
      urban
  loci of theorization, 13–16, 240, 288
  ways of knowing, 10–13, 29, 106,
      215, 230–2
urban citizenship, *see* citizenship urban
urban commons, *see* commons, urban
urban economics, *see* economics, urban
urban encounters, *see* encounters, urban
urban everyday, *see* everyday urbanism
urban governance, *see* governance,
    urban
urban growth coalitions, *see* growth
    coalitions, urban
urban (im)mobilities, *see* mobilities;
    immobilities
urban informality, *see* informality, urban
Urban Land Rent (Haila), 56, 65,
    154–64
urban nature, *see* nature, urban
urban planning, *see* planning, urban
urban political ecology, *see* political
    ecology, urban
urban political economy, *see* political
    economy, urban
urban regimes, *see* regimes, urban
urban resilience, *see* resilience, urban
urban resistance, *see* resistance urban
urban social movements, *see* social
    movements, urban
Urban Studies (journal), 50

urban sustainability, *see* sustainability,
     urban
urbanization, planetary, *see* planetary
     urbanization
utopia, 18, 20, 191, 193, 194, 293

visual culture, 24, 27, 187, 195
   and aesthetic politics, 85
   analysis of, 66, 73, 84, 86, 188,
        192–4, 209
   and ideology, 121

Wacquant, Loïc, 26, 137
Waldman, Devra, xv, 71, 266
Walker, Richard, 9, 299, 300

Ward, Kevin, 31, 35–6, 209
Washington, DC, 266, 306
water,
     see Pipe Politics; Fabric of Space
Webber, Sophie, xv, 186, 251, 323
Werner, Marion, 12, 80, 249
whiteness, 139, 183, 267
white privilege, 18
world city, 5, 269
     see also global cities
world-class,
     city, 63, 82–90, 93, 96
     aesthetics, 83–90

Zapatistas, 309